Praise from Job Seekers for the
Knock 'em Dead **Books**

"I was sending out hordes of résumés and hardly getting a nibble—and I have top-notch skills and experience in my field. I wasn't prepared for this tough job market. When I read your book, however, I immediately began applying some of your techniques. My few nibbles increased to so many job interviews I could hardly keep up with them!"

—C.S., Chicago, Illinois

"Every time I've used your book, I've gotten an offer! This book is incredible. Thanks for publishing such a great tool."

—W.Z., Columbia, Maryland

"I read and used your book, *Résumés That Knock 'em Dead*, as I searched for a job. I was called for an interview and was up against ten applicants. To make a long story short, I interviewed on Monday morning, and by Monday afternoon knew I had the job."

—E.H. (no address given)

"I've used *Knock 'em Dead* since 1994 when I graduated. It's the reason I've made it to VP—thank you!"

—P.L., Norfolk, Virginia

"After reading your book, *Résumés That Knock 'em Dead*, I rewrote my résumé and mailed it to about eight companies. The results were beyond belief. I was employed by one of the companies that got my new résumé, and received offers of employment or requests for interviews from every company. The entire job search took only five weeks."

—J.V., Dayton, Ohio

"My son called me from college last night, desperate to help a friend on her first interview. My advice? Tell her to drop everything and head to the nearest bookstore to get *Knock 'em Dead*. The book is a godsend and helped me obtain the job of my dreams eight years ago. It is by far THE best book on interviewing out there. I highly recommend it to everyone I know who asks me for help. As a Director of HR now, I know. No one should go to an interview without reading, re-reading, and re-re-reading this informative, absorbing, tremendously helpful book. It is utterly amazing. Thank you!"

—S.D., Philadelphia, Pennsylvania

"I am very grateful for your *Knock 'em Dead* series. I have read the trio and adopted the methods. In the end, I got a dream job with a salary that is almost double of my previous! By adopting your methods, I got four job offers and had a hard time deciding!"

—C.Y., Singapore

"I rejigged my résumé exactly as you outlined in your book and one employer said, 'You can tell this person has a real love of PR from his résumé.' Within three weeks I had three job offers and was able to pick and choose the perfect job for myself."

—M.W., Detroit, Michigan

"Your book is simply fantastic. This one book improved my yearly income by several thousand dollars, and my future income by untold amounts. Your work has made my family and myself very happy."

—M.Z., St. Clair Shores, Michigan

"I cannot tell you what a fabulous response I have been getting due to the techniques you describe in your books. Besides giving me the tools I needed to 'get my foot in the door,' they gave me confidence. I never thought I could secure an excellent position within a month!"

—B.G., Mountainview, California

"My job search began a few months ago when I found out that I would be laid off because of a corporate buyout. By following your advice, I have had dozens of interviews and have received three very good job offers. Your excellent advice made my job hunt much easier."

—K.C., St. Louis, Missouri

"I heard of your book right after I bombed out on three interviews. I read it. I went on two interviews after reading it. I have been told by both of those last two interviewers that I am the strongest candidate. I may have two job offers!"

—B.V., Albuquerque, New Mexico

"I read your book and studied your answers to tough questions. The first interview that I went on after doing this ended up in a job being offered to me! The interviewer told me that I was the best interviewee she'd seen! Thanks a million for writing your book. I am so thankful that I had heard about you!"

—K.P., Houston, Texas

"I just finished writing the letter I have dreamed of writing for three years: my letter of resignation from the Company from Hell. Thanks to you and the book *Knock 'em Dead*, I have been offered and have accepted an excellent position with a major international service corporation."

—C.C., Atlanta, Georgia

"After having seen you on television, I decided to order the *Knock 'em Dead* books. Your insights into selling myself helped me find opportunities in my field that would not have been attainable otherwise."

—E.M., Short Hills, New Jersey

"I just received the offer of my dreams with an outstanding company. Thank you for your insight. I was prepared!"

—T.C., San Francisco, California

"I got the position! I was interviewed by three people and the third person asked me all the questions in *Knock 'em Dead*. I had all the right answers!"

—D.J., Scottsdale, Arizona

"Thank you for all the wonderfully helpful information you provided in your book. I lost my job almost one year ago. I spent almost eight months looking for a comparable position. Then I had the good sense to buy your book. Two months later, I accepted a new position. You helped me turn one of the worst experiences of my life into a blessing in disguise."

—L.G., Watervliet, New York

"I was out of work for four months—within five weeks of reading your book, I had four job offers."

—S.K., Dallas, Texas

"I followed the advice in *Knock 'em Dead* religiously and got more money, less hours, a better hospital plan, and negotiated to keep my three weeks vacation. I start my new job immediately!"

—A.B., St. Louis, Missouri

KNOCK 'EM DEAD

RÉSUMÉS
8th Edition

Smart advice to make your online
and paper résumés more productive

Martin Yate, C.P.C.

Avon, Massachusetts

Published by Adams Media, an F+W Publications Company
57 Littlefield Street
Avon, MA 02322
www.adamsmedia.com

ISBN 10: 1-59869-674-2
ISBN 13: 978-1-59869-674-5

Printed in the United States of America.

J I H G F E D C B A

Library of Congress Cataloging-in-Publication Data
Yate, Martin John.
Knock 'em Dead Résumés / Martin Yate. -- 8th ed.
p.   cm.
Includes index.
ISBN-13: 978-1-59869-674-5
ISBN-10: 1-59869-674-2
1. Résumés (Employment) I. Title. II. Title: Knock them Dead Resumes. III.
Title: Knock 'em dead.
HF5383.Y38 2007
650.14'2--dc22
2006019730

This book is available at quantity discounts for bulk purchases.
For information, please call 1-800-289-0963.

CONTENTS

ACKNOWLEDGMENTS

In more than twenty years of publication around the world, the *Knock 'em Dead* books owe their success to millions of satisfied readers who spread the word, and four generations of dedicated professionals at Adams Media. Thank you for all of your support, and through it that greatest of honors: making a difference in people's lives all around the world.

INTRODUCTION

No one wants to write a résumé. On the list of things we "want" to do, it comes just above hitting yourself in the head with a hammer; and in part, that is because of the self-analysis involved. Although we know ourselves better than anyone else does, actually taking that knowledge and packaging it for public consumption is always an extremely difficult task.

The goal of this book is to help you accelerate your job search with an understanding of the world in which your résumé must compete, and, consequently, the tactics that will enable it to compete most effectively.

In *Knock 'em Dead Résumés,* I explain the ins and outs of putting a résumé together as painlessly as possible. I'll show you the best ways to package your background in a résumé and present it to employers. You'll understand why certain things should be in your résumé and how they should look, and why other things should never appear. Today's world of work is complex, and your circumstances are unique, so there will be situations in which what is right for one person's résumé is wrong for another's. In these cases, I'll always share with you what the experts think on the topic; and whenever industry experts disagree, I'll give you both sides of the argument, along with my reasoned solution to the dispute. That way you can make a prudent decision based on the factors that affect your particular situation. In addition, you will see a wide variety of styles and approaches that can be used within these practical guidelines to help you create a truly individual résumé.

You'll get to read real résumés from real people. Each of the résumés in this book is based on a "genuine article" that opened the doors of opportunity for its writer. Résumés are included for today's and tomorrow's in-demand jobs, as defined by the U.S. Bureau of Labor Statistics and confirmed by the professionals on the front lines: corporate recruiters and other employment-industry professionals from across the country. You are quite likely to find a résumé that reflects exactly the kind of job you are after. You should know that résumé layouts are *not* designed for specific job types; so if you see a résumé layout that works for you, don't be restrained from using it because the example you see is from another profession.

You will also find a number of résumés from people with special challenges. These reflect the pressures and needs of a modern, profession-oriented society struggling into the information age. Like the résumé that got a six-dollar-an-hour factory worker a $70,000-a-year professional sales job, or the one that helped a recovering alcoholic and drug abuser get back on his feet again. Included here are winning résumés from people changing careers, recovering from serious emotional challenges, starting over after a divorce, and even re-entering society after time in prison.

A powerful, job-targeted résumé, properly distributed, is only one element in a successful job search; for this reason, *Knock 'em Dead Résumés* is part of an integrated series of books crafted to help you land jobs and prosper in them. At times, this book will touch on subjects that are handled in greater depth elsewhere in *Knock 'em Dead*, the series of career-management books. In these instances, I will refer you to the appropriate work. For example, the self-knowledge you develop in preparing your résumé will also help you prepare for job interviews; when I touch on this topic I will refer you to the nearly 200 pages on interviewing tactics in the companion volume, *Knock 'em Dead: The Ultimate Job Seeker's Guide.*

The wide range of résumé examples here, and the nuts-and-bolts advice about résumé production and distribution, will give you everything you need to create a distinctive, professional résumé—and get it in front of the people who count!

THE POWER OF A GREAT RÉSUMÉ

Read this book with a highlighter—
it will save time as you refer back to important passages.

YOUR RÉSUMÉ IS probably the most important written document you will ever create, because it helps you understand and package yourself appropriately as a commercial commodity.

It opens the doors of opportunity for you, acts as a road map for interviewers during the selection cycle, and acts as your spokesperson long after the interviews are over. Your résumé has a major impact on the money you earn during your work life, and consequently, has a major impact on the quality of your whole life outside of work.

You didn't come to this book for a good read; you came because you are facing serious challenges of upward mobility in your professional life. Maybe you are a seasoned pro who has discovered that your current résumé no longer does the job. You are probably right; after adding job after job since those long-ago college days, your document now probably looks more like a patchwork quilt than a target-job-focused résumé. Perhaps you are fresh out of school and are wondering how you can create a professional résumé that will catapult you from paper-hat-and-name-tag jobs into the professional world. Or perhaps you have been struggling along without a résumé and simply filling out application forms, but have finally made the commitment to do it right this time.

Whatever your reason for reading this book, the following pages will help you get your act together. By the end of the process, you will not only have a knock 'em dead résumé, you will also have a much firmer grasp on crucial job-search, interviewing, and lifetime career-management skills.

The better-organized and more focused professional will always be viewed more favorably than the competition—and that is exactly what the development of your résumé will do for you. Creating a résumé helps you in your job search way beyond opening doors; it will help you understand what employers need and what you have to offer, and as a result, it will give you ammunition for handling those tough interview questions.

No one ever gets added to the payroll for the love of humanity. Management never gets up and collectively sighs, "Ah, it's a lovely day in the neighborhood . . . let's hire us some accountants." People get added to the payroll to make money, and to save money or time for the company; and they all do this at some level by anticipating and preventing problems from arising, and solving them in a timely manner when they do arise.

No résumé ever gets read, and no one ever gets interviewed or hired, unless someone somewhere is trying to solve a problem. That problem may be finding a quicker way to manufacture silicon chips, or it may be getting the telephone calls answered now that the receptionist has suddenly quit. As disparate as these examples might seem, both are still concerned with problem solving and, invariably, the problem that needs a solution is the same: productivity. Résumés that get acted on are those that position the writer as someone knowledgeable enough about the job to anticipate, prevent, and solve its problems, thus contributing positively to the bottom line.

Your résumé's job is to speak loudly and clearly about your value as a potential on-staff problem solver in a specific functional area. And this value must be clearly expressed in a few brief seconds, because that's all the attention your résumé will get in its first reading. Initially, your résumé just helps get your foot in the door, and because you can't be there to answer questions, it has to stand on its own.

The World Where Your Résumé Must Produce Results

Now, given the choice, you'd never write a résumé, but as your success depends on it, you should learn how to do it right. Résumés evolved as a solution to a productivity problem. Can you imagine what would happen to a business if everyone who applied for a job was given even a cursory ten-minute interview? The nation would simply grind to a halt, then topple into bankruptcy, because employers would do nothing but interview. The solution: find a way to get a glimpse of applicants' potentials before meeting them face to face. Thus, the résumé evolved as a screening and timesaving tool for the corporation.

You may think that writing a résumé is a tough job, but consider the realities of résumé readers for a moment. No one ever reads a résumé unless they have to; they have to because a specific job has been titled and carefully defined, a salary range has been agreed upon, the position has been budgeted and approved, and the funds released. This means that whenever anyone searches a database for résumés or actually reads one, it is being done with a specific job and very often specific language (from the job description) in mind. These simple facts tell us that simply updating a résumé with what we see as our current responsibilities probably isn't going to be very effective.

A productive résumé focuses attention on your strengths as they relate to the deliverables of a specific target job. Writing such a résumé requires that you first focus on the job you want: understanding how employers think about, prioritize, and describe the job's deliverables. Only in the light of this understanding should you begin to analyze and package your work history in support of your job goal. The entire process is one in which you take the time to look at and then package yourself as a desirable product. This also does an awful lot to help you prepare for job interviews. In a very real sense, putting a résumé together is the foundation for succeeding at the job interview; preparation for one is preparation for the other. With a résumé focused on a specific target job and built from the ground up with the employer's needs in mind, your résumé will come up far more often in database searches and it will be far more likely to grab a reader's attention and gain an invitation to interview.

For example, the interviewer's command, "Tell me about yourself" is one of those tough interview questions that almost all of us have difficulty answering without sounding like a snake-oil salesman. Were you totally satisfied with your response the last time it came up? I doubt it. This was probably because you had a sneaking suspicion that your answer didn't really seem to speak in a focused fashion to the job for which you were interviewing. You can only answer this question well if you have taken the time to analyze and package the sum of your professional experience as it relates to the targeted job. It is the only way you will ever learn to speak fluently about your background and skills in a fashion guaranteed to impress the interviewer. For this reason, *Knock 'em Dead Résumés* will kill two birds with one stone—it will help you prepare a résumé that will open all the right doors for you, and it will give you an understanding of what you have to offer when those tough questions start flying.

Many interviewers base their questions on résumé content. This means that, to a certain extent, you can guide the course of your interviews by preparing an appropriately focused résumé. Without one, you are obliged to deliver your work history on a job application form, which rarely allows a perfect representation of skills, and which gives the interviewer no flattering starting point from which to base the interview questions.

In addition to helping you get your foot in the door and easing the course of the interview, your résumé will be your final and most powerful advocate. After interviewing the candidates, interviewers review all the contenders by going over their notes and the candidates' résumés. Your résumé becomes your spokesperson long after you have left that last interview, and it has the final word on your candidacy. You can begin to see why having a résumé focused on a target job makes so much sense.

Target Job Deconstruction: A Strong Focus Leads to Positive Results

It is a mistake to think your résumé is simply a recitation of all you have done in your professional life. This will result in a résumé that lacks focus, punch, and ultimately, results. The most productive résumés start with a clear focus on the target job and look at its responsibilities from the point of view of the selection committee.

Let's start the creation of your résumé with this exercise of Target Job Deconstruction to determine the proper focus for your job-targeted résumé:

1. Collect 6–10 job postings of jobs you can do and jobs you would enjoy. Save them in a folder and also print them out. Not sure where to start? Try *www.indeed.com*, a job aggregator (or spider) that runs around thousands of job sites looking for jobs with your chosen keywords.
2. Create a new document and title it "TJD" for Target Job Deconstruction.
3. Start with a first subhead reading "JOB TITLE," then copy and paste in all the variations from your samples. Looking at the result you can say, "When

employers are hiring people like this, they tend to describe the job title with these words." This will help you come up with a suitable Target Job Title for your résumé, coming right after your name and contact information. This will help your résumé perform well in résumé database searches, and will also act as a headline, giving human eyes an immediate focus.

4. Add a second subhead titled "SKILLS/RESPONSIBILITIES/REQUIRE-MENTS/DELIVERABLES, ETC."

5. Look through all the print job postings across your desk and look for a requirement that is common to all six of your job postings. Take the most complete description and copy and paste it (with a bullet) into your TJD document. Underneath this, add any other words and phrases from the other job postings used to describe this same area. Repeat this exercise for any other requirements common to all six of your job postings.

6. Then repeat the exercise for requirements common to five of the jobs, then four, and so on, all the way down to those requirements mentioned in only one job posting.

When this is done, you can look at your work and say, "When employers are hiring people like me, they tend to refer to them by these job titles and they prioritize their needs in this way and use these words to describe them."

This means that you now know the story your résumé needs to tell to be maximally productive in the résumé databases, and when it eventually gets in front of those human eyes. You now have the proper focus for a job-targeted résumé.

The most productive résumé focuses on what has happened in your business life that enhances your ability to shine in the job you have targeted as the next logical step in your career. It is now time to start looking into your professional background to gather all the possibly relevant information you could use in such a résumé.

Here is a simple before-and-after example that will illustrate how powerful this process can be. The résumé is for a young graduate with a computer science degree looking for her first step in the professional world. When we first spoke, she had been out of school for nearly three months and had had a couple of telephone interviews and one face-to-face interview. Her search was complicated by the fact that she is a foreign national and needed to find a company that would sponsor her. This is not easy at the best of times, but in the tough job environment of early 2008, it is a significant additional challenge. The first résumé is the one she was using; the second she created after completing the Target Job Deconstruction process.

JYATITI MOKUBE

10611 ABERCORN STREET, APT 85
SAVANNAH, GA 31419
SOFTWAREGAL@GMAIL.COM
(401) 241-3703

Education

- Armstrong Atlantic State University, Savannah, GA
- MSc. Computer Science (3.5 GPA) December 2007
- University of Technology, Kingston, Jamaica
- BSc. Computing & Information Technology November 2005
- Graduated Magna Cum Laude (3.7 GPA)

Key Skills

- Programming Languages: C, C++, Java, VB.Net
- Database Programming: SQL
- Website Design
- Design Languages/Tools: HTML, CSS, JavaScript, Dreamweaver
- Problem Solving and Leadership
- Honed an analytical, logical, and determined approach to problem solving and applied this as group leader for my final year (undergraduate) research project.
- Team Player
- Demonstrated the ability to work effectively within a team while developing a Point-of-Sale system over the course of three semesters.
- Demonstrated excellent written and oral communication skills through reports and presentations while pursuing my degrees, and as Public Relations Officer for the University of Technology's Association of Student Computer Engineers (UTASCE).

Work Experience

January 2006–December 2007
- Armstrong Atlantic State University, Savannah, GA
- Graduate Research Assistant, School of Computing
- Developed a haptic application to demonstrate human-computer interaction using Python and H3D API.
- Developed an application to organize text documents using the Self-Organizing Map algorithm and MATLAB.

July–November 2005
- Cable & Wireless Jamaica Ltd, Kingston, Jamaica
- Internet Helpdesk Analyst
- Assisted customers with installing and troubleshooting modems and internet service-related issues via telephone.

July–August 2003
- National Commercial Bank Ja. Ltd, Kingston, Jamaica
- Change Management Team Member
- Generated process diagrams and documentation for systems under development using MS Visio, MS Word, and MS Excel.

Awards/Honors

- President's Pin for graduating with a GPA above 3.75 November 2005
- Latchman Foundation Award for Academic Excellence & Outstanding Character March 2005
- Nominated School of Computing student of the year March 2005
- Recognized by Jamaica Gleaner as top student in School of Computing & IT February 2005
- Nominated for Derrick Dunn (community service) Award March 2004
- Honor roll/Dean's List 2002–2005

Languages

- French (fluent), Italian (basic)

Extracurricular Activities

- Singing, acting, chess, reading
- Member of Association for Computing Machinery, AASU student chapter

References

- Available upon request.

JYATITI MOKUBE

10611 Abercorn Street, Apt 85
Savannah, GA 31419
softwaregal@gmail.com— (401) 241-3703

Talented, analytical, and dedicated Software Engineer with strong academic background in object-oriented analysis and design, comfort with a variety of technologies, and interest in learning new ones.

SUMMARY OF QUALIFICATIONS

- Excellent academic record. Achieved 3.55 GPA (Master's) and 3.77 GPA (Bachelor's, Dean's List for all eight semesters).w
- Familiarity with the software development lifecycle, from identifying requirements to design, implementation, integration, and testing.
- Familiar with agile software development processes.
- Strong technical skills in Java development and Object-Oriented Analysis and Design (OOA/D).
- Strong understanding of multiple programming languages, including C, C++, JavaScript, Visual Basic, and HTML.
- Familiar with CVS version control software.
- Excellent communications skills with an aptitude for building strong working relationships with teammates.

TECHNICAL SKILLS

Languages:	Java, JavaScript, C, C++, Visual Basic, HTML, SQL, VB.Net, ASP. Net, CSS
Software:	Eclipse, NetBeans, JBuilder, Microsoft Visual Studio, Microsoft Office Suite (Word, PowerPoint, Excel, Access), MATLAB
Databases:	MySQL, Oracle
Operating Systems:	Windows (NT/2000/XP Professional)
Servers:	Apache Server

EDUCATION

MS in Computer Science, Armstrong Atlantic State University, Savannah GA, December 2007
- Completed a thesis in the area of Computer Security (Digital Forensics: Forensic Analysis of an iPod Shuffle)

BS in Computing & IT, University of Technology, Kingston, Jamaica, November 2005

LANGUAGES

Fluent in **English**, **French**, and **Italian**

PROFESSIONAL EXPERIENCE

Armstrong Atlantic State University, Savannah, GA 01/2006–12/2007

Graduate Research Assistant, School of Computing
- Developeda haptic application to demonstrate human-computer interaction using Python and H3D API.

Cable & Wireless Jamaica Ltd, Kingston, Jamaica   07/2005–11/2005

Internet Helpdesk Analyst
- Assistedcustomers with installing and troubleshooting modems and internet service-related issues via telephone.

National Commercial Bank Ja. Ltd, Kingston, Jamaica   07/2003–08/2003

Change Management Team Member
- Generatedprocess diagrams and documentation for systems under development using MS Visio, MS Word, and MS Excel.

AWARDS/HONORS
- President's Pin for graduating with a GPA above 3.75 11/2005
- Latchman Foundation Award for Academic Excellence & Outstanding Character 03/2005
- Nominated School of Computing student of the year 03/2005
- Recognized by Jamaica Gleaner as top student in School of Computing & IT 02/2005
- Nominated for Derrick Dunn (community service) Award 03/2004

PROFESSIONAL AFFILIATIONS
Association for Computing Machinery (ACM)

REFERENCES
Available upon request.

Now what was the result of this résumé revamping? She started using it at the beginning of March 2008, and almost immediately got an invitation to interview. She subsequently relocated out of state and started work at this company on April 14.

The target-job focused résumé opened doors, positioned her professionally, told her what the employer would want to talk about, and was a powerful spokesperson after she left. The end result was a great start to a new career. It all came about because she took the time to understand how her customer—the employer—was thinking about and expressing the job she wanted to do!

DISCOVERING WHAT YOU HAVE TO OFFER

IT HAS BEEN theory up to now: This is where the rubber hits the road.

People change jobs for a multitude of reasons. Perhaps your career isn't progressing as you'd like. Perhaps you have gone as far as you can with your present employer, and the only way to take another career step is to change companies. Maybe your job has just evaporated, and you need to get back to work fast. Maybe you have been in the same job for three or more years, without dramatic salary increases or promotions, and you know that you are going nowhere, having been stereotyped, classified, and pigeonholed.

You need to know where you've been, where you are, and where you're headed. Without this stocktaking, your chances of reaching your ultimate goals are reduced, because you won't know how best to use what you've got to get where you want to go.

Believe it or not, very few people have a clear fix on what they do for a living; they miss not only their importance to an employer as part of the moneymaking machinery, but also their importance to themselves. Carefully evaluating your professional history will give you a fresh view of yourself as a professional and the important role you play in your chosen profession.

Step One: Establishing the Right Frame of Mind for Résumé Writing

Employers all want to know the same thing: How can you contribute to keeping their ship afloat and seaworthy? Everyone who ever gets hired for any job gets hired because he or she is a problem solver. Look at your work in terms of the problems you solve in the daily round, as well as the problems that would occur if you weren't there.

Go back to your TJD (Target Job Description), and for each of the bullets you noted representing employers' common requirements for this position, ask yourself:

- In this area, what problems typically arise in the normal course of the execution of my duties?
- What are some examples of where my efforts in these areas had a successful outcome to the benefit of my employer? (Such examples don't need to be of enormous proportions; they just need to catch a snapshot of you doing the job conscientiously.)

In this process of examining your work history, you will generate a mass of notes and an intimate awareness of yourself as a professional. This great mass is the raw material of your professional persona, like the sculptor's block of stone, at which they chip away to reveal the masterpiece that has been hiding there all along.

The more notes you have, the better. Just remember that whatever you write in the note-making part of your résumé preparation will never suffer public scrutiny; it is for your private consumption only. Don't let the necessity of getting it done or the fear of others' judgment cramp the creative process of capturing information. The final product can only ever be as good as the components from which you assemble it. Not all the information you discover will make it into your résumé, but all the rest will have an equal value in preparing you for the interview cycle. Remember that 50 percent of the success of any project is in the careful preparation—and this is where you are doing the spadework.

Step Two: Gathering the Raw Materials

First, set up a document titled "Résumé Questionnaire" and save it to a résumé subfolder within your career-management folder. Add all the self-revelatory information you have gathered to date and that you will gather from further exercises into this folder. You can find a résumé questionnaire document in MS Word at *www.knockemdead.com* on the résumé page, and a print version toward the end of this book.

Step Three: Identify Your Target Job Title

It's a misconception to think that a productive résumé is a simple recitation of what you have done with your professional life. On the contrary, such a résumé will seem unfocused and may well demand more effort on the part of the reader to determine if you are a worthwhile candidate.

Your résumé will be incalculably more productive if you begin by defining a clear focus on a target job that you can land and in which you can be successful. You have already done this in the TJD (Target Job Deconstruction exercise). Print out a copy of this document and keep it in front of you at all times as you gather information, as it will help focus your mind on those aspects that are most valuable to potential employers.

A résumé starts with your name and contact information, but the first thing any résumé reader looks at is the target job title. Every résumé should have one. Start by identifying what your target job title might be. Take all the title variations you collected in the TJD and come up with a couple of target job titles that work for you; you can always make the final choice later. Here are some examples taken from finished résumés:

Occupational Health Services Manager
Certified Occupational Health Nurse Specialist/Certified Case Manager/
Certified Occupational Hearing Conservationist
Senior Vice President Worldwide Operations
Nurse Practitioner   Advanced Practice Nurse   Mid-Level Practitioner

Campaign Field Director
State Senator, Maryland State Senate, **th Legislative District, Laurel, MD
Management Professional
Operations/Human Resources/Labor Relations/Staff Development
Healthcare Professional
Operations Management—Healthcare Review—Clinical Consultant
Agricultural/Environmental Manager
Horticultural Buying—International Experience

Step Four: Performance Profile or Career Summary

Most résumés today follow the target job title with a short paragraph that succinctly captures what you bring to the table. Sometimes this has a headline such as "Performance Profile" and sometimes the graphic layout of the document makes such a headline less necessary in some people's minds.

In a world where keywords are so critical to getting your résumé out of databases and in front of human eyes, some kind of Professional/Executive/Management/Career/Performance Profile or Summary is advisable. Such a profile clearly captures the essential, professional you in a few short sentences. This helps give human eyes an immediate focus on who you are and what you do. It can also increase keyword frequency in your résumé and become a critically effective branding statement.

Take a shot at creating a performance profile right now. Take a sheet of paper or a separate document on your desktop and:

1. Write 3–6 bulleted statements that capture the essential professional you
2. Reread your TJD and pull out 3–6 bulleted requirements that describe the professional you.
3. Now write a bulleted document combining all this information into just 3–6 bullets.
4. Turn the bulleted statements into no more than four to five sentences, and then check your TJD to see that it contains the words employers are using to describe their jobs.

The result will be a performance profile that captures the professional you in the words employers are most likely to use in database searches and which will resonate with human eyes when they are pulled from the databases.

Core Competencies

Over the last couple of years, the initial screening of résumés has been almost entirely taken over by the résumé tracking systems. These Spiders and Bots search for keywords that describe the position and the professional skill sets needed to execute the duties effectively. The keywords they use come primarily from formal job descriptions and the user's personal knowledge of a given job's realities.

Screen software searches for the words a user directs. For example, if a hiring manager is looking for a computer programmer, she might direct the search tool to look for words like "Information Technology," "C++," "database architecture," etc. If the manager is looking for an accountant, she might search for words like "financial analysis," "P&L," "Excel," and "accounts payable."

Your résumé, and thousands like it, can be scanned in seconds. The software will rank yours by the number of keywords it contains. The higher your ranking, the greater likelihood that your résumé will be read by a human being; and once in front of human eyes, the more relevant to the JD it will appear. The more relevant the keywords, the closer the scrutiny your résumé will receive.

A WILDLY UNSCIENTIFIC RESEARCH PROJECT

After thirty-plus years in the career management business, I know a lot of recruiters, and I often ask in conversation how many résumés they actually look at after doing a résumé database search. Here's what they've told me:

- They rarely read more than twenty résumés without generating a short list, and usually hope to achieve the list from fewer than twenty.
- They don't expect to dig for information, and they consider a candidate's ability to synthesize relevant information and make it accessible to be a critical skill. They see the résumé as a useful testing tool for this.
- The first page is critical. Like everyone else, they look for certain keywords that act as shorthand, telling them this résumé writer has a grasp of the job.

The Performance Profile/Career Summary we just addressed is a great asset in focusing a reader's attention. It does double duty, as it allows you to use critical keywords upfront then repeat them in the body of the résumé. When a Core Competency section that lists all your hard, professional skills follows this, it makes a very powerful and succinct statement about the professional you. For example, here is a Core Competency Profile of a Tax Accountant:

CORE COMPETENCIES

ASBT, C-Corporation and S-Corporation State Income Tax Returns * Vehicle Use Tax Returns * State Income Tax Budgeting and Accrual * Multistate Property Tax Returns * Federal, State, and Local Exemption Certificates * State and Local Sales, Use and Excise Tax Management * Tax Audit Management * Tax License and Bonding Maintenance * Certificates of Authority and Annual Report Filing Maintenance * State Sales and Use Tax Assessment * Federal Excise Tax Collections and Deposits * Determination of Nexus * Tax Amnesty Programs

---

You quickly get a clear idea of what this person knows—she clearly knows tax accounting. Each word in the Core Competency section helps your résumé perform well in the résumé database searches and they act as headlines for the reader: "Oh, good; she can talk about State Income Tax Budgeting and Accrual. The last guy we had was a bozo in this area." And, "Aha! So she claims to know about Federal Excise Tax Collection and Deposits. Let's examine what she knows about reconciling the Fed reports in the process." Each keyword or phrase offers the reader another topic of conversation, and the more conversation topics you can give the reader, the closer she comes to inviting you in for an interview.

A Core Competencies section adds considerable information to your résumé in a highly space-efficient way. Use it as a telegram to identify all the skill sets and experience you've developed over your work life.

Examine your TJD documents and all your résumé development notes for keywords that encapsulate your core professional competencies, and add them to a Core Competencies section in your information-gathering document. Also keep an eye open for relevant keywords you haven't used whenever you review a job posting, and add them to this section on an ongoing basis. Note that, when using keywords to extend your résumé's reach, to justify their inclusion you must have real experience in each of the areas. Including keywords in areas where you have no professional expertise may get you a telephone conversation with an employer, but will quickly reveal you as an impostor.

Your Core Competencies section can be as long as you require. There's no need for definite or indefinite articles or conjunctions; just list the keyword, starting with a capital and ending with a period, tab mark, or other standard space device that you can put between words on your list.

Where does the keyword section go? As far as the résumé-scanning computer is concerned, it doesn't matter because the computer isn't concerned with the niceties of layout and flow. However, human eyes will also see the keyword section, so it's logical to put this important information front and center, after the Profile/Summary section. Your Core Competencies section is part of the preface to your body copy, where it acts as a table of contents. The body of your résumé describes the context in which these skills have been applied.

Now, for some people, like technologists and healthcare professionals, a Core Competency Section will include that alphabet soup that spells technological literacy, and that literacy will be noted in addition to other skills. For example, this Core Competency Section addresses this networking professional's broader skill areas:

CORE PROFESSIONAL COMPETENCIES

Software Development • Life Cycle Process Automation • Vendor Management • Software Interfacing • Systems and Hardware • Analysis • Maintenance • Upgrade • Customization Modification • Client & Vendor Presentation • Employee Recruiting • Employee Mentor and Trainer • Improved Efficiency

---

A Core Technology Competencies section will identify the alphabet soup. For example:

CORE TECHNOLOGY COMPETENCIES

Operating Systems

UNIX • Solaris • IBM • AIX • HP-UX • DOS • Windows 95/98/NT/2000/XP

Languages

Java (JSP, Servlets, Applets, EJB, J2EE) • JavaScript • Visual Basic • HTML • EXL • C/C++ • COBOL • PL/SQL

Databases

Oracle • SQL • JDBC • ODBC • Microsoft Access

Software/Programs

Weblogic Application Server • Websphere Studio Application Developer • Eclipse • Fore for Java • (Sun One) • NetBeans • Visual Age for Java • MQ Series • TOPLink • CVS • RCS • Visual Source Safe • Dreamweaver • Microsoft Project • Word • Excel • Outlook • PowerPoint • FrontPage

---

Now let's look at an example of all three of these:
- Performance Profile
- Core Competencies
- Core Technology Competencies

as they might appear at the head of a résumé:

Certified Network Systems Specialist with extensive technical experience in network administration and programming. Skilled in all areas of computer technologies, including: installation, configuration, maintenance, troubleshooting, design, and conversion. Successful in implementing $300,000+ cost-reduction programs and improving operational efficiencies. Excellent organizational, team-building, and communications skills.

CORE PROFESSIONAL COMPETENCIES

Software Development • Life Cycle Process Automation • Vendor Management • Software Interfacing • Systems and Hardware Analysis • Maintenance • Upgrade Customization • Modification • Client & Vendor Presentation • Employee Recruiting • Employee Mentor and Trainer Improved Efficiency

CORE TECHNOLOGY COMPETENCIES

Operating Systems

UNIX • Solaris • IBM • AIX • HP-UX • DOS • Windows 95/98/NT/2000/XP

Languages

Java (JSP, Servlets, Applets, EJB, J2EE) • JavaScript • Visual Basic • HTML • EXL • C/C++ • COBOL • PL/SQL

Databases

Oracle • SQL • JDBC • ODBC • Microsoft Access

Software/Programs

Weblogic Application Server • Websphere Studio Application Developer • Eclipse • Fore for Java • (Sun One) • NetBeans • Visual Age for Java • MQ Series • TOPLink • CVS • RCS • Visual Source Safe • Dreamweaver • Microsoft Project • Word • Excel • Outlook • PowerPoint • FrontPage

When we see these three sections at the beginning of a résumé, it makes it perfectly clear, even to a technological Neanderthal such as me, that this guy knows his job. The rest of the résumé is wide open to repeat any or all of these keywords in context, thus dramatically improving its chances of being one of those top twenty résumés that are likely to be reviewed by human eyes.

Some job search experts argue that even professionals outside of technology should have a separate Technology Competencies Section. It helps describe the whole professional and may well reflect skills clearly sought in Job Descriptions, Job Postings, and in the awareness of hiring managers. This is a good opportunity for you to stay ahead of the curve and make your résumé stand out.

Add these **Performance Profile, Core Competencies**, and **Core Technology Competencies** sections as the lead-in to your work history and get dramatically better results.

Step Five: Capturing Your Recent Work History

With the focus you have gained from Steps 1 and 2, understanding the sort of information résumé readers are going to be looking for, it is time to start going through your work history. In this process, you'll not only be gathering all the information necessary for your résumé, but reminding yourself of all kinds of data employers are likely to require at different stages of the selection cycle. This is a time when you are going to get completely immersed in your work history.

In answering these questions, don't worry about grammar and perfect wording (that comes later), but do take the time to think about the issues. Be descriptive. Don't just say that you were a manager; say that you were a manager with fifty-five direct reports in Decatur and a further fifteen in Mumbai. Be specific whenever possible: full budgetary (with dollar amount), plus selection, development, discipline, and termination responsibilities.

Wherever you can, illustrate with real-world examples, and wherever possible, quantify those examples in terms of money earned or saved, time saved, or productivity improved. Round these examples down rather than up; always identify your role as a team member (this makes your claims more believable) and remember, to ensure a proper focus, complete your target job deconstruction exercises before looking back at your work history. Here's how to structure it:

Current Position
Company
Employment dates
Location
Standing (division, public, private)
Industry/Market Sector
What does your company do?

Example

LARA CORPORATION, INC., ORLANDO, FL, 2001 TO PRESENT

$500 Million Company—One of Largest Resort and Vacation Development/Sales Companies in U.S.—in Rapid Growth Through International Expansion, Strategic M&A, Industry Rollup, and IPO.

What were you hired to do?
Example

**WORLDWIDE DIRECTOR OF OPERATIONS,
ENTERTAINMENT IMAGING 1998–2008**

Selected to re-engineer and revitalize this $65 million business unit with accountability for thirty-two direct reports in four cities across the U.S. Established strategic vision and developed operational infrastructure. Managed supply chain, logistics/distribution, forecasting, system integration, project management, contracts administration, and third-party site operations.

Or more simply

GYPSUM, INC.—MEMPHIS, TN

2004–Present
Production Director
Drove production for world's largest wallboard plant, with 258 employees working in multiple shifts.

Next, include:

- Leadership or Membership of Executive Teams, Project Teams, or Committees
- Experience/Responsibilities/Deliverables (bearing in mind your findings in the TJD)
- When described by a professional colleague, how do you hope they would describe your most desirable professional qualities?

Deliverables

Having done a first pass in the responsibility/deliverables area, take a few moments to review your Target Job Deconstruction. Identify the ways your department or unit is expected to contribute to the bottom line (making or saving money, improving productivity).

Example

Internal auditor: to contain costs by audits to ensure adherence to company policies and financial reporting procedures

Make a bulleted list of the duties/responsibilities/deliverables in this position. Then arrange the elements from most important to least.

Step Six: Listing Your Skills and Special Knowledge

Now, for each of your identified deliverables, answer the following questions:

- What special skills or knowledge did you need to perform this task satisfactorily?

- What educational background and/or credentials helped prepare you for these responsibilities?
- What are your achievements in this area?

For each of your major areas of responsibility, you should consider both the daily problems that arose as well as those major projects/problems that stand out as major accomplishments. Think of each as a problem-solving challenge, and the analytical processes and subsequent actions you took to win the day. There is a four-step technique you will find useful here, called PSRV:

P. Identify the *project* and the problem it represented, both from a corporate perspective and from the point of view of your execution of duties.

S. Identify your *solution* to the challenge and the process you implemented to deliver the solution.

R. What was the *result* of your approach and actions?

V. Finally, what was the *value* to you, the department, and the company? If you can, define this in terms of time saved, money saved, or money earned. This is not always possible, but it is very powerful whenever you can.

The examples you come up with may appear in your résumé, but if not, they will be ready for use as real-world illustrations to the answers you give during interviews, and such examples will show you as someone who is really on top of his or her work and its relation to the company's best interests.

Step Seven: Consider Teamwork and Your Professional Profile

Next within your information-gathering document, ask yourself the following questions:

- What verbal or written comments did peers or managers make about your contributions in each area of your job?
- What different levels of people did you have to interact with to achieve your job tasks? What skills and methods did you use to get the best out of superiors? Coworkers? Subordinates?
- What aspects of your personality were brought into play when executing this duty?

Step Eight: Noting Your Professional Behaviors

How we behave at work has a major impact on how we are perceived, so to be seen as possessing desirable professional behaviors will be of great benefit to your candidacy and to your success once on the job. In order to identify what traits and abilities enable you to perform well at your work, look over the following list of twelve professional behaviors. These are behaviors that are in demand by all employers for all jobs at all levels. Going through the list, you will probably recognize that you already apply some or many of these behaviors in your work. As you read, **come up with examples of your own,** using each particular behavior in the execution of each of your major duties at this job. The examples you generate can be used in your résumé, in your cover letters, and as illustrative answers to questions in interviews.

1. *Communication and Listening Skills.* This covers your ability to communicate effectively with people at all levels in a company and refers to verbal and written skills, along with technological adeptness, dress, and body language. This is an especially important consideration when it comes to your cover letter and résumé, because these written documents are the first means an employer has of judging your communication skills. You should demonstrate that you have taken the time to craft, edit, and re-edit your résumé until it communicates what you want it to, and at the same time demonstrate that you have adequate communication skills.

   Communication embraces *Listening Skills:* listening and understanding, as opposed to just waiting your turn to talk—there is a big difference between the two. Consciously develop your "listening to understand" skills, and the result will be improved persuasive communication abilities.

2. *Goal Orientation.* All employers are interested in goal-oriented professionals—those who achieve concrete results with their actions and who constantly strive to get the job done, rather than just filling the time allotted for a particular task. Whenever possible, you should try to use an example or reference to this behavior in your letters and résumé.

3. *Willingness to Be a Team Player.* The highest achievers (always goal-oriented) are invariably team players. Employers look for employees who work for the common good and always with the group's goals and responsibilities in mind. Team players take pride in group achievement over personal aggrandizement; they look for solutions rather than someone to blame.

4. *Motivation and Energy.* Employers realize a motivated professional will do a better job on every assignment. Motivation expresses itself in a commitment

to the job and the profession, an eagerness to learn and grow professionally, and a willingness to take the rough with the smooth. Motivation is invariably expressed by the energy someone demonstrates in their work—always giving that extra effort to get the job done and to get it done right.

5. *Analytical Skills.* Valuable employees are able to weigh the short- and long-term benefits of a proposed course of action against all its possible negatives. We see these skills demonstrated in the way a person identifies potential problems and is consequently able to minimize their occurrence. Successful application of analytical skills at work requires understanding how your job and the role of your department fit into the company's overall goal of profitability. It also means thinking things through and not jumping at the first or easiest solution.

6. *Dedication and Reliability.* We are speaking here of dedication to your profession, with an awareness of the role it plays in the larger issues of company success, and of the empowerment that comes from knowing how your part contributes to the greater good. Dedication to your profession is also a demonstration of enlightened self-interest. The more engaged you are in your career, the more likely you are to join the inner circles that exist in every department and every company. You will thereby enhance your opportunities for advancement, and this dedication will repay you with better job security and improved professional horizons.

   Your dedication will also express itself in your *reliability*—showing up is half the battle; the other half is your performance on the job. To demonstrate reliability requires following up on your actions, not relying on anyone else to ensure the job is done well, and keeping management informed every step of the way.

7. *Determination.* Someone with this attribute does not back off when a problem or situation gets tough; instead, he or she is the person who chooses to be part of a solution rather than standing idly by and being part of the problem. Determined professionals have decided to make a difference with their presence every day and are willing to do whatever it takes to get a job done, even if that includes duties that might not appear in a job description.

8. *Confidence.* As you develop desirable professional behaviors, your confidence grows in the skills you have and in your ability to develop new ones. With this comes confidence in taking on new challenges. You have the confidence to ask questions, look at challenges calmly and mistakes unflinchingly, and make changes to eradicate them. In short, you develop a quiet confidence in your ability as a professional who can deliver the goods.

9. *Pride and Integrity.* Pride in yourself as a professional means always making sure the job is done to the best of your ability; paying attention to the details and to the time and cost constraints. Integrity means taking responsibility for your actions, both good and bad. It means treating others, within and outside the company, with respect at all times and in all situations. With pride in yourself as a professional with integrity, your actions will always be in the best interests of the company, and your decisions will never be based on whim or personal preference.

10. *Efficiency.* Working efficiently means always keeping an eye open for wasted time, effort, resources, and money.

11. *Economy.* Most problems have two solutions, and the expensive one usually isn't the best. Ideas of efficiency and economy engage the creative mind in ways other workers might not consider; they are an integral part of your analytical proficiency.

12. *Ability to Follow Procedures.* You know that procedures exist to keep the company profitable, so you don't work around them. Following the chain of command, you don't implement your own "improved" procedures or organize others to do so.

Employing these learnable behaviors is the key to long-term career success. If you can recognize the role each of these behaviors play in the successful execution of each of your duties, you'll not only craft a better résumé and land a better job, but you'll also be more successful in your new job and in all future ones.

Step Nine: Add Any Previous Work History at Present Employer

It is not unusual to have held different job titles with the same employer. If this applies to you, such professional progression needs to be identified on your résumé, as it speaks to your competency and promotability. For each different intermediary title, repeat these previous steps. Do not skimp on this process, because once your résumé receives careful consideration, the reader will be impressed with the story of your progression.

Step Ten: Add Work History with Previous Employers

Repeat these steps for each of your previous employers. Most finished résumés place greatest emphasis on the last three jobs, or last ten years' experience. In this developmental portion of the process, however, you must go back in time and cover your entire work history. Remember that you are doing more than preparing a résumé here; you are preparing for the heat of battle. The work you do in a careful analysis of your career to date will help prepare you for interviews through the coming years. One of the biggest complaints interviewers have about job candidates, and one of the major reasons for rejection, is unpreparedness: "You know, good as some of this fellow's skills are, something just wasn't right. He seemed slow somehow. You know, he couldn't even remember which jobs he held when!" You won't have that problem.

Step Eleven: Compile Endorsements

Looking at each of your major areas of responsibility with each of your employers, come up with whatever complimentary verbal or written commentary on your performance you can. To recall endorsements means you might be able to use one or two in your résumé, and perhaps your cover letter. They'll give you confidence, and you'll perhaps be able to use some in the interview process.

Step Twelve: Take Care of Miscellaneous Material

The hard work is done; now you just need to capture the details concerning your abilities and experience in the following areas.

Military History

Include branch of service, rank, and any special skills that could further your civilian career. Assuming you had an honorable discharge, it's worth mentioning military experience at the end of your résumé; it carries weight, and to most readers, demonstrates you are organized, can take direction, and are used to working for the good of a team.

Educational History

Start with the highest level of attainment and work backward. Give dates, schools, majors, minors, grade-point averages, scholarships, and special awards. In the final document, you might only list the school and the degree, but it is good to refresh your mind at this point.

List other school activities, such as sports, societies, and social activities. Especially important are leadership roles. Any example of how you "made a difference" with your presence could be of value to your future. Obviously, this is most important for recent graduates with little work experience, and those in the very early stages of a career.

Ongoing Professional Development

Identify all the classes and courses you have pursued during your career, including certification and accreditations; they all speak to your professional commitment and to employers' belief in your potential.

Languages

The ability to read and write foreign languages is increasingly important in a global economy. Specify your level of fluency in each.

Personal Interests

List interests and activities that could be supportive to your candidacy. For example, an internal auditor who plays chess or bridge would list these on a résumé, because they support the analytical bent so necessary to that field. Activities that challenge you physically, analytically, or as a member of a team are all regarded positively in the selection process. These aren't "must haves" in a résumé, but they can make nice little pluses when space allows, so think through this now.

Patents and Publications

Include patents that are both pending and awarded. If you have published articles, list the name of the publication, title of article, and the publication date. If you have had books published, list the title and publisher.

Professional Associations

Include membership and the details of any offices you held.

Civic Affiliations and Volunteer Work

It isn't only paid work experience that makes you valuable, so include membership in civic groups and any volunteer work you performed. In some professions and at the higher levels, community involvement is usually regarded as a positive commentary on your full engagement with life.

Miscellaneous Areas of Achievement

All professions and careers are different. Use this section to itemize any additional aspects of your history where you somehow "made a difference" with your presence.

Do Your Credentials Warrant the Target Job?

We started the information-gathering process by focusing on a target job title and then researching recruitment advertising to come up with a clear idea of what employers are typically looking for under that job title. There is a simple check-and-balance step you can take here that will benefit you in some powerful ways. You'll remember that I advised you to create a TJD that comprised a bulleted list of the desired requirements from all the recruitment postings you discovered. Now reread this document, reminding yourself that:

- No one is ever added to the payroll for the love of humanity.
- At some level, all employees are hired to do the same job: problem solution and problem avoidance within a specific area of expertise.
- No one ever reads résumés for fun.
- Résumés are always read with job titles in mind.
- Résumés are always read with a job description in mind.

Then having reread your TJD, proceed to cut and paste relevant information from each of your answers beneath each bullet. At the end of the process, you can read the TJD now enhanced with your research and answers. You'll very quickly get a picture of your relative strengths and weaknesses. Hopefully, this will tell you:

- I can do the job.
- I have a picture of what employers are going to ask me about.
- I have a blueprint for what I can talk about in response.
- I can talk about my experience in my résumé using words with which employers will be familiar.

When this is complete, you will know whether or not this is the right job for you to target, and be ready to start choosing a format for your résumé and putting all the pieces together. Remember, that to make things easier, there is a complete résumé questionnaire you can download at *www.knockemdead.com*.

CHOICES FOR RÉSUMÉ FORMAT

WE ALL HAVE different professional backgrounds and we all have the right and the obligation to package them to our greatest benefit.

Some of us have worked for only one company, and some of us have worked for eleven companies in as many years. Some of us have changed careers once or twice, and some of us have maintained a predictable career path within one profession or industry. For some, diversity broadens our potential, and for others concentration in one area deepens it. While we each require different résumé vehicles to put our work history in the most exciting light, the goals are constant.

1. To show off achievements, attributes, and accumulation of expertise to the best advantage.
2. To minimize any possible weaknesses.

Résumé experts acknowledge three major styles for presenting your credentials to a potential employer: Chronological, Functional, and Combination (Chrono-Functional). Your particular circumstances will determine the right format for you. You will see résumé books with up to fifteen different résumé styles. Such volumes are merely filling up space; in the final analysis, each additional style that such books mention is a tiny variation on the above three.

I am going to give you a brief explanation of each style with examples. They are all relevant, depending on your circumstances, and you might even try more than one version in your own job search.

The Chronological Résumé

The chronological is the most common and widely accepted résumé format. It's what most of us think of when we think of résumés—a chronological listing of job titles and responsibilities. It starts with the current or most recent employment, then works backward to your first job.

This format is good for demonstrating your growth in a single profession. It is suitable for anyone with practical work experience who hasn't suffered too many job changes or prolonged periods of unemployment. It is not always the best choice if you are just out of school or if you are changing careers, where a chronological format could then draw attention to your weaknesses (i.e., your lack of specific experience in a field) rather than your strengths.

The Work History is the distinguishing characteristic of the chronological résumé, because it ties your job responsibilities and achievements to specific employers, job titles, and dates.

There are also optional categories determined by the space available to you and the unique aspects of your professional experience. These will be discussed in Chapter 3.

Parag Gupta

104 W. Real Drive · Beaverton, OR 97006 · (503) 123-4286 · parag.gupta@technical.com

SYSTEMS ENGINEER:

Motivated and driven IT Professional offering 9+ years of hands-on experience in designing, implementing, and enhancing systems to automate business operations. Demonstrated ability to develop high-performance systems, applications, databases, and interfaces.

- Part of TL9000 CND audit interviews that helped Technical get TL9000 certified, which is significant in Telecom industry. Skilled trainer and proven ability to lead many successful projects, like TSS, EMX, and TOL.
- Strategically manage time and expediently resolve problems for optimal productivity, improvement, and profitability; able to direct multiple tasks effectively.
- Strong technical background.
- Highly effective liaison and communication skills proven by effective interaction with management, users, team members, and vendors.

Technical Skills

Operating Systems:	Unix, Windows (2000, XP), DOS
Languages:	C, C++, Java, Pascal, Assembly Languages (Z8000, 808x, DSP)
Methodologies:	TL9000, Digital Six Sigma
Software:	MS Office, Adobe Framemaker, Matlab
RDBMS:	DOORS, Oracle 7.x
Protocols:	TCP/IP, SS7 ISUP, A1, ANSI, TL1, SNMP
Tools:	Teamplay, Clearcase, Clearquest, M-Gate keeper, Exceed, Visio, DocExpress, Compass
Other:	CDMA Telecom Standards – 3GPP2 (Including TIA/EIA-2001, TIA/EIA-41, TIA/EIA-664), ITU-T, AMPS

Professional Experience

Technical, Main Network Division, Hillsboro, OR   Jan 1999–Present

Principal Staff Engineer • Products Systems Engineering • Nov 2004–Present

- Known as "go-to" person for CDMA call processing and billing functional areas.
- Created customer requirements documents for Technical SoftSwitch (TSS) and SMS Gateway products. All deliverables done on/ahead schedule with high quality.
- Solely accountable for authoring and allocation, customer reviews, supporting fellow system engineers, development and test, and customer documentation teams.
- Support Product Management in RFPs, customer feature prioritization, impact statements, and budgetary estimates.
- Mentored junior engineers and 1 innovation disclosure [patent] submitted in 2007.
- Resolved deployed customer/internal requirements issues and contributed to Virtual Zero Defect quality goal.
- TOL process champion and part of CND focus group that contributed to reducing CRUD backlog (NPR) by 25% and cycle time (FRT) by 40%.
- Recognized as the TL9000 expert. Triage representative for switching and messaging products.

Senior Staff Engineer • MSS Systems Engineering • May 2002–Oct 2004

- Led a team of 12 engineers for 3 major software releases of TSS product included around 80 features/enhancements to create T-Gate SE deliverables.

- Created requirements for TSS product, 30 features/enhancements contributing to 5 major software releases. Recognized as overall product expert with specific focus on call processing and billing.
- Played integral role in successfully implementing proprietary commercial TSS billing system.
- Supported PdM organization by creating ROMs, technical support for RFPs (Vivo, Sprint, TELUS, TM, Tata, Inquam, Alaska, Reliance, Pakistan, PBTL, Mauritius, Telefonica, Brasicel, and Angola).
- Proactively identified functional areas of improvement for requirements coverage, contributed to resolving several faults, improved customer documentation, and provided reference for future releases as well as other customers.

Senior Software Engineer • EMX Development • Aug 2000–Apr 2002

- Successfully led and coordinated the cross-functional development teams, 30 engineers, to meet the scheduled design, code, and test completion dates ensuring Feature T-Gates are met.
- Feature Technical Lead for Concurrent Voice/Data Services feature, the largest revenue-generating feature for KDDI customer.
- Feature Lead for Paging Channel SMS feature. Created requirements and design; led implementation phase of five engineers' team; supported product, network, and release testing; and created customer reference documentation.
- Performed the role of functional area lead for Trunk Manager and A1 interface functional areas. Provided 2-day Technical Workshops for internal/customer knowledge sharing and functional area transition from Caltel.
- Provided customer site testing and FOA (First Office Application) support for major EMX releases and off-hours CNRC (Customer Networks Resolution Center) support.
- Received "Bravo Award"–May 2001, Sep 2001, Jan 2002

Software Engineer • EMX Development • Jan 1999–Jul 2000

- Developed design and code for SMS feature as a Trunk Manager functional area lead for the largest FA impacted by the feature. Supported product, network, and release testing.
- Contributed to customer release documentation. Supported feature-level SMS testing at various internal labs and customer sites resulting in successful deployment at customer sites.
- Designed and coded phases for wiretap and virtual circuits feature development, initial assessment of internal and customer EMX PRs (problem reports) to route/classify issues and providing problem assessments for many of these PRs.
- Created an implementation process to serve as reference for new hires.
- Provided CNRC support during the Y2K transition.
- Received "Above and Beyond Performance Award"–Jan 2000, Dec 2000 and "Certificate of Outstanding Achievement"–Jun 1999

Education: Master of Science in Computer Engineering • University of Portland, Portland, OR • 1998

Bachelors of Engineering in Electronics • Technology and Science Institute, India •1996

Significant Trainings Include

- Open Source Software • WiMAX • Agile Management for Software Engineering
- WSG Requirements Process • Product Security

The Functional Résumé

This format focuses on the professional skills you have developed over the years and bring to a specific target job, rather than on when, where, or how you acquired them. It also de-emphasizes employers and employment dates by their placement on the second page. Job titles and employers can likewise play a minor part with this type of résumé. The focus is always on the skill rather than the context or time of its acquisition.

This functional format is suited to a number of different personal circumstances, specifically those of:

- Mature professionals with a storehouse of expertise and jobs
- Entry-level types whose track records do not justify a chronological résumé
- Career changers who want to focus on skills rather than experience
- People whose careers have been stagnant or in ebb, who want to give focus to the skills that can get a career underway again, rather than on the history in which it was becalmed in the first place
- Those returning to the workplace after a long absence
- People closer to retirement than to the onset of their careers

For any résumé to be effective, it must be conceived with a specific job in mind, and this is especially true for a functional résumé. Because it focuses so strongly on skills and the ability to contribute in a particular direction, rather than on a directly relevant work history, you must have an employment objective clearly in mind.

Though functional résumés are more free-form than chronological ones, there are certain structural features that prevent their becoming what novelist Henry James called "loose, baggy monsters" of the *War and Peace* variety:

- *A Performance Profile or Career Objective/Summary.* Different skills are needed for different jobs, so some kind of functional summary up front is where the functional résumé writer puts forward an encapsulated argument of suitability.
- *Relevant Accomplishments/Skills/Knowledge/Professional Behaviors.* Based on your target job, this is where you identify relevant accomplishments, along with the skills and behaviors that made them possible.
- *Dates.* Strictly speaking, a functional résumé needn't give dates, but a résumé without dates waves a big red flag. So if your employment history lacks stability, a functional résumé allows you to de-emphasize

Charles Chalmers

Manhattan NY 11658 • (212) 232-8269 • fineartist@earthlink.net

Senior Curator Performance Summary

My professional life is focused on art in all it embraces: drawing, painting, sculpture, photography, cinema, video, audio, performance and digital art, and art history and criticism; my personal life is similarly committed. Recently relocated to Manhattan, I intend to make a contribution to the NY arts community that harnesses my knowledge, enthusiasm, and sensibilities.

ART HISTORY

Thorough knowledge of art history from caves of Lascaux through current artists such as Bruce Nauman, Jessica Stockholder, and Luc Tuymans. Film history from Lumiere Brothers to Almodovar. Current with key critical art and film theory. Ongoing workshops and lectures with the likes of Matthew Barney, Louise Bourgeoise, and Andy Goldsworthy.

RESEARCH NEW ARTISTS

Connected to cutting-edge art and artists through involvement with the art communities and galleries of New York and Boston and the faculty, student, and alumni networks of RISD, Columbia, Boston Museum School, New England School of Art & Design, and now Mass Art. Twenty years of Manhattan gallery openings and networking with artists at MOMA, PS1, Guggenheim, Whitney, Metropolitan, Film Forum, and International Center for Photography workshops and lectures.

GATHERING ARTWORK

Through local artists, regional and global artist networks, intercultural artist exchanges, alumni groups, first-rank private collectors, personal and family networks, and Internet calls for submissions.

ART AND THE COMMUNITY

Conception and launch of themed, resourced, and sequenced shows that invigorate campus and community involvement. Reconfigure existing art spaces to create dynamic dialogue with visitors. Education and outreach programs.

INSTALLATION OF ART

Maintain fluidity of gallery space in preparing exhibitions with recognition of size/time considerations for the art, to insure a sympathetic environment for the presented works. Hang, light, and label shows in sequences that create dialogue between the works.

PR MATERIALS

Energizing invitations, comprehensive press kits, illustrated press releases, and artist binder materials. Sensitive to placing art in historical/cultural context. Photoshop.

Management Experience

Fourteen years art-staff management experience, including curriculum development. Responsible for art instructors, art handlers, maintenance crews, and working with printers, catering, and graphic arts staff.

Employment

1994–2005 Chair of Visual Arts, The Green Briar School.

Duties: Curriculum development, portfolio preparation, internal and external monthly shows, theater sets, monthly video news show, taught art history and all the studio arts, managed staff of three.

1989–2004 President Art Workshops.

Duties: Private art studio and art history curriculums, staff of four. Private groups to Manhattan museums and gallery tours.

1980–1989 Freelance artist, photographer, and editor.

Highlights include: Taught photography at Trinity School, Manhattan; photographer for the Ramones; editor of Pioneer, insurance industry trade magazine; assistant to Claudia Weill, documentary filmmaker, director of *Girlfriends*.

Education

MFA. Magna cum laude. Columbia University, 1983
   Awards: ****** ***** Prize for film criticism
   Taught undergraduate Intro to Film, under ****** ***** and ****** ******.

Subscriptions

Art in America, *Art News*, *ArtForum*, *New York Times*, *Parkett*, *Sight & Sound*, *Film Comment*, *Modern Painters*.

Memberships

MOMA/PS1, Whitney Museum, Guggenheim, Metropolitan Museum of Art, DIA.

Recent Exhibitions

2004. Corcoran Center Gallery, Southampton, NY

2005. Corsair Gallery, 37 West 33rd St. NYC

2006. Fuller Museum, Brockton, MA

2002–2007. Zeitgeist Gallery, Cambridge, MA

dates somewhat by their placement, while an absence of employment dates altogether will do anything but de-emphasize them.

• *Education.* This is always included.

The space available and the unique aspects of your background determine inclusion of other optional categories.

Functional résumés are not as popular as they once were, but in some circumstances, such as those mentioned, they really are the best choice. Below is an example of someone applying for a job as an art gallery or museum curator whose only prior experience was as an art teacher. I want you to read the first page and then ask yourself if you know what such a person does for a living. I'll give you a few more interesting insights after the example.

A couple of interesting observations about the previous résumé:

• It is more informal in tone than many examples you will see in the book, but as it reflected someone in a profession where personality is a significant part of the job, there is nothing wrong with that. Given these considerations, I decided to give the résumé a personal flavor, and the very first words after the contact information immediately draw the reader into a conversation with a passionate and committed professional: "My professional life is focused on art in all it embraces."
• There are professions where a less formal tone is more generally acceptable, usually education, the arts, and the caring professions.
• It is quite clear this person really understands the work of a curator. This résumé went out once and resulted in an interview within seventy-two hours, at which a job offer was extended at the end of the first hour.
• Now for the kicker. Everything in this résumé is absolutely true. The fact that this person had been the arts department chair of a private elementary through middle school was never an issue, because he so clearly understood the demands of the target job, and that was possible because his TJD research had allowed the résumé to be properly focused and prepared him for exactly the topics that would come up at interview.

This functional résumé was successful because the writer took the time to go through the TJD process we have been discussing and was able to recognize what it was that made a successful curator. He then demonstrated that he had exactly the credentials needed.

The Combination Résumé

For the upwardly mobile professional, this is becoming the résumé of choice. It has all the flexibility and strength that come from combining both the chronological and functional formats, and it allows you to clearly demonstrate your thorough grasp of the job and its deliverables.

- *A Career Summary or Performance Profile.* The combination résumé, more often than not, has either a Career Summary or a Performance Profile, where you spotlight yourself as a professional with a clear sense of self, and a history of relevant contributions. It might include a power-packed description of skills, achievements, and professional behaviors. In the example here, the variation is "Executive Summary."

  Alternatively, it may contain a "Job Objective" (not nearly such a powerful headline as an inducement for the reader's attention) that doesn't so much announce what you want in a job, but rather showcases your thorough understanding of the target job and its contribution to the target endeavor.

  This section comes right after the target job title at the very top of the résumé. You will also see from examples later in the book that some résumés do without the Performance Profile/Career Summary altogether, the argument being that coming right after the target job title it is a given that this paragraph is a performance profile. The choice is yours, but if in doubt, add the headline "Performance Profile"—it gives the reader an immediate positive focus.

- *A Description of Functional Skills.* This is where the combination of styles comes into play. Following the summary, the combination résumé starts out like a functional résumé and highlights achievements in different categories relevant to the job/career goals.

- *A Chronological History.* Then it switches to the chronological approach and names companies, dates, titles, duties, and responsibilities. This section can also include further evidence of achievements or special contributions.

John William Wisher, MBA

2541 Bainbridge Blvd.
West Chicago, IL 60185

jwisher@ameritech.net

630.878.2653 630.377.9117

Expert leadership in cost effective supply chain, vendor, and project management within *Fortune* organizations.

EXECUTIVE PROFILE

A visionary, forward-thinking SUPPLY CHAIN AND LOGISTICS LEADER offering 20+ years of progressive growth and outstanding success streamlining operations across a wide range of industries. Excellent negotiation and relationship management skills with ability to inspire teams to outperform expectations. Proven record of delivering a synchronized supply chain approach through strategic models closely mirroring business plan to dramatically optimize ROI and manage risk.

Supply Chain Strategy:—Successfully led over 500 supply chain management initiatives across a wide spectrum of businesses, negotiating agreements from $5K to $27M. Implemented technology solutions and streamlined processes to reduce redundancies and staffing hours, improving both efficiency and productivity. Industries include: automotive and industrial manufacturing, consumer goods, government and defense, healthcare, high tech, and retail.

Industry Knowledge:—Extensive knowledge base developed from hands-on industry experience. Began career in dock operations with experience in Hub and Package Operations, multi-site retail operations management, to custom supply chain strategy development over twenty-one-year career with UPS.

Supply Chain Process Costing:—Built several information packets on total cost of ownership (TCO) and facilitated several C-level negotiations to identify and confirm opportunities. Worked to increase awareness among stakeholders on efficiencies and cost-saving measures ROI. Delivered $3.75M total cost savings to client base over three-year period.

Operations Reorganization:—Designed and implemented new sales force alignment and reporting structure; increased daily sales calls by 20%, reduced travel mileage 23%, and head count by nine; total annual cost savings of $920K.

Logistics:—Experienced across all modes of transportation: ocean, air freight, LTL, TL, mail services, and small package. Performs complex analysis to develop strategy based on cost and delivery requirements.

Project Management:—Implemented complete $1.2M redesign of 11 new UPS Customer Centers. Managed vendor and lease negotiations, developed budgets, training, and sales structure. All 11 centers up and operational on time and on budget.

Cost & Process Improvements

- Implemented complete warehouse redesign for a large optical distributor. Optimized warehouse operations through engineering a new warehouse design, integrating and automating technology, and synchronization of goods movement through ocean, air, ground, and mail services. Reduced transportation expense by 15%, increased production levels by 25%, reduced inventory by 15% and staffing by 20%.

- Built custom supply chain for a nationally recognized golf club manufacturer. Improved service levels by 30%, reduced damage by 45%, and integrated technology to support shipping process automation, reducing billing function staffing hours 50%.

Trust-Based Leadership

Vendor/Client Negotiations

Cross-Functional Collaboration

Supply Chain Mapping

Financial Logistics Analysis

Contingency Planning

Risk Management

Competitive Analysis

Haz Mat Compliance

Inventory Planning, Control, & Distribution

Recruiting/Training/Development

Project Management

Organizational Change Management

Distributive Computing

Budget Management

Labor Relations

PROFESSIONAL BACKGROUND

United Parcel Service (UPS), Addison, IL   1986 to Present
World's largest package-delivery company and global leader in supply chain services, offering an extensive range of options for synchroniz-
ing the movement of goods, information, and funds. Serves more than 200 countries and territories worldwide and operates the largest
franchise shipping chain, the UPS Store.

DIRECTOR/AREA MANAGER—SUPPLY CHAIN SALES, 2005–Present

Promoted to lead and develop a cross-functional sales force of 18 in consultative supply chain management services to Chicago-area businesses. Directs development of integrated supply chain management solutions across all modes of transportation, closely mirroring client business plans. Mentors team in Demand Responsive Model, a proven methodology to quickly align internal and external resources with changing market demands, situational requirements, and mission critical conditions. Manages $100M P&L.

Accomplishments:
- Implements over 100 multimillion-dollar supply chain integrations per year with 14% annual growth on 8% plan.
- Develops future organizational leaders; four staff members promoted through effective mentoring and development.
- Choreographed a supply chain movement from the Pacific Rim for a global fast-food chain to deliver 300k cartons to 15k locations all on the same day. Utilized modes of ocean, TL, air, and ground services, allowing for a national release synchronized to all locations on the same release date.
- Designed and implemented an automated reverse logistics program for a nationally recognized health food/supplement distributor. Automated returns process to reduce touches and costly staffing hours. Eliminated front-end phone contact using technology and web automation.

MARKETING MANAGER   2004 to 2005

Fast tracked to streamline sales processes, increasing performance. Performed analysis of sales territory, historical data, operations alignment, reporting structure, and sales trends to devise solutions. Managed and coached area managers in business-plan development and execution of sales strategies. Delivered staff development in cost-reduction strategies and compliance requirements. Accountable for $500M P&L.

Accomplishments:
- Drove $500M+ in local market sales. Grew revenues 2004/2005 revenues 12% and 7% respectively.

RETAIL CHANNEL/OPERATIONS MANAGER   2002 to 2004

Charged with turning around this underperforming business unit. Managed development and implementation of new retail strategy across northern Illinois. Rebranded UPS Customer Centers and the UPS Store. Performed vendor negotiations and collaborated with nine regions to support additional implementations.

Accomplishments:
- Developed key revenue-generating initiatives across multiple channels. Attained 65% growth in discretionary sales. Several strategies adopted across the national organization.
- Re-engineered inventory for over 1,000 dropoff locations, reduced lease expenses by 45% and inventory levels by 40% through weekly measurement, inventory level development by SKU, order process automation, and order consolidation.
- Implemented new retail sales associate structure in 1,100 locations; scored highest national service levels by mystery shoppers.
- Selected as Corporate team member on Mail Boxes Etc. acquisition integration.

PROJECT MANAGER   2001 to 2002

Selected to support several underperforming business areas. Managed key segments of district business initiatives and compliance measures for 1,000 dropoff locations. Reported on status to corporate management. Supervised office staff of 16. Negotiated vendor and lease agreements.

Accomplishments:
- Rolled out and managed ongoing Haz Mat compliance program for all locations.
- Generated $6M in sales through cross-functional lead program and increased participation from 20% to 100%.
- Attained union workforce sponsorship of support-growth program through careful negotiations and persuasion.

SENIOR ACCOUNT MANAGER   1999 to 2001

Delivered $2.8M in growth on $1.1M plan, rated 3rd of 53 managers in revenue generation

ACCOUNT MANAGER   1997 to 1998

Top producer out of 53; $1.3M sales on $500K plan.

John William Wisher, MBA

SERVICE PROVIDER   1994 to 1996
Top producer out of 53; $1.3M sales on $500K plan.

SUPERVISOR OF PACKAGE OPERATIONS   1994
Managed 65 full-time service providers. Performed post-routine analysis, operating strategy development, compliance, payroll, service failure recovery, and new technology implementation. Met 100% DOT and Haz Mat compliance. Reduced post-delivery staffing time by 50% and missed pickups by 65%.

SUPERVISOR OF HUB OPERATIONS   1988 to 1994
Managed up to 100 union employees and staff processing 75K pieces per day involving 40+ outbound bays. Performed complex staff scheduling and maintained low turnover rates. Designed new management reporting format, reducing administrative time by 20% and improved load quality by 30%.

OPERATIONS DOCK WORKER AND TRAINING LEAD   1986 to 1987

EDUCATION
MBA

National Louis University, Wheaton, IL, *4.0 GPA*

BA, Business, Supply Chain Management

Elmhurst College, Elmhurst, IL, *3.84 GPA, Magna cum laude*

Additional Specialized Courses:
- Supply Chain Mapping, 20 Hours
- Financial Logistics Analysis (FLOGAT), 10 Hours
- Hazardous Materials, 20 Hours
- Labor Relations, 30 Hours
- Managers Leadership School, 100 Hours
- Hazardous Materials, 20 Hours
- Managing from the Heart, 30 Hours

THE BASIC INGREDIENTS

TECHNOLOGY CONTINUES TO create new professions overnight, and with them, new career opportunities. The content of these new professions and careers has made the employment world dramatically different from that of just a few years ago.

What used to be strictly off-limits in all résumés is now acceptable in many and required in some. One example that comes to mind: Your résumé's performance in résumé database searches now demands that they should be heavy with keywords and, where necessary, technical jargon.

Writing a résumé is like baking a cake: In most instances, the ingredients are essentially the same; what determines the flavor is the order and quantity in which those ingredients are blended and how the final confection is presented. There are certain ingredients that go into almost every résumé, others that rarely or never go in, and those added as special touches depending on your personal tastes and requirements.

If a certain ingredient must always go in or always stay out, you will know why. In circumstances where the résumé-writing world holds conflicting views, I will explain the divergence so that a reasoned judgment can be made.

First, let's look at the ingredients that are part of every successful résumé.

What Must Always Go In

You should create a template for your résumé, so that as you proceed and read that an item must go in, go right ahead and add it as you read, making any changes necessary for your particular circumstances. You will find lots of résumé templates at *www.knockemdead.com*.

Name

We start with the obvious, but there are other considerations about your name besides remembering to put it on your résumé. Give your first and last name only. It isn't necessary to include your middle name(s). My name is Martin John Yate, but my résumé says simply Martin Yate, because that is the way I would introduce myself in person. Notice also that it isn't M. J. Yate, because that would force the reader to play Twenty Questions about the meaning of my initials. Even if you are known by your initials, don't put them on your résumé. If you use quotation marks or parentheses, those on the receiving end might think it a little strange. Better that it comes out at the interview when the interviewer asks you what you like to be called; at the very least, you'll have some small talk to break the ice.

It is not required to place Mr., Ms., Miss, or Mrs. before your nam, unless yours is a unisex name like Gayle, Carroll, Leslie, or any of the other names that are used for members of either sex. In such instances, it is acceptable to write Mr. Gayle Jones or Ms. Leslie Jackson.

Finally, if you are the II, III, Junior, or Senior holder of your name, and if you always add Jr. or III when you sign your name, or if that is the way you are addressed to avoid confusion, go ahead and use it. Otherwise, it is extraneous information on the résumé, and therefore not needed.

Address

Give your complete address. Do not abbreviate unless space restrictions make it mandatory. If you do abbreviate—such as with *St.* or *Apt.*—be consistent. The state of your residence, however, is always abbreviated to two capitalized letters (for example, MN, WV, LA), according to post office standards. The accepted format for laying out your address looks like this:

Maxwell Krieger
9 Central Avenue, Apartment 38
New York, NY 23456

Notice that the city, state, and zip code all go on the same line, with a comma between city and state. If space is an issue, you can put your contact information on a single line; use your judgment.

It is acceptable to omit/fictionalize both name and address if you are creating a sanitized résumé that protects your identity; important if you are both employed and professionally visible.

Telephone Number

Always include your telephone number; few businesses will send you an invitation for an interview in the mail. Including your area code is important even if you have no intention of leaving the area. In this era of decentralization, your résumé might end up being screened in another part of the country.

Unless your current employer knows of your job search and approves, leave your work number off the résumé; if your circumstances dictate, put it in your cover letter. Good cover letters do this with a short sentence that conveys the information and demonstrates you as a responsible employee. For example, something like this can work very well:

"I prefer not to use my employer's time by taking personal calls at work, but with discretion you can reach me at 202/555-5555, extension 555, to initiate contact."

If you are employed, it is entirely acceptable to replace the name of your current employer with something more generic. I will show you how best to do this in a few pages.

Most telephone companies allow you to have more than one telephone number, and each number you have can have its own distinctive ring. It might not be a bad idea to use one of these numbers as a permanent career-management contact; whenever it rings, you can be sure to finish chewing the Doritos before picking it up.

E-Mail

Your e-mail address is an integral part of your contact information. Never use your work e-mail address. It increases the odds of your boss learning that you are looking at broader horizons; you don't want that to happen. Nowadays, it is common for an IT worker to be assigned to monitor appropriate use of company computers, and that always includes tracking Internet and e-mail usage. Using company e-mail outside regular working hours won't work either; the trail is still there for prying eyes to see. Please stay away from company telephone and e-mail usage for your job search. It can be, and often is, regarded as theft of company time and services; as such, it's not only cause for dismissal from your current job, but it also sends the wrong message to potential employers.

Your ISP will allow you to have a number of different e-mail addresses. Take advantage of this and create one that you will only use for career-management initiatives, and come up with something that speaks to your profession: *finebiochemist@earthlink.net* or *supersales@aol.com*.

This protects your identity and acts as a tempting headline to the potential reader.

Target Job Title

It is astounding how many résumés in this day and age do not carry a target job title. A target job title, coming right after the contact information, helps your résumé perform in the database searches and acts as a headline to give the reader a focus and starting point. Think about it: Have you ever read a book or a magazine article or watched a television show or a movie that didn't have a title to draw the reader or viewer in? Your résumé has to perform in a similarly competitive marketplace. Here are some of the target job titles we looked at earlier:

- Occupational Health Services Manager
- Certified Occupational Health Nurse Specialist/ Certified Case Manager / Certified Occupational Hearing Conservationist
- Senior Vice President Worldwide Operations
- Nurse Practitioner   Advanced Practice Nurse   Mid-Level Practitioner
- Campaign Field Director _____ for State Senate—Montana State Senate, **th Legislative District, Boise, MT
- Management Professional

- Operations / Human Resources / Labor Relations / Staff Development
- Healthcare Professional
- Operations Management—Healthcare Review—Clinical Consultant
- Agricultural/Environmental Manager
- Horticultural Buying—International Experience

Career Summary or Performance Profile

Without a Career Summary or Performance Profile, a résumé can have no focus, no sense of direction. If you don't have a target job, you can't write a targeted résumé, because the body copy has nothing to support. In this day and age, a job-targeted résumé is going to be dramatically more productive.

Both a Career Summary and Performance Profile are acceptable. Regardless of the heading, your objective is to show your possession of exactly the kinds of skills that employers seek when hiring this type of person. This paragraph should summarize your value proposition, and is a powerful way to open your résumé. It gives the reader a clear focus and summary of who you are and what you bring to the table.

Additionally, this paragraph allows you to repeat critical keywords and phrases that will help your résumé's ranking in database searches, plus overworked résumé screeners are given a ready focus for their evaluation.

These job objectives appear at the top of a résumé, as a headline and attention grabber. They focus on skills, achievements, and relevant personal behaviors that summarize the argument of your target job title.

The inclusion of Performance Profiles and the like has just as much relevance for résumé databases as they do for people. In a best-case scenario, the résumé reader is looking for someone just like you. The Target Job Title and Performance Profile will quickly demonstrate that you are a fit and the reader will continue with the rest of the résumé. Then, in this best-case scenario, you will get a call asking you to interview right away.

But what happens if, as happens more often than not, your résumé immediately gets logged onto the résumé database without ever being seen by human eyes? With a Target Job Title and Career Summary/Performance Profile describing the target job and using the right keywords to describe the work, your résumé will be retrieved and reviewed by human eyes with greater frequency.

Employment Dates

Employment dates belong in your résumé, and they need to be accurate, as they are quite likely to be checked. Résumé readers are often leery of résumés without employment dates. If you expect a response, you can increase your odds dramatically by including them—in one form or another.

With a steady work history and no employment gaps, you can be very specific (space allowing) and write:

January 11, 2004 to July 4, 2008 or 1/11/04 to 7/4/08

Or, to be a little less specific:

January 2004–July 2008

But if there are short employment gaps, or the occasional job with short duration, you can improve the look of things by writing:

2007–2008

instead of:

December 12, 2007–January 23, 2008

There is no suggestion here that you should lie about your work history, but it is surprising just how many interviewers will be quite satisfied with such dates.

While this technique can effectively hide embarrassing employment gaps, and it may get you in for an interview, you should be prepared, without any hesitancy, with a forthright answer to questions on this topic. Even if such questions are posed, you will have the opportunity to explain yourself in person, and that is a distinct improvement over being peremptorily ruled out by some faceless nonentity before you get a chance to speak your piece. The end justifies the means, in this case.

If you abbreviate employment dates, be sure to do so consistently. It is acceptable to list annual dates, rather than month and year. Remember, when references get checked, the first things verified are dates of employment and leaving salary.

Untruths in either of these areas are grounds for dismissal with cause, and that can dog your footsteps into the future.

All Important Keywords

If computers have helped streamline your job-search activities, they have done the same for the recruitment work of many human resource departments. Understanding how your résumé is stored and retrieved will dramatically affect your chances for success in your job search.

While electronic résumé distribution makes your life easier, it has created an avalanche of electronic paper on the other side of the desk. If a company once had to deal with 100 résumés a day, it now probably sees ten times that number. With the high cost of human handling, the wholesale adoption of résumé screening and tracking systems by businesses is a given. When computer screening replaces human judgment, the whole game changes. The computer program can't use human logic; instead, the computer searches for keywords that describe the position and the professional skills needed to execute the duties effectively.

It works like this: The company representative sits down at the keyboard and opens the database program and keys a job title into a dialogue box (immediately, we see the value of that Target Job Title). The program then offers an extensive selection of words that can be used to describe that job. The user scrolls through the list clicking on the keywords that best describe the current needs and also has the option to add additional key words and phrases to the search. At the end of the sequence, the user hits a "Search" button and the program goes to work. A bot, or electronic spider, searches the résumé database for all résumés that mention any of the selected keywords. When this is done, it weights the list (just like a Google search), with those résumés with the greatest frequency of the selected keywords ranked first.

Your résumé—and a millions like it—can be scanned for the necessary keywords in seconds.

In 2008, all three of the largest job sites (Careerbuilder, Monster, and Hotjobs) had in excess of 25 million résumés in their databases. With such a huge number to pick from, recruiters have gotten into the habit of only looking at the top twenty résumés in any given search; this is usually adequate to fulfill their needs.

Almost instantaneously, the user receives a weighted list of the résumés that contain the appropriate keywords. The greater the number of relevant keywords in your résumé, the higher your ranking on the list. The higher your ranking, the greater the likelihood that your résumé will be rescued from the avalanche and passed along to human eyes for further screening. This has led directly to the denser résumés we are seeing today and the increasing prevalence of keyword sections.

In some of the résumé examples later in the book, you'll see a section that lumps a string of keywords together. This is often referred to as Core Competencies, Special Knowledge, Professional Skills, Technical Skills, or Areas of Expertise. Here's what the Core Competencies section of a taxation specialist's résumé looks like:

AREAS OF EXPERTISE

SBT, C-Corporation and S-Corporation State Income Tax Returns * Vehicle Use Tax Returns * State Income Tax Budgeting and Accrual * Multistate Property Tax Returns * Federal, State, and Local Exemption Certificates * State and Local Sales, Use and Excise Tax Management * Tax Audit Management * Tax License and Bonding Management * Certificates of Authority and Annual Report Filing Maintenance * State Sales and Use Tax Assessment * Federal Excise Tax Collection and Deposits * Determination of Nexus * Tax Amnesty Programs

---

A Core Competencies (my personal choice for most powerful headline for this section of your résumé) section not only dramatically increases your chances of getting the computer's attention, recruiters and HR people appreciate them as a brief synopsis of the whole résumé. Each keyword or phrase acts as an affirmation of a skill area and as a possible topic of conversation. Confirming lots of topics to talk about so early in the screening process is a big bonus for your candidacy.

A Core Competencies section also allows you to succinctly identify skill sets that might not otherwise make it into your résumé by acting as a series of topic headlines about skills with which you have experience.

One last point. This approach also allows you to repeat highly important keywords that appear in the body of your résumé. This repetition of keywords that speak to especially relevant competencies can improve the ranking of your résumé in the weighted list, because the search programs count the frequency with which keywords are used as part of the weighting process.

Job Titles

The purpose of a job title on your résumé is not to reflect exactly what you were called by a particular employer, but rather to provide a generic identification that will be understood by as many employers as possible. So if your current title is Junior Accountant, Level Three, realize that such internal titling may well bear no relation to the titling of any other company on Earth.

To avoid painting yourself into a career corner, you can be "specifically vague" with job titles like:

Administrative Assistant   *Accountant*
instead of   instead of
Secretary   *Junior Accountant Level II*

It is imperative that you examine your current role at work, rather than rely on your starting or current title. Job titles within companies change much more slowly than the jobs themselves, so a job change can be an opportunity to escape stereotyping and the career stagnation that accompanies it. This approach is important because of the way titles and responsibilities vary.

This obviously doesn't pertain when you apply for a job in certain kinds of professions, such as health care. A cardiologist wouldn't want to be specifically vague by tagging herself as a Health Aide; use your professional judgment here.

Company Name

The names of your employers should be included. There is no need to include the street address or telephone number of past or present employers, although it can be useful to include the city and state.

When referring to work for a multiple-division corporation, you may want to list the divisional employer. Bell Industries might not be enough, so you could perhaps add Computer Memory Division. By the way, it is quite all right to abbreviate words like "Corporation" (Corp.), "Company" (Co.), "Limited" (Ltd.), or "Division" (Div.), but remember to be consistent in your editing process.

Here is how you might combine a job title, company name, and address:

Design Engineer
Bell Industries, Inc., Computer Memory Div., Mountain View, CA

The information you are supplying is relevant to the reader, but you don't wish it to detract from space usable to sell yourself. If, for instance, you live in a nationally known city, such as Dallas, you need not add "TX" if space is at a premium.

There is a possible exception to these guidelines. Employed professionals are justified in omitting current employers when their industry has been reduced to a small community of professionals who know, or know of, each other, and where a confidentiality breach is likely to have damaging repercussions. This usually happens to professionals on the higher rungs of the ladder. Of course, if you don't quite fit into this elite category but are still worried about identifying your firm, you are not obliged to list the name of your current employer.

One approach is simply to label a current company in a fashion that has become perfectly acceptable in today's business climate.

A National Retail Chain
A Leading Software Developer
A Major Commercial Bank

A company name can be followed by a brief description of the business line, and this can be an asset when it talks to a specific targeted job.

Example:
Lara Corporation, Inc., Orlando, FL 1997 to present
$500 Million Company—One of Largest Resort and Vacation Development/Sales Companies in U.S.—in Rapid Growth Through International Expansion, Strategic M&A, Industry Rollup, and IPO

Responsibilities

The area where you address your responsibilities and achievements is the meat, or body copy, of the résumé. It's the area where you list not only your responsibilities, but also your special achievements and other contributions.

Endorsements

Remember when you got that difficult job finished so quickly that your boss couldn't stop complimenting you about your work? Well, in a résumé you can very effectively quote him, even if the praise wasn't in writing (though of course it is best to quote directly). A line such as, "Praised as 'most innovative and determined manager in the company'" is a nice comment to be able to add to your résumé.

These third-party endorsements are not necessary, and they most certainly shouldn't be used to excess; but used sparingly, an endorsement or two can be very impressive.

Such endorsements become especially effective when they support your quantified achievements.

Here is an example of a Target Job Title followed by performance profile, without the subhead. Its placement makes it obvious, and finishes the résumé with a string of endorsements from evaluations; in the original the endorsements within the quotes were also printed in blue, which made them stand out even more.

REGISTERED NURSE

Compassionate nursing professional qualified by a Bachelor of Science in Nursing, RN Licensure, and numerous certifications including ACLS, BLS, and CNC. Provide high-quality nursing care and unsurpassed patient service.

Competent in infectious-disease containment with proper universal precautions for tuberculosis; hepatitis A, B, and C; VRE; MRSA; West Nile; meningitis; necrotizing infections; and others.

Procedure expertise—intubation/extubation, ventrulostomies, chest-tube placement, lumbar punctures, thorocentises, paracentesis, tracheostomy exchanges, central-line insertions, swan guiding, arterial-line insertions, peritoneal dialysis, continuing hemodialysis.

Excellent **critical thinking skills** utilized throughout career on a daily basis.

" . . . functions effectively in an emergency situation, including Code Blue procedures . . . independent worker who needs little supervision . . . can be counted on to complete assignments . . . thoughtful and courteous . . . is an important contributor to the morale and success of the MICU team. . . ."

—Excerpts from performance evaluations

Charts and Graphs

A picture is worth a thousand words, so if you can use a graphic to make a powerful point, do so; otherwise leave them out. Here is an example of a graphic insert that shows increasing sales achievements.

Revenue Growth—Maintained consistent, year-over-year pattern of increasing revenues through robust and downturn economies, from $50,000 to $1.2 million as illustrated below:

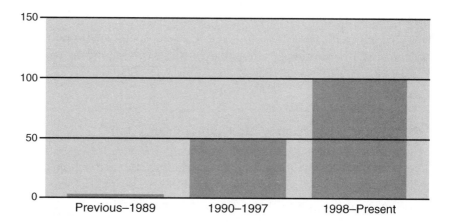

Accreditation and Licenses

Many fields of work require professional licensure or accreditation. If this is the case in your line of work, be sure to list everything necessary. If you are close to a particular accreditation or license (a C.P.A., for example), you would want to list it with information about the status:

Passed all parts of C.P.A. exam, September '06
(Expected certification March '07)

Professional Affiliations

Your affiliation with associations and societies related to a profession demonstrates a commitment to your career. Membership is also important for networking, so if you are not currently a member of one of your industry's professional associations, give serious consideration to joining. Note the emphasis on "professional" in the heading. An employer is almost exclusively interested in your professional associations and societies. Omit references to any religious, political, or otherwise potentially controversial affiliations, unless your certain knowledge of that specific company assures that such affiliations will be positively received.

An exception to this rule is found in those jobs where a wide circle of acquaintance is regarded as an asset. Some examples might include jobs in public relations, sales, marketing, real estate, and insurance. In these cases, include your membership/involvement with community organizations, charities, and the like, as such involvement demonstrates a professional involved in the community, and this fact speaks to having a wide circle of contacts.

By the same token, a seat on the town board, charitable cause involvement, or fundraising work are all activities that show a willingness to involve oneself and can often demonstrate organizational abilities through titles held in those endeavors. Space permitting, these are all activities worthy of inclusion because they show you as a force for good in your community.

These activities become more important, as companies who take their community responsibilities seriously often look for staff who feel and act the same way.

As for method of inclusion, brevity is the rule and placement is at the tail end of your résumé.

American Heart Association: Area Fundraising Chair

If you are a recent entrant into the workplace, both your scholastic achievements and your contributions have increased importance. List your position on the school newspaper or the student council, memberships in clubs, and recognition for scholastic achievement; in short, anything that demonstrates your potential as a productive employee. As your career progresses, however, prospective employers care less about your school life and more about your work life.

Civil Service Grade

If you have a civil service job in your background, you will have been awarded a civil service grade. So, in looking for a job with the government, be sure to list it. This is also important if you are applying for jobs with government contractors, subcontractors, or employers doing business with state or federal agencies.

Publications and Patents

Such achievements are usually found toward the end of the résumé. While their importance varies from profession to profession, they make a powerful statement about creativity, organization, determination, and follow-through on any résumé. They tell the reader that you invest considerable personal time and effort in your career and are therefore a cut above the competition. Publication carries more weight in some industries and professions (where you hear phrases like "publish or perish"), while patents are a definite plus in the technology and manufacturing fields. You will notice in the résumé examples in this book that the writers list dates and names of publications, but do not include copyright information.

"Radical Treatments for Chronic Pain." 2002. *Journal of American Medicine.*
"Pain: Is It Imagined or Real?" 2000. *Science & Health Magazine.*

Languages

Technology allows all companies the opportunity to become global in their activities, and many companies have a vibrant international presence. Therefore, knowing a foreign language might give you just the edge you need. If you are fluent in a foreign language, don't hide your light under a bushel. If you understand a foreign language, but perhaps are not fluent, still mention it.

Fluent in Spanish and French   Read German
Read and write Serbo-Croatian   Understand conversational Mandarin

Education

Educational history is normally listed wherever it helps your case the most, although the exact positioning of the information can vary according to the length of your professional experience, the relative strength of your academic achievements, and your profession.

If you are recently out of school with little practical experience, your educational credentials, which probably constitute your primary asset, will appear near the beginning of the résumé.

As you gain experience, your academic credentials become less important in most professions, and gradually slip toward the end of your résumé. The exception to this is found primarily in certain professions where academic qualifications dominate a person's career—medicine and law, for instance. This does not mean that your educational efforts are unimportant in any way; on the contrary, the educational section of your résumé can show a commitment to ongoing professional education. This makes a powerful statement about both your competency and commitment, finishing your résumé on a high note.

The highest level of attainment always comes first, followed by the lesser levels. In this way, a doctorate will be followed by a master's degree, then a bachelor's. For degreed professionals, there is no need to go back further into educational history; it is optional to list your prestigious prep school. Those who did not achieve the higher levels of educational recognition will list their own highest level of attainment.

A word on attainment is in order here. If you graduated from high school and attended college, but didn't graduate, you may be tempted to list your high school diploma first, followed by the name of the college you attended. That would give the wrong emphasis: It says you are a college dropout and focuses on you as a high school graduate. In this instance, you would, in fact, list your college and omit any reference to earlier educational history.

While abbreviations are frowned on in most circumstances, it is normal to abbreviate degrees (Ph.D., M.A., B.A., B.S., etc.). In instances where educational attainment is paramount, it is acceptable to put that degree after your name; traditionally, this has been the privilege of doctors and lawyers, but there is absolutely no reason that your name shouldn't be followed by, for example, MBA:

Paul Ruffino, MBA

Those with scholarships and awards should list them, and recent graduates will usually also list majors and minors (space and relevancy permitting). The case is a little more confused for the seasoned professional. Many human resources professionals say it makes life easier for them if majors and minors are listed, so they can further sift and grade the applicants. That's good for them, but it might not be good for you. All you want the résumé to do is get you in the door, not slam it in your face. So, as omitting these minutiae will never stop you from getting an interview, I urge you to err on the side of safety and leave 'em out, unless they speak directly to the target job.

Technology is rapidly changing the nature of all work, so if you aren't learning new skills every year, you are being paid for an increasingly obsolescent skill set. Employers really appreciate people who invest in their future. Here's some proof from the U.S. Department of Education:

Of postsecondary students who enrolled in any A.A. degree program but didn't graduate, 48 percent received better job responsibilities and 29 percent received raises! If they actually graduated, it gets even better: 71 percent gained improved job responsibilities and 63 percent got raises. Clearly, being enrolled in ongoing education looks good on a résumé; you have nothing to lose and everything to gain by committing to your career. Being enrolled in an advanced educational program is cheap, and all other things being equal, may well help you overcome an otherwise mandatory requirement.

Avoid exaggerations of your skills, accomplishments, and educational qualifications. Research has now proven that three out of every ten résumés feature inflated educational qualifications. Consequently, verification, especially of educational claims, is on the increase. If, after you have been hired, it is discovered that you exaggerated your educational accomplishments, it could cost you your job.

Changing times have also changed thinking about listing fraternities and sororities on résumés. A case could be made, I think, for leaving them off as a matter of course. If such organizations are important to an interviewer, he or she will ask. My ruling, however, is that if the résumé is tailored to an individual or company where membership in such organizations will result in a case of "deep calling to deep," then by all means, list it. If, on the other hand, the résumé is for general distribution, forget it.

Professional Training

Under the educational heading on smart résumés, you will often see a section for continuing professional education, focusing on special courses and seminars attended. For example, if you are computer-literate, list the programs you are familiar with. Such a section demonstrates your and your employers' commitment to your professional development.

Military

If you have a good military record, include it with your highest rank. Military experience speaks to your determination and your understanding of teamwork, policies, and procedures. Always list your military experience—it's a plus in just about every employer's mind.

Summer and Part-Time Employment

This should only be included when the résumé writer is either just entering the work force or re-entering it after a substantial absence. The entry-level person can feel comfortable listing dates and places and times. The returnee should include the skills gained from part-time employment in a fashion that minimizes the part-time aspect of the experience—probably by using a functional résumé format.

What Can Never Go In

Some information just doesn't belong in résumés. Make the mistake of including it, and at best, your résumé loses a little power; at worst, you fail to land the interview.

Titles: Résumé, Fact Sheet, Curriculum Vitae, etc.

It should not be necessary to use any of these variations on a theme as a heading. Their appearance on a properly structured résumé is redundant. If it isn't completely obvious from the very look of your document that it is a résumé, it needs further work. Such titles take up a whole line, one that could be used more productively. You can either use the space for information with greater impact, or buy yourself an extra line of white space to help you with more accessible formatting.

Availability

All jobs exist because there are problems that need solutions, and interviewers rarely have time for interviews that don't potentially help them solve the problem at hand. Statements about your availability for employment on a résumé are redundant. If you are not available, then why are you wasting everyone's time? The only justification for including this item (and then only in your cover letter—see Chapter 8 of *Knock 'em Dead Cover Letters*) is if you expect to be finishing a project and moving on at such and such a time, and not before. In such a case, your enlightened self-interest demands that you always have your eyes and ears open for better career opportunities. You aren't forced to act on those opportunities, but you are best advised to at least know about them. If leaving before the end of a project could affect your integrity and/or references, okay, but say so when you have an offer in hand or when one is about to be extended. There's a lot to be said for not burning your bridges, and as careers progress, it's surprising how many of the same people you bump into again and again.

As a rule of thumb, let the subject of availability come up at the face-to-face meeting. After meeting you, an employer is more likely to be prepared to wait until you are available, but will usually pass on an interview if you are not available now.

Reason for Leaving

There is no real point to stating your reasons for leaving a job on a résumé, yet time and again they are included—to the detriment of the writer. The topic is always covered during an interview anyway; if the employer isn't interested, why should you raise an issue that could turn into a negative? You can usually use the space more productively; however, if you have been caught in a couple of downsizings, there is an argument for listing the reason to countermand any perception of willful job-hopping.

Salary

Leave out all references to salary, past and present—it is far too risky. Too high or too low of a salary can knock you out of the running even before you hear the starting gun. Even in responding to a job posting that specifically requests salary requirements, don't give them on your résumé. A good résumé will still get you the interview, and in the course of the discussions with the company, you'll certainly talk about salary anyway. If you somehow feel obliged to give salary requirements, simply write "Competitive" or "Negotiable," and then only in your cover letter—never put salary on a résumé.

Mention of Age, Race, Religion, Sex, and National Origin

Government legislation was enacted in the 1960s and 1970s forbidding employment discrimination in these areas under most instances. It is wisest to avoid reference to these unless they are deemed relevant to the job.

Photographs

In days of old, when men were bold and all our cars had fins, it was the thing to have a photograph in the top right-hand corner of the résumé. Today, the fashion is against photographs; including them is a waste of space that says nothing about your ability to do a job. Obviously, careers in modeling, acting, and certain aspects of the media require photos. In these instances, your face is your fortune.

Health/Physical Description

You are trying to get a job, not a date. Unless your physical health (gym instructor, for example) and appearance (model, actor, media personality) are immediately relevant to the job, leave these issues alone and let the reader take it for granted.

Early Background

I regularly see résumés that tell about early childhood and upbringing. To date, the most generous excuse I can come up with for such anecdotes is that the résumés were prepared by the subject's mother.

Weaknesses

Any weakness, lack of qualifications, or information likely to be detrimental to your cause should always be avoided. Never tell résumé readers what you don't have or what you can't or haven't had the opportunity to do yet—they might never ask.

Demands

You will never see demands on a good résumé. Don't outline what you feel an employer is expected to give or to provide. The time for making demands is when the employer extends a job offer with a salary and job description attached. That is when the employer will be interested and prepared to listen to what you want. Until then, concentrate on bringing events to that happy turn by emphasizing what you can bring to the employer. In your résumé, you should, to paraphrase John F. Kennedy, ask not what your employer can do for you, but rather what you can do for your employer.

Judgment Calls

Here are some areas that fall into neither the do nor the don't camp. Whether to include them will depend on your personal circumstances.

Personal Flexibility, Relocation

If you are open to relocation for the right opportunity, make it clear. It will never, in and of itself, get you an interview, but it won't hurt. Conversely, never state that you aren't open to relocation. After all, that factor usually comes into play only when you have a job offer to consider. Let nothing stand in the way of a nice collection of job offers! You can always leverage a job offer you don't want into an offer you do; you can learn how in Chapter 21 of *Knock 'em Dead: The Ultimate Job Seeker's Guide.*

References

It is inappropriate and unprofessional to list the names of references on a résumé—you will never see it on a top example. Why? Interviewers are not interested in checking them before they meet and develop a strong interest in you—it's too time-consuming. In addition, the law forbids employers to check references without your written consent (thanks to the 1970 Fair Credit and Reporting Act), and they have to meet you first in order to obtain your written permission.

You typically grant this permission when you fill out an application form; in fact, it is usually the reason you are given an application form to complete when you already have a perfectly good résumé. There, at the bottom of the backside of the form, is the space for your signature, and above it, a block of impossibly small type. Your signature below that type is granting permission for the reference check. This is why companies frequently require that you fill out an application form even though you have a perfectly good résumé. What they really want is permission to check your references when the time comes, which won't be until immediately before or after the offer is made.

One further note on filling out an application form when you have a perfectly good résumé: You can usually get away with filling in the employer information and writing, "See résumé" for other information. As long as they have your signature, most potential employers will be quite happy with this.

Employers assume that references are available anyway, and if they aren't available, boy, are you in trouble! For that reason, there's an argument to be made for leaving that famous line—References Available Upon Request—at the end of your résumé, but only if space allows; however, if you had to cut a line anywhere this would be one of the first to go. It may not be absolutely necessary to say that references are there for the asking, but those four extra words certainly don't do any harm and may help you stand out from the crowd. Including the phrase sends a little message: "Hey, look, I have no skeletons in my closet."

Name Changes and Your References

A brief but important aside: If you have ever worked under a different surname, you must take this fact into account when giving your references. A recently divorced woman I know of wasted a strong interview performance because she was using her maiden name on her résumé and at the interview. She forgot to tell the employer that her references would, of course, remember her by a different last name. The results of this oversight were catastrophic: Three prior employers denied ever having heard of anyone by the name supplied by the interviewer.

Marital Status

If you think mention of your marital status will enhance your chances (if you are looking for a position as a long-distance trucker, marriage counselor, or traveling salesperson, for example), include it. In all other instances, leave it out. Legally, your marital status is of no consequence. Also, see above item on name changes and your references.

Written Testimonials

It is best not to attach written testimonials to your résumé. Of course, that doesn't mean that you shouldn't solicit such references for your files. Instead, you might consider using them as a basis for those third-party endorsements we talked about earlier; then you can produce the written testimonials at the interview with the comment that they will support the claims made on your résumé. This way, you get to use them twice to good effect. This will be especially helpful to you if you are just entering the work force, or re-entering after a long absence, because the content of the testimonials can be used to beef up your résumé significantly.

Personal Interests

A Korn Ferry study showed that executives with team sports on their résumés were seen to be averaging $3,000 a year more than their more sedentary counterparts. Now, that makes giving a line to your hobbies worthwhile, if they fit into certain broad categories. These would include team sports, determination activities (running, climbing, bicycling), and "brain activities" (bridge, chess). The rule of thumb, as always, is only to include activities that can, in some way, contribute to your chances of being hired.

Personal Activities

Here and there throughout the résumé section of this book, you will see résumés that include—often toward the end—a short personal paragraph that gives you a candid snapshot of the résumé writer as a person. Done well, these can be exciting, effective endings to a résumé, but they are not to everyone's taste. Typically, they refer to one or two personal traits, activities, and, sometimes, values . . . although that is a term that has been much tainted and devalued in recent years. These are often tied in with skills required for the particular job sought.

The idea is to make the reader say, "Hey, there's a real person behind this piece of paper, let's get him in here; he sounds like our kind of guy." Of course, as no one can be all things to all people, you don't want to go overboard in this area.

Putting the Résumé Pieces Together

CHAPTER · CHAPTER · CHAPTER · CHAPTER · CHAPTER ·

RÉSUMÉS DEPART FROM the rules that govern all other forms of writing. First and last, they are urgent business communications that no one wants to read, so they must be succinct and to the point.

You can assume that the potential employer has a position to fill and a problem to solve, and that he or she is buried in an avalanche of résumés.

For the next fifteen minutes, imagine yourself in one of your target companies. You are in the HR department on résumé detail, you have just completed a résumé database search and have twenty résumés from that to read, plus half a dozen that came directly to HR, and the morning mail has just landed another four résumés on your desk to be read. Go straight to the example section now and try to read thirty résumés without a break, and then return to this page.

With some idea of what it feels like to screen résumés, you probably felt a little punch-drunk, but you also learned a very valuable lesson: Brevity and focus are to be desired above all other things.

Choose a Layout

You have seen the basic examples of chronological, functional, and combination résumés in Chapter 3, and you have browsed through the résumés. If you didn't do so before, now is the time to find one that strikes your fancy and fits your needs, and use it as your model. Remember, there are plenty of résumé templates at *www.knockemdead.com.* As résumé layouts are NOT designed with particular professions or jobs in mind, the template you choose need not reflect your field of professional expertise. Your job will be to load the template with your professional details as you have gathered them as we went along. You will need to put in your own contact information and job objective, add the details of each of your jobs, and add your unique details, as necessary.

Filling In the Picture

This first step is just like painting by numbers. Go through the template and fill in the obvious slots—name, address, telephone number(s), e-mail address, employer names, employment dates, educational background and dates, activities, and the like. Shazam! You immediately have a document that is beginning to look like a résumé.

Chronological Résumés

Performance Profiles

You will focus the Performance Profile/Career Summary/Executive Profile etc. on what you can do for the company. You can use the Target Job Deconstruction document you developed to craft a synopsis of the professional you in the language that employers are using to describe your target job. This will help both human eyes and database spiders find your résumé attractive.

The Company's Business

Now, for each employer, edit your response from material you collected in Chapter 4 (or from the electronic questionnaire you downloaded from *www.knockemdead.com*) to outline that company's services or products. Make it one short sentence; this is not necessary if the company name, like Microsoft, is a household name. As you get to the polishing phase of your résumé and space becomes an important factor, this will be one of those lines you can put in a smaller font to save space.

Job Titles

Remember what we said in Chapter 4: There is nothing intrinsically wrong with listing your title as Fourth-Level Administration Clerk, Third Class, as long as you are prepared to wait until doomsday for it to be considered by someone who understands what it means and is able to relate it to current needs. Make sure that you use job titles that will be commonly understood.

Responsibilities

In a chronological résumé, the job title is sometimes followed by a short sentence that helps the reader visualize you doing the job. If you choose to do this, get the information from the completed questionnaire and do a rough edit, getting it down to one short sentence; don't worry about perfection now, you can polish it later.

The responsibilities and contributions you list here are those functions that best relate to the needs of the target job; if you have focused on a target job in which you can be successful, this should not pose a problem. They do not necessarily correspond with how you spent the majority of your working day, nor are they related to how you might prefer to spend your working day. It can perhaps best be illustrated by showing you part of a résumé that came to my desk recently. It is the work of a professional who listed her title and duties for one job like this:

> *Motivated a sales staff of six, recruited, trained, managed. Hires improved sales. Sales Manager increased sales.*

If you prioritize the importance of the above statements, you will see that the writer mistakenly listed everything in the reverse order of importance, not in relation to the items' relative importance to a future employer. She also wasted space stating the obvious for a sales manager: improving sales. Let's look at what subsequent restructuring achieved:

> *Sales Manager: Hired to turn around stagnant sales force. Successfully recruited, trained, managed, and motivated a sales staff of six. Result: 22 percent sales gain over first year.*

Notice how this is clearly focused on the essentials of a sales manager's job: to increase income for the company.

Hired to turn around stagnant sales force. (Demonstrates her skills and responsibilities.)

Successfully recruited, trained, managed, and motivated a consulting staff of six. Result: 22 percent sales gain over first year. (Shows what she subsequently did with the sales staff, and just how well she did it.)

By doing this, her responsibilities and achievements become more important in the light of the problems they solved. Be sure to itemize your responsibilities to an employer's stated needs and priorities; and YES, you should take the time to customize each résumé you send when you have specifics about the job.

An important word about "contributions": Business has very limited interests. In fact, those interests can be reduced to a single phrase: making a profit. Making a profit is done in just three ways: by saving money in some fashion for the company; by saving time through some innovation at the company, which in turn saves the company money and gives it the opportunity to make more money in the time saved; or by simply making money for the company. That does not mean that you should address only those points in your résumé and ignore valuable contributions that cannot be quantified, but it does mean that you should try to quantify as much as you can.

Achievements

Pick two to four accomplishments for each job title and edit them down to bite-size chunks that read like a telegram. Write as if you had to pay for each entry by the word—this approach can help you pack a lot of information into a short space. The resulting abbreviated style will help convey a sense of immediacy to the reader.

Here is an example:

Responsible for new and used car sales. Earned "Salesman of the Year" awards, 2006 and 2007. Record holder for: Most Cars Sold in One Year.

Here's another example from a fundraiser's résumé:

- *Created an annual giving program to raise operating funds. Raised $2,000,000.*
- *Targeted, cultivated, and solicited sources including individuals, corporations, foundations, and state and federal agencies. Raised $1,650,000.*
- *Raised funds for development of the Performing Arts School facility, capital expense, and music and dance programs. Raised $6,356,000.*

Now, while you may tell the reader about these achievements, never explain how they were accomplished; the key phrase here is "specifically vague." The intent of your résumé is to pique interest and to raise as many questions as you answer. Questions mean interest, and getting that interest satisfied requires talking to you!

Next, prioritize the listing of your accomplishments as they relate to your target job, and be sure to quantify your contributions wherever possible and appropriate.

If you can, now is the time to weave in some of those laudatory quotes. Put in all that you have right now, but when you come to the final editing phase, you will want to cut it back; one or two will be fine, although I have seen résumés where each job entry is finished with a complimentary quote. For example:

- Sales volume increased from $90 million to $175 million. Acknowledged as "the greatest single gain of the year."
- Earnings increased from $9 million to $18 million. Review stated, "always has a view for the company bottom line."

In a functional or combination résumé, you will have identified the skills and attributes necessary to fulfill the functions of the target job, and will highlight the appropriate attributes you have to offer. In this format, you will have headings that apply to the skill areas your chosen career path demands, such as: Management, Training, Sales, etc. Each will be followed by a short paragraph packed with selling points. These can be real paragraphs, or an introductory sentence followed by bullets. Here is an example of each style:

COLLECTIONS:
Developed excellent rapport with customers while significantly shortening payout terms. Turned impending loss into profit. Personally salvaged and increased sales with two multimillion-dollar accounts by providing remedial action for their sales/financial problems.

COLLECTIONS:
Developed excellent rapport with customers while significantly shortening payout terms:

- *Evaluated sales performance; offered suggestions for financing/merchandising, turned impending loss into profit.*
- *Salvaged two multimillion-dollar problem accounts by providing remedial action for their sales/financial problems. Subsequently increased sales.*

Whenever you can, keep each paragraph to a maximum of four lines. This ensures that the finished product has plenty of white space so that it is easy on the reader's eye. If necessary, split one paragraph into two.

Editing Your Résumé

Over the next few pages, we are going to go through a process that will turn your rough notes from the résumé questionnaire into polished "résumé-speak."

Sentences gain power with verbs that demonstrate an action. For example, a woman with ten years at the same law firm in a clerical position had written in her original résumé:

I learned to use a computer database.

After discussion of the circumstances that surrounded learning how to use the computer database, certain exciting facts emerged. By using action verbs and an awareness of employer interests, this sentence was charged up, given more punch:

I analyzed and determined the need for automation of an established law office. Responsible for hardware and software selection, installation, and loading. Within one year, I had achieved a fully automated office.

Notice how the verbs show that things happen when you are around the office. These action verbs and phrases add an air of direction, efficiency, and accomplishment to every résumé. They succinctly tell the reader why you did it and how well you did it.

Now look at the above example when a third-party endorsement is added to it:

I analyzed and determined need for automation of an established law office. Responsible for hardware and software selection, installation, and loading. Within one year, I had achieved a fully automated office. Partner stated, "You brought us out of the dark ages into the technological age, and in the process neither you nor the firm missed a beat!"

Now, while the content is clearly more powerful, the presentation is still clunky and it takes up too much space. Read on, and in the next few pages you will see how you can speed up and shorten paragraphs like this further.

Keywords

With the prevalence of electronic résumé screening, it's critical to choose and use specific keywords in your résumé. Internal job descriptions are usually built of nouns and verbs that describe the skill sets required for the job. Your résumé should be built the same way, with nouns that identify the skill sets and verbs and action phrases that describe your professional behavior and achievements with these skill sets.

This is an important distinction in the initial screening process: Screening software focuses on the skill sets, which invariably are nouns. If you are a computer programmer, the screening device might search for words like "HTML"; if you are an accountant, it might search for words like "financial analysis." Only when the computer has identified those résumés that include matching skills, do human eyes enter into the picture, and only then can the verbs and action phrases that describe your competencies and achievements have the desired impact. With an electronic résumé, the nouns and skill sets are the skeleton, while the verbs and action phrases are designed to put flesh on the bones for human eyes hungry for talent.

Keywords are the words commonly used to describe the essential skill sets and knowledge necessary to carry out a job successfully. They are likely to include:

- Skill sets, abilities, and competencies
- Application of these skill sets
- Relevant education and training

Your résumé is a living document, and its content may well change as your job search progresses. Whenever you come across keywords in job postings that reflect your capabilities, but those words are not in your résumé, it is time to add them in; if nowhere else, at least in your Core Competencies section.

You'll want to weave the nouns and verbs describing your professional competencies into the main body of your résumé as much as possible. However, that won't always be possible. The flow of your résumé—or insufficient space—might prevent you from using the keywords in multiple places. That's where a separate Core Competencies (keyword) section comes in handy. It is the perfect spot to list the technical acronyms and professional jargon that you can't fit into the body copy; but whenever possible, try to repeat keywords from your performance profile and Core Competencies section in the body of your résumé as well. This allows you to put the skill within the context of a specific job and use the keyword multiple times, which helps your résumé database ranking.

Think of your Core Competencies section as an electronic business card that allows you to network with computers! Here's an example of a core competencies/keyword section from a sales management professional:

SPECIFIC KNOWLEDGE AND SKILLS

Market Trend Analysis * Profit & Loss * Multi-Site Management * Needs Analysis *
Budget * Employee Motivation * Business Savvy * Sales * Performance Evaluations *
Contract Negotiation * Technical Expertise * Team Training

A Core Competencies section in your résumé allows you to add a host of additional information to your résumé in a space-efficient way—use as many keywords as you like.

Using one in your résumé will increase the odds of a résumé spider making multiple matches between your résumé and an open job requisition.

Where does the core competencies/keyword section go? As far as the computer is concerned, it doesn't matter. The computer doesn't care about the niceties of layout and flow. However, human eyes will also see this section, so there is a certain logic in putting it front and center, before any Performance Profile.

This section acts as a preface to the body copy, in effect, saying, "Hey, here are all the headlines. The stories behind them are immediately below." To put it another way, the keyword section acts as a table of contents for your résumé, while the body—with its action words and phrases—explains and expands upon this table.

There's no need to use definite or indefinite articles or conjunctions. Just list the word, starting with a capital—"Forecasting," for example—or a phrase, such as "Financial modeling."

Action Verbs

Here are over 175 action verbs. See which ones you can use to give punch to your résumé writing by using them to show exactly what you did with those keyword nouns.

accepted	advised	assisted	calculated
accomplished	allocated	attained	cataloged
achieved	analyzed	audited	chaired
acted	appraised	authored	clarified
adapted	approved	automated	classified
addressed	arranged	balanced	coached
administered	assembled	budgeted	collected
advanced	assigned	built	compiled

completed	evaluated	launched	regulated
composed	examined	lectured	rehabilitated
computed	executed	led	remodeled
conceptualized	expanded	maintained	repaired
conducted	expedited	managed	represented
consolidated	explained	marketed	researched
contained	extracted	mediated	resolved
contracted	fabricated	moderated	restored
contributed	facilitated	monitored	restructured
controlled	familiarized	motivated	retrieved
coordinated	fashioned	negotiated	revamped
corresponded	focused	operated	revitalized
counseled	forecast	organized	saved
created	formulated	originated	scheduled
critiqued	founded	overhauled	schooled
cut	generated	oversaw	screened
decreased	guided	performed	set
defined	headed up	persuaded	shaped
delegated	identified	planned	solidified
demonstrated	illustrated	prepared	solved
designed	implemented	presented	specified
developed	improved	prioritized	stimulated
devised	increased	processed	streamlined
diagnosed	indoctrinated	produced	strengthened
directed	influenced	programmed	summarized
dispatched	informed	projected	supervised
distinguished	initiated	promoted	surveyed
diversified	innovated	proposed	systemized
drafted	inspected	provided	tabulated
edited	installed	publicized	taught
educated	instigated	published	trained
eliminated	instituted	purchased	translated
emended	instructed	recommended	traveled
enabled	integrated	reconciled	trimmed
encouraged	interpreted	recorded	upgraded
engineered	interviewed	recruited	validated
enlisted	introduced	reduced	worked
established	invented	referred	wrote

Use these words to edit and polish your work and to communicate, persuade, and motivate the reader to take action.

Varying Your Sentences

Most good writers are at their best when they write short, punchy sentences. When writing a résumé, where space is limited, this advice is especially relevant. Keep your sentences under about twenty words, and if one runs longer, try to shorten it by editing out unnecessary words, or by making two sentences out of one. Lawyers and doctors whose frequent professional needs for obfuscation should pay special attention to this need for simplicity and clarity.

At the same time, you don't want the writing to sound choppy, so vary the length of sentences when you can. You can also start with a short phrase and follow with a colon:

- Followed by bullets of information
- Each one supporting the original phrase

These techniques are designed to enliven the reading process. Here's the simple example from a few pages back that we have gradually been improving:

I analyzed and determined need for automation of an established law office. Responsible for hardware and software selection, installation, and loading. Within one year, I had achieved a fully automated office. Partner stated, "You brought us out of the dark ages into the technological age, and in the process neither you nor the firm missed a beat!"

Now, let's take this "punching-up" process a step further, removing personal pronouns and using bullets, and see what the result looks like:

Analyzed and determined need for automation of an established law office:

- Responsible for hardware and software selection.
- Coordinated installation database and workstations.
- Operated and maintained equipment and trained users.
- Achieved full automation in one year.

Partner stated, "You brought us out of the dark ages, and neither you nor the firm missed a beat!"

The result is not only more organized to the eye, it also speaks of a professional who knows the importance of getting to relevant information fast.

Just as you use short sentences, you should also use common words; they are easy to understand and communicate effectively. Remember:

Short words in short sentences help
Make short, gripping paragraphs:
Good for short attention spans!

Voice and Tense

The voice you use in your résumé depends on a few important factors: getting a lot said in a small space, being factual, and packaging yourself in the best way.

The voice you use should be consistent throughout the résumé. There is considerable disagreement among the experts about the best voice.

Sentences can be truncated (up to a point) by omitting pronouns—I, you, he, she, it, they—and articles—a or the. In fact, many authorities recommend the dropping of pronouns as a technique that both saves space and allows you to brag about yourself without seeming boastful, because it gives the impression that another party is writing about you. Many people feel that to use the first-person pronoun—"I automated the office"—is naive. These experts suggest you use either the third person, as in "He automated the office," or leave the pronoun out altogether: "Automated office."

At the same time, there are others who feel that writing in the first person makes you sound, well, personable; and I have seen the occasional résumé like this that really does work. In fact, we had an example of a functional résumé earlier in the book with just such a personal tone that worked almost magically for the professional. Use whatever style works best for you. If you do use the personal pronoun, try not to use it in every sentence—it gets a little monotonous and takes up valuable space on the page.

A nice variation I have occasionally seen employed is the use of a third-person voice through the résumé, followed by a few final words in the first person appended to the end of the résumé, to give an insight into your values. Here are examples:

Regular third person:
James Sharpe is a professional who knows Technical Services from the ground up. He understands its importance in keeping a growing company productive, and takes pride in creating order in the chaos of technology.

First person:
I am accustomed to accepting responsibility and delegating authority, and am capable of working with and through people at all levels. Am able to plan, organize, develop, implement, and supervise complex programs and special projects. All of this requires sound communication and people management skills and a commitment to timely, cost-effective results.

Many people mistake the need for professionalism with stiff-necked formality. The most effective tone is one that mixes the conversational and the formal, just the way we do in our jobs. The only overriding rule is to make it readable.

Length

The accepted rules for length are one page for every ten years of your experience. If you have more than twenty years under your belt, many of the skills from those early days are now irrelevant; so on the whole, the "two-page maximum" rule is still a sensible guideline. However, this is only an editing guideline to help keep your résumé focused; your résumé can be as long as it needs to be to tell a concise story. Just be sure that anyone can tell from the first page alone that you are fully capable in the target job.

With the increased complexity of all our technology-impacted jobs, the need to demonstrate competence and the exigencies of electronic database manipulation make exceeding the traditional two-page mark not only necessary, but often desirable. Now, while brevity and focus are still the very soul of a productive résumé, that $350,000-a-year EVP of Marketing résumé is going to have to be read by someone in a position to hire you, so squeezing everything onto two pages for the sake of accepted norms defeats your purpose. Assuming that the first page clearly demonstrates a thorough understanding and of competency in the target job, you can feel comfortable taking that third, and sometimes fourth, page. In the chapter of sample résumés, you'll see two examples of justifiably longer executive résumés, starting on page 249.

You'll find that thinking too much about length considerations while you write is counterproductive. Think instead of the story you have to tell, and then layer fact upon fact until it is told. When that is done, you can go back and ruthlessly cut it to the bone. Ask yourself the following questions:

- Can I cut out any paragraphs?
- Can I cut out any superfluous words?

- Can I cut out any sentences?
- Where have I repeated myself?
- Are all statements as relevant to the target job as possible?

If in doubt, cut it out—leave nothing but facts and action words!

The Proofreading Checklist for Your Final Draft

There are really two proofreading steps in the creation of a polished résumé. The first is one you do at this point: to make sure that all the things that should be there are there, and that all the things that shouldn't, aren't. In the heat of the creative moment, it's easy to miss critical components or mistakenly include facts that give the wrong emphasis. Check your résumé against the following points:

Contact Information

Is the pertinent personal data—name, address, personal telephone number, and e-mail address—correct? You will want to make sure that this personal data is on every page.

Performance Profile

- Does it give a concise synopsis of the professional you as it relates to the target job?
- Does the language reflect that of typical job postings for this job?
- Is it prioritized in the same way employers are prioritizing their needs in this job?
- Is it no more than five lines long, so that the block of type remains accessible?
- Does it include reference to some of your personality or behavioral traits that are critical to success in your field?

Core Competencies

- Do you have experience in each of the areas you've listed?
- Can you illustrate your experience in conversation?
- Is the spelling and capitalization correct? (It's easy to make mistakes here, especially with acronyms.)
- Are there any other justifiable keywords you should add?

Body of Résumé

- Is your most relevant and qualifying work experience prioritized throughout the résumé to the employer's needs as they have prioritized them, lending strength to your application?
- Have you avoided wasting space with unnecessarily detailed employer names and addresses?
- Have you been suitably discreet with the name of your current employer?
- Have you omitted any reference to reasons for leaving a particular job?
- Have you removed all references to past, current, or desired salaries?
- Have you removed references to your date of availability?

Education

- Is education placed in the appropriate position? It should be at the beginning of the résumé if you have little or no work experience, and, in most professions, at the end if you are established in your field and your practical experience now outweighs your degree.
- Is your highest educational attainment shown first?
- Have you included professional courses that support your candidacy?

Chronology

- If you've done a chronological résumé, is your work history stated in chronological order, with the most recent employment coming at the head of the résumé?
- Within this chronology, does each company history start with details of your most senior position?
- Have you avoided listing irrelevant responsibilities or job titles?
- Does your résumé emphasize contributions and achievements?
- Can your body copy include one or more third-party endorsements of your work?
- Have you avoided poor focus by eliminating all extraneous information?
- Have you included any volunteer or community service activities that can lend strength to your candidacy?
- Is the whole thing long enough to whet the reader's appetite for more details, yet short enough not to satisfy that hunger?
- Have you left out lists of references and only included mention of the availability of references if there is nothing more valuable to fill up the space?

- Have you avoided treating your reader like a fool by highlighting the obvious—i.e., heading your résumé, "RÉSUMÉ"?

Writing Style

- Have you substituted short words for long words? And one word where previously there were two?
- Is your average sentence no more than twenty words? Have you made sure that any sentence of more than twenty words is shortened or broken into two?
- Have you kept every paragraph under five lines, with many paragraphs considerably shorter?
- Do your sentences begin, wherever possible, with powerful action verbs and phrases?

Crossing the T's, Dotting the I's

Before your résumé is finished, you have to make sure that your writing is as clear as possible. Incorrect spelling and poor grammar are guaranteed to annoy résumé readers. Go back and check all these areas; spell checkers are NOT infallible. This done, you should also send your résumé to third parties for their input on grammar and spelling.

It simply isn't possible for even the most accomplished professional writer to go directly from final draft to print, so don't try it. Your pride of authorship will blind you to the blemishes, and that's a self-indulgence you can't afford.

You need some distance from your creative efforts to gain detachment and objectivity. There is no hard-and-fast rule about how long it takes to come up with the finished product. Nevertheless, if you think you have finished, leave it alone as long as you can—at least overnight—then you can come back to it fresh and read it almost as if it were meeting your eyes for the first time.

More Than One Résumé?

Do you need more than one type of résumé? Probably. With just a few years' experience, most people have a background that qualifies them for more than one job. But this is not an argument for having a general, unfocused, and one-size-fits-all résumé. Look at all the jobs you can do (they are all probably closely related in some way) and choose your best shot and build your prime résumé around this skill set and relevant target job postings.

Then, as necessary, create specific résumés for each of the subsequent jobs you can do. The process is as simple as changing your target job focus, doing a quick target job deconstruction exercise on the next target job, as we have discussed, and then creating the new résumé along the lines explained in this chapter.

Much of the information is likely to remain the same, so it will largely be a matter of editing. You will already have a layout, and even with a different focus, much of the information will remain the same, so it shouldn't feel like you are back to square one. With a computer-based template, this shouldn't be too much of a headache; you will also need an e-mail version for each print résumé.

There is also a case for having résumés in more than one format. I was once engaged in an outplacement experiment for a group of professionals. With a little work, we developed chronological, functional, and combination résumés for everyone. The individuals sent out the résumé of their choice. Then, in those instances where there was no response, a different version of the résumé was sent. The result from just a different format: 8 percent more interviews. So if your chronological résumé isn't getting results, maybe try a little reformatting and send it out as a combination-style résumé.

THE FINAL
PRODUCT

WHEN IT COMES to clothes, style has a certain feel that everyone recognizes but few can define. Fortunately, with résumés, there are definite rules to follow.

By some accounts, upward of 95 percent of résumés are stored in and retrieved from electronic databases. Even if this number is unscientific, we can still accept that the percentage is indeed substantial. Your résumé may be an aesthetic marvel, but if it goes into the computer as gobbledygook, it won't do you much good. This chapter will cover the "traditional" résumé—the résumé designed for human eyes. The other kind, the "computer-friendly" résumé, is designed to get through a computer scanner with data intact. It is so vital in today's job market that I have devoted a separate chapter to it. The two kinds of résumés do have certain basics in common.

Avoiding the Circular File

Your résumé will get only thirty to forty seconds of initial attention, and then only if it's laid out well and looks accessible to a tired pair of eyes. What are the three biggest complaints about those résumés that reach the trash can in record time?

1. *Impossible to read.* They have too much information crammed into too little space with too small a font. Remember, you can go longer than one or two pages now if your needs demand it; just remember to keep the focus and the writing tight.
2. *No coherence.* Their layout is unorganized, illogical, and uneven. They look shoddy and slapdash.
3. *Typos.* Thay are riddled wiht misspelings. (See how annoying that last sentence is?)

Here are some tips that will help your résumé rise above the rest.

Fonts

Business is rapidly coming to accept the likes of Bookman, New York, Times New Roman, and Palatino as the norm. When choosing your font, stay away from heavy and bold for your body copy (although you may choose to take a more dramatic approach with keywords or headlines). Bold type takes space, so use it sparingly to begin with. You should bold those things you want to jump out, and that would certainly include any words the company may have used in recruitment advertising; you'll notice examples later that use consistent bolding of specific keywords throughout the résumé to tell a complete story to even the most cursory résumé screener.

Avoid "script" fonts similar to handwriting; while they look attractive to the occasional reader, they are harder on the eyes of people who read any amount of business correspondence. That said, you will see examples of just this sort of font. For example, in the arts, education, and healthcare are areas where the warmer and more personal look of a script font can work and still present a professional-looking résumé. Use with discretion.

Capitalized copy is tough on the eyes, too; Many people think it makes a powerful statement, when all it does is cause eyestrain and give the reader the impression that the writer is shouting at him or her.

How to Brighten the Page

Once you decide on a font, **stick with it**, because more than one on a page looks confusing. You can do plenty to liven up the visual impact of the page within the variations of the font you have chosen.

You will notice from the examples that the clearest and most successful résumés use just a couple of typographic variations and stick with them.

Proofing

When you have the printed résumé in hand, you must proofread it.

- Is everything set up the way you want it?
- Are there any typographical errors?
- Is all the punctuation correct?
- Has everything been underlined, capitalized, bolded, italicized, and indented, exactly as you desire?

Once you read the résumé, get someone else to review it. A third party will always provide more objectivity, and can catch errors you might miss.

Appearance Checklist

- The first glance and the first feel of your résumé make a powerful impression. What's your immediate reaction to it?
- Have you used only one side of the page? Never print a résumé on two sides of a single piece of paper.
- If more than one page, did you paginate your résumé ("1 of 2" at the bottom of the first page, and so on)?
- Does the first page of the résumé clearly announce that you understand and can do the target job?

Choosing Your Paper

While you should not skimp on paper cost, neither should you be talked into buying the most expensive available. Indeed, in some fields (health care and education come to mind), too ostentatious a paper can cause a negative impression. The idea is to create a feeling of understated quality.

Every résumé should be printed on standard, 8½" x 11" (letter-size) paper. Paper comes in different weights and textures. Good résumé-quality paper has a weight designation of between 20 and 25 pounds. Lighter, and you run the risk of appearing nonchalant and unconcerned; heavier, and the paper is unwieldy. Most office supply stores carry paper and envelopes packaged as kits for résumés and cover letters.

As for color, white is the prime choice. Cream is also acceptable, and I'm assured that some of the pale pastel shades can be both attractive and effective. Personally, I think that most professionals don't show up in the best light when dressed in pink—call me old-fashioned if you will. White and cream are straightforward, no-nonsense colors.

Cover-letter stationery should always match the color and weight of your résumé. To send a white cover letter—even if it is written on your personal stationery—with a cream résumé looks uncoordinated, and detracts from the powerful statement of attention to detail you are trying to make.

It is a good idea to print some cover-letter stationery when you produce your résumé. The letterhead can be in a different font but on the same kind of paper, and it should have the same contact information as your résumé.

Why You Need Printed Résumés

E-mail has not spelled the end of the printed résumé by any means; you will still need them.

- To take to interviews so that you have a measure of control over the docs your interviewers are reviewing
- To mail in addition to your e-mail delivery of résumés

This last is worthy of a little explanation. Everyone gets most of their information by e-mail today, and everyone gets far less traditional mail. At the same time, opening mail is still something that all humans still like to do, unless it is the monthly bills. So, when you send your résumé by traditional mail as well as by e-mail, you dramatically improve your chances of it being reviewed by human eyes. Make it stand out by sending it in a larger envelope that doesn't require your résumé to be folded.

The Final Checklist

- Have you used good-quality paper?
- Does the paper size measure 8½" x 11"?
- Have you used white, off-white, or cream-colored paper?
- If your résumé is more than one page, have you stapled the pages together (one staple in the top left-hand corner)?
- Is your cover letter written on stationery that matches your résumé?

E–Résumé Concerns

TODAY, VIRTUALLY ALL companies (except perhaps some of the smallest locally focused companies) use the Internet as a primary means of recruitment.

Searching résumé banks and social networking sites like Linkedin and Myspace now occupy a substantial part of many a recruiter's day. For you, the Internet offers an array of opportunities to get your résumé on the desks of thousands of companies and recruiters. Unless you are sending the résumé directly to a specific person, you will need to upload it into résumé databases in ways that will increase the likelihood of it being selected for download and serious review by human eyes, and perhaps give your résumé its own website.

Keep Your Résumé Always Fresh in the Résumé Databases

Your résumé is probably the most important document you will ever create, and having done so, you will want to keep it current and relevant.

When an employer needs to find résumés for likely job candidates, she or he goes to the keyboard, types in a job title, and is presented with a list of descriptors—keywords describing different aspects of a particular job—from which she or he chooses those most relevant to the vacancy being filled. After selecting the preferred keywords, the software program searches in the company's database and ranks the résumés that contain any of those keywords. The more keywords your résumé matches, the better your chances are of having it read, because the program ranks the generated list, putting the most keyword-heavy résumés at the top.

As you use job postings to find open positions, pay attention to the keywords that you see repeated in job descriptions for positions that interest you and fit your qualifications, and add them to your résumé on an ongoing basis. Remember that your résumé is a living document, vital to your professional success. Also, update those versions of your résumé that are already hosted in résumé databases with these same fresh keywords.

This ongoing review and update of your résumé will help you keep focused on what employers want to hear about, and updating your posted résumés has the effect of making them brand-new documents for résumé spiders and bots. This is a good thing, as recruiters have ways to restrict their searches—for example, by date posted. Let's take this thought a little further: If there is a site or two where you always want to be maximally visible, you should make an edit on your résumé every week or two. If there are no relevant new keywords or phrases to add, you can simply delete a word, log out, log back in, and rewrite the word you deleted. To the résumé spider, this is a new résumé, and you stay maximally visible to the recruiters.

Your Résumé Will Be Used in Different Formats

Sometimes, you will send your résumé as an MS Word or PDF attachment. Other times, you will choose to paste an ASCII version of your résumé into the body copy of your e-mail message, and you will most probably need to cut and paste an ASCII version of your résumé into the résumé templates required for uploading into many résumé databases. You may even decide to create an HTML résumé to upload on those sites that accept them, or even as a web-based résumé to be hosted on its own simple website.

Types of E-Résumés

For our purposes, an e-résumé is one delivered via e-mail to the recipient or one uploaded into a résumé database or otherwise accessed and viewed by someone using their computer and the Internet. The different formats to use for sending your résumé electronically are:

1. ASCII plain text or with line breaks
2. Formatted in Microsoft Word or as a PDF file
3. Web-based/HTML

You may not need all three, but you will definitely need at least the first two. Here is a quick review of the major formats:

1.   Plain text or ASCII: This is the simplest version of the three. We're talking just the basics: only text; letters, numbers, and a few symbols found on your keyboard. ASCII (American Standard Code for Information Interchange) résumés are important because this is the only format that any computer, whether PC or Macintosh, can read. The reader will not need a word-processing program such as Microsoft Word or WordPerfect, and their software or printer compatibility isn't a consideration.

An ASCII résumé looks like the average e-mail message you receive. I will show you how to create two separate versions of an ASCII résumé, one best suited for pasting into the body of an e-mail message, the other for cutting and pasting into résumé-bank résumé templates.

2.   Formatted Electronic Résumé: A formatted electronic résumé is usually your résumé as created in a word-processing document, most often in MSWord, which has become the standard word-processing format. This is a résumé that is also sent via e-mail, but as an attachment. It is normal when sending résumés, without a prior conversation to determine that the recipient expects the attachment, to paste your résumé into the body of your e-mail with a notation that a copy is also attached. You paste your résumé into the body of the e-mail and attach it as an MS Word document because some employers will not open attachments from people they do not know, for fear of viruses. It is sensible to work with Microsoft Word, which is the world's word-processing program of choice.

Alternatively, you might attach your résumé in PDF format. The layout is fixed and will appear exactly as you send it (which can't always be said of MS Word docs). Both ways are acceptable, and there are even people who attach their résumé in both formats to give the reader a choice.

3.   Web or HTML Résumé: A web résumé is not a "must have" for everyone. Essentially, an HTML résumé is one that can have additional features such as visuals and video and sound, and be uploaded in certain instances to résumé banks and social networking sites, or even housed on the Internet at its own URL. There are some advantages; for example, you can include audio and video clips, music, and pictures. If you are in a creative profession and would typically have a portfolio, a web résumé can allow access to your work samples. Likewise, if you are a web-page design professional or HTML guru, then by all means, use the Internet to show your creative and electronic abilities. We'll look at the steps for quickly creating the ASCII versions of your résumé and then say more about a possible multimedia or HTML résumé.

How to Convert Your Formatted Résumé to ASCII

This is a really simple process that anyone can do. Start by opening your MS Word formatted version of your résumé and I'll walk you through this process:

PATRICIA JOHNSON

1234 Murietta Ave. • Palmdale, CA 93550

Residence (661) 555-1234 • Mobile (661) 555-9876 • *PatJohnson@email.com*

FINANCE / ACCOUNTING PROFESSIONAL
Internal Auditor / Financial Analyst / Staff Accountant

Detail oriented, problem solver with excellent analytical strengths and a track record of optimizing productivity, reducing costs, and increasing profit contributions. Well-developed team building and leadership strengths with experience in training and coaching coworkers. Works well with public, clients, vendors, and coworkers at all levels. Highly motivated and goal orientated as demonstrated by completing studies toward B.S. in Finance, graduating with honors concurrent with full-time, progressive business experience.

—*Core Competencies*—

Research & Analysis / Accounts Receivable / Accounts Payable / Journal Entries / Bank Reconciliations
Payroll / Financial Statements / Auditing / General Ledger / Artist Contracts / Royalties / Escalation Clauses

PROFESSIONAL EXPERIENCE

MAJOR HOLLYWOOD STUDIO, Hollywood, CA • 2000 to Present

Achieved fast-track promotion to positions of increasing challenge and responsibility

Royalty Analyst—Music Group, Los Angeles, CA (2005–Present)

Process average of $8–9 million in payments monthly. Review artist contracts, licenses, and rate sheets to determine royalties due to producers and songwriters for leading record label. Ensure accuracy of statements sent to publishers in terms of units sold and rates applied. Research, resolve, and respond to all inquiries.

- Resolved longstanding problems substantially reducing publisher inquiries and complaints.
- Promoted to "Level 1" analyst within only one year and ahead of two staff members with longer tenure.
- Provided superior training to temporary employee that resulted in her being hired for permanent, Level 1 position after only three months.

Accounts Payable Analyst—Music & Video Distribution (2002–2005)

Processed high volume of utility bills, office equipment leases, shipping invoices, and office supplies for 12 regional branches. Assisted branches with proper invoice coding and resolving payment disputes with vendors.

- Identified longstanding duplicate payment that resulted in vendor refund of $12,000.
- Created contract-employment expenses spreadsheet; identified and resolved $24,000 in duplicate payments.
- Gained reputation for thoroughness and promptness in meeting all payment deadlines.

- Set up macro in accounts payable system that streamlined invoice payments.
- Consolidated vendor accounts, increasing productivity and reducing number of checks processed.

Accounts Receivable Analyst—Music & Video Distribution (2000–2002)

Processed incoming payments, received and posted daily check deposits, reviewed applications for vendor accounts, distributed accounting reports, and ordered office supplies. Handled rebillings of international accounts for shipments by various labels.

- Hired as permanent employee from temporary position after only three months.

Additional Experience: Billing Clerk / Accounting Clerk / Bookkeeper (*details available upon request*)

EDUCATION

B.S. in Finance; **Graduated with Honors** • CALIFORNIA STATE UNIVERSITY, Northridge, CA; 2005
Completed Studies Concurrent with Full-Time Employment

Computer Skills: Windows, Microsoft Office (Word, Excel, PowerPoint), Peachtree, J.D. Edwards, Tracs

Step One

Step one will convert the Word résumé to an ASCII (or text) format. It will remove all graphic elements, convert the font to a standardized font, and remove bolding, italics, and underlining. The purpose of doing this step is to produce a document that can be read by all operating systems (Mac, PC, Linux, etc.), all ISPs (Internet service providers), and résumé-tracking software systems. You will use it to upload and insert into career and company websites.

1. Save résumé using File/Save As feature.
2. In "Save As" window, use identifiable name such as "NameE-Résumé."
3. In "File Type," scroll to and select "Plain Text."
4. Make sure that "Insert Line Breaks" is NOT checked.

5. Make sure that "Allow Character Substitution" IS checked.
6. Save and close.

Step Two

The purpose of step two is to make sure that the ASCII document is "clean" and that all information is left-justified to optimize readability by résumé-tracking systems.

> Open the NameE-Résumé file. All information will be in simple text and characters will show keyboard characters.

Your résumé will now look like this:

PATRICIA JOHNSON
1234 MURIETTA AVE. * PALMDALE, CA 93550
RESIDENCE (661) 555-1234 * MOBILE (661) 555-9876 * PATJOHNSON@EMAIL.COM

FINANCE / ACCOUNTING PROFESSIONAL
INTERNAL AUDITOR / FINANCIAL ANALYST / STAFF ACCOUNTANT
DETAIL ORIENTED, PROBLEM SOLVER WITH EXCELLENT ANALYTICAL STRENGTHS AND A TRACK RECORD OF OPTIMIZING PRODUCTIVITY, REDUCING COSTS, AND INCREASING PROFIT CONTRIBUTIONS. WELL-DEVELOPED TEAM BUILDING AND LEADERSHIP STRENGTHS WITH EXPERIENCE IN TRAINING AND COACHING COWORKERS. WORKS WELL WITH PUBLIC, CLIENTS, VENDORS, AND COWORKERS AT ALL LEVELS. HIGHLY MOTIVATED AND GOAL ORIENTATED AS DEMONSTRATED BY COMPLETING STUDIES TOWARD B.S. IN FINANCE, GRADUATING WITH HONORS CONCURRENT WITH FULL-TIME, PROGRESSIVE BUSINESS EXPERIENCE.

-CORE COMPETENCIES-
RESEARCH & ANALYSIS / ACCOUNTS RECEIVABLE / ACCOUNTS PAYABLE / JOURNAL ENTRIES / BANK RECONCILIATIONS
PAYROLL / FINANCIAL STATEMENTS / AUDITING / GENERAL LEDGER / ARTIST CONTRACTS / ROYALTIES / ESCALATION CLAUSES

PROFESSIONAL EXPERIENCE

MAJOR HOLLYWOOD STUDIO, HOLLYWOOD, CA * 2000 TO PRESENT
ACHIEVED FAST-TRACK PROMOTION TO POSITIONS OF INCREASING CHALLENGE AND RESPONSIBILITY

Royalty Analyst–Music Group, Los Angeles, CA (2005–Present)
Process average of $8–9 million in payments monthly. Review artist contracts, licenses, and rate sheets to determine royalties due to producers and song-writers for leading record label. Ensure accuracy of statements sent to pub-lishers in terms of units sold and rates applied. Research, resolve, and respond to all inquiries.

* Resolved longstanding problems substantially reducing publisher inqui-ries and complaints.
* Promoted to "Level 1" analyst within only one year and ahead of two staff members with longer tenure.
* Provided superior training to temporary employee that resulted in her being hired for permanent, Level 1 position after only three months.

Accounts Payable Analyst–Music & Video Distribution (2002–2005)
Processed high volume of utility bills, office equipment leases, shipping invoices, and office supplies for 12 regional branches. Assisted branches with proper invoice coding and resolving payment disputes with vendors.

* Identified longstanding duplicate payment that resulted in vendor refund of $12,000.
* Created contract–employment expenses spreadsheet; identified and resolved $24,000 in duplicate payments.
* Gained reputation for thoroughness and promptness in meeting all pay-ment deadlines.
* Set up macro in accounts payable system that streamlined invoice payments.
* Consolidated vendor accounts, increasing productivity and reducing number of checks processed.

Accounts Receivable Analyst–Music & Video Distribution (2000–2002)
Processed incoming payments; received and posted daily check deposits, reviewed applications for vendor accounts; distributed accounting reports, and ordered office supplies. Handled rebillings of international accounts for shipments by various labels.

* Hired as permanent employee from temporary position after only three months.

Additional Experience: Billing Clerk / Accounting Clerk / Bookkeeper (details available upon request)

EDUCATION
B.S. IN FINANCE; GRADUATED WITH HONORS * CALIFORNIA STATE UNIVERSITY, NORTHRIDGE, CA; 2005
COMPLETED STUDIES CONCURRENT WITH FULL–TIME EMPLOYMENT
COMPUTER SKILLS: WINDOWS, MICROSOFT OFFICE (WORD, EXCEL, POWERPOINT), PEACHTREE, J.D. EDWARDS, TRACS

1. Open résumé file. All information will be in simple text and characters will show keyboard characters.
2. Set margins to 1" left, 2" right, 1" top and bottom.
3. Align all information to the left.
4. Check for strange keyboard-character substitutions such as dollar signs. Usually the substitution will automatically default to asterisks, which is fine. Make changes as appropriate.
5. Correct any strange line breaks.
6. Separate sections using all caps for headings and lines composed of keyboard characters such as hyphens, equal signs, asterisks, tildes, etc.
7. Save but don't close. Again, make sure that "Insert Line Breaks" is NOT checked and that "Allow Character Substitution" IS checked.

Your e-résumé will now look like this.

PATRICIA JOHNSON
1234 MURIETTA AVE.
PALMDALE, CA 93550
RESIDENCE (661) 555–1234
MOBILE (661) 555–9876
PATJOHNSON@EMAIL.COM
==
==
FINANCE / ACCOUNTING PROFESSIONAL
INTERNAL AUDITOR / FINANCIAL ANALYST / STAFF ACCOUNTANT
DETAIL ORIENTED, PROBLEM SOLVER WITH EXCELLENT ANALYTICAL STRENGTHS AND A TRACK RECORD OF OPTIMIZING PRODUCTIVITY, REDUCING COSTS, AND INCREASING PROFIT CONTRIBUTIONS. WELL–DEVELOPED TEAM BUILDING AND LEADERSHIP STRENGTHS WITH EXPERIENCE IN TRAINING AND COACHING COWORKERS. WORKS WELL WITH PUBLIC, CLIENTS, VENDORS, AND COWORKERS AT ALL LEVELS. HIGHLY MOTIVATED AND GOAL ORIENTATED AS DEMONSTRATED BY COMPLETING STUDIES TOWARD B.S. IN FINANCE, GRADUATING WITH HONORS CONCURRENT WITH FULL–TIME, PROGRESSIVE BUSINESS EXPERIENCE.

==

-Core Competencies-
Research & Analysis / Accounts Receivable / Accounts Payable / Journal Entries / Bank Reconciliations / Payroll / Financial Statements / Auditing / General Ledger / Artist Contracts / Royalties / Escalation Clauses

==
==

PROFESSIONAL EXPERIENCE

MAJOR HOLLYWOOD STUDIO
Hollywood, CA
2000 to Present
Achieved fast-track promotion to positions of increasing challenge and responsibility
~~Royalty Analyst-Music Group, Los Angeles, CA
~~(2005-Present)
Process average of $8-9 million in payments monthly. Review artist contracts, licenses, and rate sheets to determine royalties due to producers and songwriters for leading record label. Ensure accuracy of statements sent to publishers in terms of units sold and rates applied. Research, resolve, and respond to all inquiries.
* Resolved longstanding problems substantially reducing publisher inquiries and complaints.
* Promoted to "Level 1" analyst within only one year and ahead of two staff members with longer tenure.
* Provided superior training to temporary employee that resulted in her being hired for permanent, Level 1 position after only three months.
~~Accounts Payable Analyst-Music & Video Distribution
~~(2002-2005)
Processed high volume of utility bills, office equipment leases, shipping invoices, and office supplies for 12 regional branches. Assisted branches with proper invoice coding and resolving payment disputes with vendors.
* Identified longstanding duplicate payment that resulted in vendor refund of $12,000.
* Created contract-employment expenses spreadsheet; identified and resolved $24,000 in duplicate payments.
* Gained reputation for thoroughness and promptness in meeting all payment deadlines.
* Set up macro in accounts payable system that streamlined invoice payments.

* CONSOLIDATED VENDOR ACCOUNTS, INCREASING PRODUCTIVITY AND REDUCING NUMBER OF CHECKS PROCESSED.
~~ACCOUNTS RECEIVABLE ANALYST–MUSIC & VIDEO DISTRIBUTION ~~(2000–2002)
PROCESSED INCOMING PAYMENTS; RECEIVED AND POSTED DAILY CHECK DEPOSITS, REVIEWED APPLICATIONS FOR VENDOR ACCOUNTS; DISTRIBUTED ACCOUNTING REPORTS AND ORDERED OFFICE SUPPLIES. HANDLED REBILLINGS OF INTERNATIONAL ACCOUNTS FOR SHIPMENTS BY VARIOUS LABELS.
* HIRED AS PERMANENT EMPLOYEE FROM TEMPORARY POSITION AFTER ONLY THREE MONTHS.

ADDITIONAL EXPERIENCE: BILLING CLERK / ACCOUNTING CLERK / BOOKKEEPER (DETAILS AVAILABLE UPON REQUEST)

===
===
EDUCATION

B.S. IN FINANCE; GRADUATED WITH HONORS
CALIFORNIA STATE UNIVERSITY
NORTHRIDGE, CA
2005
COMPLETED STUDIES CONCURRENT WITH FULL–TIME EMPLOYMENT
COMPUTER SKILLS: WINDOWS, MICROSOFT OFFICE (WORD, EXCEL, POWERPOINT), PEACHTREE, J.D. EDWARDS, TRACS

Step Three

Step three will create a résumé that you will use to cut and paste directly into e-mails. While it appears to be the same as the previous version, this step will insert line breaks at the end of each line. Since the margins have already been set at 1" left and 2" right, the new file WITH line breaks will contain no more than 65 characters across. This is the standard width of e-mail windows, and will fit into a standard screen shot. If you cut and pasted the original e-résumé into an e-mail without this step, the lines would scroll off the page and be hard to read.

1. Save again, using the "Save As" command, this time making sure that "Insert Line Breaks" IS checked, as well as allowing character substitution. Use a save name such as NameE-MailRésumé.
2. This version will have line breaks and will fit a standard screen shot. Remember, this is the version to cut and paste directly INTO e-mail.

The résumé will look like this:

PATRICIA JOHNSON
1234 Murietta Ave.
Palmdale, CA 93550
Residence (661) 555–1234
Mobile (661) 555–9876
PatJohnson@email.com
==
==
FINANCE / ACCOUNTING PROFESSIONAL
Internal Auditor / Financial Analyst / Staff Accountant
Detail oriented, problem solver with excellent analytical strengths and a track record of optimizing productivity, reducing costs, and increasing profit contributions. Well–developed team building and leadership strengths with experience in training and coaching coworkers. Works well with public, clients, vendors, and coworkers at all levels. Highly motivated and goal orientated as demonstrated by completing studies toward B.S. in Finance, graduating with honors concurrent with full–time, progressive business experience.
==
–Core Competencies–
Research & Analysis / Accounts Receivable / Accounts Payable / Journal Entries / Bank Reconciliations Payroll / Financial Statements / Auditing / General Ledger / Artist Contracts / Royalties / Escalation Clauses
==
==
PROFESSIONAL EXPERIENCE

MAJOR HOLLYWOOD STUDIO
Hollywood, CA
2000 to Present
Achieved fast–track promotion to positions of increasing challenge and responsibility
~~Royalty Analyst–Music Group, Los Angeles, CA
~~(2005–Present)
Process average of $8–9 million in payments monthly. Review artist contracts, licenses, and rate sheets to determine royalties due to producers and songwriters for leading record label. Ensure accuracy of statements sent to

publishers in terms of units sold and rates applied. Research, resolve, and respond to all inquiries.

* Resolved longstanding problems substantially reducing publisher inquiries and complaints.
* Promoted to "Level 1" analyst within only one year and ahead of two staff members with longer tenure.
* Provided superior training to temporary employee that resulted in her being hired for permanent, Level 1 position after only three months.

~~Accounts Payable Analyst–Music & Video Distribution
~~(2002–2005)

Processed high volume of utility bills, office equipment leases, shipping invoices, and office supplies for 12 regional branches. Assisted branches with proper invoice coding and resolving payment disputes with vendors.

* Identified longstanding duplicate payment that resulted in vendor refund of $12,000.
* Created contract-employment expenses spreadsheet; identified and resolved $24,000 in duplicate payments.
* Gained reputation for thoroughness and promptness in meeting all payment deadlines.
* Set up macro in accounts payable system that streamlined invoice payments.
* Consolidated vendor accounts, increasing productivity and reducing number of checks processed.

~~Accounts Receivable Analyst–Music & Video Distribution
~~(2000–2002)
Processed incoming payments; received and posted daily check
deposits, reviewed applications for vendor accounts; distributed accounting reports, and ordered office supplies. Handled re-billings of international accounts for shipments by various labels.
* Hired as permanent employee from temporary position after only three months.

Additional Experience: Billing Clerk / Accounting Clerk / Bookkeeper (details available upon request)

==
==

EDUCATION

B.S. in Finance; Graduated with Honors
CALIFORNIA STATE UNIVERSITY
Northridge, CA
2005
Completed Studies Concurrent with Full–Time Employment
Computer Skills: Windows, Microsoft Office (Word, Excel, PowerPoint),
Peachtree, J.D. Edwards, Tracs

HTML Multimedia Résumé Considerations

We have already noted that an HTML or multimedia résumé can be a sensible option if you work in a field where visuals and sound and or graphics represent critical skills. This option is also a nice plus if you work in any other field, as a logo of your university or from a widely recognized professional accreditation is an instance of a picture worth a thousand words.

Again on the plus side, about 50 percent of résumé banks and social networking sites accept HTML résumés; plus a simple HTML résumé can be created by using the "Save as HTML" feature you can access when you save and name your documents.

You can also add a hotlink in your e-mail that takes the reader to your web-hosted résumé (rather than adding an attachment or pasting in a résumé), and they will then see your background positioned as ideally as you could wish it.

Drawbacks to This Résumé Format:

- Adding the graphics and visuals and video and audio is a time consuming process, and can be expensive if you hire someone to do it for you.
- If you want your HTML résumé to be web-based, you'll need to build a website or have one built. This website will then have to be hosted somewhere and you'll have registration fees and hosting fees and announcement fees (elementary optimization) to host it. Apart from paying to have such a site built, these costs are usually small, but they are ongoing and do add up.
- If you build it yourself without any experience, there is a learning curve involved.
- Because the content is more complex, these documents take longer to open and work through, so the content needs to be compelling if you are going to hold anyone's attention.
- You can't expect recruiters to flock to it because anything to do with résumés is fiercely competitive in terms of achieving page rankings

(only 1 in 200 typically get to the third page of a Google search). So unless you spend a small fortune on optimization, you can't realistically expect much traffic. You will build it because you hope to send people to see it.

Essential HTML & Multimedia Résumé Considerations

- The look of the HTML résumé or website needs to look clean and professional; this is no place for your creative, out-of-work personality to seep through. Remember the end user and don't be seduced by the design capabilities.
- Use the technology to make life easier for the visitor. Your e-mail address must be a hotlink, so that clicking on it immediately launches the user's e-mail to contact you.
- If the HTML résumé ends up being a complex document with its graphics and sound and video, additional hotlinks (think navigation bar) are going to be needed on the home page for topics such as education, core competencies, technical competencies, work samples, etc.
- Don't start from ground zero; find an example you like and emulate it.
- Hotlink for a print version that allows the user to print out that beautifully formatted PDF version of your résumé.

So is an HTML or web-based résumé a waste of time? Not really, and much depends on your situation and what you are trying to sell by way of skills sets. It will always be a nice thing to have, but not mandatory. Best approach is to get your MS Word résumé completed along with the necessary ASCII text versions, get your job search up to speed, and then decide if you need to develop this third variation.

Remember to Proofread and Test E-mail All Versions of Your Résumé

Before you send any version of your résumé, take time to save and proofread it carefully. Send your electronic cover letters and résumé attachments to yourself and to a friend or family member. Ask them for printouts of your practice e-mail messages and résumés to ensure that what you intended to send is actually what was received. Often, this exercise will help you find mistakes, bloopers, or larger problems incurred during the conversion process. You shouldn't be finding spelling errors at this stage, and if you do, reward yourself with a smack up the side of the head for being sloppy.

Posting Your Résumé and Tricks to Online Questionnaires

Job sites have evolved tremendously over the last few years. There are thousands of job sites on the Internet, from mega-sites and aggregators (such as Indeed.com) to very focused sites that cater to a specific geographical location or profession. Even radio stations and newspapers are launching online résumé and job banks.

Most of the larger sites offer free delivery of relevant job postings as they appear, and résumé-posting services. For the delivery of job postings, you just select a few criteria and jobs matching your specifications are automatically sent to your inbox. With the résumé banks, your résumé goes into a database for employers and recruiters to search by keywords.

If you are currently in a full job-search mode, and spending time browsing job postings, start with broad-based search criteria; you might even eliminate salary or geographical requirements at the outset. This enables you to uncover the maximum number of opportunities. Even if the specific job opening isn't a great match or you aren't planning to relocate, you'll be able to check your résumé against the requirements being advertised and the keywords being used to describe them. Additionally, you'll become aware of these companies for future reference.

Résumé banks allow employers to find you while you are sleeping, playing, or working—it never rests. It sounds great and it works—if you understand the rules of the game.

Registering on Job Sites

Not all job sites and résumé banks work the same way. On some, you will simply copy and paste your résumé into dialog boxes as directed. On others, you will be completing a profile or questionnaire that the site has developed. This is where knowing the rules comes into play—knowing which to abide by and which to bend to your own best interests.

Job sites are usually free for you to use, but the employers are paying to post their job openings, just as they are also paying to search the résumé bank. These same paying customers want to control their search time, and the job sites work with them to develop even more efficient screening tools. By making you, the jobseeker, fill out profiles and answer questionnaires that ask for very specific information, you are helping them screen you in—or screen you out.

Whenever you are filling out a profile or questionnaire, you must keep two things in mind:

1. Who will be reading this, and for what purpose?
2. What are they really asking me?

Let's look at the Monster résumé builder, because it is also a screening tool they have created to assist the employer.

In the following illustration, we'll follow an Applications Programmer who has chosen to use the Monster site in her online strategy. Once on the site, she follows buttons for new users and, like the millions before her, starts to set up her free My Monster Account, filling out her name, address, career level, and degree, all of which are required fields.

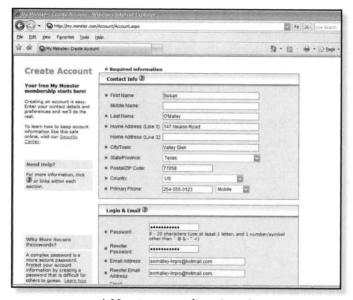

A Monster.com online résumé

Now, one of the great features of Monster is that it will allow you to maintain five different résumés or profiles—this is useful for people competent in more than one professional area. When sites allow you to do this, take advantage of it, creating edited versions of your résumé to focus on each specific target job.

The Monster résumé builder is typical in that it breaks up the résumé and profile into thirteen specific areas, including Work Experience, Target Job, Target Location, Salary, Work Status, Skills, Accomplishments, References, and Education; you will have to address similar subject areas in most online profiles and registrations.

One of the first screens Susan is asked to complete includes her "Title" and work experience. The site offers examples to help you fill in answers to these questions—but the advice is not in your best interest. Remember, the employer pays Monster to save them time in the recruitment process by screening you out. Monster advises you to list a position title that describes what type of position you are looking for. You have to think beyond the question if you want to increase your visibility. Every field you fill out is a keyword opportunity. Instead of simply completing the "Title" field as "Application Programmer," Susan utilizes the amount of space she has and makes a list of all the languages, software, and systems that she knows.

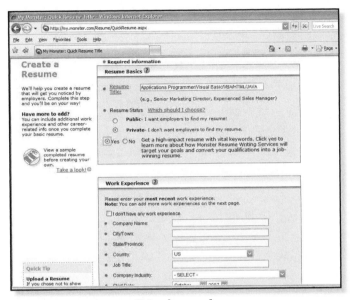

Using keywords

Always use the Work Experience areas of questionnaires to include illustrative stories about what you've done. Sometimes you are required to describe responsibilities; detail your responsibilities and reporting relationships, then follow with accomplishments and or keywords that apply within the context. You can test how much space is really available by pasting in blocks of dummy text and seeing how much the dialog box will accept.

Additionally, employers and recruiters are often looking for candidates who either are working for, or have worked with, certain companies or industry competitors. So with space not being a problem here, take the time to list customers, partners, and companies you did business with. If you have sanitized your current employer, you can pop that information into this list.

Understand that while answering these questions, you are really building your résumé again, so you must use plenty of keywords and highlight your past success stories as you build your profile. You will find a huge database of keywords in Appendix C.

The important point to remember is that you are not always limited to one answer—not even if the directions on the screen indicate you are.

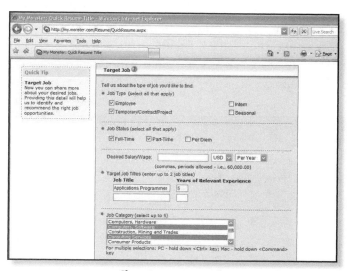

Choosing a target job

Susan was also asked about her salary requirements. We all dread this question, and as a pre-employment screening profile, nothing could be worse. But guess what? Although the salary question is sandwiched between "required" fields, it's not itself required, so Susan can, and should, leave it blank. In instances where you are forced to answer the question, use a salary range, not a single figure.

When completing questions about relocation, don't jump at an answer. Make sure you have to respond to the question at all; and if you do, select the broadest option that you can. Even if you have the ability to list many preferred locations, don't. Instead, keep your response broad. Any company or recruiter only interested in local candidates will use the address on your résumé as the search parameter.

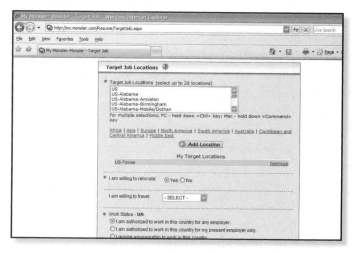

Relocation

Although our user is madly in love with her fiancé, and they both have family and friends in California, she should select "No preference." Here's the rule: You can always say "no," but you can't say "yes" unless you've been asked. For the right job, right opportunity, and right money, we would all move to Possum Trot, Kentucky. Besides, what isn't right for your career today may be tailor-made for a situation in the future; and with your own electronic career-management database, you can store all these possibilities for future reference. Plus, any jobs you interview for, but reject, will only enhance your interviewing skills!

You are most likely to come across online questionnaires and profiles in these situations:

- Registering with a job site
- Posting a résumé to a job board
- Applying for a job with a company
- Registering with a recruitment firm

In each case, you must always consider who is asking you the question and why they are asking it. Each audience is trying to screen you in, or out, so consider your responses carefully. Always read the screen instructions, avoid questions on salary and relocation if you can, and add as many keywords as possible.

These online questionnaires and profiles will affect your job search just as your résumé will. Treat this process with the respect it deserves; don't rush it. Proofread and spell check anything new that you must compose, and only post to sites that will allow you to edit and update your material at any time.

Always test the word limits of a particular category. For example, you might be told that your entry in a particular section must be limited to 500 characters—don't necessarily believe this. If it turns out that this part of the form will actually take 2000 characters, you can simply enter your info four times, giving you that many more valuable keyword hits.

COVER LETTERS

A JOB SEARCH is all about getting into conversation with people in a position to hire you.

So if all you are going to do is load your résumé into résumé databases, a cover letter isn't going to do you a whole lot of good. But if you intend to make the effort to execute a comprehensive job search that will get you into conversation with decision makers (see *Knock 'em Dead: The Ultimate Job Search Guide*), a cover letter can make a big difference.

When an e-mail or envelope is opened, your cover letter is the first thing seen; it is the device that can get your résumé an initial read with something like serious attention. Now, the writing of cover letters for résumés, as well as all the other letters you can write during the course of a job search (there are about nine different kinds that can advance your candidacy), is not a topic that can be properly addressed in the few short pages we have available in this book. You can get complete comprehensive advice, with lots of samples, in the companion book to this one, *Knock 'em Dead Cover Letters*. The following will get you moving.

Your cover letter is the personalizing factor in the presentation of an otherwise essentially impersonal document—your résumé. A good cover letter sets the stage for the reader to accept your résumé as something special.

Your target is someone who can either hire you or refer you to another who can; a management title always offers you a more direct contact with the ultimate decision maker, but an HR name is just as good, for different reasons. The HR contact can't make the hiring decision (although he or she can have a strong influence), but their pivotal position makes them aware of all areas within a company that could use your skills. The moral is, that any name is better than no name, and with the Internet at your fingertips there are plenty of ways of finding names that go with your target titles.

Your cover letter will either be sent to someone as a result of a prior conversation or sent "cold"—with no prior conversation. You will see how to handle both of these situations as we progress through the chapter.

Building a Cover Letter

The following four steps will help you create the body of the letter:

Step One

There are four basic building blocks to creating a productive cover letter, and the underlying rules of effective written communication embodied in these four steps can be applied to any memo or business letter you ever write.

Your first step is to grab your reader's ATTENTION. You do this with the appearance of your letter: The type is large and legible enough for others to read (a 12-point font is standard), it is free of misspellings, and it is well laid out so that it is easy on the eye; and if that letter is going by mail as well as e-mail (highly recommended), you will grab attention by using quality stationery and matching envelopes available at any office supply superstore. When your message is crafted with this attention to detail and convenience for the reader, it reflects the kind of professional who just might have something to say. Here is an example that immediately builds a bridge between writer and reader, then cuts right to the point:

Recently, I have been researching the leading local companies in data communications. My search has been for companies that are respected in the field and who provide ongoing training programs. The name of DataLink Products keeps coming up as a top company.

I am an experienced voice and data communications specialist with seven years experience in networked environments. If you have an opening for someone in this area, you will see that my résumé demonstrates a professional of unusual dedication, efficiency, and drive.

My experience and achievements include:

- *The complete redesign of a data communications network, projected to increase efficiency companywide by some 12 percent.*

- *The installation and troubleshooting of state-of-the-art callback security systems.*

I enclose a copy of my résumé, and look forward to examining any of the ways you feel my background and skills would benefit DataLink Products. While I prefer not to use my employer's time taking personal calls at work, you can reach me on my cell phone at (213) 555-5555. I am someone who likes to make a difference with my day. Let's talk!

Yours,
[SIGNATURE]
[TYPED NAME]

Step Two

Your second step is to generate INTEREST with the letter's content. The first opportunity you have to do this is by addressing the letter to someone by name (research approaches explained in *Knock 'em Dead: The Ultimate Job Search Guide*). The first couple of sentences grab attention, and the rest of the paragraph introduces your candidacy. The secret is to introduce yourself with conviction; if you don't believe in the professional product that is you, how can you expect anyone else to believe?

Use research to get your letter off to a fast start; with Google and other search engines, anyone can search the web for articles and visit the employer's own site. Here's another example:

I've been meaning to contact you ever since I saw that article in the online edition of Newsweek *last month about your new product line directions (attached in case you missed it). It encouraged me to do a little research. I am now convinced of two things: that you are the kind of company I want to be associated with, and that I have the kind of qualifications that might be successfully applied to your current development projects.*

On a company's website, you will find lots of eye-opening information, including news and press clippings. You can use Google to find interesting information about the company by typing in the company name as a keyword. You should also try "Google News," which tracks mentions of your keywords in the media; the news link is just above the regular Google search box. Once you find a relevant article:

- With an e-mail, paste the article and attach it.
- With a traditional letter, enclose a copy of the article.

Of course, not every company you approach will have been mentioned in *Newsweek*, but if there is no mention in the press, the chances are still good that their website can give you some insight that can be turned to similar advantage. Here are some real-life examples that you can adapt to your own needs:

I have been following the performance of your company in Mutual Funds Newsletter. *With my experience working for one of your direct competitors, I know I could make significant contributions. . . .*

Recently, I have been researching the local _____ *industry. My search has been for companies that are respected in the field and . . . which prize a commitment to professional development. I am such an individual and you are clearly such a company.*

*Within the next few weeks, I will be moving from New York to*_____. *Having researched the companies in* _____ *I know that you are the company I want to talk to. . . .*

The state of the art in _____ *changes so rapidly that it is tough for most professionals to keep up. I am the exception, and I am eager to bring my experience to bear for your company.*

Step Three

Now, having built a bridge between you and the reader, the intent is to turn that INTEREST into a DESIRE to learn more. First, tie yourself to a specific job category or work area. Use phrases like:

I am writing because . . . or *My reason for contacting you . . .*

. . . should this be the case, you may be interested to know . . .

If you are seeking a _____, *you will be interested to know. . . .*

I would like to talk to you about your staffing needs for _____ *and how I might be able to contribute to your department's goals.*

If you have an opening for someone in this area, you will see that my résumé demonstrates a person of unusual dedication, efficiency, and drive.

You might next call attention to your merits with a short paragraph that highlights one or two of your special contributions or achievements:

I have an economics background from Columbia and a quantitative analysis approach to market fluctuations. This combination has enabled me to consistently pick the new technology flotations that are the backbone of a growth-oriented technology fund.

Similar statements applicable to your area of expertise will give your letter more personal punch. Include any qualifications, contributions, and attributes that prove you are someone with professional commitment and talent to offer. If an advertisement or a telephone conversation with a potential employer reveals an aspect of a particular job opening that is not addressed in your résumé, you can use the cover letter to fill in the gaps. For example:

I notice from your advertisement that training experience in a distance-learning environment would be a plus. In addition to the qualifications stated in my enclosed résumé, I have over five years of experience writing and producing sales and management training materials in new media.

It is through this third step that you want the reader to say, "Wow, this man/woman really understands the job. I need to read on and learn more."

Step Four

Here's where your letter turns a DESIRE to know more into ACTION. The action you're shooting for is that the reader will dash straight on to your résumé, then call you in for an interview. You achieve this with brevity—always leave the reader wanting more. Offer too much information, and you may be ruled out of consideration; so whet the reader's appetite, but leave them asking questions. Make it clear to the reader that you want to talk. Explain when, where, and how you can be contacted. You can also be proactive, by telling the reader that you intend to follow up at a certain point in time if contact has not been established by then. Just as you worked to create a strong opening, make sure your closing carries the same conviction. It is the reader's last personal impression of you, so make it strong, make it tight, and make it obvious that you are serious about entering into meaningful conversation.

Useful phrases include:

It would be a pleasure to give you more information about my qualifications and experience. . . .

I look forward to discussing our mutual interests further. . . .

While I prefer not to use my employer's time taking personal calls at work, with discretion I can be reached at _____ .

I will be in your area around the 20th, and will call you prior to that date. I would like to arrange . . .

I hope to speak with you further, and will call the week of _____ to follow up.

The chance to meet with you would be a privilege and a pleasure, so to this end I shall call you on _____ .

I look forward to speaking with you further, and will call in the next few days to see when our schedules will permit a face-to-face meeting.

May I suggest a personal meeting where you can have the opportunity to examine the person behind the résumé?

My credentials and achievements are a matter of record that I hope you will examine in depth when we meet . . . you can reach me at _____ .

I look forward to examining any of the ways you feel my background and skills would benefit [name of organization]. I look forward to hearing from you.

Résumés help you sort out the probables from the possibles, but they are no way to judge the caliber of an individual. I would like to meet you and demonstrate that I have the professional personality that makes for a successful _____ .

I expect to be in your area on Tuesday and Wednesday of next week, and wonder which day would be best for you. I will call to determine. In the meantime,

I would appreciate your treating my application as confidential, since I am currently employed.

With my training and hands-on experience, I know I can contribute to _____, and want to talk to you about it in person. When may we meet?

After reading my résumé, you will know something about my background. Yet, you will still need to determine whether I am the one to help you with current problems and challenges. I would like an interview to discuss my ability to contribute to your company.

You can reach me at [home/alternate phone number] to arrange an interview. I know that your time investment in meeting with me will be repaid amply.

Thank you for your time and consideration; I hope to hear from you shortly.

May I call you for an interview in the next few days?

A brief phone call will establish whether or not we have mutual interest. Recognizing the demands of your schedule, I will make that call within the week.

Some people feel it is powerful in the closing to state a date—"I'll call you on Friday if we don't speak before"—or a date and time—"I'll call you on Friday morning at 10 A.M. if we don't speak before" when they will follow up with a phone call. The logic is that you demonstrate that your intent is serious, that you are organized, and that you plan your time effectively (all desirable behavioral traits).

On the other hand, at least one "authority" has said that an employer would be offended by being "forced" to sit and await your call. Frankly, with over thirty years of involvement in the hiring process, I have never met anyone who felt constrained to wait by the phone for such a call. What sometimes does get noticed, though, is the person who doesn't follow through on commitments as promised. Therefore, if you use this approach, keep your promise.

Writing the Cover Letter

Keep your sentences short—an average of twenty words per sentence is about right. Likewise, your paragraphs should be concise and to the point. In cover letters, paragraphs can often be a single sentence, and should never be longer than five lines. This makes the page more inviting for the harried reader, by providing adequate white space to ease eyestrain.

Short words work best, as they speak more clearly than those polysyllabic behemoths that say more about your self-image problems than your abilities.

Never write a letter and send it; your writing can always be tightened. Make the time to edit it at least three or four times over a couple of days, each time trying to shorten or punch up a sentence.

While abiding by accepted grammatical rules, punctuate for readability rather than strictly following *The Elements of Style* or *The Chicago Manual of Style*. Get by on commas, dashes—and periods. And in between the punctuation marks, use the action verbs and phrases that breathe life into your work.

Necessarily brief as this chapter has had to be, you can find a complete guide to writing the many types of letter you will use in a successful job search in *Knock 'em Dead Cover Letters*.

THE BALANCED JOB SEARCH AND HOW RÉSUMÉS GENERATE JOB OFFERS

YOUR RÉSUMÉ IS the first step in bringing that next strategic career move from dream to reality. It is an integral part of every approach to the job-search, and continues its job throughout the interview and selection cycle.

It may surprise you to discover that your résumé's job doesn't end once you get a foot in the door. If you followed my advice and focused your résumé first on a specific target job, and then went about deconstructing the deliverables of that job from relevant job postings, you now have a résumé that not only opens doors, but that helps you prepare for the interview cycle.

After all, you created a job description based on those developed by employers, and your résumé reflects this focus. Consequently, you already know the areas that employers are going to want to discuss, and you know what you have to offer in these areas and even have real-world examples ready. Because your résumé has been built with the needs of the employer in mind, tailored to their needs and reflective of their language, there is a much greater likelihood that your résumé will set a positive tone for your meetings, and may well be used as a roadmap for the interviewers' questions. So your work in creating the résumé in the ways I have laid out for you is going to give you a modicum of control over the interview process.

You should always take multiple copies of your résumé with you to interviews. Often, you can attach it to those annoying application forms and then just write on the form, "See attached résumé." You can have one on your lap during the interview to refer to, as the interviewer has one on his desk; it makes you look organized and helps keep you from doing anything awkward or socially unacceptable with your hands. You can also offer copies to subsequent interviewers. Your *Knock 'em Dead* résumé will even work for you long after the last interview is finished. Right before the hiring decision is made, hiring managers usually sit down with the dossiers on leading candidates as a last refresher, so that a target-job focused résumé will open doors of opportunity, prepare you for the interview, and guide the course of that interview. It will also be your last and most powerful spokesperson right before the decision is made. Fifty percent of the success of any project in life is in the preparation, and all the effort you put into creating your résumé will repay you with more interviews, more job offers, and a better professional future.

Résumé First Then the Job Search

In a competitive market, you need to make use of every tool you can to land that ideal job; you cannot rely on just sending résumés in response to job postings and uploading your résumé to databases.

Apart from these approaches, there are proven and effective techniques for networking, tools to research and approach employers directly, productive ways to use print resources, techniques for tapping into the different headhunter communities, and many more, but no single channel of search is a guaranteed "silver bullet." Any one of them could turn up the ideal opportunity for you and your future, so your plan of attack should embrace as many of these approaches as is practical to your situation.

The statistics say that, on average, over a career you might well change jobs about every four years. So anyone with an IQ above room temperature would be smart to commit to learning how to build an intelligent résumé and execute an effective job search. You are well on your way to having a lock on the résumé part of the equation.

Job search is a critical career survival skill, and one that cannot be shared in a couple of pages; it is a skill and a topic all its own. *Knock 'em Dead: The Ultimate Job Search Guide*, updated every year, is a book I have devoted to honing your job search and interviewing skills.

Now, take a little time to read through all the résumé samples in the next pages with your highlighter, flagging those phrases, words, and layouts that you feel might work for you when adapted to your profession and particular work experience. Please do NOT restrict yourself to looking only at résumés for your profession; look at them all for words, phrases, structure, and layout that will work for you in your unique situation.

THE RÉSUMÉS

THE RÉSUMÉS ON the following pages are based on the genuine articles, the ones that really did the trick for someone who had to translate his or her fantastic skills and background into a single, compelling document. Whether or not your background is represented in the following sample, use the résumés reproduced here as a starting point for composing your own.

Clinical Nurse Assistant

To emphasize Chantile's objective, a title was used in place of a statement along with a tag line to highlight the medical units where she has worked. Her jobs are grouped together to make it easier to read while allowing the résumé to remain on one page.

Chantile Fausett
500 La Villa • Brentwood, New York 11717 • (631) 555-2233 • ERNurse@med.net

CLINICAL NURSE ASSISTANT

ER...Shock/Trauma...Immediate Care...Triage

- Two years experience as a Clinical Nurse Assistant in ER, Shock/Trauma, Immediate Care, and Triage units.
- Hardworking and energetic; adapt easily to change, stressful environments, and flexible work schedules.
- Maintain strong observation, assessment, and intervention skills essential to providing competent patient care.
- Advocate for patients/family rights; effectively communicate a patient's needs and concerns to medical team.

Education

Western Community College, Brentwood, New York
Currently enrolled in Liberal Arts Program with a concentration in Nursing, 2005 – Present
Coursework: Anatomy and Physiology, Chemistry, Psychology, Sociology, Statistics

North Brentwood School of Nursing, Brentwood, New York
Clinical Assistant Skills Upgrade Program, 2007

Licenses & Certifications

New York State Certified Clinical Nurse Assistant, 2005
Basic EKG and Phlebotomy

Professional Experience

Clinical Nurse Assistant, North Brentwood Hospital, Brentwood, New York	4/04 – Present
—prior positions: Hospital Attendant; Pharmacist Assistant	Evening/Night Shifts
Pharmacist Assistant, One Way Pharmacy, West Islip, New York	6/02 – 10/03
Customer Service Representative, Safeway Transportation, Islip, New York	5/02 – 6/03

- Work with a team of nurses and physicians throughout Emergency Room, Shock/Trauma, Immediate Care, and Triage departments for Brentwood Hospital, one of the only Level I Trauma hospitals on Long Island.
- Care for up to 200 patients per shift within a 29-bed Emergency Room Unit, and for patients in a 7-bed Trauma Unit; assist with intubating of patients, life support systems, and general postmortem procedures.
- Provide direct patient care in areas of vital signs, phlebotomy, EKGs, treatment of surgical wounds, gynecological examinations, activities of daily living, and patient transportation within the hospital.
- Prepare patients for transfer to all critical care units, demonstrating quick thinking skills and ability to multitask while remaining focused and calm under pressure.
- Under the direction of the staff nurse, perform initial assessments of patients upon admission within a fast-paced Triage unit, and establish a Plan-of-Care for all patients.
- Assist orthopedic physicians with splinting, casting, positioning, and setup of tractions.
- Closely monitor and report changes in patients' conditions and malfunctioning of medical equipment.

Registered Nurse

Cheryl used this résumé to land her first RN position right out of college.

Cheryl Bloom, R.N.

89 Pine Road • Monrovia, NY 95777 • (555) 555-5555

Registered Nurse

- ✓ Strongly motivated graduate with experience in hospital, sub-acute, and other health care settings.
- ✓ Clinical skills combine with dedication to excellent patient care, compassion, and professionalism to integrate patients' medical and emotional care.
- ✓ Able to relate to patients quickly and work effectively with physicians, peers, and other health care professionals. Conscientious, team-oriented, and eager to learn.

Education, Licensure, and Certification

B.A. in Nursing, 2005
Chenneworth College, Croton, NY

Registered Nurse, New York State License, 2006

Basic Life Support with Automatic External Defibrillator, American Heart Association
CPR, American Heart Association
Certified Nursing Assistant, New York Nursing Assistant Registry, 2003

Additional: Math and Sciences courses, Flynn Community College, Monrovia, NY

Areas of Knowledge & Skills

- Physical Assessments
- Vital Signs/Blood Glucose
- Catheter Insertion
- Finger Sticks
- Patient & Family Education

- Dispensing Medications/Intravenous Therapy
- Documentation/Care Maps
- Nasopharyngeal & Oral Suctioning
- Application of Dressings/Wound Care
- Cast Care/Pin Care/Traction Care/Tracheotomy Care

Clinical Training

Acquired hands-on clinical experience and knowledge in nursing procedures while completing several rotations at the following facilities. Experience with patients ranging from pediatric to geriatric.

Medical-Surgical	Rockport General Hospital
OB/GYN	Melville Memorial Hospital
Pediatric	Montessori School
Gerontology	Evergreen Health Care Center, Mediplex, Kimberly Hall, Meadowbrook

Employment in Healthcare

Patient Care Technician – Jackson Memorial Hospital, Croton, NY 2003–present
Provide post-operative care to patients on an 80-bed Medical-Surgical Unit. Diverse responsibilities include: monitoring vital signs, blood glucose and tube intake/output, collecting specimens, assisting with personal hygiene and feeding, and recording patient status. Transport patients to medical procedures and operate portable electrocardiogram. Educate patients and family members on home care.

Prior Employment

Wait Staff, Calinda's Restaurant, Monrovia, NY   1998–2005

Earned reputation for dependability, accuracy, and delivering superior customer service by providing well-timed, professional service. Demonstrated skills in communication, organization, and problem solving, as well as ability to work efficiently in a fast-paced environment. Gained computer skills.

Trauma Treatment

Richard is transitioning out of the Navy, where he gained a great deal
of experience in trauma treatment and crisis management.

RICHARD P. ISAACS, RN, BSN

529 SPRINGDALE ROAD
SPRINGWATER, NEW YORK 14560
585-555-6184
RICHI@CS.COM

....

DISASTER RESPONSE • ACUTE & CRITICAL PATIENT CARE • MEDICAL/SURGICAL CARE
Pediatrics / Geriatrics / Post-Surgical / Nuclear & Biological Hazards

Health care professional with over eight years' intensive experience in fast-paced military hospital
environments. Demonstrated capacity to provide direct patient care and effectively supervise support
staff in a variety of clinical settings. Specialized training in dealing with nuclear and biological exposure, as well as experience treating patients with infectious diseases including typhoid, meningitis,
AIDS, and other contagions. Proven capacity to function well in crisis situations, plus excellent ability
to relate to patients from diverse cultural backgrounds and various age groups.

....

PRIMARY CLINICAL EXPERIENCE:

LIEUTENANT, UNITED STATES NAVY (2003 – Present)
US Naval Hospital; Tokyo, Japan
*Patients encompass infants through geriatrics, with conditions including a broad range of
infectious diseases and physical injuries.*
Staff Nurse / Charge Nurse – Adult & Pediatric Care   **May 2007 – Present**

- Provide bedside care to patients; administer medications and implement physician orders.
- Confer with physicians and other care team members on treatment plans for various patients.
- Address the needs of patients in isolation with typhoid, meningitis, and other contagious diseases.
- Train and provide leadership for staff of seven RNs and LPNs in Charge Nurse role.
- Participate in field exercises to maintain readiness for combat deployment in support of
  Marine units.

Key Accomplishment:
*Restructured medical supplies inventory and wrote new Standard Operating Procedures
(SOPs) to improve departmental efficiencies.*

Staff Nurse / Division Officer – Post-Anesthesia Care Unit   **May 2006 – May 2007**

- Served needs of post-operative patients, addressing special concerns of post-anesthesia recovery.
- Otherwise supported surgical teams in treating patients with a broad range of medical conditions.

US Naval Hospital; Annapolis, Maryland
*Patient base included military dependents and retirees, as well as active military personnel,
including several "VIP" patients.*
Staff Nurse – Medical / Telemetry Acute Care Unit   **Apr. 2003 – Apr. 2006**

- Addressed acute care needs of medical patients, including oncology and infectious disease patients.
- Cared for patients in isolation wards with tuberculosis, AIDS, and other contagious diseases.
- Monitored cardiac activity of patients using state-of-the-art telemetry technology.

Accomplishment:
Selected to serve as part of Humanitarian Relief Response Team.

Richard P. Isaacs, RN
Résumé – Page Two

PRIMARY CLINICAL EXPERIENCE *(continued)*:

LONG ISLAND GENERAL HOSPITAL; Riverhead, New York
Suburban/rural facility (eastern Long Island, New York) providing full range of medical services.
Staff Nurse / Charge Nurse – Medical / Surgical Unit **2000 – 2003**

- Provided direct patient care including telemetry monitoring.
- Served needs of incarcerated individuals in conjunction with Suffolk County (NY) Sheriff's Office.

ADDITIONAL CLINICAL EXPERIENCE:

EXPOSERVE MEDICAL SERVICES; Annapolis, Maryland
Per Diem Registered Nurse – Maryland Children's Center **2003 – 2006**
- Served the needs of pediatric patients in a clinical outpatient setting.

HEARTLAND NURSING SERVICES; Riverhead, New York
Per Diem Registered Nurse **2002 – 2003**
- Cared for burn victims, cardiac patients, post-surgical patients, ICU patients, and the terminally ill.

EDUCATION:

MICHIGAN STATE UNIVERSITY; East Lansing, Michigan
Master of Science, Community Service *Anticipated May, 2007*

STATE UNIVERSITY OF NEW YORK AT ALBANY; Albany, New York
Bachelor of Science, Nursing **May 2001**
Sigma Theta Tau Honorary / Gold Key Award / Silver Key Award

JOHNSON & WALES UNIVERSITY; Providence, Rhode Island
Associate of Science, Hotel & Restaurant Management **June 1986**

CERTIFICATIONS / SPECIALIZED TRAINING:

Registered Nurse
Advanced Cardiac Life Support (ACLS); Basic Life Support (BLS)
Pediatric Advanced Life Support (PALS I)
Intravenous Conscious Sedation (IVCS)

Nuclear & Biological Hazard Medical Training
Mass Casualty Training; Field Hospital Training; Shipboard Hospital Training
Suturing; Chest Tube Insertion

References Provided On Request

Ophthalmic Doctor Assistant/Technician

Career transition: This former sales representative attained her ophthalmic certification and then obtained successful employment in her new field.

THERESA R. KEEBLER
404-555-6822 • 3248 Derry Lane, Decatur, GA 30035

OPHTHALMIC DOCTOR ASSISTANT / TECHNICIAN
Building organizational value by assisting with diagnostic and treatment-oriented procedures

Technical Skills:
Precise Refracting/Work Up
Scribing
Goniometry
Sterile Techniques

Procedures & Treatments:
Chalazion Surgery
Glaucoma Treatments
Conjunctivitis
Diabetes Monitoring
Retinopathy of Prematurity
Macular Degeneration
Strabismus
Cataracts
Palsy
NLD Obstruction
Blepharplasty

Equipment:
A Scans
Lasers
Tonometry
Slit Lamp
Lensonetry
Keratometer
Visual Fields
Topography

QUALIFICATIONS SUMMARY

Personable and capable professional experienced in conducting diagnostic tests; measuring and recording vision; testing eye muscle function; inserting, removing, and caring for contact lenses; and applying eye dressings. Competently assist physicians during surgery, maintain optical and surgical instruments, and administer eye medications. Extensive knowledge in ophthalmic medications dealing with glaucoma, cataract surgery, and a wide variety of other diagnoses.

PROFESSIONAL EXPERIENCE

AUGUSTA EYE ASSOCIATES, Decatur, Georgia — since 2005
Hired as a **Technician/Assistant** for a cornea specialist in a large ophthalmic practice. Performed histories, vision screenings, pupil exams, and precise manifest refractions. Assisted with a variety of surgical procedures. Quickly build trust and rapport and streamline processes to ensure physician efficiency.

GUGGINO FAMILY EYE CENTER, Atlanta, Georgia — 2004 to 2005
Taught customer service techniques and promoted twice within two months to an **Ophthalmic Doctor Assistant** for a pediatric neurology ophthalmologist performing scribing, taking histories, preparing patients for examination, and educating patients on treatment procedures.

DAVEL COMMUNICATIONS, Atlanta, Georgia — 2001 to 2003
Recruited as a **Regional Account Manager** and promoted within 3 months of hire to **National Account Manager**. Contributed to the company doubling in size within 10 months; maintained a 100% satisfied customer retention rate.

CHILI'S BAR & GRILL, Decatur, Georgia — 1995 to 2000
Hired as a **Hostess** and quickly promoted to **Server**.

EDUCATION

Bachelor of Science, Organizational Communication — 2001
University of Georgia, Athens, Georgia

CERTIFICATION

Certified Ophthalmic Assistant (COA) — expected July 2006

Dental Assistant

Burton wanted a position with a larger practice. The résumé highlighted his extensive training and certifications as well as experience. It contains lots of information, in a great layout.

Burton Roberts, CDA

DENTAL ASSISTANT
CDA, EFDA, CPR CERTIFIED

GENERAL OR SPECIALTY PRACTICE
ORAL SURGERY ▪ PERIODONTICS ▪ ENDODONTICS ▪ ORTHODONTICS

Highly skilled, energetic, and flexible dental professional with experience in 4-handed dentistry, radiology, sterilization, laboratory, and office duties. Adept at earning patient's trust and confidence. Demonstrated initiative and commitment, and a proven asset to a growing practice.

DENTAL SKILLS SUMMARY

- 4-Handed Dentistry
- Preventative Care
- Instrument Sterilization
- Diagnostic X-Rays

- Infection Control
- Oral Surgery/Extractions
- Emergency Treatment
- Prosthetics/Restorations

- Teeth Whitening
- Casts/Impressions
- Root Canals
- Patient Education

CHAIRSIDE EXPERIENCE

- Prepare tray setups for dental procedures. Obtain dental records prior to appointment.
- Prepare patients for procedures – ensure comfort and develop trust; calm distressed patients; instruct patients on postoperative and general oral health care; take and record medical and dental histories.
- Oversee cleanliness of operatories and instruments; ensure safe/sanitary conditions using autoclave, ultrasound, and dry heat instrument sterilization.
- Assist dentist with extractions, fillings, and sealants. Take casts and impressions for prosthetics/restorations.

LABORATORY EXPERIENCE

- Prepare materials for impressions and restorations.
- Pour models and make casts.
- Expose radiographs and process X-ray film.

OFFICE EXPERIENCE

- Greet patients; arrange and confirm appointments; keep treatment records.
- Order dental supplies and materials; maintain stock in accordance with monthly budgets.
- Develop and document office policies and procedures. Share best practices with staff.

PROFESSIONAL HISTORY

Chairside Assistant, Dr. George Rose, Denver, CO, January 2005 – Present
Student Intern/Chairside Assistant, Dr. Victoria Mercer, Denver, CO, September 2004 – December 2004
Student Intern/Nitrous Oxide/Oxygen Administration, Dr. John Mann, Denver, CO, October 2004

EDUCATION AND PROFESSIONAL DEVELOPMENT

CPR Certification – Adult, Infant, and Child, American Red Cross, January 2005 – January 2007
Tooth Bleaching, Home Study Educators (ADA Continuing Education Recognition Program), 2006
Certified Dental Assistant, Front Range Community College, 2005
Expanded Function Dental Assistant (EFDA), University of Colorado School of Dentistry, 2005
Schuster Center for Professional Development, 2005
Colorado Radiology Certification, 2004
Nitrous Oxide/Oxygen Administration Certification, 2004
ADA Midwinter Dental Conventions, 2003 – 2006
Photocopier Technician Certification, 1996

B.B.A. University of Tacoma, Tacoma, WA, May 1993

123 W. Main Street ▪ Denver, CO 00000 ▪ 303.555.1234 ▪ burtrob@aol.net

119

Medical Assistant

Jennifer's actual paid experience was minimal and dated; her skills needed to be brought to the forefront. This new résumé was presented at a job fair where she was hired on the spot.

Jennifer Martin
(555) 555-5555
email@address.com
1234 West Street
Hometown, NY 01234

MEDICAL ASSISTANT

Triage	Injections	Patient Scheduling
Medical Terminology	Phlebotomy	Chart Updating
Patient Intake	Vital Signs	ICD and CPT Coding
Dosage Calculations	Infection Control	Insurance Claims
Sterilization Procedures	Urinalysis	Accounts Payable/Receivable
Blood Smears and Blood Tests	Hematocrit	Collections
Lab Equipment Operation	EKG	Data Entry

EXPERIENCE

Patient Care
- Cared for in-home patients with complex, multi-symptom illnesses for three years
- Eased patient discomfort by conducting accurate assessment and drawing techniques
- Fostered healthy environment for diabetic patient through meal preparation, medication dispensing, and glucose level monitoring

Administrative
- Improved cash flow by recovering uncollectible accounts in excess of $1,000,000
- Increased accuracy of patient files by designing and implementing new patient update sheet
- Exceeded daily quotas and minimized overhead expenses with effective scheduling and management of part-time employees

Computer Skills
- Microsoft Windows, Word, Excel, and Works
- Corel Word Perfect
- Medical software including Medical Manager and Great Plains

---

EDUCATION

College of Medical Careers, San Diego, CA
Medical Assistant Certificate, 1999
Valedictorian

High School, Anytown, PA
Diploma – Science Emphasis, 1997

RELATED EMPLOYMENT HISTORY

Billing Specialist, Bookkeeper, Medical Assistant (various – Indiana and Somerset, PA)	1999–2000
Medical Assistant (Internal Medical Office – San Diego, CA)	1999
Long-term/Acute Care Provider (self-employed – Anytown, PA)	1995–1998

Occupational Health Services Manager

Susan was successful in finding an Occupational Health Services management position in another industry after being a casualty of airline downsizing.

SUSAN BROWN, RN, COHN-S/CM

Manchester, NH
Mobile: 603-555-9944
Pager: 800-555-3642 PIN#1937761
E-mail: susanbrown81@hotmail.com

OCCUPATIONAL HEALTH SERVICES MANAGER

Certified Occupational Health Nurse Specialist / Certified Case Manager / Certified Occupational Hearing Conservationist / Case Management / OSHA & DOT Compliance / Ergonomics / Workers' Compensation / Corporate Safety / Training / Customer Service / Problem Solving / Quality Assurance / Sales & Marketing

- 10 years direct experience developing innovative occupational health programs and establishing clinics.
- 14 years experience in trauma centers and critical care units.
- Success in driving revenue stream and cost-saving initiatives through strong combination of business management and clinical skills.
- Licensed Registered Nurse: New Hampshire and Massachusetts
- Proficient in Sign Language, Microsoft Office, and Outlook.

PROFESSIONAL EXPERIENCE

Supervisor, Occupational Health Services, Southwest Air Lines, Manchester, NH   2001–Present

Recruited to implement and manage Southwest's first onsite employee health clinic in eight years. Accountable for care of work-related and non-occupational injuries and illnesses for 5000 airport employees (from baggage handlers to pilots). Coordinated care for another 1500 employees in New Hampshire and 1000 employees in Chicago. Hired and directly supervised 13 registered nurses. Managed $1,000,000 budget. Assisted with the launch of new Southwest clinics in four other airports. Standardized policies and procedures and created training programs.

Developed position to also encompass system-wide responsibilities, and established self as the resource for OSHA-related matters, insourcing opportunities, ergonomic issues, and post-job offer testing programs. Updated operational managers on daily events, occupational health program progression, new programs, ongoing testing, compliance achievement, drug testing program, etc.

Achievements

- Overcame resistance and established first-ever Manchester airport onsite clinic as an integral part of operations. Planned the department design, oversaw the architect and contractors, hired and trained staff, and developed an orientation manual from scratch.
- Conceived and implemented matrix to document value of occupational health services to Southwest. Demonstrated an average of 55% ROI each month.
- Generated annual revenue of $120,000 by spearheading a drive to insource business from other airport companies, promoting the utilization of the Southwest clinic instead of an offsite clinic.
- Initiated joint venture with Comair and opened a lucrative satellite clinic in Manchester for Comair employees.
- Innovated a post-job offer functional testing program to address the high percentage of injuries among new hires. Worked closely with Southwest Legal and Human Resources and researched vendors.
- Negotiated inpatient services volume discount with most utilized hospital system that will save $60,000+ per year.
- Developed an improved nurse orientation process and a charting quality assurance program.

- Coordinated availability of appropriate emergency care for passengers aboard flights that were diverted to Canada on 9/11. Arranged for medical providers to meet over 17 staggered flights and 1100 passengers that arrived over the course of the next 6 days following the event.

Trainer, Manchester, NH   1999–Present

Provided continuing education, with CEU's approved by New Hampshire Board of Nurses, on Workplace Violence Guidelines for Health Care Workers, Nuts and Bolts of Occupational Health Nursing, OSHA Compliance and the Occupational Health Nurse, and Workers' Compensation Fraud Prevention and Update.

Program Supervisor, Allied Health Corporation, Boston, MA   1998–2001

Accountable for providing a broad range of quality services in a convenient, efficient, and cost-effective manner for this 8,000-employee Hospital Based Occupational Health Services Program dedicated to "Business Health." Supervised staff of 50 at 35 different companies.

- Managed successful start-up of 8 freestanding occupational medicine walk-in clinics.
- Instrumental in winning $600,000 in new business through marketing the placement of clinics, doctors, and/or nurses at company sites.

Manager, Occupational Health Services, Cumberland Farms, Salem, NH   1995–1998

Managed department, workers' compensation benefits, OSHA compliance issues, and health and wellness initiative for this multi-million dollar division of Sara Lee Industries with 1,000 employees.

- Decreased compensation costs by 66% over three years.

Occupational Health Nurse, Granite Industrial Constructors, Boston, MA   1994
Provided occupational health and case management services to this large construction company.

Previous experience working at several medical centers and a trauma center providing direct emergency nurse care as a lead trauma nurse and charge nurse.

EDUCATION & TRAINING

Associate's Degree, Nursing, University of New Hampshire, Durham, NH   1983

Select Ongoing Professional Development (attended numerous occupational health and case management continuing education programs):

- 28 hours toward Bachelor of Science, Nursing, University of New Hampshire and Manchester Community College
- Certification Programs for Occupational Health Nurse Specialist, Certified Case Manager, and Occupational Hearing Conservationist
- 50 hours of OSHA Training

PROFESSIONAL MEMBERSHIPS

- Member, American Association of Occupation Health Nurses (AAOHN)—10 years
- International Airline Occupational Health Nurse Association
- American Board of Occupational Health Nurses (ABOHN)

COMMUNITY SERVICE
Manchester Association for the Hearing Impaired (1995–Present)

Pharmaceutical Sales and Service

Catherine was a bright sales and service specialist who was growing in her career responsibilities and accomplishments and wanted to move into more advanced management positions.

Catherine Atree

1441 Meadowbrook Road #A12 • Novi, Michigan 48375
248.555.6101 • catherineatree@yahoo.com

EXPERTISE:
PHARMACEUTICAL SALES & SERVICE

High energy sales professional with experience developing product awareness through building business relationships. A proven performer with a track record of outperforming sales goals, delivering high levels of customer service, and achieving successful sales results built on key strengths of:

- **Consultative Sales Skills** — experience and education involving custom pharmaceutical and consumer products
- **New Business Development / Territory Management** — prospecting and building a territory; identifying and capitalizing on opportunities, knowledge of sales cycles
- **Customer Retention / Relationship Building** — excellent communication (listening, speaking) and interpersonal skills
- **Goal Setting** — experience in setting and achieving both independent and team-driven targets

PROFESSIONAL EXPERIENCE

QUALIFIED HEALTHCARE INCORPORATED; Grand Rapids, Michigan
Largest domestic contractual sales and marketing partner providing solutions to pharmaceutical & healthcare industries
Pharmaceutical Sales Specialist, 2003–current
Manage team-driven pharmaceutical sales responsibilities in southeast Michigan territory. Interact with physicians, nurses, physician assistants, and medical professionals to represent a premier product line. Interact with other sales reps to do strategic planning, problem solving, and collaborative thinking. Manage 35–40 weekly calls on physicians to increase market share in territory.

- Coordinated product launch for new acid reflux drug (AstraZeneca).
- Petitioned physicians to contact their HMOs and recommend formulary status; received formulary standing in January 2005.
- Member of market-leading Prilosec sales team.
- Consistently over sales quota; won highest call activity contest. Regional sales leader for hypertensive drug.

OFFICE MAX [2000–2003]; Columbus, Ohio
Multibillion-dollar global retailer of office supplies, furniture, and technology
Business Development Specialist, 2001–2003
Promoted to develop new business while maintaining current business in competitive southeastern and central Michigan territories; focused on small to medium-size companies. Managed complete sales cycle from initial contact, through presentation and consultation, to close of sale. Acted as liaison between sales center rep team and corporate office in Boston.

- Consistently maintained above-expected goal percentage in regional and corporate sales.
- Trained new reps in all areas of product presentation, solution selling, and customer service.

Sales Representative, 2000–98
Managed sales and account maintenance with companies. Independently maintained relationships with company personnel to increase visibility and credibility. Developed leads through cold calls; met with customers to identify needs.

- Developed new customers; maintained high goal percentages; recruited to higher position.

EDUCATION & TRAINING

UNIVERSITY OF MICHIGAN; Ann Arbor, Michigan
Bachelor of Science degree in Interdisciplinary Studies/Social Science with a focus in Health & Humanities; Minor: Psychology, 1998
Seminars: Leadership Sales, Presentations Skills

References available on request

Medical Sales Representative

Jennifer went out of her way to display her yearly achievements right up front.

Jennifer J. Rogers

116 N.E. 229th Street
Vancouver, Washington 88888

555-555-5555
jrogersmed@earthlink.com

Medical Sales Representative

Professional Profile

Impressive 17-year **Medical Sales Representative** career with proven track record in prospecting, consultative sales, new business development and account retention. Proficient in sales presentations, introducing and detailing products, conducting inservices with physicians and nursing staffs. Strong assessment abilities with outstanding perception of customer needs and ability to recommend effective solutions. Well-developed closing skills for large capital purchases. Experienced sales trainer providing training classes in a corporate classroom setting as well as field training. Highly motivated, enthusiastic, and committed to professional excellence.

Achievements – percentage of plan by year

2004 – 183%	2001 – 105%	1998 – 90%	1995 – 164%
2003 – 78%	2000 – 159%	1997 – 92%*	1994 – 110%
2002 – 100%	1999 – 138%	1996 – 111%	

*started new territory

Professional Experience

Experience includes the sales of medical supplies and capital equipment. As a Senior Monitoring Consultant, worked with sales representatives throughout the Western US to assist in the presentation and closing of large systems deals. Outstanding achievements include securing multiple orders for patient monitoring systems in excess of $1 million. Possess excellent product knowledge with quick learning abilities. Demonstrated a commitment to long-term customer relationships evidenced by strong repeat business.

Career Progression

WelchAllyn Monitoring • prior to 2003 known as Protocol Systems • Beaverton, Oregon

Senior Representative • *1999–Present*
Position achieved by recommendation of Sales Director and President

Sales Trainer/Sales Representative • Northwest – based in Portland, Oregon • *1997–Present*
Territory includes Oregon, Washington, Idaho, Hawaii, and Alaska

Medical Sales Representative • Southern California – based in Orange County • *1993–1997*
Co-Medical • Seattle, Washington – Territory based in Portland, Oregon

Medical Sales Representative • *1985–1993*
Providence Hospital Pharmacy Department • Portland, Oregon

Technician Coordinator • *1981–1985*

Medical Equipment Sales

Erik is seeking to transition from pharmaceutical sales to sales of medical equipment. The résumé demonstrates a track record of accomplishments and outstanding sales and account development capabilities.

ERIK CLAYTON
erikclayton@email.com

5555 W. 55th St.
New York, NY 10024

Residence (212) 555-1234
Mobile (212) 555-4321

MEDICAL EQUIPMENT SALES

Top-producing sales professional with five years progressive experience, including three years in pharmaceutical sales. Natural communicator with expertise in forging solid working relationships with professionals at all levels. Proven ability to identify and capitalize on market opportunities to drive revenues and capture market share. Strong closer who consistently exceeds targets in a consultative sales environment.

—Core Competencies—

Sales & Marketing • Business Development • Account Development & Retention
Client Relations • Team Building & Leadership • Training & Educating
Prospecting & Closing Negotiations • Consensus Building
Problem Solving • Presentations • Public Speaking

PROFESSIONAL EXPERIENCE

Sales Representative • 2003 to Present
INDUSTRY-LEADING PHARMACEUTICAL CO., New York, NY
Represent leading pharmaceutical company in consultative sales of select medications to MDs, Pharmacists, Pharmacy Technicians and Pharmacy Managers throughout Metro New York area.

- Call on 250 accounts monthly; consistently exceed company targets.
- Increased product market share from 25%-46%.
- Educated clients on launch of product, achieving 35% market share within three months.
- Selected by District Manager, out of 12 representatives, to anchor and train new hires.
- Placed #2 in nation for sales of main product out of 2,500 reps.
- Achieved #1 in district two consecutive years, 2005, 2006.
- Nominated for *Representative of the Year* award (2005).
- Nominated for company's most prestigious award (2004).

Account Executive • 2001 to 2003
COMPUTER MASTER, New York, NY
Gained valuable sales and client relations experience with $5 million computer sales company.

- Serviced existing accounts and developed new business, including several major corporations.
- Increased territory gross sales by 20%.

EDUCATION

B.S. in Communications
NEW YORK UNIVERSITY, New York, NY; 2001

Professional Development
Company Sponsored Sales Training; 2005
Team Train the Trainer (Company home office, one week); 2005

Computer Skills: Windows, Microsoft Word, PowerPoint

Pharmaceutical Sales Representative

Melanie Moore

459 Birch Avenue * Austin, IL 60000
(555) 555-2809 * mmoore@yahoo.com

WHAT I CAN OFFER **CROSLEY** AS YOUR **NEWEST PHARMACEUTICAL SALES REPRESENTATIVE**

Meeting demanding customers' needs * "Selling" ideas to doctors * Communicating to get results under tough conditions * Using creative ideas to solve problems on my own

RECENT WORK HISTORY WITH EXAMPLES OF PROBLEMS SOLVED

Investigator *promoted from six eligibles to* **Hospital Liaison;** *promoted to* Training Supervisor *and* Hiring Manager, Illinois Department of Protective and Regulatory Service, Austin, IL 00–Present

CAPABILITY: Well informed, senior, busy judges and **doctors usually approve my recommendations quickly because I've built their trust** without the benefit of formal training.

CAPABILITY: Regularly **win the day** with my ideas, even **after** penetrating **cross-examination** by some of the best attorneys in the business.

CAPABILITY: Persuaded senior decision makers to help us deliver better quality, reduce turnover, and make our employees more effective. Our **clients were served even better.**

CAPABILITY: My new training program lowers **costs, despite our diverse workforce. Team members** now **master training** that once intimidated them.

Child Specialist, State of Missouri, Division of Family Services, Kansas City, MO   99–00

CAPABILITY: Convinced a decision maker that **my plan would help his patient stay with a demanding treatment protocol.** Patient and her unborn child protected.

Account Manager, Dunhill Staffing, Austin, IL   98–99
Dunhill provided temporary clerical and light industrial workers to local employers.

CAPABILITY: Boosted our client's productivity and made us more productive at the same time. **Complaints fell to zero** and stayed there.

EDUCATION

B.S., University of Illinois, Austin,   97
Earned this degree while working up to 20 hours a week. GPA: 3.2.

COMPUTER SKILLS

Expert in Word and Excel; proficient in proprietary customer information software suite and Outlook; familiar with Internet search protocols

Biochemistry Researcher

Young professional making first job change with a powerful and well-focused résumé.

SOPHIA L. MEYERS

15993 Mayfair Court
West Bloomfield, MI

(248) 555-8520
sophialmeyers@aol.com

Talented young professional with skills and training in:
NEUROBIOLOGY AND BIOCHEMISTRY RESEARCH

Highly-accomplished, quick learner with an impressive **hands-on knowledge base** encompassing the entire spectrum of **neurobiological research**, with special expertise in Organic, Inorganic, Analytical, Solutions, Instrumental Analysis, and Physical Chemistry. Regarded by peers and mentors as an overachiever who is **committed to excellence in this field**, as demonstrated by **outstanding academic achievement**. Demonstrate thorough and detailed research capabilities. *Experience and academic preparation include:*

- Molecular Theory
- Quantum Mechanical Modeling
- Mathematical Modeling
- Particle Location and Density
- DNA Analysis and Separation

- Reagent Preparations
- EDTA Titration Process
- Electron Neutron Diffraction
- Electrophoretic Techniques
- Thermodynamic Principles

- Ethology
- Blood Typing
- Diffusion Principles
- X-Ray Diffraction
- GCMS/MS

EDUCATION

Bachelor of Science in Biology and Biochemistry
Michigan State University, East Lansing, MI ~ Graduated with the Highest Honors ~ 2006

RELEVANT EXPERIENCE & EMPLOYMENT

Scheduling Coordinator ~ Oakland Radiology Consultants, Oak Park, MI ~ 5/2006 to present
Neuroscience Intern ~ Michigan State University, East Lansing, MI ~ 8/2005 to 5/2006
Medication Care Manager ~ Sunrise Assisted Living, East Lansing, MI ~ 2/2003 to 7/2005

Clinical Trials: Administered a significant drug trial and established a dosage response curve for the identification of invertebrate behavior using neuromodulators.

Medication Management: Completed state requirements training to confidently, legally, and safely administer patient medication and effectively document their immediate reaction. Managed a staff of 10, ordered and controlled the administration of all narcotics.

Ethology: Performed pet care behavioral science medical procedures, including the administration of both local and general anesthesia, catheters, IV, and injectables. Confidently handle x-rays and assess behavior modifications due to hormones, neuroreceptors, and neurotransmitters.

Quality Assurance and Statistical Analysis: Delivered 3+ years in-depth reagent preparation and reaction writing capstone project culminating in and solidifying expertise in testing chemicals to determine molarity of any solution.

Spectroscopy: Trained in Chemical Detection Methods including UV detection, chromotrography, and polarity, as well as finding unknown chemicals by running samples using search criteria.

Gamete Shedding/In Vitro Fertilization: Oversaw a developmental biology project devoted to the in vitro fertilization of insects, rats, and invertebrates, whereby deliberate injection led to gamete shedding, fertilization of eggs in petri, and ultimately the reintroduction of eggs into animals.

PRESENTATIONS & CONFERENCES

Presented Topic: "Octopomine vs. Serotonin as a Neuromodulator and Neurotransmitter" Society for Neuroscience National Conference - 2005 and West Virginia Academy of Science - 2006

MEMBERSHIPS, CERTIFICATIONS & AFFILIATIONS

Society of Neuroscience ~ American Chemical Society for Analytical Inorganic and Organic Chemistry
Sigma Phi Epsilon Fraternity ~ National Honor Society ~ MENSA ~*Who's Who* Listed

Registered Nurse

Clean layout, plenty of white space, easy on the eyes. The serif fonts don't detract here (they show a caring professional). The original had all the serif headings in blue and the employer endorsement near the top of the page. Eye-appealing and works well.

Laraine Brook Elliott, RN, BSN

nurse_elliott@yahoo.com

1234 Rexwood Drive ◆ Columbus, Ohio 43230 ◆ 614.555.0000

Registered Nurse

Compassionate nursing professional qualified by a **Bachelor of Science in Nursing**, RN Licensure and numerous certifications including ACLS, BLS and CNC. Provide high quality nursing care and unsurpassed patient service.

- ◆ Competent in **infectious disease containment** with proper universal precautions for tuberculosis; hepatitis A, B and C; VRE; MRSA; West Nile; meningitis, necrotizing infections and others

- ◆ **Procedure expertise**—intubation/extubation, ventrulostomies, chest tube placement, lumbar punctures, thorocentises, paracentesis, tracheostomy exchanges, central line insertions, swan guiding, arterial line insertions, peritoneal dialysis, continuing hemodialysis

- ◆ Excellent **critical thinking skills** utilized throughout career on a daily basis

" ... functions effectively in an emergency situation, including Code Blue procedures ... independent worker who needs little supervision ... can be counted on to complete assignments ... thoughtful and courteous ... is an important contributor to the morale and success of the MICU team ..." ~ Excerpts from performance evaluations

Education & Licensure

MT. CARMEL COLLEGE OF NURSING, Columbus, Ohio (May 2005)
Bachelor of Science in Nursing

Licensure & Certification
- ◆ RN License – State of Ohio, License #1234567
- ◆ Advanced Cardiac Life Support (ACLS)
- ◆ Continuous Renal Replacement Therapy (CRRT)
- ◆ Code Nurse Coordinator (CNC)
- ◆ Basic Life Certified (BLS)
- ◆ Disaster Relief Certificated with the American Red Cross

Related Professional Experience

BSN, Registered Nurse
THE OHIO STATE UNIVERSITY MEDICAL CENTER, Medical Intensive Care Unit, Columbus, Ohio (July 2005–present)
Provide superior care for patients with critical and/or life-threatening illnesses/injuries in a 25-bed intensive care unit.
- ◆ Serve as Code Nurse Coordinator (CNC) for hospital and assist with codes on my unit patients as well as others.
- ◆ Perform numerous procedures ranging from intubation/extubation to central and arterial line insertions while maintaining sterile environment and managing/maintaining lines.
- ◆ Issue medications, perform lab draws, specimen cultures, wound care and maintain wound vacs.
- ◆ Withdraw life support providing comforting care for patients and comfort and counsel for grieving families.
- ◆ Perform post-morgue care and transport bodies to morgue.

Nurse Resident
THE OHIO STATE UNIVERSITY MEDICAL CENTER, Nurse Residency Program, Columbus, Ohio (August 2005–August 2006)
Year resident involved in research of new graduates analyzing progression the first year out of nursing school with a guided program compared to new graduates without the program.
- ◆ Gave presentations on legal issues and numerous issues encountered during first year as an RN with strong focus on professionalism and dealing effectively with other members of medical team.

Laraine Brook Elliott, BSN, RN
Page 2

Related Experience (cont'd)

Nurse Intern
THE OHIO STATE UNIVERSITY MEDICAL CENTER, Nurse Internship, Columbus, Ohio (July–September 2005)
Rotated throughout surgical intensive care, medical intensive care and emergency room care units to gain insight and experience in all areas of operation and patient care

Patient Care Assistant (PCA)
MT. CARMEL MEDICAL CENTER, Columbus, Ohio (May 2004–May 2005)
Provided prescribed medical treatment and personal care services to ill, injured, convalescent and handicapped persons maintaining high standard of excellence throughout department
- Performed a variety of care including taking vitals, applying compresses and ice bags, administering medications and wound care.
- Cared for patients with chest tubes, central venous catheters, peripheral inserted central catheters, dialysis AV shunts and ventilators
- Observed patients and reported adverse reactions to medication or treatment to medical staff.
- Assembled and used equipment such as catheters, tracheotomy tubes, oxygen suppliers and SCDs with TED hose.
- Examined and passed food trays for prescribed diets.
- Inventoried and requisitioned supplies.

Dental Assistant
RACINE DENTAL CLINIC, Racine, Ohio (August 1998–August 2001)
Rotated throughout clinic providing assistance in various areas as needed.
- Performed central sterilization and processed dental impressions.
- Reviewed patient history and prepared patients for procedures.
- Scheduled appointments and assisted with clerical support functions.

Community Involvement/Activities

- Numerous hours of community service work with Mt. Carmel College of Nursing in various settings including Columbus Public Schools
- Mt. Carmel College of Nursing – Member of softball team (two years) and volleyball team (one year)
- Volunteer at Faith Mission – Prepared and served meals at homeless shelter
- American Red Cross Volunteer – Volunteer for disaster relief gathering supplies and updating medications
- Mission Trip to Mexico – Helped set up a clinic for the relief and medical care of people in Nuevo Progresso

Trauma Coordinator

Clean layout, easily readable subject headings, and well focused.

FIONA PATTERSON

Address	Phone
City, State Zip	Email Address

CAREER TARGET: TRAUMA COORDINATOR

Experience in Coordinating and Executing Outreach Programs to Meet Preventive Education Goals; Strong Background in Training, Mentoring, and Supporting Employees; Effective Communicator, Fluent in Spanish

Dedicated, resourceful health care professional with previous success in planning and implementing programs that emphasize preventive measures for injuries and illnesses. In-depth knowledge of principles, methods, and procedures of trauma and medical care. Strong advocate of health care organization's role as teacher within society. Knowledge and skill areas include:

*Program Development & Implementation • Training Development & Delivery • Public Speaking & Presentations
Data Analysis & Evaluation • Community Outreach Initiatives • Trauma System Procedure Standardization
Emergency Medical Services Processes • Local, State, and Federal Regulations • Quality Assurance*

Education & Credentials

Bachelor of Science in Nursing, In Progress: Lubbock Christian University, Lubbock, TX / Expected **Associates Degree in Science:** Eastern New Mexico University, Roswell, NM

Certifications: ACLS, BLS, PALS, TNCC, ENPC
Affiliations: Member, Emergency Nurse Association
Attended National ENA Convention for the past 3 years
Currently serve as Injury Prevention Chairperson for local and state chapters

PROFESSIONAL EXPERIENCE

COVENANT MEDICAL CENTER – Lubbock, TX   2001 – Present
Staff Registered Nurse

In charge of implementing instructional outreach program. In addition to nursing responsibilities within 43-bed Emergency Room (over 40 nurses at any given time), perform Relief Charge Nurse duties at least once per week. Match patients with nurses at various levels and direct ambulances to different stations. As senior nurse within unit, serve as official mentor for organization, trainer for new graduates, and resolution specialist to address conflicts between staff members. Sat on Nurse Staff Council for the Emergency Department over the past 2 years, functioning as liaison between nurses and management.
Challenges: Implementing strategies for upholding high level of morale within under-staffed, stressful situations while maintaining optimal patient care.

KEY CONTRIBUTIONS & ACHIEVEMENTS:

❑ **Coordinated successful, well-received Injury Prevention Outreach Program. Landed Academy and Master Locks** as sponsors for events, oversaw Health Fairs to address various topics/issues, and worked with local fire departments (spanning from Ransom Canyon to Levelland) to disseminate information regarding fireworks safety measures.

❑ **Served as key member of Student Advocacy Subcommittee, ensuring proper training for high school, nursing, and** EMT students. Took on educator role with students circulating through ER, contributing to improved capabilities.

❑ **Assisted unit in ensuring fulfillment of standards for JCAHO, as well as improving Quality Assurance and Safety** objectives. Maintained and improved morale through continual communications and team building exercises.

❑ **Earned "Excellent" ratings on performance evaluations and received acknowledgment from multiple patients for** high level of care and personal attention. Leveraged bilingual background to serve Spanish-speaking population.

** Prior position as Staff Registered Nurse with the Eastern New Mexico Medical Center, Roswell, NM, 1997–2001. Performed various nursing duties, including those revolving around Emergency Room. Participated in extreme trauma cases.

Medical Assistant

Minimalist one-pager that still packs in a great deal of relevant information focused on the target job.

SALLY WILLIAMS

Anywhere, CA • C: 555-555-5555 • H: 666-666-6666 • swilliams@anyserver.com

Tools for Transition Sample Résumé

EXPERIENCED MEDICAL ASSISTANT

Broad background in different medical disciplines. Able to perform all types of assistant functions, and learns new skills quickly. Gets along well with patients, doctors, and medical staff. Able to multitask for individual patient care, physician communication, and managing all necessary paperwork. Develops good rapport with patients and provides motivational support to them and their families.

Clinic Experience:

- Cardiology
- Family Practice
- Dermatology
- Neurology
- Neurosurgery

- OB/GYN
- Orthopedics
- Pain Management
- Podiatry
- Urology

Medical Experience:

- Anatomy & Medical Terminology
- EKG Testing Procedures
- File & Record Maintenance
- Front Desk Registration
- Instrument Handling
- Insurance Benefits / Authorizations
- Patient Relations

- Pharmacy Communications
- Physician Assistance
- Sterile Environments
- Supply / Inventory Control
- Surgery / Appointment Scheduling
- Urinalysis & Hemoccult
- Venipuncture & Injections

PROFESSIONAL BACKGROUND

ACADEMIC SABBATICAL	2006 – 2007
CONFIDENTIAL MEDICAL GROUP	1995 – 2006
Private practice with up to 7 physicians **Medical Assistant**	
ALTOS CARDIOVASCULAR MEDICAL ASSOCIATES, Los Altos, CA	1994 – 1995
Private practice with 4 physicians **Medical Assistant** (including EKG Technician duties)	
STANFORD UNIVERSITY CLINIC, Stanford, CA	1993 – 1994
Multiple specialty clinics on campus **Medical Assistant III** (Clinic Relief Staff)	
WANG UROLOGY CLINIC, Vacaville, CA	1991 – 1993
Single physician practice **Medical Assistant** (on call), 1992 – 1993 **Medical Assistant**, 1991 – 1992 **Medical Assistant Externship**, 1991	

EDUCATION, TRAINING, & CERTIFICATIONS

American Red Cross: CPR, Community First Aid & Safety

Ohlone College, Fremont, CA, 2005 – 2007

Selected Coursework:

Medical Terminology, Microbiology, Nutrition, Psychology, Anatomy & Physiology, Sociology

Med-Help Training School, Concord, CA

Administrative Medical Assistant Program (9 months)

Certified Medical Assistant

EKG Technician

Solano Community College, Fairfield, CA

Associate of Science, Computer Programming

TECHNICAL SKILLS

MEDIC

Microsoft: Word, Excel

Hospital Management Professional

Clean layout, generic target job title followed by three key strengths
relevant to job and a core competency section

Dianne Martino

555 Gayle Avenue • Los Angeles, California 90049
Residence (310) 555-1234 • Mobile (310) 555-5678 • DianneMartino@email.com

HOSPITALITY / HOTEL MANAGEMENT
Strengths in Operations / Sales / Marketing

Top-flight hospitality management professional with 10+ years progressive experience and
a track record of delivering measurable revenue and profit contributions. Team building
and leadership strengths with proven ability to hire, train, and motivate top performing
teams. "Big-picture" thinker, highly organized, with the ability to multitask in a fast-paced
environment and respond quickly and effectively to problems. Learns quickly and thrives
on challenges.

—Core Competencies—

Customer Service / Client Relations / Team Building / Hiring, Training, & Motivating
Operations Management / Marketing / Advertising / Time & Task Management / Policy &
Procedures
Revenue Optimization / Cost Containment / Productivity Enhancement / Problem Solving

PROFESSIONAL EXPERIENCE

STAR CITY RESTAURANT, Los Angeles, CA
*Achieved fast-track promotion to positions of increasing responsibility at world-renowned
establishment.*

Assistant General Manager—Hollywood (2004–Present)
Oversee day-to-day food and beverage operations of $5+ million fine-dining establishment
that averages 250 covers daily. Train, manage, and mentor cross-functional team of 60+,
ensuring highest standard of customer service and brand integrity. Supervise food & beverage
inventories, manage costs and maximize profitability, monitor safe handling best practices
& procedures; prepare sales and labor forecasts. P&L accountability. Payroll responsibility.
Accounting & POS support.

• Orchestrated scheduling initiative that minimized overtime, captured 10% increase in
  productivity, and reduced payroll by over 10%.
• Hired, trained, and supervised cross-functional front- and back-of-the-house staff of 60
  with minimum turnover; achieved impact ratio over 100%.
• Generated mystery shopper score of 90+% annually.
• Slashed food cost by over $150,000 annually.
• Created marketing strategies that increased top line sales.
• Consistently ensured excellent service within critical time frame for 300+ pre-theater
  patrons as required.
• Organized liquor perpetual inventory and streamlined daily procedures, capturing cost
  reduction of 2%.

Administrative Manager—Hollywood (2002–2004)
Promoted after nine months to initiate and manage administrative affairs for new location including daily cash and credit reconciliations, employee file maintenance, accounts payable, office administration, benefits administration, new hire processing, etc.
- Achieved 95% or better on all audits
- Appointed as corporate administrative trainer; trained six managers during tenure.
- Authored Positouch Procedural Guide for use at all locations.
- Designed employee file initiative that was adopted for use companywide.
- Implemented side work, floor plan, and scheduling charts to organize restaurant opening.
- Assumed responsibility for OSHA and Workers' Comp that resulted in perfect scores on corporate audits.

Bartender—Santa Monica (2000–2001)
Hostess—Santa Monica (2000)

PROFESSIONAL EXPERIENCE, continued
CARLA'S DINNER HOUSE, Los Angeles, CA • 1996–2000
Shift Supervisor / Bartender / Server
Advanced to shift supervisor with responsibility for opening/closing, scheduling staff, maintaining inventory, purchasing, reconciling cash drawer, etc., for busy Upper East Side restaurant.
- Gained valuable experience in all aspects of restaurant operations.
- Developed "spotter" system to eliminate theft that has been implemented by other establishments throughout the area.
- Increased sales through "door to door" advertising program.

Additional Experience—*Worked Part-time as Server/Hostess at various establishments concurrent with University studies*

EDUCATION
UNIVERSITY OF CALIFORNIA, Los Angeles, CA
BA in Humanities
Professional Development / Certifications
Stellar Service Training (Phoenix, 2004)
Servsafe, FMP (Food Management Professionals) Certified Trainer

ADDITIONAL INFORMATION

Professional Affiliations—Member, NAWBO (National Association of Women's Business Owners)

Computer Skills—(PC and Macintosh), Word, Excel, Databases, POS Systems (Positouch, Squirrel, Micros), Restaurant Magic

Foreign Language Skills—Conversational Spanish in the Workplace

Teacher

Normally I'm against warm and fuzzy fonts like this, but for this teacher, they work. Note how clean and professional the rest of the layout is.

1234 Dove Lake Road
Athens, Ohio 45701
740.555.3996
sjkramer@hotmail.com

Shannon J. Kramer
Elementary School Teacher

Excerpts from Letters of Recommendation

"…her enthusiasm for teaching, love for children, and ability to plan creative and effective lessons will be definite assets …"

~Dr. Diane J. DePeal
Ohio University Professor and
Mentor, Chauncey Partnership

"…extremely organized …very helpful with room set-up …eager to learn as much as possible … seeks resources to help her accomplish her goal … great knowledge on the computer–uses it as a tool to support classroom management … excellent rapport with students, their families … communicates well with other teachers … aware of what it takes to be the best teacher she can be!"

~Amy Martin
Cooperating Teacher
Barrington Elementary School

Summary of Qualifications

- Self-directed, resourceful and enthusiastic teaching professional with a genuine interest in fostering students' cognitive and social growth
- Skilled in the design of developmentally-appropriate, enriching, innovative and hands-on activities and lessons to meet social and emotional needs of students as well as state standards
- Combine strong passion for literacy, motivation and inspiration to create a fun and challenging learning environment with strong connections to community
- Active team member effectively communicating and collaborating with all levels of staff to ensure optimum learning environment for students

Education & Certification

OHIO UNIVERSITY, Athens, Ohio (November 1999)
Bachelor of Science in Elementary Education • Reading Endorsement

Certification
State of Ohio Five-Year Professional License (1-8) with K-12 Reading Endorsement (Effective June 2007)

Related Teaching Experience

First and Second Grade Multi-Age Teacher
HIGHLAND PARK ELEMENTARY SCHOOL, Grove City, Ohio (August 2000–June 2002)
- Integrated first and second grade curriculum while establishing an independent, self-directed multi-age classroom. Conducted Developmental Reading Assessments (DRAs) as well as other routine assessments setting individual student performance goals based on results. Successfully implemented new science curriculum. Developed home/school relationships with communication through weekly newsletters and grading period conferences. Utilized a variety of teaching methods including Guided Imagery, Process Drama and hands-on sensory activities to facilitate learning process.

Long Term Substitute/First Grade Classroom
BARRINGTON ELEMENTARY SCHOOL, Upper Arlington, Ohio (February–June 2000)
- Developed and implemented weekly lesson plans and units in absence of regular classroom teacher. Created and fostered a child-centered, literacy rich environment. Established individual student goals across curriculum. Scheduled daily parent involvement and held parent/teacher conferences.

Shannon J. Kramer
Elementary School Teacher

1234 Dove Lake Road
Athens, Ohio 45701
740.555.3996
sjkramer@hotmail.com

Page 2

Related Teaching Experience (cont'd)

Student Teacher
BARRINGTON ELEMENTARY SCHOOL, Upper Arlington, Ohio (Fall 1999)
- Assumed full teaching responsibility in first grade classroom developing, planning and implementing weekly lesson plans and units. Assisted cooperating teacher with assessments. Completed DRA and Everyday Math training; integrated Everyday Mathematics into lesson plans. Attended staff meetings, parent information night and parent/teacher conferences.

Ohio University Literacy Partnership (400 hours)
CHAUNCEY ELEMENTARY SCHOOL, Chauncey, Ohio (September 1998–June 1999)
- Collaborated with both 2nd and 6th grade teachers and students in challenging school demographic of 30% IEP and 25% identified students. Taught individual small group and whole class assignments. Created and taught lessons using rich text aligned with thematic units. Used various reading assessments to set reading goals, develop lessons with appropriate reading strategies to support students' literacy growth and track progress throughout the year.

Technology Skills

Competent in both Microsoft Windows and Macintosh OS X operating systems and the following software packages:

- Microsoft Word and Powerpoint
- WordPerfect
- AutoCAD
- Scholastic Reading Inventory
- Power Media Plus
- Chalkwaves
- Internet and e-mail packages
- Working knowledge of Quicken

Current Professional Experience

Designer/Sales Associate
KITCHEN CREATIONS & RENOVATIONS, Athens, Ohio (January 2007–present)
- Coordinate sales and manage large- and small-scale projects from initial design through final install. Projects range from kitchen remodels to custom cabinetry layouts.

Computer Support Technician

Joshua is a recent graduate of a computer help desk/computer support technician program, and his résumé demonstrates commitment to excellence, team spirit, and customer focus—all qualities needed in his new line of work.

Joshua Michael Peterson

4 Borderland Court • Montclair, NJ 12345 • tel: 555-555-5555 • petersonjm22@aol.com

OBJECTIVE: HELP DESK / COMPUTER SUPPORT TECHNICIAN

PROFILE
- ✓ **Recent computer center graduate with proven technical abilities.**
- ✓ Demonstrated track record of achieving goals in a team environment.
- ✓ Highly motivated and dependable. Proven skills in problem solving, customer relationship management, and organization.

EDUCATION

The Computer Learning Center, **Skillman, NJ**   **2005 – 2006**

Computer Coursework completed in:

✓ **Networking Essentials**	✓ Beginning Windows NT
✓ A+ Certification	✓ Administering Windows NT
✓ Intermediate Word 2003	✓ Windows NT Core Technologies
✓ Beginning Word 2003	✓ Windows NT Support by Enterprise
✓ Beginning Access 2003	✓ Beginning Business on the Internet
✓ TCP/IP Protocol	✓ Beginning FrontPage 2003

Montclair University, **Montclair, NJ**   **2003 – 2004**

General first-year courses in Bachelor's Degree program (24 credits).

EMPLOYMENT A Cut Above, **Montclair, NJ**   **2002 – 2006**

Receptionist / Cashier
- Successfully handled front desk and three incoming telephone lines for busy, upscale hair salon. Greeted and logged in steady stream of customers, coordinating appointments with hairdresser availability.
- Developed cooperative, team-oriented working relationships with owners and co-workers in this 12-station salon.
- Managed customer problems and complaints with tact and attention to prompt customer service. Received team and customer service awards.
- Experience gained in opening and closing procedures, cash register receipts, counter sales, light bookkeeping, and telephone follow-up.

Pro Soccer Camp, **Princeton, NJ**   **Summers 1999 – 2002**

Trainer / Coach
- Assisted Women's Soccer Coach in 200-participant soccer camp. Asked to return as trainer for 3 seasons. Worked with individuals, as well as teams, to improve their attitude and resulting soccer performance.

ACTIVITIES Jersey Waves **Soccer Semi-Pro Team**   **1999 – 2003**

✓ **Team consistently ranked in top 10 semi-pro teams in the nation.**

Washington Crossing High School Soccer Team   **1998 – 2001**

✓ Captain of team that won State Soccer Title in 2000
✓ Recognized as one of the top two mid-fielders in the state in 2001

Software Developer/Project Manager

Jackson A. Lewis

1532 W. 35th Terrace, Dallas, Texas 75032 Phone: 276-555-7225 Email: jacklew@sbc.global.net

SOFTWARE DEVELOPMENT / PROJECT MANAGEMENT

Expertise

Software Development Life Cycle, Process Automation, Vendor Management, Software Interfacing
Systems and Hardware Analysis, Maintenance, Upgrade, Customization, & Modification
Client & Vendor Presentations / Employee Recruiting / Employee Mentor and Trainer, Improved Efficiency

Operating Systems

UNIX, Solaris, IBM AIX, HP-UX, DOS, Windows 95/98/NT/2003/XP

Languages

Java (JSP, Servlets, Applets, EJB, J2EE), JavaScript,
Visual Basic, HTML, XML, C/C++, COBOL, PL/SQL

Databases

Oracle, SQL, JDBC, ODBC, Microsoft Access

Software/Programs

Weblogic Application Server, Websphere Studio Application Developer, Eclipse, Forte for Java
(Sun One), NetBeans, Visual Age for Java, MQ Series, TOPLink, CVS, RCS, Visual Source Safe,
Dreamweaver, Microsoft Project, Word, Excel, Outlook, PowerPoint, FrontPage

SUMMARY OF EXPERIENCE

SBC Corporation, Dallas, Texas
Software Engineer IV, April 2003 – Current
Software Engineer III, October 2001 – April 2003
Software Engineer II, July 2000 – October 2001

Integrated communications provider serving 85 million customers,
and employing a workforce of 90,000 worldwide.

- **Lead Analyst** for **multiple projects** and **subprojects** (with Regional, National, and International clients and vendors), performing supervisory functions, including task assignment, quality assessment, scheduling, and employee evaluation.
- Vendor development and management, including **Cingular Wireless, Telcordia,** and **RLG Systems.**
- Designed and developed Web-based production job scheduling system with multi-threaded server component, **automating scheduling process.**
- Managed Customer Records Database project, interfacing with vendor software, affecting **1 Million+** SBC customers and **700** internal personnel.
- **Improved** operational **efficiency** of Sierra Online Scheduling, **reducing personnel by 50%.**
- **2004 SBC Award of Distinction.**
- **Multiple Monthly SBC Awards of Distinction,** including May 2006, December 2005, March 2005, April 2004, August 2003, November 2002, July 2001, and September 2000.
- Developed **configuration management process** allowing multiple team members to access system without interference to other users.
- Created and presented seminar for EDP (Enterprise Development Project) process to client and software team. Implemented **customization or updating processes** to meet team needs.
- **Trained** over **40 employees** in use of systems and processes.
- **Mentored 20 employees** in technical and professional business aptitude, including associates in Sales and Marketing Systems, Operational Systems Support, and Resolution Support Services departments.

- Experienced in managing hardware-related projects.
- Maintain existing systems, upgrade existing hardware and operating systems, establish new hardware, and provide on-call support.

BPC, Ft. Worth, Texas
Programmer/Analyst, May 1998 – July 2000

*Medical-based applications company marketing software to
healthcare industry, including hospitals, laboratories, pharmacies, and doctors.*

- 24/7 **on-call crisis management** for all clients accessing Patient Management Systems.
- **Enhanced Patient Management software** with additional functionalities, utilizing COBOL, and Discern Explorer.
- **Modified** Patient Management software to correct flaws/errors.
- Planned and executed all phases of **project management,** including design, coding, testing, and implementation.
- Analyzed and resolved client software issues.
- Educated clients during **troubleshooting** process in **resolution of software issues,** while preparing them to independently repair similar issues in the future.
- Assisted management team in **selection of new associates,** including interview process.
- **Lead Developer** for Patient Management Team, guiding other developers and software specialists.

CIVIC CONTRIBUTIONS

Habitat for Humanity, May 2006

Grande Point Homeowners Association, Vice President 2004, Member 2002 – Present

EDUCATION & PROFESSIONAL DEVELOPMENT

Baylor University, Waco, Texas

B.S. Business Administration – Computer and Office Information Systems, May 1998

SBC Corporation, Dallas, Texas

"Advanced Project Management" April 2004
"Project Management Principles and Practices" May 2003
"Negotiations" August 2002
"Process Analysis and Maturity" January 2002
"Advanced C++" December 2001
"C++" November 2001
"Conflict Prevention and Resolution" October 2001
"Presentation Skills" March 2001
"Managing Basic Projects (Project Management)" February 2001
"Seven Habits of Highly Effective People" January 2001
"Java Workshop" December 2000
"Visual Basic" December 2000
"UNIX: Advanced Shell Programming" November 2000
"UNIX: Shell Programming" November 2000
"Oracle for Application Developers" September 2000

Network Administrator

David wants to transition his impressive and broad experience from technical consulting with the military to commercial endeavors in the corporate sector.

DAVID J. WAGNER, MCP

217 Magnolia Court, Oakland, NJ 07436
(201) 405-5555 Home • (201) 405-8888 Mobile • djwagner@csn.com

---

Networks / Systems
Hardware Configuration:
Windows, UNIX, Cisco
Software Configuration
Systems Integration
Systems Configuration
Router Configuration
Intrusion Detection Systems
Frame Relay Networking
Network Planning
Network Firewalls
Peer-to-peer Networks
Ethernet Networks
Telephony & Fiber Optics
Internet Information Server
Switches & Hubs
ISDN/T1 Lines

Media & Peripherals
Voice & Data
TCP/IP

Project Management
Technology Consulting
Technology Management
Networking Infrastructures
Systems Implementation
Virtual Team Leadership
Relationship Management
Advanced Communications
Telecommunications
Security Analysis
Security Development
Applications Development
Evaluation & Testing
Troubleshooting
Resource Utilization
Inventory Management
Technology Training
End-User Training
Knowledge Transfer
Executive Presentations
Strategic Planning
Project Team Development
Team Building
Client Relations
Quality Assurance
Problem Solving

TEAM LEADER • PROJECT MANAGER • DEPARTMENT MANAGER
Network Administration • Systems Security Technology

✓ **Microsoft Certified Professional. A+ Certification.**
Accomplished technology consultant and project manager adept in desktop and network security / systems architecture planning, design, installation, configuration, maintenance, and smooth project delivery.

✓ Accustomed to supporting multi-user networks, as well as leading high-performance technology and telecommunications solutions. Successfully employ technology to improve operations efficiency, reduce costs, and meet reliability and security goals and deadlines.

✓ Proven track record in team leadership and training, supplying a balanced mix of analytical, management, coaching, and technical skills.

PROFESSIONAL EXPERIENCE

Senior Computer Scientist   2003 – present
S5 Systems Group (US Army technology consulting firm), Stockton, NJ

Technical Lead – Army Computer Systems Office (2004 – present)
Focus: Rollout of Army Partnership Tool Suite (APTS) system, implementing new functionality into live networks and systems.

- Lead Consultant and liaison (chosen by government project manager) in 7-member cross-functional team deploying integrated networks, systems, and technologies. Introduced real-time, peer-to-peer collaboration via new application, bringing far-flung team together and eliminating disconnects.
- Key player in development, testing, and implementation process, including custom tool suite development, to fit client needs. Integrate configuration, and supply installation support for pioneering technology collaboration.

Lead Network Engineer
Information Systems Engineering Office (2003 – 2004)
Focus: $24 million Communications Update & Planning System (CUPS). Evaluated, selected, and integrated advanced communications and networking products for the Communications Collaboration Team.

- Key role (network engineer/administrator/technician) leading 6-member team. Honed end-to-end project management and presentation skills.
- Pioneered first-ever use of security hardware/software, including intrusion detection systems (IDS), Cisco routers, and network management apps.
- Designed robust, mobile communications (and upgrades) to facilitate efficient network convergence and bandwidth utilization. Developed network management tools for real-time monitoring and troubleshooting.
- Field-tested flying local area network (FLAN), utilizing wireless Ethernet technology, which interconnected en route aircraft to ground-based units.
- Proposed equipment purchasing savings of $2.5 – $6 million through services analysis, reducing duplication of physical space and equipment.
- Introduced new traffic routing method (tech) utilizing a defense satellite channel for communications, enabling netmetting in worldwide locations.

continued

HARDWARE:
Sun Microsystems
IBM PCs & compatibles
SCSI & IDE Hard Drives
Cisco Routers & Switches
3COM Switches & Hubs
Ascend Pipeline Series
Netgear Hubs
RAID Arrays (Sun)
Ethernet NICs
Printers, Scanners
CD-ROMs, Modems
CD-R & CD-RW Drives
Sound Cards, TV Cards
Tape Drives

Software (UNIX):
Solaris, Linux
HP UNIX, SCO UNIX
Cisco Works Essentials
BIND 4 & 9 (DNS)
X-Windows, Open Windows
SSH, Lynx, Pine, ELM
sh, csh, bash
ftp servers & clients
Eagle Raptor Firewall
Apache, Sendmail, IRC

Software (PC):
Windows, DOS
Novell Netware
MS Office, MS Outlook
WordPerfect, FrontPage
IRC, IE, Netscape
FTP Servers & Clients
Norton, Cisco
HyperTerminal, Kermit
HP Openview
Cisco Works Essentials
Carbon Copy
Seagate Backup Exec.
SCO Xvision

Software (Cisco IOS):
Internetworking OS
Network Address Trans.
Access Lists
Context Based Access
Intrusion Detection
Remote Syslog Logging
Routing Protocols

Signal Officer   1994 – present
113th Signal Battalion, NJ Army NG, Stockton, NJ

- Platoon Leader – Mobile Subscriber Equipment Company. Lead, develop, and motivate 40 soldiers. Oversee inventory management of $4.8 million in vehicles, weaponry, security, and communications equipment.
- Mission – establish mobile subscriber equipment network (mobile phone network for combat soldiers in the field).

Computer Scientist   2001 – 2003
Computer Development Services, Inc., Oakland, NJ

- Lead technical consultant – Computer Services Security Branch (U.S. Army) for setup, testing, and evaluation of networks/systems security technologies. Established configuration, installation procedures, and network topologies for all support tasks. Tech reports used as management measurement tool.
- Designed secure test bed network/domain on UNIX, Windows, and Cisco IOS providing e-mail, DNS, firewalls, routing, file serving, and accounting.
- Selected to serve as test bed manager for dry run and official testing, personally resolving testing challenges and intrusion issues.

Systems Administrator   2000 – 2001
Technical Solutions & Services Corporation, Oakland, NJ

- Installation, configuration, and troubleshooting software (UNIX, Linux, Windows, Solaris) on HP workstations, Toshiba laptops, and servers (Compaq, Diversified, HP, Sun). Prepared backups on multiple platforms and provided 24/7 technical support to data warehousing center.
- Oversaw corporate telecomm system, LAN physical extension, and technical purchasing (POs, quoting, authorizations, and receiving).

Technology Consultant   1999 – 2000
Campbell & Cohen (legal firm), Trenton, NJ

- Systems and network troubleshooting (Windows & Novell Netware) at multiple locations. Peer-to-peer training. Proposed LAN and equipment recommendations to stay ahead of the curve, which were implemented.

Systems Instructor / Client Support   1998 – 1999
Healthcare Information Group, Oakland, NJ

EDUCATION & CERTIFICATIONS

MS, Telecommunications Management, Rutgers University – in progress
BS, Accounting, The College of New Jersey, Ewing, NJ – 1998

Microsoft Certified Professional – Windows NT, Network Essentials
A+ Certification – Computer and Network Repair
Cisco Switching 2.0 & Routing 2.0 – towards CCNP in progress
Building Scalable Cisco Networks (BSCN) course – in-house training

PROFESSIONAL ASSOCIATION

Institute of Electrical & Electronics Engineers (IEEE)

Computer and IT

Software Designer

Regina updated her résumé after being off from work for quite some time due to surgeries after an accident. She wanted an updated résumé just in case (after being away from work for over a year) the company decided to downsize her.

Regina Pierce

1974 Paramount Way
Toledo, OH 43623
Phone: 419.555.5555
Email: reginapierce@msn.com

* SOFTWARE DESIGN ENGINEER *
DELIVERING SOFTWARE TO REDUCE COSTS AND INCREASE EFFICIENCIES

Detail-oriented, highly motivated SYSTEMS SOFTWARE CONSULTANT with 8+ years of successful experience in designing, developing, and implementing software solutions to support strategic business objectives. Keen **problem-solving skills** evidenced by the implementation of innovative technologies across dissimilar architectures and multiple platforms to provide quality product functionality. An **effective communicator** who can easily interface with end-users, technical teams, and professionals on all levels.

Technology Expertise Includes:

- Astute strategic understanding of mainframe, client/server, and Internet environments.
- Experience in Object-Oriented design and development.
- Empirical knowledge of all system development life cycle phases and a structured approach to project management. Accurately develop end-user documentation.
- Proven ability to acquire knowledge rapidly and to apply new technologies for process improvement.
- Functional knowledge of the finance, billing, and operations areas of **Customer Information Systems.**

KEY PROJECT MANAGEMENT & LEADERSHIP

ERNST & YOUNG – * LEAD TECHNICAL ANALYST *
Customer Information System for Southeastern Utility Company

Challenge: To identify and resolve critical errors of newly developed software in the Primary Test region before migrating online and batch programs to Regression Testing region.

Action: Extensively used problem-solving skills while interacting with eight-member team, Software Engineers, Data Conversion, project manager, and end-users to understand client requirements. Executed and analyzed test suites resulting in quality assessments that verified product requirements and high quality code.

Result: Delivered high quality software that exceeded client expectations and was specifically requested to stay on as Technical Analyst of the Regression Test Team, supporting both test teams through first- site implementation.

ERNST & YOUNG – * CUSTOM DEVELOPMENT LEAD / SUPERVISOR*
Customization of Client / Server Customer Information System

Challenge: To resolve technical issues of the Open Client architecture that were slowing progress on the development of a $1.8M CIS system at a Canadian utility company. To develop a detailed design of Powerbuilder software modifications in the Operations area.

Action: (1) Supervised two developers in identifying the cause of the Open Client issues and in the completion of software modifications to resolve those issues.
(2) Developed detailed design of Powerbuilder software modifications to increase functionality and efficiency.

Result: My team successfully identified and resolved the Open Client issues ahead of schedule, streamlining the rest of the project back to schedule.

COMPUTER TECHNOLOGIES

Languages: SQL, SQL*Plus, PL/SQL, Transact SQL, C, Java, HTML, COBOL, Pascal, Scheme ▪ **Databases:** Oracle 8.x, DB2, Sybase, MS Access ▪ **Environments:** Microsoft Windows 95/98/NT/2003, DOS, UNIX, VMS, CICS ▪ **CASE Tools:** ADW 1.6, ADW 2.7 ▪ **Development Tools:** JDeveloper v.2.0, Oracle Designer v.6.0, Oracle Developer 2003 v.2.0, Oracle Forms v.5.0, Oracle Reports v.2.5, Dreamweaver 3.0 ▪ **Methodologies:** Oracle's Applications Implementation Methodology (AIM) & Custom Development Methodology (CDM); Ernst & Young's Application Implementation Methodology (SMM).

PROFESSIONAL EXPERIENCE

Corporate Affiliations: Oracle, Healthnet, Bell South, Eaton Corporation, Kellogg Company, Kelly Services Corporation, Price Waterhouse, Niagara Mohawk Power Co., Alabama Gas Co., Atmos Energy, Consumers Gas, Consolidated Natural Gas

ORACLE CORPORATION, **Senior Consultant / Technical Analyst**   2000 – 2006
Installed and configured Oracle Financial Applications at five large North American companies to enhance the accuracy, availability, and timeliness of financial data for strategic planning and reporting. Identified, designed, developed, and documented customizations and interfaces to Oracle applications. Delivered excellent results to each client. Consistently commended for ability to work independently or as a team member to complete assignments on time and under budget.

- Designed and developed online Help for a customized installation of Oracle's iBill – iPay system, a $1.2M Oracle initiative. Extensive use of Dreamweaver 3.0 to develop 16 HTML Web pages.
- Developed work plans for a $2.5 million implementation of the Oracle CPG/Oracle Financials solution using Project Workbench and Microsoft Project '98.
- Developed Configuration Management Standards for a $1.5 million global implementation of Oracle Applications at a large international temporary services agency. Developed initial template of the project's global work plan.

ERNST & YOUNG LLP, **Consultant / Programmer Analyst**   1996 – 2000
Demonstrated outstanding technical skills in design, development, and implementation of a large Customer Information System package at five North American companies.

- Conducted analysis of Finance System on the CIS project of a large utility holding company. Prepared and presented Joint Application Design sessions, creating modification control reports, and proposing and estimating solutions for complex system enhancements in the following areas of Finance: Credit and Collections, Accounts Receivable, and Payment Processing.
- Programmer/Analyst. Modified existing batch and online (CICS) programs and constructed new programs to support general ledger journaling and credit collection processes in the implementation of a COBOL/DB2 Customer Information System at a northeastern electric and gas company.

EDUCATION & TRAINING

BOWLING GREEN STATE UNIVERSITY, Bowling Green, OH
Bachelor of Science in Computer Information Systems

ORACLE PRODUCT TRAINING:

Oracle CRM eCommerce 3i (iStore)
Java Programming with JDeveloper v.2.0
Developer/2003 Release 2: Build Forms I and Report Builder v.3.0
Oracle Receivables Release II
Oracle Financials 10.7 SC Bootcamp: General Ledger, Purchasing, Payables, Receivables, &
Application Implementation Methodology (AIM) 2.0
Ernst & Young MCS Information Technology Individual Study (MITIS 1) & Study 2 (MITIS 2)

Technical Support Specialist

Gloria needed to present her technical, project management, and technical training/ supervisory qualifications for an upcoming promotion possibility within her department.

Gloria Bartlett

6463 Apple Valley Road, Stevens Point, WI 54481
(715) 555-5555 Home ▪ (715) 555-8888 Mobile ▪ gloriabar@bol.com

Application Support Administrator / Technical Support Specialist / Desktop Support

Technologically sophisticated, bilingual (Spanish / English) IT Support & Training Specialist with hands-on experience in project life-cycle management for technical and intranet applications, Web site development and maintenance, and workgroup support. Proven desktop and network troubleshooting skills. Expertise in:

✓ Help Desk & Hardware Support	✓ First-Level PC Support	✓ Project Management
✓ System Upgrades / Conversions	✓ LAN / WAN Architecture	✓ Escalation Resolution
✓ Peer-to-Peer User Groups	✓ Web Content Upgrades	✓ Customer Service

TECHNOLOGY SUMMARY

Networking – LAN / WAN, Windows 2000 / NT 4.0 Server, TCP/IP, SQL Server

Operating Systems – Windows 95 / 98 / 2000 / XP, Windows 2003 / NT 4.0 Server, DOS 6.0

Applications – MS Office Suite 97/2000/2002 (Word, Access, Excel, PowerPoint), MS FrontPage 2003, Macromedia Dreamweaver 3.0, Adobe Acrobat 5 and PDF, Flash 4.0, Novell GroupWise 5.5, Adobe Pagemill 3, Lotus Suite 96, Corel Suite 96, Corel 9, Adobe PhotoShop, Kodak digital software, Symantec pcAnywhere 32, Internet Explorer, Netscape Communicator, and WinZip

Programming – HTML code, CGI, Java, JavaScript, C Programming, RPG 400, SQL, Visual Basic 5.0, Visual InterDev 6.0, AS/400, ASP code

PROFESSIONAL EXPERIENCE

WISCONSIN STATE TREASURY DEPT., DIV. OF TAXATION, Madison, WI   1998 – present
Senior Technician, MIS – Technical Support Activity (2004 – present)
Promoted to provide help desk support for 2003+ end-users (including remote users) in 9 locations throughout Wisconsin, as well as project management team leadership for special technical assignments. First-point-of-contact (Tier 1 Help Desk Technician) for support incidents, as well as end-user training.

- **Help Desk.** Ensure effective "one-stop" technical support for mainframe, WAN, LAN, and remote system. Install and update software, and set up, configure, and troubleshoot Reach Center equipment. Track and de-escalate technology and workflow problems, and assist Desktop Support Group and other IT groups.
- **Web Site Development.** Project-managed Division of Taxation's Web site redesign to text-only version, enabling fast and easy access for all users, including vision-impaired. Supervised staff of 8.
- **Intranet Development.** Key player in creation, launch, and maintenance of Division of Taxation intranet site, providing management with easily retrievable, up-to-date information for operations decisions. Initiated, created, and maintain Access users group intranet to facilitate information sharing and learning.
- **Project Management.** Led WIX CD-ROM project for 2 years, delivering interactive CD-ROMs with 1000+ tax-law-verified documents for simplified tax preparation (tax years 2004 & 2005) on schedule.
- **ASP Development.** Played pivotal role in beta-test programming and development of causal sales application (upgraded Alpha 4 database into back-end of Access 2000 and SQL Server, front-end into Internet Explorer via ASP programming).
- **End-User Training.** Expanded Reach Center offerings by designing, developing, and delivering advanced programs and manuals for MS Office, GroupWise, Novell Network, and Internet, making information easily understood and usable. Manage all Access courses, training and supervising 5 adjunct team instructors.

WISCONSIN STATE TREASURY DEPT.– continued
Technical Assistant, MIS – Technical Support Activity   (2002 – 2004)
First-level technical support for software installation, as well as setup and configuration of new equipment used in Division of Taxation (PCs, laptops, printers, scanners, projectors, digital & video).

- **IT Software Training.** Designed curriculum and materials, and delivered technical training, for introductory programs in Microsoft Office Suite (Word, Excel, Access), as well as Windows 95, keeping staff motivated and focused while improving job satisfaction and productivity.
- **Web site Support.** Functioned as Web Editor for Division of Taxation's Internet/intranet Web site, proofing and updating Web site information on a daily basis.
- **Database Maintenance.** Upgraded and maintained link-shared employee Access database with Chief of Staff's office, ensuring data integrity for training. Created database reports for management evaluation.
- **Technical Development Project.** Pioneered development and implementation of storage, archive, and retrieval system for electronic presentations used throughout Division of Taxation.

Principal Clerk – Technical Education   (2000 – 2002)
Promoted to provide installation, configuration, and troubleshooting support for new equipment and software in REACH Center, as well as evaluation and modification of skills assessment.

- **Training Center Database.** Initiated and implemented data gathering system in Access to compile, store, and retrieve statistics on computer training classes. Researched and wrote monthly reports used to evaluate training trends and staff training needs.
- **WI Saver Rebate Program.** Key team participant in initial, large-scale data compilation for WI Saver Rebate Program, including retrieval, distribution, quality control, and storage of data.

Senior Clerk Typist, Clerk Typist – Corporation Business Tax   (1998 – 2000)
Assisted auditors by researching taxpayer information on mainframe, ordered work files for Supervising Auditor using HLLAPI information system, and prepared report statistics using Excel spreadsheets.

WISCONSIN STATE DEPT. OF BANKING, Madison, WI (temp contract)   1997 – 1998
Data Entry Specialist / Legal Secretary
Front office support for attorneys and accountants: records management, legal document preparation, purchasing, and equipment maintenance. Used IS software for research and to process taxpayer complaints.

FIRST AMERICAN BANK, Stevens Point, WI   1993 – 1996
Customer Service Representative / Supervisor Teller
Instructed employees in use of computerized banking systems and procedures. Verified and audited financial reports and balance sheets. Cash management responsibility exceeded $100,000.

EDUCATION

Instructor Certification, **HRDI, Blue Bell, PA – 2003**
Courses: Curriculum Design, Performance Consulting, Training Presentations, Design Surveys and Questions, Determining Training Needs, and Active Techniques for Teaching.

Certificate in Computer Programming, The Computer Institute, Madison, WI – 2002
Courses: HTML, CGI, Java Programming, JavaScript Programming, RPG 400, C Programming, SQL, Visual Basic 5.0, AS/400 Subfiles & Common Language Queries, MS Office, Windows NT 4.0

Ongoing Professional and Technical Development in-house and at vendor locations (1998 – present)

Web Developer/Programmer

Here's an example of a young technologist creating a powerful one-two punch.

Kelly L. Hillman

225 Springdale Drive   Pittsboro, WA 12345   (888) 555-2200

Web Developer / Programmer or Database Programmer

Highlights of Qualifications

Accomplished and innovative Web Development / Programming Professional with a proven track record of effective database / Web-page design for high-profile, technical companies and governmental organizations. Experienced in all aspects of architecture and accessibility techniques; hands-on working knowledge of Section 508 and W3C Standards. Skilled analytical problem-solver with the ability to quickly learn new technologies. Polished communication, presentation, training, and client relations skills; able to relate effectively to people at all levels and convey complex technical information in an understandable manner.

Technical Skills

Programming/Scripting Languages: HTML, XHTML, DHTML, CSS Stylesheets, ColdFusion, Fusebox, Perl, JavaScript, CGI Scripting, XSSI, Java, Java Servlets, JSP, JDBC, Swing
Database Applications: SQL, SQL / PL, Oracle, Access, Database Design and Architecture
Software Applications / Programs: Dreamweaver, Flash, Fireworks, Adobe PhotoShop
Operating Systems / Platforms: UNIX and Windows 95 / 98 / 2003 / NT

Professional Experience

Web Developer / IT Specialist, EXCEL SYSTEMS / EPA (Formerly LOCKHEED-MARTIN) – RESEARCH Triangle Park, WA (2005 to Present): Manage the maintenance, development, and enhancement of a Coldfusion application that interfaces with an Oracle database. Create, update, and maintain 11,000 Web pages / templates while ensuring compliance with section 508 and EPA Web guidelines. Perform JavaScript and PDF conversions; resize, create, and maintain high quality graphics; compile a monthly report listing all Web pages, URLs, titles, and updates; produce content; integrate dynamic popup menus; and update employee Web-based information. Trained a temporary employee in all aspects of conversion operations and Dreamweaver applications.

> Managed the complete conversion of 20,000 EPA Web pages to meet section 508 Web site guidelines in both appearance and compatibility.
> Instrumental in successfully meeting all critical and stringent deadlines.
> Recognized by management for advanced skill level and efficiency.

Web Development / Maintenance – Pittsboro, WA (2004 to 2005): Oversaw all aspects of client Web site development. Performed a wide range of design and coding projects utilizing HTML, DHTML, XHTML, JavaScript, and Flash. Updated and maintained content and graphics for both new and previously existing sites.

> Spearheaded and managed all business, technical, and client relations functions.
> Developed and launched numerous high-impact Web sites in addition to successfully redesigning existing sites to create additional market exposure.

Junior Systems Programmer / Analyst, MCTC – Research Triangle Park, WA (2002 to 2004): Hired to develop and code Web-based applications and user interfaces in transmitting / integrating data with Oracle databases for a comprehensive governmental occupational network database. Served as a member of a technical team in developing multiple Web, database, data search, and retrieval applications.

> Recruited for a part-time position, promoted to full-time.
> Pioneered the research and development of guidelines for people with disabilities.

Marketing / Technical Support Assistant, URKG CORPORATION – Morton, WA (2000 to 2001)

Educational & Training

MS Computer Information Technology (Expected 5/03), REGIS UNIVERSITY – Colorado Springs, CO (GPA 3.96)
Bachelor of Arts in Sociology (2000), UNIVERSITY OF NORTH CAROLINA – Chapel Hill, NC (GPA 3.7)
Information Systems Programming (2002), DURHAM TECHNICAL COMMUNITY COLLEGE – Durham, NC (GPA 4.0)
HTML _ Advanced HTML _ Advanced Online JavaScript Training _ Sun's sl285 Hands-on Java Workshop _ XML Certification Training _ Applied Systems Analysis and Design _ Object-Oriented Software

Network Architecture Specialist

John has just been laid off and needs to find another job. He is looking to stay in his field, and he wants a position that will utilize and compensate him for his Cisco Networks Certification and experience.

JOHN A. CHRISTOPHER

11 Barbara Lane • Simi Valley, California 80932 • (805) 555-3787 • fax (805) 555-9741 jacla@aol.com

Applications
Adaptec Easy CD Creator
Adaptec Direct CD
Carbon Copy
Cc Mail
Clarify
HP Colorado Backup
MS Active Sync
MS Office Professional
MS Outlook 98 and 2003
MS Internet Explorer
NetAccess Internet
Netscape
Norton Ghost
Partition Magic
PC Anywhere
Rainbow
Reflection 1
Reflection X
Remedy-ARS
Symantec Norton Antivirus
Visio
Windows CE

Operating Systems
Microsoft Windows 2000
Microsoft Windows NT 4.0
   Workstation and Server
Microsoft Windows ME
Microsoft Windows 95, 98
Cisco Router/Switch IOS
MS-DOS
UNIX

Hardware
Intel-based Desktops
Intel-based Mobile Computers
HP Colorado Tape Backup
Cisco 2500 Series Router
Hewlett Packard Pro Curve
Switches
CD Writer

Protocols & Services
TCP/IP
DHCP
DNS
NetBEUI
Remote Access Service
WINS

Networking
Ethernet
Token Ring
Microsoft Networking

Network Architecture Specialist
Cisco Certified Network Associate

Results-driven, self-motivated professional with solid experience supporting hundreds of users in multiple departments in the corporate environment. Recognized for outstanding support and services, process development, and project management. Able to manage multiple projects simultaneously and to move quickly among projects. Capable of leading or collaborating. Areas of expertise include:

- Network architectures and networking components
- Software and operating system deployment in corporate environments
- PC hardware installation/repair and disk imaging
- Troubleshoot complex operating system problems
- Call tracking, case management, solution integration

Accomplishments

- Reduced help desk calls by developing end-user training and knowledge database.
- Led migration for 3000+ client/server email accounts from HP Open Mail to MS Exchange.
- Developed data collection protocol for BLM Natural Resource Inventory.
- Mentored teammates on technical materials and procedures.
- Built relationships to quickly resolve business-critical issues.

Certifications

Technical Certification for MS Network Support Program, 9/02
CCNA – Cisco Certified Network Associate, 8/02

Work History

Technical Support Engineer, ABC Technologies (Holt Services), 4/03 – Present
E-mail Migration Specialist, ABC Technologies (Holt Services), 11/02 – 4/03
PC Technician, RBM (The Cameo Group), 5/02 – 11/02
Customer Support Specialist, Center Partners, 9/01 – 5/02
Recycle Technician, RBM (WasteNot Recycling), 2/01 – 9/01
Soil Scientist, Bureau of Land Management, 5/00 – 10/00

Education

Pacific Institute Workshop – Goal Setting, Achievement, Motivation, 1/01
B.S., Soil Science: Environmental Mgt. – CA Polytechnic State University, 12/00
A.A., Mathematics, Mira Costa College, 7/97

Awards and Honors

ABC Shining Star Award for Outstanding Customer Service, October '04
Outstanding Services to Technical Services Division, January '03
High Quality Customer Service Award, RBM Technical Support March & April '02

Systems Engineer

Technical Skills section (Core Competencies) is right up front on this engineer's résumé. It tells the story quickly, and the body copy fills in the details.

PARAG GUPTA

104 W. Real Drive • Beaverton, OR 97006 • (503) 555-4286 • parag.gupta@technical.com

SYSTEM ENGINEER

Motivated and driven IT professional offering 9+ years of hands–on experience in designing, implementing, and enhancing systems to automate business operations. Demonstrated ability to develop high-performance systems, applications, databases, and interfaces.

➤ Part of TL9000 CND audit interviews which helped Technical get TL9000 certified which is significant in Telecom industry. Skilled trainer and proven ability to lead many successful projects, like TSS, EMX, and TOL.

➤ Strategically manage time and expediently resolve problems for optimal productivity, improvement and profitability; able to direct multiple tasks effectively.

➤ Strong technical background with a solid history of delivering outstanding customer service.

➤ Highly effective liaison and communication skills proven by effective interaction with management, users, team members, and vendors.

TECHNICAL SKILLS

Operating Systems:	Unix, Windows (2000, XP), DOS
Languages:	C, C++, Java, Pascal, Assembly Languages (Z8000, 808x, DSP)
Methodologies:	TL9000, Digital Six Sigma
Software:	MS Office, Adobe Framemaker, Matlab
RDBMS:	DOORS, Oracle 7.x
Protocols:	TCP/IP, SS7 ISUP, A1, ANSI, TL1, SNMP
Tools:	Teamplay, Clearcase, Clearquest, M-Gatekeeper, Exceed, Visio, DocExpress, Compass
Other:	CDMA Telecom Standards – 3GPP2 (Including TIA/EIA-2001, TIA/EIA-41, TIA/EIA-664), ITU-T, AMPS

PROFESSIONAL EXPERIENCE

Technical, Main Network Division, Hillsboro, OR   Jan. 1999 – Present

Principal Staff Engineer • Products Systems Engineering • Nov. 2004 – Present

✓ Known as "go-to" person for CDMA call processing and billing functional areas.

✓ Create customer requirements documents for Technical SoftSwitch (TSS) and SMS Gateway products. All deliverables done on/ahead schedule with high quality.

✓ Solely accountable for authoring and allocation, customer reviews, supporting fellow system engineers, development, and test and customer documentation teams.

✓ Support Product Management in RFPs, customer feature prioritization, impact statements, and budgetary estimates.

✓ Mentored junior engineers and 1 innovation disclosure (patent) submitted in 2007.

✓ Resolve deployed customer/internal requirements issues and contribute to Virtual Zero Defect quality goal.

✓ TOL process champion and part of CND focus group that contributed to reducing CRUD backlog (NPR) by 25% and cycle time (FRT) by 40%.

✓ Recognized as the TL9000 expert. Triage representative for switching and messaging products.

✓ Achieved 'CND Quality Award' for contribution to quality improvement in May 2007.

Senior Staff Engineer • MSS Systems Engineering • May 2002 – Oct. 2004

- ✓ Led a team of 12 engineers for 3 major software releases of TSS product included around 80 features/ enhancements to create T-Gate SE deliverables.
- ✓ Mentored newer engineers to get up to speed on TSS product.
- ✓ Created requirements for TSS product, 30 features/enhancements contributing to 5 major software releases. *Recognized as overall product expert with specific focus on call processing and billing.*
- ✓ Played integral role in successfully implementing proprietary commercial TSS billing system.
- ✓ Supported PdM organization by creating ROMs, technical support for RFPs (Vivo, Sprint, TELUS, TM, Tata, Inquam, Alaska, Reliance, Pakistan, PBTL, Mauritius, Telefonica, Brasicel and Angola).
- ✓ Proactively identified functional areas of improvement for requirements coverage, contributed to resolving several faults, improved customer documentation, and provided reference for future releases as well as other customers.
- ✓ *Received 'Above and Beyond Performance Award' – Oct. 2003.*

Senior Software Engineer • EMX Development • Aug. 2000 – Apr. 2002

- ✓ Successfully led and coordinated the cross-functional development teams, 30 engineers, to meet the scheduled design, code, and test completion dates ensuring Feature T-Gates are met.
- ✓ Feature Technical Lead for Concurrent Voice/Data Services feature, the largest revenue-generating feature for KDDI customer.
- ✓ Feature Lead for Paging Channel SMS feature. Created requirements and design; led implementation phase of five engineers' team; supported product, network, and release testing; and created customer reference documentation.
- ✓ Performed the role of functional area lead for Trunk Manager and A1 interface functional areas. Provided 2-day Technical Workshops for internal/customer knowledge sharing and functional area transition from Caltel.
- ✓ Provided customer site testing and FOA (First Office Application) support for major EMX releases and off-hours CNRC (Customer Networks Resolution Center) support.
- ✓ *Received 'Bravo Award' – May 2001, Sep. 2001, Jan. 2002*

Software Engineer • EMX Development • Jan. 1999 – Jul. 2000

- ✓ Developed design and code for SMS feature as a Trunk Manager functional area lead for the largest FA impacted by the feature. Supported product, network, and release testing.
- ✓ Contributed to customer release documentation. Supported feature-level SMS testing at various internal labs and customer sites resulting in successful deployment at customer sites.
- ✓ Designed and coded phases for wiretap and virtual circuits feature development, initial assessment of internal and customer EMX PRs (problem reports) to route/classify issues and providing problem assessments for many of these PRs.
- ✓ Created an implementation process to serve as reference for new hires.
- ✓ Provided CNRC support during the Y2K transition.
- ✓ *Received 'Above and Beyond Performance Award' – Jan. 2000, Dec. 2000 and 'Certificate of Outstanding Achievement' – Jun. 1999*

EDUCATION

Master of Science in Computer Engineering • University of Portland, Portland, OR • 1998

Bachelors of Engineering in Electronics • Technology and Science Institute, India • 1996

Significant Trainings Include

- Open Source Software
- WSG Requirements Process
- WiMAX
- Product Security
- Agile Management for Software Engineering
- Fagan Inspection and Moderation

Computer and IT

Information Technology Manager

A good technical résumé that worked for the owner. Notice the technical skills at the end of the résumé. While this doesn't matter in the résumé database, it would have been more helpful to human eyes had it come after the Core Competencies section on the first page.

Dan Newcomb, PMP

82 Nowhere Ave. • Nowhere, NJ 08820
Cell: 732.555.1212 • arésumésolution.com

INFORMATION TECHNOLOGY MANAGEMENT

Hands-on technology manager with multifaceted experience in mainframe and client server environments with multiple relational databases; Informix, Oracle Sybase, and SQL server. Exceptional team building and management capabilities. Strong background in relational database management, performance tuning, and high availability techniques. Skilled project manager with ability to obtain project requirements and implement solutions that drive bottom line. Talented in providing technology risk management. Leverages wide-ranging talents in computer technology, staff leadership, and SDLC to effectively manage organizational change, mitigate risk, infuse new ideas, and deliver large-company capabilities.

➢ Excellent ability to analyze business needs and implement cost-effective solutions meeting business objectives.
➢ Solid record of achievement building and aligning organizations with strategic IT business objectives to achieve dramatic bottom-line results.
➢ Expertise providing project management, technology expertise, and staff leadership.
➢ Demonstrated talents in database architecture, design, and maintenance.

KEY COMPETENCIES

– $MM Project Management	– Staff Leadership
– Process Management	– Release & Change Management
– Software Development Lifecycle	– Disaster Recovery Management
– Telecom Systems	– Vendor Management
– Client Relationship Management	– Database Administration

PROFESSIONAL EXPERIENCE

XYZ FINANCE COMPANY, Parsippany, NJ 2003 – Present
Consumer division of Cleveland based 92 billion key bank providing lending/leasing of auto and home mortgages to customers all across America.

Application System Team Manager

Provides team leadership and project management for IT projects with price ranging in value from $50K to $1.5M, ensuring timely completion. Directs and mentors four Application/Database Designers, providing prototype, design, development, and implementation of database architecture and strategies and 24/7 support of databases and applications. Oversees organizational change management functions, providing support and approval of over 100 change requests in one release cycle. Designs and implements ETL solutions for XML-based interface of Origination data. Assists audit organizations, providing engineering and architecture changes to necessary applications, databases, and servers for SOX compliance. SME for origination data and ensures persistence of data across downstream systems. Provides 24/7 support for back applications.

Accomplishments:
• Increased client leads by 20% through development and implementation of lead registration system.
• Directed team in development and implementation of Disaster Recovery Planning efforts, providing quick restoration of critical applications.
• Spearheaded major 18 month application and database design project for implementation of application and database security ensuring SOX compliance for entire organization with budget of $1.5M.

NEW MORTGAGE, Parsippany, NJ   2001 – 2003

Leader in sub-prime lending in Tri-state area with presence in 22 states subsequently acquired by key bank.

<u>Database Consultant</u>

Designed and implemented the Enterprise wide Data Warehouse and reporting framework for the mortgage line of business with departmental data mart. Performed Dimensional data modeling to implement the data warehouse. Managed the Application and Physical DBA role for Enterprise wide Oracle and Informix databases ranging from 50 GB to 250 GB size. Established database backup and recovery strategies using RMAN and ONBAR utilities.

Performed expert object management technique like object partitioning. Performed capacity planning based on transaction volume and expected growth. Developed and implemented shell scripts, stored procedures, functions, and triggers. Ensured all databases were functioning appropriately and resolved any issues on a timely basis.

Accomplishments:
- 10% reduction of time between receipts of inquiry to funding with the help of availability of daily Sales, appraisal effectiveness reports.

TELCORDIA TECHNOLOGIES, Piscataway, NJ
Leading provider of technology solutions for Telecom Industries around the globe.   2000 – 2001

<u>Senior Database Consultant</u>

Developed and maintained telecom clearinghouse software for telecom services providers to manage 1 million customer requests per day. Directed team of developers in support and maintenance for Exchange Link project running on an Oracle 8-I database with capacity of over 200 GB. Performed application and database tuning with object and index redesign resulting in 66% improvement in application performance. 24/7 support of application in an ASP model. Handled configuration management, change management, business analysis, and project management.

Accomplishments:
- Increased customer satisfaction through improved application support, increasing revenue from $1M to $10M.

ABC TECHNOLOGIES, Somerset, NJ   1998 – 2000

Leading provider of software for telecom service providers.

<u>SAP Production Support Database Administrator</u>

Served as Oracle database administrator for large 600GB database, providing 24/7 support of numerous SAP R/3 systems. Learned and quickly adapted to new technology. Analyzed and resolved complex issues with over 1000 batch jobs in SAP R/3 environment. Developed and implemented shell scripts, providing escalations based on procedure and severity. Provided support for end users on complex issues. Configured and maintained various files. Ensured application security and provided user administration.

Accomplishments:
- Key member of team that turned six-month pilot SAP project to company-wide implementation, providing coordination between vendors, clients, and implementation team.

EDUCATION

Bachelor of Science, Engineering

Regional Engineering College, St. Louis, MO

Training:
   ~ Certified training in COBOL, DMSII, UNIX, C, and Oracle
   ~ Certified training in "Structured Systems Analysis and Design"

TECHNICAL SKILLS

Databases:	SQL Server2000, DMSII, Sybase, Oracle 7, 8, 9I, 10G Informix 7.3/9.X, SQL Server 7.0
Systems:	HP9000 (HP-UX 11, 10.20), SUN SPARC-Enterprise 2000(Solaris 2.5), SUN SPARC 6500 (Sun OS 5.6), Sun Fire 880, AIX, Linux, UNISYS A series, Windows NT
Languages:	C, COBOL74, SQL, Oracle Pro*C, PRO*COBOL, PL/SQL, VB, ASP
UNIX Programming:	Shell scripting, AWK/SED Scripting
DB Tools:	Oracle (Enterprise Manager), SQL*DBA, Import, Export, SQL Loader, SQL (Report Writer), Microsoft SQL Server Data Transformation Service, Oracle RMAN
CASE Tools:	ERWIN/ERX (both IE and IDEF1X)
Methodologies:	UML, Rational Unified process, SCRUM, Agile

Computer and IT

Graphic Designer/Illustrator

Today every résumé needs to be data-dense and appealing to the eye, and never more so than with a graphic designer, a beautiful example of form following function.

NORA PATTERSON

Address
City, State Zip

Phone
Email Address

ILLUSTRATOR ✍ GRAPHIC DESIGNER ✍ VISUAL ARTIST

CORE SKILL AREAS:

Textbook Illustration

❖ ❖ ❖

Scientific Drawings

❖ ❖ ❖

Museum Exhibits
Illustration

❖ ❖ ❖

Storybook Illustration

❖ ❖ ❖

Cartoon Image Design

❖ ❖ ❖

Greeting Card Design/
Illustration

❖ ❖ ❖

Artifact Replications

❖ ❖ ❖

Surface Coloration
Restoration

❖ ❖ ❖

Original & Production
Artwork

❖ ❖ ❖

Visual Aid Preparation

❖ ❖ ❖

Photo-Realistic
Illustration

❖ ❖ ❖

Logo Design

❖ ❖ ❖

Full-Figure Drawing

❖ ❖ ❖

CAREER PROFILE

Creative, diverse illustrator and artist with extensive experience in designing and developing broad range of visual pieces to meet business and program objectives of both employers and their clients. Particularly adept in creating original, vibrant artwork that captures attention from serious and casual viewers. Additional skills:

- *Developing Products* — Able to translate concepts into well-designed products by integrating various elements, including illustration, formatting, photography, and typography. Combine innovative thinking with logical design elements.
- *Conveying Messages* — Create illustrations that articulate key ideas and earn recognition for aesthetic quality. Excel in reinforcing positive messages.
- *Meeting Expectations* — Maintain consistent track record of fulfilling organizational goals. Highly adaptable to changing needs and requirements.

SELECTED WORKS *(a full portfolio is available for immediate review)*

Marketing Material & Product Design

- International Colloquium for Biology of Soricidae — **Logo, image, and product development** for line of merchandise used in international conference.
- Carnegie Museum of Natural History — **Sweatshirt** *The American Mastodon* for the museum's gift shop. Designed and produced original artwork for full line of products sold in association with the Walton Hall of Ancient Egypt. Created full-sized, full-color paintings for children's area the Discovery Room.
- H. J. Heinz Pittsburgh Historical Center — **Photo-mural retouching** activities to enhance key display areas.
- Tucson Children's Museum — Initial design and development of **cartoon images** for outside banner/T-shirt image and other museum merchandise.

Book & Magazine Illustrations

- *The Carnegie Magazine, Pittsburgh Magazine* — Miscellaneous illustrations and graphics.
- *The New York Times, Time, Johns Hopkins Magazine, others* — Widely published illustrations through the United Press International.
- Dr. L.E. McCullough — Instructional drawings for *The Making and Playing of Uilleann Pipes*, including musical notation.
- Dr. Sandra Olson — Reconstruction illustration of Paleolithic horse fetish for *Horses Through Time*.

Scientific Illustrations

- *National Geographic* — 11"x14" acrylic reconstruction of *Eosimias sinesis*.
- Cultural & Environmental Systems — Artifacts for Technical Series #56.
- Walton Hall of Ancient Egypt — Scientifically accurate recreation of 18th dynasty tomb walls and entire hall as graphics artwork. Built complete scale models, coordinated all illustration production with various collaborators, and earned commendation from Egyptologists for accuracy of reconstruction.

TESTIMONIALS

"Nora is a dedicated and highly talented artist….[her] ability to work in close collaboration with others, together with her innate artistic talents, were the key elements that allowed her to produce such stunning works of art…"
K. Christopher Beard, PhD
Associate Dean of Science,
Carnegie Museum of Natural History

"Nora's passion for a subject comes across in her artwork…[she] is a talented illustrator able to work in a variety of media…more importantly, she is a team player used to dealing with multiple aspects of a project to effect a successful outcome…"
- James R. Senior
Chairman, Division of Exhibits, Carnegie Museum

"In addition to her skills, Nora has proven to be extremely dedicated and a very amiable coworker and colleague. I am quite happy to recommend her as an excellent candidate for a wide range of positions in which precision, talent, patience, and attention to detail are important assets.
- Sandra Olsen
Curator of Anthropology, Carnegie Museum

"I strongly recommend Nora at the highest level… has very well-developed critical thinking skills… novel ideas for designs…a true artist with great creative ability."
- Sankar Chatterjee
Professor of Geology, Curator of Paleontology, Museum of Texas Tech

SELECTED PROFESSIONAL EXPERIENCE *(in order of professional importance)*

Illustrator/ Exhibits Preparator, The Carnegie Museum of Natural History

Built distinguished record of achievement and extensive portfolio of work for one of the 4 museums comprising the Carnegie Museums of Pittsburgh family. Employed with museum for 20+ years until 1998.

- *Work Summary* – Served as exhibits/scientific illustrator and designer for installation of traveling and temporary exhibits. Collected, researched, and accurately reproduced artifacts (both for 3-dimensional and 2-dimensional venues) and vegetation for permanent installations.
- *National/Global Recognition* – Collaborated with Dr. K. Christopher Beard on production of life restoration for 40 million-year old fossil primate *Eosimias centennicus*, featured in *Science* magazine (1996) and receiving global coverage in the following:

National Geographic, Science et Vie (Paris), *Earth, U.S.A Today,* Pittsburgh *Post-Gazette, Dallas Morning-News.*

- Leadership Role – Supervised gallery technicians, staff, and volunteers in general and specific activities, providing expertise and support to facilitate project completion.

Freelance Artist, Various Clients

Contracted to design and develop illustrations and artwork for broad range of companies, organizations, and individual buyers. Period spanned from 1985 to 1999.

- Satisfying Requirements – Aligned client/employer needs with artwork to ensure satisfaction, leading to frequent repeat and referral business.
- Meeting Deadlines – Worked often under tight timelines; consistently exceeded expectations in delivering work on time with zero effect on quality.
- Earning National Recognition – Received placement in national, well-respected publications and garnered recognition for breadth/quality of creations.

Preparator, The Texas Tech Museum

Oversee preparation and surface treatment of dinosaur cast exhibit specimens for university museum in Lubbock, TX. Arrange artwork for display in large and small exhibits, prepare works on paper for exhibitions, and perform accurate replications of surface coloration for cast specimens. Work jointly with internal team members and external partners to ensure success of exhibitions. Hired in 2003; currently held position.

Held additional positions with J.C. Penneys, S-K Designs, Cultural & Environmental Systems, and Holland Gardens, among others. A full employment history will be provided on request.

EDUCATION & CREDENTIALS

Bachelor of Fine Arts ❖ Major in Drawing, Minor in Painting
TEXAS TECH UNIVERSITY, Lubbock, TX

Former Affiliations
- Member, Guild of Natural Science Illustrators
- Member, Society for the Preservation of Natural History Collectors
- Member, National Association of Museum Exhibitors

Computer Summary
- Appleworks 6, Photoshop 7 (rudimentary level), Internet research

Guidance Counselor

Sharon wanted to get into another district closer to her home,
as she had a daily commute of over one hour.

SHARON WISE

500 Nottingham Street ~ Plymouth, MI 48170
444.555.1111 ~ sharon _wise@hotmail.com

SCHOOL GUIDANCE COUNSELOR

Dedicated elementary, middle, and high school guidance counselor, skilled at providing positive direction for students' academic, social, and emotional well-being. Work effectively with children with ADHD and with multicultural and diverse populations. Counseling Skills include:

Guidance Curriculum: Classroom Guidance Lessons; Career Awareness; Conflict Resolution/Social Skills; Developmental Awareness

Individual Planning: Student Assessments; Student Placement & Scheduling; New Student Transition; Academic & Career Advisement

Responsive Services: Mental Health; Family & Teacher Consulting; Crisis Intervention & Grief Management; Psycho-Educational Support Groups

Systems Support: Program Evaluation; Program Development & Coordination; Needs Assessment; Committee Participation

EDUCATION / CERTIFICATION

MA, *School Counseling,* UNIVERSITY OF DETROIT-MERCY, Detroit, MI
MA, *Teaching,* MARYGROVE COLLEGE, Detroit, MI
BA, *Teaching – Social Studies/French,* MICHIGAN STATE UNIVERSITY, East Lansing, MI

Certified – *Counseling* – K–12 – State of Michigan
Certified – *Social Studies & French* – grades 7–12 – State of Michigan
Certified – *LLPC* – expected completion 7/03

PROFESSIONAL EXPERIENCE

HARTLAND COMMUNITY SCHOOLS, Hartland, MI   2005 – 2006
SCHOOL COUNSELOR

Provide individual and small-group counseling sessions and large-group counseling presentations within classroom and guidance office environments for a school with 800 students. Participate in parent/teacher meetings to discuss and develop emotional and behavioral strategies for students with physical, mental, and emotional challenges.

- Developed 45-minute Bully-Proofing classes and presented them to each of 30 classes in the building.
- Wrote a monthly article for the school newsletter on a topic of relevance.
- Facilitated students participating in the Midwest talent search for the Gifted & Talented program.
- Held orientation for new students and their parents, providing them with a schedule of classes and showing them around the building.
- Created 30-minute Career Awareness/Exploration sessions so students would become exposed to various career options. Organized a Career Day, arranging for 40 speakers in various fields to talk with the students about their profession.
- Facilitated support groups dealing with social and coping skills, and conducted needs assessment and program evaluation with staff and students.
- Designed a survey for students and teachers to evaluate the guidance program.
- Hung a display of bully-proofing pledges in the shape of the American flag, with children earning hearts instead of stars for "acts of kindness."

- Participated as a team member for the School Improvement Team (SCIT).
- Performed Title I coordinator duties, planning and organizing initial structure mailings, assigning students to teachers, adhering to budgets, and scheduling classes.

NOVI COMMUNITY SCHOOLS, Novi, MI　　　　　　　　　　　　　　　　2003 – 2005
GUEST TEACHER

Substituted in the middle school and high school, teaching most subjects, including special ed. Immediately tried to develop a rapport with students and engage in discussion of relevant topics. Facilitated the discussion to steer towards daily lesson plan. Discussion and debate kept students centered, entertained, and open to learning.

- Given long-term teaching assignment for students with disabilities. Taught math, science, and social studies in grades 6–8 for a full semester. There were 5 – 10 students in each of four classes, ages 11–13; many students had ADHD. Wrote lesson plans, graded assignments, and consulted with parents.

DETROIT PUBLIC SCHOOLS, Detroit, MI　　　　　　　　　　　　　　　1996 – 2003
FRENCH & SOCIAL STUDIES TEACHER

Taught five classes each day, with each class having between 30 – 35 students, engaging their curiosity and research abilities in structured classroom activities. Provided lectures, notes, study guides and projects for courses in American History, Government, Economics, World Geography, Global Issues, and French.

- Devised an effective structure for parent communication.
- Gathered resources as supplemental materials to be used in conjunction with assigned texts to give students a richer experience.
- Assigned different subjects each year, showed flexibility in providing first-rate learning experience for each subject.
- Developed a system to track work and assignments while moving to different rooms for each class period.
- Provided students with practical experience, such as making menus and calendars in French.
- Member of School Improvement team and on the committee to improve student self-esteem.

PROFESSIONAL MEMBERSHIPS

- American Counseling Association
- American School Counselor Association
- Michigan Counseling Association
- Michigan School Counselor Association

RECENT CONFERENCE PARTICIPATION

Launching Career Awareness – Oakland Education Service Agency
Legal Issues for School Counselors – Washtenaw County Counselors Association
Counseling Groups in Crisis – Michigan Association of Specialists in Group Work
A.D.H.D in the New Millennium – Oakland Schools
Bully-Proofing Your School – Oakland Schools
The Human Spirit & Technology – Michigan Counseling Association
Understanding Attachment Disorders – Medical Educational Service
Grief Counseling Skills – Cross Country University

Social Work and Counseling

Paralegal

Jody needed to highlight her formal training as well as her transferable experience as she transitioned from law enforcement to paralegal work.

Jody Gilroy
4321 E. 129th #J8 ■ Denver, CO 00000
555.555.5555 ■ jgil@attol.com

PARALEGAL

Skilled office professional with exceptional interpersonal and communication skills. Highly organized and detail-oriented; efficiently manages time and projects with close attention to deadlines. Effective in stressful situations and able to successfully work with diverse populations. Persuasive and tenacious.

EXPERIENCE

- Drafting legal documents, affidavits, and preparing orders
- Conducting independent interviews and investigations without supervision
- Serving as liaison between attorneys, investigators, court clerks, and judges
- Researching case law using the library and Internet
- Proofreading for accuracy and consistency
- Opening and maintaining case files
- Proficient in Microsoft Office and scheduling applications

FORMAL TRAINING AND COURSEWORK IN CIVIL AND CRIMINAL LAW

Civil Litigation	Drafting of pleadings, preparation of motions, discovery and pretrial data certificates, and trial notebooks
Ethics	Client confidences, conflicts of interest, unauthorized practice of law
Contracts	Offers, acceptance, consideration, illegal contracts, third-party contracts, contractual capacity, remedies, Uniform Commercial Code, discharge of obligations, provision
Research	Statutes, digest, case law, citators, encyclopedias, dictionaries, online databases
Torts	Negligence, intentional torts, strict liability, personal injury litigation, settlements
Criminal Law	Statutory and common law, criminal theory and interpretation of statutes
Public Law	Business and economic regulation and ethical considerations

EDUCATION

A.G.S. Pikes Peak Community College, Westminster, CO, May 2006

PROFESSIONAL DEVELOPMENT

- Leadership Training
- Administrative Plan, Policies, Procedures, and Programs
- Interviewing and Interrogation (Reid Technique)
- Conflict Management

WORK HISTORY

Peace Officer/Investigator, Boulder County, Boulder, CO 2003 – 2005
Communications/Correction Officer, Adams County, Denver, CO 2002 – 2003
Trainee, Southwestern Louisiana Criminal Justice Academy, 2000 – 2001
Intelligence Analyst, U.S. Army, Fort Caron, LA 1998 – 2000
DUI Technician, New Orleans County Sheriff's Office, New Orleans, LA 1996 – 1997
Intelligence Analyst, U.S. Marine Corps, Jacksonville, FL 1993 – 1996

Law Enforcement Officer

Because James is a recent graduate, his education section needed to come first; however, he also wanted to emphasize his experience as a trainer and team leader.

JAMES BURLINGTON

9803 Clinton Avenue
Lubbock, TX 79424

(806) 555-9900
jamesb@door.net

Career Profile

GRADUATING STUDENT
Career Targets: Law Enforcement ■ Criminal Justice
Dependable, service-focused professional with strong background knowledge in Human Services and Criminal Justice, complemented by work experience reflecting promotion, excellent service delivery, and meticulous attention to detail. Able to manage multiple tasks and responsibilities in fast-paced, demanding environments; exercise calm approach in pressure situations.

Areas of Ability

- Customer Service
- Team Leadership
- Business Ethics
- Quality Standards

- Law & Rules Enforcement
- Public Service Delivery
- Public Speaking
- Team Collaboration

- Problem Solving/Resolution
- Workplace Organization
- Multi-Task Management
- Classroom Presentations

Education

Texas Tech University, Lubbock, TX
BSOE in Human Services, Emphasis in Criminal Justice
Completed August, 2006

Selected Upper-Level Coursework:
- Police Administration
- Minority Relations
- Criminal Investigations

- Vice & Narcotics
- Theories of Personality
- Introduction to Social Work

- Organized Crime
- Police-Community Relations
- Forensic Psychology

Work Experience

Certified Trainer / Bartender / Team Leader (2002 – Present)
Orlando's, Lubbock, TX
Promoted from original busser position to train staff of eight bussers in all duties; hand-selected by management to work bartending shifts in addition to training schedule. Provide hands-on instruction to new and established bussers; team with management to ensure fulfillment of all service and quality goals. As Bartender, interact directly with guests and team members, including servers, kitchen personnel, hosts, and managers; handle large amounts of cash on each shift.

Key Contributions/Accomplishments:
- Contribute comprehensive, quality training for diverse group of bussers; demonstrate patience with new employees and provide assistance during busy periods.
- Place uncompromising focus on guest service delivery; commended by management team for positive attitude and attention to guests' needs.

Garden Shop Associate (2001 – 2002)
Sutherland's, Lubbock, TX
Held responsibility for organizing garden shop, with emphasis on outside garden area; worked with team of five in arranging tables, displays, product placement, and inventory storage areas. Maintained area cleanliness and assisted customers as needed.

Key Contributions/Accomplishments:
- Earned consistently favorable performance evaluations and recommendation for promotion to Lead Associate position based on training and mentoring abilities.
- Maintained well-organized, attractive outside garden area to secure attention of customers and influence buyer decisions for key product offerings.

Volunteer – University Medical Center, Lubbock, TX. Worked in outpatient pharmacy for 18-month period; assisted with verifying inventory and filling prescriptions.

Transportation Security Specialist

This is a résumé for a federal job, so it includes information you won't normally find in commercial sector jobs. It's also six pages long; here are the first two pages.

Edward William Hastings

7896 White Pine Lane

Kingston, New York 12401

Day Phone: (518) 444-3456

Secondary Phone: (518) 555-6789

Social Security Number:	xxx-xx-xxxx
Citizenship:	U.S. Citizen
Veteran's Status:	N/A
Federal Civilian Status:	N/A
OBJECTIVE:	Transportation Security Specialist (ASI), SV-4357-A
	Vacancy Announcement Number TSA-R-0274D
	Albany International Airport, Albany, New York
	Department of Homeland Security
	Transportation Security Administration

PROFILE:

Experienced Police and Security Specialist with 20 years of expertise, excellence and outstanding service as a Patrolman, Investigator and Sergeant in the Albany City Police Department, and 4 years of specialized experience as a Security Officer and Supervisor at the Albany International Airport.

EXPERTISE:

- 24 years experience as a city police officer with high level of expertise as a criminal investigator and firearms trainer. Six years experience as a Police Sergeant responsible for up to 35 officers in the line of duty.
- Expertise as security/police supervisor at the Albany Airport in daily security of airport buildings, facilities, and personnel through use of Federal, state, local, and FAA regulations.
- Expert knowledge in use and deployment of physical security systems to safeguard airport buildings, facilities, staff, and travelers.

AWARDS & RECOGNITION:

- Received many commendations for Recognition of Service in situations including making burglary arrests, gun arrests, and homicide arrests. Awarded two medals for heroism.
- Ranked second in the city in arrest/conviction rate in the first year on the job.
- Recipient of Mayor's Achievement Award for saving several people from a burning building.

PROFESSIONAL HISTORY:

Albany Police / Albany International Airport

North Albany, New York 14708 11/01 – Present

SERGEANT/SUPERVISOR, PATROL OFFICER (Airport)
Part time: 20 hours/week Col.
Salary: $XXXXX/year

Conduct Albany Police Department law enforcement and security operations at the Albany Airport, ensuring the daily safety and security of hundreds of passengers and employees of the Albany Airport.

Sergeant/Supervisor:

- Oversee a staff of four security officers during the day shift, ensuring officers are at their assigned posts, and coordinating breaks to assure that all posts are continually manned.
- Responding to all potential arrest situations to assure that all state and federal procedures are followed. In the event of a major incident I am responsible for notifying and deploying the proper personnel to various locations as needed.
- Make crucial decisions when situations call for immediate attention.

Patrol Officer:

In addition to being a supervisor I have worked at four different posts at the airport, involving:

- Assisting the Transportation Security Administration (TSA) employees with weapons and contraband discovered during their screening process, and taking custody of any weapons or contraband to determine if that person possessed it legally or if they were in violation of federal or state law.
- Monitoring all vehicle traffic as it entered in front of the terminal. Conducted over five hundred vehicle inspections ensuring nothing hazardous was brought into the terminal area by means of a motor vehicle.
- Monitoring all vehicle traffic entering airport service entrances, including jet fuel trucks, construction vehicles, airport personnel vehicles, sanitation trucks, and United Parcel Service vehicles. Verifying the drivers' identification, and, where applicable, visibly checking the contents of the vehicle to ensure it matched the manifest presented to me. Checking all deliveries entering the restricted Airport grounds that were eventually brought into the Airport terminal and on the airplanes. Checking the validity of the drivers' identification and then visibly checking the contents of the delivery truck, and contacting the appropriate Airport divisions to respond and escort delivery vehicle into restricted areas.
- Checking and verifying identifications from all truck drivers entering restrictive areas during the construction phase of the Airport runways and pads, inspecting over 60 vehicles a day.

Law Enforcement Manager

Strong résumé for a seasoned professional in the public eye for thirty years and looking for a promotion.

EDWARD ROYCE

1400 Everett Street
San Jose, CA 95111

e.royce@mindspring.com

408-555-2222 (cell)
408-555-1212 (home)

LAW ENFORCEMENT MANAGEMENT

Moving organizations forward by putting people before paper and projects

More than 29 years of law enforcement experience, with a track record of consistently delivering improved results in each new assignment. Successful performance as acting Captain in 3 divisions during the absence of division commanders. Commitment to achieving high standards, both personally and for subordinates, to ensure providing outstanding public service. MA in Leadership and BA in Management.

Core Strengths & Expertise

- Large-scale event planning & management
- Community outreach
- Emergency & incident management
- Risk assessment

- Community & media relationship management
- Group training & public presentations
- Peer-to-peer & inter-organization collaboration
- Personnel counseling & investigations

PROFESSIONAL EXPERIENCE

San Jose Police Department, San Jose, CA   1979–Present
Lieutenant, Investigations (current)

As Investigations Lieutenant, oversee and manage 6 sergeants, 6 officers, 1 community service officer, and 2 office specialists. Coordinate daily operations of the Investigations Division, which includes managing major investigations, performing case assignments, conducting personnel counseling and background investigations, controlling narcotics "flash funds," and informally supervising an undercover unit. Previous assignments as Lieutenant: Media Relations; Administrative Services / Community Services; Field Operations; Honor Guard.

Special Accomplishments:

Managed the planning and completion of a new custody facility within 9 months versus expected 18-month time-frame.

Orchestrated successful planning and completion of July 4th festivities attended by about 100,000 people. Coordinated development and implementation of a plan involving 4 police departments, 1 fire department, 65 personnel, and 10,000 residents and business owners.

Developed an effective Public Information Officer unit with 24-hour availability. Major actions and benefits included the following:

- Achieved broader community outreach through diverse composition of the unit, including male, female, gay, white, and bilingual Hispanic, Vietnamese, and Korean members.

Established and fostered beneficial relationships with 135 media agencies.

Created a media resource book for future reference.

Formed and motivated a volunteer team that achieved the most successful Special Olympics fundraising campaign in the agency's history. Inspired commitment in team members and others to achieve challenging goals and negotiated support from corporate sponsors. Garnered positive media coverage, both print and television.

Spearheaded a project to provide detectives with an electronic investigation facility that incorporated all required elements. Identified remedial actions, instituted training, and established accountability for outside vendors and department personnel. Achieved a working, digitally recorded interview system that included 4 interview rooms and extensive equipment.

Sergeant: Field Operations; Administrative; Detective; Department Training; Traffic / Motors; Patrol;
Services Division; Honor Guard; TAC Squad; Field Training
Major actions and results as Sergeant included the following:
Selected as first person to hold Administrative Sergeant position, which required defining its responsibilities. Coordinated construction, creation, and implementation of the department's first temporary holding facility, from policy-manual writing through equipment acquisition.
Created and facilitated curriculum for the 3 most successful Advanced Officer Trainings in the department's history. Established strong new relationships with vendors, private industry, and city staff. Through successful budgetary control, helped increase training budget by 50% and returned 66% of training dollars spent through a variety of reimbursement processes.

EDUCATION & PROFESSIONAL DEVELOPMENT

Master of Arts in Leadership & Bachelor of Arts in Management, University of Santa Clara, Santa Clara, CA: graduated with Honors; achieved Distinction for Top Research Project
Level 1 Management Certificate, West Valley College, Saratoga, CA
POST Management Certificates including **Supervisory, Advanced, & Reserve,** POST Supervisory Leadership Institute, Class 46, Sacramento, CA; selected as Auditor for Class 56
POST Executive Development Course, San Mateo, CA
21st Century Leadership Course, City of San Jose, San Jose, CA
Crisis Communication **#1, #2 & PIO Certificates,** California Specialized Training Institute, Shell Beach, CA
FEMA ICS Training, San Jose, CA / Online
7 Habits of Highly Successful People, Covey Leadership Center, San Jose, CA

AWARDS & RECOGNITION

Distinguished Service Award, San Jose Police Department
"Top Cop" Award, Santa Clara County Criminal Justice Training Center
Silver & Gold Medals, Northern California Special Olympics Fundraising / Coordination

PROFESSIONAL AFFILIATIONS & CONTRIBUTIONS

Vice-President, Santa Clara County Training Managers Association
Co-Chair, South Bay Regional Criminal Justice Training Center Academy Advisory Committee
Associate Member, International Association of Chiefs of Police
Board Member, San Jose Police Officers Association
Speakers' Bureau Member, representing San Jose Police Department at diverse functions
Member, International Police Officers Association & Santa Clara County Peace Officers Association

COMMUNITY INVOLVEMENT

San Jose Kiwanis: current member; past member of Board of Directors
Special Olympics: past Chairman, Santa Clara County Law Enforcement Torch Run
San Jose High School Grad Night Committee Member, 2004

Security Guard

For a moment, imagine that you're a Hollywood star in need of a bodyguard and driver. Now read the first third of the page.

JOHN HARRISON

12345 Gilbert Street, #140 • North Hollywood, California 91442
Residence (818) 555-1111 • Mobile (818) 555-8998 • josehern1@email.com

SECURITY GUARD / DRIVER

—*Bilingual English / Spanish*—

- Over 20 years experience in all aspects of security including transport of goods and protection of residential and commercial properties.
- Possesses a strong work ethic with a verifiable record of perfect attendance and punctuality.
- Professional in appearance and work habits.
- Experienced in training and supervision.

CERTIFICATIONS

Security Guard License
Mace & Baton Certification
Gun Permit (.38. 98 mm 42 mm)
Health/Drug Certificate

Class B Driver's License
Forklift Certificate
Licensed Auto Mechanic
CPR / First Aid Certified

EXPERIENCE

Security Guard • 1999 to Present
FARGO, INCORPORATED, Van Nuys, CA
- Promoted to Messenger with full responsibility for security of armored truck, crew performance, and custody of goods.
- Coordinate daily activity of crew and truck; ensure safekeeping and security of shipments; control safe.
- Supervise crew members in safe and efficient performance of duties; assist in training new hires.

  Recognition / Awards:
  - 10 Year Anniversary Award for Contributions to the Success of Company, 2005
  - Recipient of Safe Worker Awards 1995, 1998, 2000, 2005
  - Inside Sales Manager/Office Manager

Armed Security Guard • 1997 to 1999
ESTELLA NIGHT CLUB, Sylmar, CA
- Maintained security of patrons and premises (including parking lots) at popular night club.
- Checked IDs; searched male patrons for weapons; assisted law enforcement agencies as required.

Security Guard • 1995 to 1997
NORTH VALLEY HOSPITAL, Granada Hills, CA

Inside Sales Manager-Office Manager

Catherine M. Sipowicz

36 Algonquin Drive • East Brunswick, NJ 08816 • 732.555.5555 • jcsipowicz2006@yahoo.com

INSIDE SALES MANAGER ~ OFFICE MANAGER

Professional Inside Sales Manager and Office Manager with over 10 years experience in all phases of the business cycle. Consistently exceed objectives and increase bottom-line profits for employers. A quick learner and an excellent communicator with an ability to perform well in a multi-tasking environment.

Extensive experience in the sales process from order entry through customer service. Thrive in manufacturing and production arenas; a detail-oriented individual, friendly and personable, a self-starter with a willingness to work well as a member of a team.

Creative and skilled analyst with strong problem-solving skills offering outstanding systems expertise (conversions, upgrades, and training), excellent computer and Internet skills.

Areas of Expertise:
- Office Management
- Project Management
- Customer Service
- Customer Sales Profiles
- Inventory Control
- Credit and Collections
- Problem Identification/Solutions
- Sales Management Support
- Commission Reporting
- Inside Sales

Professional Experience

AMERICAN BOUQUET COMPANY, INC. – *Edison, New Jersey (1993 to 2006)*
Inside Sales Account Manager (2001–2007)
Responsible for maintaining $7 million of current business and coordinating all functions between the outside sales staff and the internal departments of the company.
- Directed and coordinated activities concerned with the sales organization including screening and evaluating new customers, performing credit authorizations, verifying client's sales history, and compiling monthly sales comparisons.
- Appointed as inside Sales Account Manager to handle a major supermarket chain buying $3 million of floral products, resulting in a 23% sales increase in the first year.
- Provided sales forecasts for holidays and special events which greatly increased the efficiency and accuracy of production schedules and purchasing requirements.
- Designed an innovative program to evaluate effectiveness of new marketing campaigns. Hired and supervised a merchandiser to track the program on a weekly basis.
- Developed an automated monthly sales comparison analysis with the IT department reducing the report generation time from 8 hours to 1 hour.

Office Manager (1996–2001)
Manage a multitude of tasks contributing to the daily operations of American Bouquet Company. Responsible for hiring, training, motivation, and supervision of the telemarketing staff.
- Developed and implemented various systems for optimizing production resources and increasing efficiency. Designed Excel spreadsheets and standardized forms for use by all departments.
- Enhanced interdepartmental communications resulting in reduced production and billing errors.

Administrative Assistant (1993–1996)
Coordinated communications between sales and production. Performed credit checks, collections, and resolved price discrepancies. Responsible for inventory, price lists, and customer lists.
- Project Manager for developing, implementing, and maintaining an inventory control system that utilized coding to correlate new orders with production scheduling.

Education

BA in Political Science, **RUTGERS UNIVERSITY,** New Brunswick, New Jersey – 1993

International Sales/Marketing Manager

Meghan had worked her way through a fast-track entry-level program and was ready to strike out on her own with another company.

MEGHAN M. ENGLAND

327 Bristol Circle • New Fort, NY 12345 • (888) 555-2200 • email@email.com

INTERNATIONAL SALES/MARKETING MANAGER
Strategic Planning/Staff Supervision & Training/Business Development

Highly accomplished and innovative marketing professional with key domestic and international experience in penetrating new markets, expanding existing accounts, and boosting profits. Fluent in English and Spanish. Results-oriented and visionary leader with proven success in new market identification, regional advertising, branding, and competitor analysis. Skilled in staff supervision and training, client relations, and strategic planning. Polished communication, presentation, negotiation, and problem-solving skills. Thrive in an intensely competitive, dynamic environment.

Core competencies include:

- Strategic Business Planning
- Budget Management
- Business Development/Planning
- Staff Training & Development
- Marketing Program Design

- Market Identification
- Team Building & Leadership
- Account Relationship Management
- International Client Relations
- Key Networking Skills

PROFESSIONAL EXPERIENCE

SAP AMERICA/SAP CHILE/LATIN AMERICA
Fast-track progression through the following key international marketing management positions:

Latin American Marketing Manager, **TAPP LATIN AMERICA – Newton Square, NY (2003 to Present)**
Direct and manage 360 degree company marketing programs throughout Argentina, Bolivia, Brazil, Chile, Colombia, Mexico, Paraguay, Peru, Puerto Rico, Venezuela, Uruguay, and the Caribbean Islands for the third largest software company worldwide. Oversee all aspects of Latin American regional marketing operations with broad responsibility for strategic planning and the indirect supervision of a staff of four marketing managers and various partner PR/advertising agencies.

Initiate, develop, and nurture new leads to generate additional sales revenues; collaborate with sales representatives to turn over leads and establish key relationships. Accomplish marketing goals by launching comprehensive marketing, advertising, and branding plans. Manage PR marketing functions through press releases, C-level executive interviews, press conferences, professional networking, and by creating an educational focus to allow greater company exposure. Ensure top-level customer satisfaction; collaborate with various outside agencies to administer and analyze customer surveys.

Develop and manage a $3 million marketing budget encompassing strategic industries such as banks, the public sector, and utility companies, as well as strategic solutions involving customer relationship management, enterprise resource planning, supply chain management, and small to mid-sized businesses. Design and implement regional advertising/branding strategies, and analyze progress through brand-tracking studies and competitive reports. Pioneer and manage key relationships with high-profile industry analyst firms. Interact with an outside global advertising agency to effectively leverage internationally syndicated relationship marketing campaigns. Serve as a company representative, liaison, and central point-of-contact for providing vital information, managing market research, and resolving issues at all levels.

Key Accomplishments:

- Spearheaded and manage a highly effective electronic quarterly newsletter, resulting in increased communications among Latin American employees.

- Directed an extensive 8-month regional team project in successfully training and educating all Latin American marketing personnel on the newly implemented CRM system in the areas of budgeting/planning, campaign planning, preparation, execution/analysis, lead management, and reporting.
- Developed and initiated the first regional budget with the global marketing team.
- Pioneered the centralization of advertising, resulting in greater discounts and significant savings.
- Accomplished greater recognition for the company including the first, and many additional publications of the company president in regional magazine articles.

Marketing Manager, **TAPP CHILE – Santiago de Chile (2001 to 2003)**

Spearheaded, built, and launched the first marketing department for the company's Chilean subsidiary, with full responsibility for hiring, training, scheduling, supervising, mentoring, and evaluating marketing coordinator and marketing analyst staff members. Managed an $800,000 Enterprise Resource Planning marketing budget. Interacted directly with the sales team to implement marketing strategies and meet goals. Managed extensive market research and analysis functions by collaborating with a local agency to conduct focus group interviews in evaluating both company and competitor solutions. Involved in all aspects of production, public relations, sales, relationship building, and customer service.

Key Accomplishments:

- Created and implemented a lead-generation program, resulting in an increased amount of qualified leads for Account Executives and improved revenues due to shorter sales cycle.
- Built solid PR operations by developing and managing high-impact press strategies; concurrently continued to initiate key media relationships, conduct press conferences and executive interviews.

Latin American Coordinator, **TAPP LATIN AMERICA – Wayne, NY (1998 to 2001)**

Managed the international roll-out and training for the company's Sales and Marketing Information System. Traveled extensively to various international locations to oversee all implementation and training functions. Concentrated on providing a full range of support to Finance and Marketing Directors.

Spanish Teacher, **CHASE CHEMICAL CORPORATION – Exton, NY (1998)**
Taught Spanish to top-level corporate executives.

Education & Credentials

BS in International Studies
EDUCATIONAL UNIVERSITY – Ross, NY (1997)

Language Studies
Seville/Segovia, Spain (1997)

Comprehensive Spanish Language Studies
Adelaide, Australia (1996)

Additional Professional Training in Business and Communications

Private Pilot License with instrument and commercial ratings

– Excellent Professional References Available on Request –

Sales and Marketing

Database Administration

Jackie enjoys most the database administration portion of her current job and will be targeting employers that will give transition from database marketing to database administration.

Jacqueline Alois

188-17 Greenway, Salt Lake City, UT 00000
000-000-0000
jacqueline@alois.net

Database Management ◆ Marketing Communications ◆ E-mail Template Design

Profile

Sales and Marketing Support Professional with more than 14 years of experience in time-sensitive, fast-paced environments. Highly developed skills in oral and written communications, multitasking, attention to detail, and perseverance to completion. Keen insight into clients' perspectives, goals, and target audiences. Proficient with various software programs including Word, Excel, Access, and Goldmine.

Key strengths include:

- Database administration
- Market research
- Sales lead qualification
- Proactive problem solving
- Promotional copywriting

- Internal/external customer service
- Computer and procedural training
- Project coordination
- Relationship building
- New account development

Professional Employment History

GRAYROCK COMMUNICATIONS INC., BEAR CREEK, UT   2002–PRESENT

Database Marketing Coordinator for trade-show design firm

- Assist the President, Creative Director, and sales force of 7 in developing targeted messages to promote company's services (trade-show display design and client training seminars). Contribute ideas in brainstorming sessions and translate concepts into persuasive written materials (brochures, Web pages, and e-mail templates).
- Generate leads through extensive phone contact, which has facilitated the closing of numerous sales by determining clients' interests and addressing their specific needs or concerns.
- Enter and update all pertinent information for up to 500 clients and prospects on Goldmine system; create profiles and periodically send electronically distributed promotional pieces to keep company in the forefront for future business.
- Initially train new sales consultants on data mining to their best advantage as well as empower them for success in prospecting and cold calling. Organize sales assignments to avoid duplication of efforts.
- Coordinate all pre- and post-sale details with various departments.
- Demonstratedversatility and talent in several areas; was retained on staff despite 2 company downsizings.

QUIGLEY & VANCE, CARRINGTON, UT   2000–2002

Inside Sales Representative for graphic arts supply company

- Performed duties of sales liaison, assistant purchasing agent, and customer service representative.
- Streamlined department by automating the quote process and systematizing sales literature.

Education

Westview County College, Randolph, UT – A.A.S., Marketing Communications, 2000
Shelton Institute, Shelton, UT – Applied Writing and Database Administration courses, 2001

Sales Executive

Mary Ann was a recent college grad looking for a job
while she continued training as a performer in New York.

MARY ANN BURROWS
123 Randolph Street
Wilmington, Delaware 19801
(555) 555-5555

Outside Sales/Account Manager/Customer Service

Energetic and goal-focused sales professional with solid qualifications in large account management and customer relationship building/maintenance. Proven ability to develop new business and increase sales within established accounts and mature territories. Self-confident and poised in interactions across all business hierarchies; a persuasive communicator and assertive negotiator with strong deal-closing abilities. Excellent time-management skills; computer-literate. Areas of demonstrated value include:

- Sales Growth / Account Development
- Commercial Account Management
- Prospecting & Business Development
- Customer Liaison & Service
- Consultative Sales / Needs Assessment
- Territory Management & Growth

PROFESSIONAL EXPERIENCE

Morris Mtr. Co., Wilmington, DE   1998 – Present
SALES EXECUTIVE (2000 – Present)
Promoted and challenged to revitalize a large metropolitan territory plagued by poor performance. Manage, service, and build existing accounts; develop new business, establishing both regional and national accounts. Serve as key liaison for all customers and work as the only outside sales representative in the company. Produce monthly reports for major national accounts.

Selected Results
- Reversed a history of stagnant sales; delivered consistent growth and built territory sales 22%, to $4.75 million annually, in less than 2 years.
- Surpassed quota by a minimum of 20% for 14 consecutive months.
- Personally deliver 95% of all sales generated for the company's main site.
- Prospected aggressively and presented products to key decision-makers during cold calls; opened more than 60 new commercial accounts.
- Improved account service and applied consultative sales techniques; grew sales in every established account a minimum of 15%.

MANAGER, Harrisburg Store (1998 – 2000)

MANAGER TRAINEE, Wilmington Store (1998)
Initially recruited as a management trainee and rapidly advanced to management of a retail location generating $1 million annually. Supervised and scheduled 12 employees. Budgeted and produced advertising, oversaw bookkeeping, and set/managed sales projections and growth objectives.

EDUCATION AND CREDENTIALS

B.S., BUSINESS MANAGEMENT, 1998
Wilmington College, New Castle, DE

Additional Training

Building Sales Relationships, 2001
Problem Solving Skills, 2001

Professional & Community Associations

Member, Chamber of Commerce, 1999 – Present
Member, Country Club and Women's Golf Association, 1999 – Present
Youth Soccer Coach and FIFA Certified Referee, 2002 – Present

Sales Manager

Although the costs of book publishing won't allow color printing in *Résumés That Knock 'em Dead*, this résumé jumped out at me because every relevant keyword has been highlighted in yellow. Try this when customizing a résumé to a specific set of requirements.

MAX STERN

22225 Mayfair Way • Reston, VA 20190 • cell: (703) 555-2406 • *maxstern234@aol.com*

NATIONAL SALES MANAGER / PARTNER ACCOUNT MANAGER
Internet....High-Tech....Software Industries

Award-winning and dedicated sales manager with over a decade of success generating revenue and securing high-profile clients for industry leading companies, such as AOL Time Warner and Monster, with excellent levels of retention. Recipient of numerous prestigious sales awards for consistently exceeding sales goals and forecasts, and creating win-win client solutions. Utilize a consultative approach to assess client needs and provide solutions that meet the client's strategic goals. Expertise in:

❖ New Business Development	❖ High-Expectation Client Relations	❖ Relationship Management
❖ Key Account Management	❖ Consultation and Solution Sales	❖ Contract Negotiations
❖ Strategic Alliance/Partners	❖ Sales Training & Team Leadership	❖ Vertical Channel Sales

Proficient in all sales cycle phases from lead generation and presentation to negotiation, closing, and follow-up. Excel in training and mentoring teams to outperform the competition. Possess a high level of discipline, professional integrity, a passion for achieving organizational success, and a desire to always play on a "winning team."

PROFESSIONAL EXPERIENCE

TELCORDIA TECHNOLOGIES - Sterling, VA   10/2005 – Present
Telcordia Technologies provides trusted, neutral, and essential addressing, interoperability, infrastructure, and other clearinghouse services for communication service providers and enterprises worldwide.

National Sales Manager   3/2006 – Present
Promoted from Account Executive to National Sales Manager in eight months due to the consistent attainment of breakthrough sales results. Oversee national sales programs and supervise 15 sales representatives. Recruit, interview, hire, and train staff and evaluate performance for regional placements. Conduct quarterly sales meetings, develop goals, and coordinate all local, regional, and national training efforts.

- **Sales Performance.** Achieved **100% of sales quota despite a 60% reduction in staff.**
- **Awards & Recognition. Received 2005 Polaris Award, Neustar's most prestigious distinction,** which rewards superior performance and strong commitment to operational excellence. Nominees undergo a rigorous nomination and selection process, and awards are granted to the **"top-talent" (less than 5%)** of the company.
- **People Leadership.** Empowered staff and built a focused and loyal national sales team that consistently generated higher-than-budget sales.
- **New Business Development.** Key player in cultivating relationships with national clients including Nutrisystem, Expedia, and Mediacharge. Personally conducted assessment interviews with prospective clients to identify needs and formulate appropriate solutions.

Account Executive   10/2005 – 3/2006
- **Vertical Sales Campaign Management.** Through rigorous cold-calling and prospecting, launched company into the online advertising vertical, setting the stage for colleagues to follow. As a result, an impressive 65% of all online advertising currently comes through Neustar, and recurring monthly revenue exceeds $150,000.

HOTJOBS.COM – Annandale, VA
Yahoo! HotJobs has revolutionized the way people manage their careers and the way companies hire talent, and puts job seekers in control of their careers, making it easier for employers and staffing firms to find qualified candidates.

Southeast Account Executive   6/2004 – 9/2005
Aggressively sold Monster business solutions including database, web job hosting, and job posting packages within the Mid-Atlantic and Southeast Regions. Applied a solutions selling methodology to the sales cycle, promptly completing proposals and sales activities, closing sales opportunities quickly and efficiently, and completing necessary paperwork steps to successfully set projects in motion.

- **Revenue Generation.** Consistently exceeded monthly revenue target of $15,000. Cold-called and closed new business with major retail clients including Safeway and Wal-Mart.

TNS SOLUTIONS – Herndon, VA
TNS is the trusted source for the complete Oracle suite of data-centric solutions, including database, Oracle Fusion Middleware, and packaged applications.

Account Executive   1/2004 – 6/2004
Managed Sales for Oracle's 9iAS and Collaboration Suite, and developed new territory in district, including several key accounts such as RSA and Comstore. Managed a staff of 25 sales representatives.

- **Marketing.** Generated $1 million in new business development by creating local and state-wide marketing programs to generate buzz around Symantec products and DLT's Commonwealth of Virginia contract.
- **Campaign Management.** Prospected for new business through various marketing campaigns, including telemarketing, direct mail, targeted seminars, and partnerships with leading software firms.
- **New Business Development.** First to sell the hosted Collaboration Suite product to the Armed Forces Retirement Home, and secured the RSA relationship at DLT.
- **Trade Show Participation.** Networked extensively throughout the business community at industry trade shows, obtaining over 7,000 leads on average per event.
- **Awards and Recognition.** Generated the highest volume of accounts company-wide and was recognized with the DTL's prestigious "Sales Leader Award."
- **Partner Development.** Liaised with DLT staff and Oracle team to successfully manage the Symantec relationship.

AOL TIME WARNER – New York, NY
AOL Time Warner is a leading media and entertainment company, whose businesses include interactive services, cable systems, filmed entertainment, television networks, and publishing.

National Account Sales Manager   3/1998 – 10/2003
Sold print and online advertising across all AOL Time Warner properties (159 websites and publications) including People, Time Inc, Fortune, Netscape, and Compuserve. Interfaced directly with C-Suite executives, negotiated high-dollar contracts, and coordinated implementation. Managed accounts in three major verticals (retail, travel and tourism, and online gaming) and orchestrated post-sale professional services and resources. Recognized market needs and provided clients with new solutions, ultimately expanding their customer base.

- **Revenue Generation.** Booked $2.3 million in new revenue from a previously dormant category, exceeding $1.8 million revenue quota within eight months.
- **New Business Development.** Created $1.5 million in new business opportunities through presentations, cold calling, and successful final negotiations.
- **Training Course Development.** Designed and implemented a live prospecting training class focused on topics such as utilizing unique online tools (ad relevance and niche online sites, etc.) and capturing contact information from prospects and leads.
- **Customer Relations and Retention.** Forged strong partnerships with both clients and ad agencies, and increased advertisers' retention rates by encouraging collaboration between both groups.
- **Sales Presentations.** Completed intensive national sales and presentation training, and ranked #1 (out of 30) and #7 in the country in both 2000 and 2001, based on number of deals closed.

EDUCATION & TRAINING

Advanced Leadership Program

Telcordia Technologies • Sterling, VA • 2008
Bachelor of Arts in Business Administration
George Mason University • Fairfax, VA

Salesperson

The first page tells a strong, focused story. Notice the MBA after the name. Some object to this as not traditional. My view? Hard-earned and well-respected, it makes a powerful statement about the candidate. If you've got it, flaunt it!

SARA FERNANDEZ, MBA

22451 Blue Onyx Way • Fairfax, VA 22033 • cell: (703) 555-8791 • *sara123@comcast.net*

EXPERIENCED MULTIMEDIA SALES PROFESSIONAL
Advertising, Communications, and Media Industries
Strategic Sales & Marketing / New Product Launch / Advertising Strategy / Team Building

Ambitious, high-performing sales professional with a twenty-year track record of success generating revenue and securing high-profile clients for "best in class" companies. Recipient of **numerous prestigious sales awards** for consistently **exceeding sales goals and forecasts,** and creating win-win client solutions. Utilizes a consultative approach to assess client needs and provide "turnkey" solutions and programs that meet the client's strategic goals. Possesses deep expertise in branding, managing and positioning product lines, and implementing innovative solutions that drive revenue and bring unique products to the community. Expertise in:

❖ Business Development	❖ High-Expectation Client Relations	❖ Overcoming Objections
❖ Relationship Management	❖ Employee Communication Strategy	❖ Contract Negotiations
❖ Strategic Alliance/Partners	❖ Staff Motivating and Mentoring	❖ Channel Sales Strategies

Gifted sales strategist and tactician who excels in driving revenue through innovative channel development programs. Candidate differentiators include: the ability to produce ROI with passion, tenacity, and an ethical, compliance-based stance that nurtures respect and supports growth. Excels in training and mentoring teams to outperform the competition. Possesses a high level of personal and professional integrity, a passion for achieving organizational success, and a desire to **always play on a "winning team."**

VALUE LINE, INC. - Alexandria, VA • 3/2007 - Present
Sr. Sales Account Executive
Promoted and sold online advertising packages for leading investment and personal finance website. Identified and targeted key accounts and built relationships with senior level, often C-suite, clients and advertising agencies, building for them a "soup to nuts" online campaign and suite of services that generated results. Charged with delivering $1-3 million in advertising revenue, by analyzing existing sales channel relationships and developing a new strategy focused on market leaders.

THE LOUDOUN EASTERNER – Ashburn, VA • 7/1998 - 3/2007
Account Manager (3/2006 - 5/2007) • **National Ad Agency Channel Sales Representative** (2/2005 - 5/2006)
National Recruitment Sales Representative (7/1998 - 2/2005)

Aggressively recruited to develop, revitalize, and nurture productive relationships with *Fortune* 1000 companies and government agencies such as Inova Healthcare, BAE Systems, Lockheed Martin, and the FBI and CIA. Packaged and sold targeted multimedia integrated talent solutions and services to maximize effectiveness and reach to key clients.

Key Accomplishments:

➢ **Multimedia Campaign Development.** Offered existing clients an opportunity to "fish in a different pond" by developing and recommending new and alternative multimedia account strategies targeted at niche and passive candidate markets. Packaged and sold nontraditional campaigns from non-print sources targeted at key audiences.

➢ **Product Development.** Credited for designing and spearheading the execution of a cutting edge hotjobs.com product offering whereby keyword searches served up product-related ads along the margins of the website, generating more than $50K in incremental revenue per year.

➢ **Increased Advertiser Revenue.** Through a combination of face-to-face visits to 13-15 domestic markets, the creation of various telephone sales programs, and multiple e-mail marketing campaigns, grew Easterner JOBS Advertising Unit by $10 million, an increase of 25%, representing one-third of all sales for the unit.

➢ **Sales Performance.** Consistently met and exceeded quarterly and annual sales revenue goals, up to 131% above quota.

➤ **Awards & Recognition.** Recipient of Presidents Club Year End Award for demonstrating a commitment to customers that is reflected in business performance, a high-level of sales achievement, and customer satisfaction. Recipient of several prestigious awards including two Vice Presidents Club Awards, three Sales Achievement Awards, two Sales Excellence Awards, and a Publishers Award for Sales Excellence.

HOTJOBS.COM - Annandale, VA • 1991 - 1998
Vice President/General Manager - (1997 - 1998) • **Director of Client Services** - (1996 - 1997)
Account Executive - (1991 - 1996)

Progressed rapidly through and promoted into positions with increasing responsibility during tenure with HotJobs. com. Directed all aspects of sales, marketing, and operations functions, and managed full P & L ($10 million in revenue) for Washington, D.C., office. Generated significant new client business and produced employer-branded recruitment and retention advertising campaign and execution strategies.

Key Accomplishments:

➤ **Cost Containment.** Spearheaded key cost-containment initiatives, saving thousands of dollars, resulting in a Top 10 (out of 35) "managerial profitability" ranking for the Washington, D.C., office.

➤ **New Business Development.** Partnered with the HotJobs sales channel in the design and implementation of a "business case building" sales contest, increasing HotJobs revenue by $2 million.

➤ **Sales Productivity.** Noted for driving $1 million in new business development in one year.

➤ **Process Improvement.** Spearheaded from conception to implementation an employee retention initiative. Launched monthly new hire performance appraisals (30/30's), which fostered a welcoming new hire experience, and drastically improved retention. Hired, trained, and supervised a staff of 12 account managers, and provided ongoing staff mentoring and support enabling them to grow company's client base.

➤ **High Expectation Client Relations.** Painstakingly researched and subsequently instituted the recommended solutions outlined in the business book classic *The Nordstrom Way: The Inside Story of America's #1 Customer Service Company* to maximize HotJob's customer satisfaction.

➤ **Employer Branding.** Partnered with senior level Human Resources clients in the design and development of uniquely branded corporate recruitment advertising strategies. Recommended tactical approaches for campaign execution.

➤ **Marketing Solutions.** Presented competitively positioned employee communication solutions and executed delivery of solutions such as collateral development, diversity strategies, university/college relations, and creative ad design to maximize employee communication programs.

Education

Masters of Business Administration
The Kogod School of Business – American University
Fully financed way through Business School

Bachelor of Science in Marketing
Michigan State University – East Lansing, MI

Member - National Society of Hispanic MBAs

Sales Account Manager

All I need to see before calling this candidate is the target job titles, the first two subheads, and three demonstrative graphics (graph bars in blue in the original). A picture is worth a thousand words in this instance.

TODD GUNDERSON

945 Main St. ♣ Lubbock, TX 79400 ♣ 806-555-9900 ♣ *todd_gunderson34@yahoo.com*
♣ Relocating to Las Vegas region

SALES DEVELOPMENT ♣ ACCOUNT MANAGEMENT ♣ CUSTOMER SERVICE

Career Overview:
Determined, customer-driven sales professional with extensive experience and track record of success in B2B sales and account management within the vending product industry, demonstrating ability to gain customer trust and secure win-win results. Build strong "partnerships" with individuals ranging from small business owners to decision-makers within high-profile customers (e.g. Wal-Mart, McLane) and business partners (Coca-Cola, Pepsi). Recognized for overachieving goals and delivering exceptional service. Quick, on-the-spot learner.

Knowledge & Skill Areas:

❖ Consumer Product Sales	❖ Prospecting & Lead Generation	❖ Account Management/Retention
❖ Customer Relationships	❖ Order Writing & Fulfillment	❖ Backroom Inventory Management
❖ Product Merchandising	❖ Point-of-Sale Advertising	❖ Customer Needs Fulfillment

PROFESSIONAL EXPERIENCE

VENDING, INC., Lubbock/Amarillo, TX
Specializing in sales, installation, and maintenance of vending machines throughout Texas.
Sales Representative / Account Executive (1989 – Present)
Gained increase in responsibilities as business grew from wholesale liquor distributor to include sales and service of vending machines. Conduct extensive field research to determine optimal locations for machines; develop and deliver presentations to prospective customers detailing how merchandise will add to their bottom line. Negotiate contract terms and handle all closing and follow-up service activities. Additionally serve as Acting Manager in overseeing performance of 12 team members. *Key Contributions & Accomplishments:*

- *Revenue Growth* – Maintained consistent, year-over-year pattern of increasing revenues through robust and downturn economies, from $50,000 to $1.2 million as illustrated below:

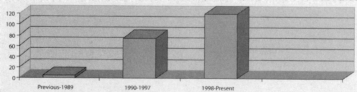

- *Product Placement & Market Share* – Grew number of machines from **1** to **450** from 1989 to 1998 prior to Lubbock opening; expanded inventory from **89** machines in 1998 to **780** by 2004, buying out some of the largest vendors in the area. Earned position as one of top vendors market-wide.

- *Key Account Management* – Built strong, sustainable relationships with broad range of accounts, including: **X-Fab of Texas • Industrial Molding • McLane • Owens-Corning • Wal-Mart**

- *Customer Service* – Provided excellent service for customer companies throughout tenure, characterized by immediate, thorough resolution of problems with equipment and friendly service.

* Prior roles as Sales Associate and Service Worker with Quality Vending. Played key role in expanding company's market presence and driving sales growth from **zero** to **$50,000** in annual revenues.

PROFESSIONAL DEVELOPMENT

Sales Training: Attended seminars and workshops featuring highly recognized speakers, including:
Zig Ziglar • Paul Tracy • Anthony Robbins
Technical Skills: Able to operate forklift, pallet jack, and other equipment. Skilled in MS Office and Internet tools.

Sales Account Manager

The entire first third of the page consists of highly relevant keywords relating to the job's deliverables. The sales chart breaks up the text, draws the eye, and packs a serious punch.

Thomas Vargas

3799 Millenia Blvd. Miami, FL **** | Phone: ***-***-*****

revenuedriver@aol.com

Account Management | **Product Marketing** | **Program Management**—IT Industry

Skillfully combining sales cycle management and technical expertise to drive revenue growth

LEADERSHIP PROFILE

Profit-driver and technology-expert professional with more than eight years' experience exceeding sales quotas, generating increased revenue, managing highly technical projects, and developing executive relationships. Well-rounded knowledge of the telecommunications industry with strong academic preparation: Master of Business Administration with Marketing and Management Information Systems majors; Cisco technical certifications.

Areas of Strength

Sales Goals | Territory Sales | Marketing | Executive Presentations | Emerging Technologies | Prospecting
Consultative Sales | Negotiations | Public Speaking | New Client Acquisition | Market Assessment
Competitive Market Intelligence | Corporate Communications | Account Management | Long-term Planning
Customer Service | Networking | Product Solutions | Vendor Relations | Strategic Initiatives

~ Solid career history of sales goal deliveries ~

Projection	Sales	Percentage
$240,000	$425,000	177%
$90,000	$106,200	118%
$102,000	$114,000	112%
$114,000	$123,120	108%
$185,000	$192,816	104%
$120,000	$121,000	102%

Top performing professional with a unique ability to implement technology knowledge into sales presentations. Technical expertise: install, configure, operate, and troubleshoot medium-size routed and switched networks, including implementation and verification of connections to remote sites in a WAN.

PROFESSIONAL EXPERIENCE & ACHIEVEMENTS

Corporate Account Manager III, WorldCom, Orlando, FL   2002–Present

Sales, Marketing, and Revenue Generation:
Prospect, qualify leads, and gain new business with persuasive presentations. Lead high-powered negotiations with corporate executives; develop proposals and create enticing sales presentations that include in-depth product education and executive briefings. Combine efforts with marketing specialists to study market trends, create customized and effective marketing strategies.
- Influenced prospective clients of *Fortune* 1000 companies; convinced them to close on multi-million-dollar, long-term contracts by demonstrating value over the competition.
- Managed total revenue of $5M and more than $250K per month customer revenue base.
- Grew revenue by 10% within one year by building and strengthened relationships with existing customers.

Technology Projects:
Design and lead complex network-implementation projects. Demonstrate expertise in Wide Area Networking including IPVPN, Private IP (MPLS), Frame Relay, ATM, and Private Line; local voice and private branch exchange service including class 5 and class 3 switching technologies. Introduce emerging technologies such as VoIP, VoFR, PoE, FCoIP, hosted IP Centrex, and Managed IP PBX.
- Increased profits by selling entire suite of telecommunication products and services, leveraging partner vendors like Cisco, Nortel, Avaya, and Checkpoint.

Network Solutions Consultant, Business Solutions, Houston, TX   2001–2002

Devised sales plans to cater to new and existing customer base and yielded higher revenue. Provided consultation on sales strategies, emerging technologies, existing line of products, and small networks to large client servers. Combined effort to work on projects that included WAN technologies, both data bandwidth and telephony solutions multiple platform networks.

- Developed new marketing techniques that increased sales opportunities and propelled sales from $110,000 in 2000 to $425,000 in 2001.

Network Design Consultant, Network Media, Austin, TX   2000–2001

Designed, installed, and maintained structured voice and data cabling projects, both Inside Plant and OSP. Prepared bids and estimations for structured cabling projects per RFP and RFQ.
- Collaborated and played an instrumental role in the winning bid for a $1.5M structured cabling job with the State of Texas Corrections Department.

EDUCATION

UNIVERSITY OF TEXAS AT DALLAS, Richardson, TX
MBA, dual concentration in Management Information Systems and Marketing, 2002
Activities and Societies: National Scholars Honor Society, UTD MBA Society, AITP

TEXAS A&M UNIVERSITY, College Station, TX
Bachelor of Business Administration in Information and Operations Management, 2000

CERTIFICATIONS

Cisco Certified Network Associate | Cisco Sales Expert

Senior Account Executive

All the right component parts. Of interest is the Selected Achievements section, which acts as a focusing tool for the reader who reads "achiever."

Bob M. Smith

résumés@arésumésolution.com

#2 Nowhere St. • New York, NY
Home: 973.555.1212 • Mobile: 973.555.1313

Sr. Account Executive

❖ ❖ ❖

Highly qualified professional with strong background in sales, sales management, new business development, and account management in collaborative environments. Skilled in Enterprise Software Sales, Enterprise Content Management (ECM), Business Process Management (BPM), and Business Process Outsourcing (BPO). Increased sales by developing strong relationships with clients, staff, partners, and management from initial contact through implementation. Demonstrated talents in building name brand awareness through various marketing techniques.

- Exceptional ability to research, analyze, and translate information to diverse audiences.
- Skilled in developing and implementing marketing techniques that drive revenue and increase sales.
- Excellent communicator with a consultative sales style, strong negotiation skills, and a keen client needs assessment aptitude.
- Strong background in selling to C-level executives of large organizations.

Key Proficiencies Include:

➤ Business Process Analysis ➤ Contract Negotiations ➤ Order Management

➤ Sales & Marketing ➤ Relationship Development ➤ Strategic Accounts

➤ Document Management ➤ Technical Sales ➤ Business Development

SELECTED ACHIEVEMENTS

- ✓ Created a niche market at Pyramid Solutions, providing a repeatable business process management (BPM) solution for national financial services and mortgage industries, utilizing FileNet technologies. Project resulted in significant increase in deal profit margin by 35%.
- ✓ Awarded FileNet's "Innovative Solution of the Year" at Pyramid Solutions for development of a repeatable Business Process Management Solution in financial services industry. (2002)
- ✓ Met and exceeded quota by 103% and added (4) new named accounts in 2006 at Thunderhead Limited.
- ✓ Recognized as "Top Partner - Kofax Midwest Region" at Pyramid solutions. (2001 – 2004)
- ✓ FileNet Presidents Club Achiever 125% > of Quota. (1991-1996)

PROFESSIONAL EXPERIENCE

Thunderhead, Ltd. – London, England

Senior Sales Executive / Business Development Director   **2005 - Present**

Performs direct software sales for organization which specializes in 100% Open Standards-based Enterprise Document Generation. Focuses on financial services and government programs, including lending and unemployment insurance. Negotiates contracts with new vendors and partners. Cultivates relationships from initial contact through implementation with partners, clients, staff, and management.

- Hired as first direct sales staff member in for start-up operations in North America, gaining four new named accounts in first year
- Organized "Lunch & Learn" program for FileNet System Consultants and integration partners to provide product education.
- Established strategic partnerships with UNISYS, BearingPoint, and IBM Global Services, as well as several other system integrators.

TECHNICAL SOLUTIONS, INC. – New York, NY

DIRECTOR OF SALES & MARKETING   2001 – 2005

Charged with providing sales and marketing for systems integration and professional services organization. Increased brand awareness through development of comprehensive marketing materials. Analyzed business needs and implemented solutions that drove business growth. Created new pricing model and product structure. Provided sales and deployment of ECM and BPM solutions nationwide. Managed relationships with FileNet, Captiva, and Kofax. Implemented Business Process Analysis methodology that analyzed and documented customer's current processes, and how the technology could streamline these processes. Customers included: Flagstar Bank, Sun Trust, PMI, Comerica, Washtenaw County, Muskegon County, Oakland County.

- Awarded FileNet's "Innovative Solution of the Year" for development of Business Process Management Solution in financial services industry. (2002)
- Exceeded quota by over 100% two out of four years.
- Earned membership in FileNet's ValueNet Partner Million Dollar Club. (2002 – 2004)
- Developed and implemented new change management marketing program, assisting companies with installation of complex technology.

NEW SYSTEMS, INC. – New York, NY

REGIONAL SALES DIRECTOR   1997 – 2001

Directed and managed sales staff throughout the United States. Oversaw and managed budget of $6.2M. Created and implemented new value-based sales process for rapid prototyping technology. Developed and installed Rapid Manufacturing Application within the Aerospace industry. Provided global sales support for Ford Motor Company, DaimlerChrysler, and GM. Trained sales and engineering staff members. Oversaw all regional operations, including deals and resources on a national basis. Established and managed relationships with Business Process Outsourcers (BPO).

- Reduced operating costs for field operations by combining facilities.
- Facilitated professional sales training boot camps.
- Discovered highly complex application, resulting in creation of InVisiLine braces.
- Transformed 3D Solutions sales force from product focus to solutions-oriented focus, through process analysis, training, and ROI models.
- Grew annual sales 15% by focusing sales teams on solution sales.

ABC CORPORATION – New York, NY

DISTRICT MANAGER / SENIOR ACCOUNT EXECUTIVE   1990 – 1997

Promoted from Senior Account Executive in 1995. Provided direction and management to 14 staff members, charged with providing large enterprise document management and BPM solutions. Gained new channel partners with application providers and consulting vendors. Charged with selling $MM solutions to C-level executives at large organizations, including GE Aircraft Engines, Medical Mutual of Ohio, Goodyear Tire and Rubber, Steelcase, Dow, Ford Motor Credit, U of M Health Systems, Comerica, Huntington Banks, and Key Banks.

- Increased indirect sales channels by 100%.
- Awarded "Presidents Club" for exceeding quota by 125%, 1991 – 1996.
- Earned "Rookie of the Year," 1990.
- Received "Eastern Region Top Producer," 1993.

EDUCATION

Bachelor of Science, Business Administration • The Ohio State University
– Columbus, OH

Brand/Product Manager

I like this résumé targeted to a specific job and taking part of the job posting as the content for what otherwise might be an objective/summary/profile. It works well for human eyes and will come out tops in the employer's database searches.

Jackie Byrd

Address City, State Zip
Home Phone Cell Phone E-mail Address

Career Target

BRAND/PRODUCT MANAGEMENT, GAMING INDUSTRY

Brand/Product Manager, WizKids.com

Looking for experienced Brand Manager to direct product lines, develop strategic marketing promotions, product research & positioning, and cross-departmental interfacing. Minimum 3 years management/marketing experience. A+ with game marketing experience.

Qualifications

Over 15 years of overall experience in sales and marketing leadership positions. Demonstrate strong commitment to maintaining highest level of product quality while driving revenue growth through multiple marketing and promotional strategies. Able to identify and convey Unique Selling Proposition (USP) to customers/business partners. Skilled in all core marketing and business development disciplines, with particular strength in product evangelism. Hold deep passion and interest in gaining market share for gaming company. <u>Certified HeroClicks Facilitator.</u>

- As key point of distinction, recognized as lifelong participant in the field of gaming, with experience in the '80s working for gaming pioneer Chaosium under the tutelage of renowned game designers Sandy Petersen and Greg Stafford. Completed all editing, mapping, layouts, and writing for SuperWorld Companion of SuperWorld; worked on supplemental modules for Cthulhu. In addition, managed gaming store during similar time period; eventually sold business that remains profitable two decades later. *

Knowledge & Skill Areas

Strategic Marketing & Promotional Campaigns ¡ Branding & Competitive Positioning ¡ Game Marketing
Product Research & Analysis ¡ Customer Relationship Building ¡ Team Building & Leadership
Product Line Management ¡ Point-of-Sale Displays ¡ Collateral Material Development
Sales Prospecting & Lead Generation ¡ Presentations, Negotiations & Closing

Professional Experience

Marketing Manager (2000 – Present)

ANVIL BUSINESS DEVELOPMENT, Seattle, WA
In charge of developing company marketing plan, managing vendor relationships, hiring/training sales staff, evaluating team performance, and completing sales in hands-on account executive role. Contract with companies to develop market presence for telecommunications products and services, working with broad range of clients that includes retailers, software development firms, and real estate developers.
- Redeveloped Web site and all marketing materials for key client Pacific Rich Homes. Tracked results of advertising placements, created sales/marketing plan, and secured exposure in *Everett Business Journal.*
- *Results: Increased sales and established pre-selling pattern affecting every community.*
- Improved management of product line (profile assessments) by writing brochure for customization to **5 industries,** including health care and non-profit organizations.

Account Executive   (2000 – 2001)
ESCHELON / ICM COMMUNICATIONS

Oversaw all aspects of sales in both employment positions, with focus on medium-sized companies. Scope of responsibility included making cold calls, conducting fact-finding research, delivering presentations, securing new accounts, and creating referral partner network.

- Introduced sales and marketing strategies that contributed to product improvement and revenue growth in downturn, heavily competitive market.

Account Executive   (1996 – 2000)
NORTHWEST WIRELESS, Seattle, WA

Directed sales and marketing initiatives for business clients. Managed all phases of sales cycle, transitioning to consultative selling approach as company increased lines to accommodate customers.

- Played key role in driving company from start-up to Nextel New Dealer of the Year recognition in 1998. Assisted in migrating company from one to multiple carriers.

Broker   (1994 – 1996)
AFLAC, Seattle, WA

Represented supplemental insurance programs to companies and their employees.

- Created "package" approach to sell multiple insurance lines simultaneously, resulting in **228%** revenue increase and average sales growth from **$360** to **$820** annual premium.
- Earned formal recognition as Number One Producer for largest supplemental insurance company worldwide; received commendations for opening most new groups in WA/OR regions in 1995.

Senior Partner   (1985 – 1993)
RESOURCE MANAGEMENT CENTER, Seattle, WA

Initially hired as Sales Manager and earned subsequent promotions to GM and Senior Partner, respectively. Delivered consulting and training seminars in all areas of business management, including finance and accounting, business growth, personnel law and management, taxes and reporting, and personal development.

- Spearheaded company's expansion into computer market to offer high-end accounting systems, wide area networks, centralized processing solutions, and ISDN to customers.

Professional Experience

Professional Training Courses:

Dale Carnegie Sales Training ¡ Brian Tracy-Strategic Sales Training ¡ Tom Hopkins Sales Training ¡ Nextel Basic, Advanced, and Consultative Selling Training ¡ Certified PSI Disk Cashing Controllers ¡ Certified PC Multi-User Operating System ¡ Certified Novell Netware ¡ License in Insurance for Health, Life and Disability / Certified & Certified Trainer in Cafeteria Plans/Section 125 ¡ Telecommunications Training Courses: PBX Trunks, Digital Switched Service, Digital Data Service, ISDN, Frame Relay Service, Self-Healing Network Service, DS1 (includes SHARP/SHARP+), DS3, Analog Private Line

Computer Skills: Skilled in Excel, Word, PowerPoint; experienced with sales programs Onyx, Gold Mine, & ACT
Community Involvement: Community Advocate, Role Playing Game Association (RPGA). Work with at-risk youths in running games on late Friday and Saturday nights, providing fun, appealing alternative to prohibited activities.

* Certified HeroClicks Facilitator; run demos of CreepyFreaks (under company's authorization) and promote Pirates of the Spanish Main, both products by the WizKid Corporation *

Sales Professional

Strong one-page sales résumé with a layout that packs in lots of data and keywords. The chart speaks loudly of a young, motivated professional who can close the deal.

MARK BIENLICH

SALES REPRESENTATIVE

Clinical Sales • Territory Sales • Customer-focused Selling Strategies

SUMMARY OF QUALIFICATIONS

Performance-focused sales professional, recognized for consistently increasing sales in challenging territories. Track record exceeding sales goals and generating more than $4M in combined revenue throughout career.

More than ten years' experience in all aspect of sales cycle management: lead generation, customer needs assessment, multimedia presentation, negotiation, closing, follow-through, relationship management, and development of customer loyalty. Experienced in pharmaceutical sales and preparing engaging clinical presentations, which include visual and audio appeal. Computer literate: MS Access and PowerPoint.

Areas of Strength:

➢ Sales Presentations	➢ Revenue Growth	➢ Product Demonstration
➢ Sales Closing	➢ Consultative Sales	➢ Staff and Customer Training
➢ Direct Sales	➢ Customer Retention	➢ Account Development

PROFESSIONAL EXPERIENCE & ACCOMPLISHMENTS

Account Manager, O'BRIEN PAINT CORPORATION, Minneapolis, MN — 2005–Present
Manage 130 accounts in 12 Midwestern states and three Canadian provinces. Gain new accounts, prepare proposals, and negotiate aggressively. Report to the district manager of one of the top manufacturers in America with an annual revenue over $1B.
- Reached sales goals, consistently increased sales by 12% each year:

	2005	2006	2007
Sales Revenue Growth	$1M	$1.12M	$1.25M

- Gained 11% market share by renegotiating and convincing clients to extend contracts on existing accounts from six months to three years.
- Improved customer service by 32% for 2006 by following up after the sale, leveraging position with customers, and reassuring their decisions.
- Generated 65 new accounts and $50K additional revenue on existing accounts by leading-high-powered negotiations.

Sales Representative, CIM CLARK-SHEEHAN, Chicago, IL — 2002–2005
Sold multiple pharmaceuticals for a multimillion-dollar corporation. Generated leads, cold called, made clinical presentations, nurtured customer relationships, and managed accounts.
- Produced $450K sales increase and surpassed company's record quota by 9%.
- Earned salesman of the year for three consecutive years by driving revenue growth via enticing, client-focused product presentations.
- Converted new hires into strong sales closers that became top-territory producers.

EDUCATION

Bachelor of Science Degree, SOUTHERN ILLINOIS UNIVERSITY, Carbondale, IL, 2001

PROFESSIONAL DEVELOPMENT

Seminars: Situational Leadership | Successful Selling | Sales and Motivation Skills
2122 S. Main St., Jacksonville, IL 62650 • Home: 217-555-0098 • Cell: 827-555-7629 • Email: *mark2@aol.com*

Bank Branch Management

SCOTT E. BOWMAN

19 Harrington Lane • Manalapan, NJ 07726 • 555.770.8956 • boman4765@hotmail.com

FINANCE ~ BANKING
Branch Management/Customer Service

Well-qualified and results-oriented **Finance and Banking** professional with experience and demonstrated accomplishments developing corporate growth, stability, and financial performance. Skilled analyst with strong organizational and communication abilities, and proven leadership qualities. Broad-based understanding of financial needs at all levels of business including evaluating, analyzing, and communicating financial data. Demonstrated broad-based strengths and accomplishments in:

Finance & Banking	Project Management	Teller Operations
Marketing Financial Services	Customer Service Relations	Loan/Account Origination
Team Management	Sales Management	Problem Solving
eBusiness Management	Communications	Continuing Education
Supervision/Leadership	Branch Management	Strategic Management

Recipient ~ Commerce Capital Markets Referral Award ~ July/August 2004

PROFESSIONAL EXPERIENCE

COMMERCE BANK, New Brunswick, NJ ~ 2004 to Present
CUSTOMER SERVICE REPRESENTATIVE (CSR)
Counsel clients in the selection of financial products in order to meet their financial planning and banking needs. Create and process client accounts providing excellent customer service. Sell and refer bank products based on specific sales focus (Commerce Capital Markets, Commerce National Insurance and Residential Mortgage). Identify prospective clients and develop and implement presentations for clients. Originate and process consumer and mortgage loan applications. Extensive knowledge of bank lending policies, practices, compliance, and underwriting criteria. Familiar with processing collateral loans, unsecured personal loans, asset-based loans, and mortgage-based loans. Process a myriad of loan documentation performing research activities when necessary.

Accomplishments:

- Consistently met and exceeded sales quotas and standards by cross-selling and up-selling bank products and services.
- Increased branch loan production volume.
- Sold a variety of loans by pulling CBA, creating loan worksheets, and making recommendations to lenders upon request.
- Ensured that loan policies and procedures were followed in accordance with audit guidelines.

STAR FIRE AUTOGRAPHS, Manalapan, NJ ~ 1999 to Present
BUSINESS MANAGER/PRINCIPAL
Established and currently manage Internet and mail order entertainment media business. Implemented strategic marketing programs successfully retaining clients and achieving market position. Instituted pricing structure after conducting extensive marketing research utilizing industry resources. Explored marketing and advertising opportunities adding value to new initiatives. Tracked data and improved business operations accordingly.

Accomplishments:

- Grew annual revenues to $30K.
- Authored inventory item descriptions and managed customer service relations.

EDUCATION/TRAINING

FAIRLEIGH DICKINSON UNIVERSITY, Madison, NJ
BA – History, Minor – Politics

COMMERCE UNIVERSITY BANK COURSES
Finance, Supervision, Business Management, Consumer Lending, Customer Service, Loan Products, Privacy Compliance, Loan Underwriting, BSA/AML, Foreign Assets Control, Bank Secrecy, etc.

COMPUTER SKILLS

Microsoft Office, Lotus Notes, dBase, Basic, HTML

Credit and Collections

James is a bank executive who wanted to relocate to the Dallas/Fort Worth area. This particular format showcased his credentials in a straightforward, results-driven manner.

JAMES HOFFMAN

2212 Gate Drive _ Phoenix, AZ 85001 _ 928.444.0888

PROFESSIONAL OBJECTIVE

Opportunity with a Dallas-based financial services organization where expertise in commercial collections, credit administration, and financial analysis/structuring contributes to increased profits.

PROFILE

- Extensive general business experience in the financial services industry, with credentials in both line and staff positions. Areas of expertise:

  - credit/portfolio administration
  - asset structuring/restructuring
  - commercial collections
  - loan documentation
  - regulatory compliance

  - financial analysis
  - risk assessment/underwriting
  - problem asset resolution/loan work-outs
  - operations/information integration
  - lender liability issues

- Background in diverse environments ranging from major regional financial holding companies to large and small community banks.
- Driving force in the establishment of a newly chartered commercial bank in the Phoenix area.
- Customer-focused professional whose philosophy is to "do it right the first time."
- Viewed by clients as an individual who is worthy of their trust, and who holds their best interests paramount.
- Effective at building sound internal/external relationships to support client and organizational goals.
- Actively involved in leadership roles focused on community development.

EDUCATION

M.B.A. **Financial Administration**
Northwestern University, Evanston, Illinois, 1982

B.A. **Business-Economics**
Vanderbilt University, Nashville, Tennessee, 1980

Executive Professional Development Programs:

- Northwestern University – Management School for Corporate Bankers
- University of Texas – National Commercial Lending Schools
- Certified Commercial Lender – American Bankers Association
- Computer School for Executives – Bank Institute of America
- Leadership and Lending – National Credit Executives Association

EXPERIENCE

RIVCOM STATE BANK, Phoenix, Arizona   1998 – Present
- Founder/Charter Director/Executive Vice President and Senior Lending/Compliance Officer.
- Member of three-person team that founded and organized a new state-chartered FDIC insured commercial bank. Established nine-member Board of Directors.

Key Accomplishments:
- Led efforts in generating $17.2 million in start-up capital.
- Grew bank into a profitable organization with $120 million in assets, while maintaining strong loan quality.
- Personally managed 70% of the bank's borrowing client base and 60% of $72 million in total loans outstanding.

U.S. LEASING COMPANY, Fort Worth, Texas   1995 – 1998
- Senior Vice President, Leasing – Managed lease origination process for a national leasing company. Offerings included private label programs for five *Fortune* 500 companies. Trained, supervised, and developed new team members.

Key Accomplishment:
- Introduced commercial bank quality underwriting procedures to correct prior portfolio deficiencies for leases averaging $75,000 per transaction.

STATE BANK AND TRUST, Springfield, Illinois   1989 – 1995
- Vice President and Senior Lending Officer – Responsible for bank's credit administration and management of commercial, consumer, and residential lending. Chaired loan and Community Reinvestment Act (CRA) committees.

Key Accomplishment:
- Developed and implemented new credit culture, achieving an all-time bank record of 1.12% ROA, from a negative .67%.

COMMERCIAL BANK, Chicago, Illinois   1983 – 1985
- Commercial Lending Officer – Special Loan Division – Established and managed new loan workout activity to support the bank's domestic commercial lending group.

Key Accomplishment:
- Directed reduction of internally classified credits and nonperforming assets by 70% each.

CIVIC AND PROFESSIONAL ACTIVITIES

- Board of Directors and Past President, Local Chamber of Commerce
- International Association of Bank Executives, Charter Member and Board of Directors
- Senior Board Member, National Banking Institute of Arizona

Finance Manager/Accountant

A strongly focused résumé that tells a compelling story in just one page.

Patricia Johnson

1234 Murietta Ave. • Palmdale, CA 93550
Residence (661) 555-1234 • Mobile (661) 555-9876 • PatJohnson @*email.com*

FINANCE / ACCOUNTING PROFESSIONAL
Internal Auditor / Financial Analyst / Staff Accountant

Detail-oriented problem-solver with excellent analytical strengths and a track record of optimizing productivity, reducing costs, and increasing profit contributions. Well-developed team building and leadership strengths with experience in training and coaching coworkers. Works well with public, clients, vendors, and coworkers at all levels. Highly motivated and goal orientated as demonstrated by completing studies toward B.S. in Finance, graduating with honors concurrent with full-time, progressive business experience.

—*Core Competencies*—

Research & Analysis / Accounts Receivable / Accounts Payable / Journal Entries / Bank Reconciliations
Payroll / Financial Statements / Auditing / General Ledger / Artist Contracts / Royalties / Escalation Clauses

PROFESSIONAL EXPERIENCE

MAJOR HOLLYWOOD STUDIO, Hollywood, CA • 2000 to Present
Achieved fast-track promotion to positions of increasing challenge and responsibility.

Royalty Analyst—Music Group, Los Angeles, CA (2005–Present)
Process average of $8–9 million in payments monthly. Review artist contracts, licenses, and rate sheets to determine royalties due to producers and songwriters for leading record label. Ensure accuracy of statements sent to publishers in terms of units sold and rates applied. Research, resolve, and respond to all inquiries.
• Resolved longstanding problems, substantially reducing publisher inquiries and complaints.
• Promoted to "Level 1" analyst within only one year and ahead of two staff members with longer tenure.
• Provided superior training to temporary employee that resulted in her being hired for permanent, Level 1 position after only three months.

Accounts Payable Analyst—Music & Video Distribution (2002–2005)
Processed high volume of utility bills, office equipment leases, shipping invoices, and office supplies for 12 regional branches. Assisted branches with proper invoice coding and resolving payment disputes with vendors.
• Identified long-standing duplicate payment that resulted in vendor refund of $12,000.
• Created contract employment expenses spreadsheet; identified and resolved $24,000 in duplicate payments.
• Gained reputation for thoroughness and promptness in meeting all payment deadlines.
• Set up macro in accounts payable system that streamlined invoice payments.
• Consolidated vendor accounts, increasing productivity and reducing number of checks processed.

Accounts Receivable Analyst—Music & Video Distribution (2000–2002)
Processed incoming payments; received and posted daily check deposits, reviewed applications for vendor accounts; distributed accounting reports and ordered office supplies. Handled re-billings of international accounts for shipments by various labels.
• Hired as permanent employee from temporary position after only three months.

Additional Experience: Billing Clerk / Accounting Clerk / Bookkeeper (*details available upon request*)

EDUCATION
B.S. in Finance; Graduated with Honors • CALIFORNIA STATE UNIVERSITY, Northridge, CA; 2005
Completed Studies Concurrent with Full-Time Employment

Computer Skills: Windows, Microsoft Office (Word, Excel, PowerPoint), Peachtree, J.D. Edwards, Tracs

Intern

This is an internship résumé that will fast-track the start of any career.

Dan Tranner

San Jose, CA   444.444.4444   *dantranner@anyserver.com*

QUALIFICATIONS FOR BANK OF AMERICA INTERNSHIP

- Committed to a career combining formal education in economics with practical work. Experienced with analysis for project management, including budgets, labor resources, and timelines. Prepared and delivered numerous presentations on project status to city and PG&E officials. Researched and presented options to property owners and investors for construction materials.
- History of taking on responsibility and successfully managing personnel for multimillion-dollar project. Excellent communication with individuals, businesses, municipalities, and professional firms. Conversational Spanish.

EDUCATION

SAN JOSE STATE UNIVERSITY, San Jose   UNIVERSITY OF CALIFORNIA, Davis
Masters, Economics   Bachelor of Arts, Economics, 2005
Expected completion December 2008

PROFESSIONAL BACKGROUND

CONFIDENTIAL, San Jose, CA   2006 – 2008
Installer of wet and dry underground utilities for new developers and municipalities

Project Manager
- Managed $3.6M project to install new underground dry utilities and new street lights on Main Street in Santa Cruz. Worked with city, PG&E, telephone and cable companies. Project took approximately 1-1/2 years for planning, execution, and completion. Averaged approximately 15 full-time crew, including both union and non-union.

INDEPENDENT CONTRACTOR   2005, 2006
DAVÉ CONSTRUCTION   2005
Residential and investment property new construction and renovation

Construction Manager / Project Manager
- Functioned as general contractor for construction of new $2M, 4,700 sq. foot residential property. Hired and managed approximately 300 subcontractors and vendors over the course of the project.
- Obtained building permits, and worked with general contractors and clients on architectural plans. Oversaw daily construction, and handled accounting, including paying all subcontractors.
- Worked with owner to convert 1,000 sq. foot home to 3,200 sq. feet. Same duties noted as above. Sale of home resulted in net profit of almost $400K for property owner.

RISK MANAGEMENT SOLUTIONS (RMS), Newark, CA
Global provider of expertise to manage catastrophic risk
Software Upgrade Aide   Summer 2001
Accounts Receivable Clerk   Summer 2000

LEADERSHIP EXPERIENCE

PHI DELTA THETA, Davis, CA   2000 – 2005, Consecutively

President / Vice President / House Manager / Treasurer

Financial Manager

You read this résumé and immediately know that the career direction is no accident.
I fully expect to see this focused young professional submitting
a résumé for a VP position within twelve years.

Norman Stanley

5555 Ficus Lane #555
Los Angeles, California 90049

(310) 555-5555
nstanley@email.com

Target Positions—FINANCIAL SALES / PORTFOLIO MANAGEMENT
Strengths in Research / Analysis / Client Relations / Financial Planning

RECENT GRADUATE with demonstrated leadership strengths and proven ability to manage multiple responsibilities in a fast-paced environment with critical deadlines… Worked throughout college to partially self-finance education… Well organized with attention to detail… Works well independently as well as collaboratively in a team setting… Proven ability to "think outside the box" in identifying problems and implementing innovative solutions.

——*Areas of Strength*——

Sales & Market Research & Analysis • Competitive Intelligence • Strategic Planning • Project Management
Budget Management • Team Building & Leadership • E-commerce • Website Maintenance

EDUCATION
UNIVERSITY OF SOUTHERN CALIFORNIA, Los Angeles, CA; 12/ 2007
Bachelor of Science in Business Economics; Minor in Accounting
GPA: 3.8

Activities: Treasurer—Alpha Beta Gamma Fraternity… President—Student Accounting Society…
Vice President—Business-Economics Society

PROFESSIONAL EXPERIENCE

PORTER WARNER, INC., Century City, CA • Jan. 2006 to Nov 2007—*Concurrent with Studies*

Portfolio Manager / Finance Assistant to Senior Portfolio Managers
Set up and managed client accounts to ensure compliance with established policies and procedures. Collaborated with other financial institutions to facilitate money and account transfers. Conducted in-depth research utilizing Internet, Bloomberg, and direct corporate contact, etc.

- Implemented and maintained detailed database to accurately track clients and prospects.
- Streamlined client communication process.
- Collaborated with support staff to maintain account compliance and reduce missing documents.

INTERNAL REVENUE SERVICE, Los Angeles, CA • 2005, 2006, 2007 *(Tax Seasons)*

Volunteer Income Tax Assistance (V.I.T.A.)
Prepared income tax returns for low-income families and students; provided step-by-step instruction to guide taxpayers in filling out future returns.

ZEMAN & YOUNG, C.P.A.'s, INC., Los Angeles, CA • Oct. 2004 to Jan. 2006 *(Concurrent with Studies)*

Jr. Accountant
Prepared individual and corporate income tax returns; audited company records to identify fraud; investigated, compiled, and summarized data to support records for IRS audit.
- Maintained client books through financial statement preparation.
- Prepared investment proposal for start-up company.

Previous Experience: Camp Counselor *(Summers 2001 to 2003)*

Computer Skills—Microsoft Word, Excel, PowerPoint, Access, Outlook, Peachtree, QuickBooks, Turbo Tax
Foreign Languages—Proficient in Oral and Written Spanish, including business terminology
Community Activities—Little League Coach, Big Brothers

General Ledger Accountant

Powerful punch on the first page. The résumé's organization gives fast access to the credentials of someone who clearly lives up to the target job title.

CURTIS SMITH

Confidential, CA   curtis.smith@comcast.net   C: 999.999.9999

EXPERIENCED GENERAL LEDGER ACCOUNTANT

Strong general ledger experience supported by accounts payable background. Takes leadership role in systems conversions, process improvement, and establishing better vendor relations. Communicates well with team members, purchasing department, and operations employees.

Selected Career Accomplishments – Confidential Corporation

- Team Lead in successful 1-1/2 year conversion to global SAP Purchase to Pay module.
- Reconciled $3.2M vendor discrepancy that was over one year old by working closely with another confidential location in the Netherlands. Researched and reviewed every individual invoice and payment, and corrected each transaction that had not been properly recorded.
- Eliminated significant backlog of past-due invoices, including establishing improved procedures to prevent future problems. Rebuilt vendor relations.

CORE COMPETENCIES

General Accounting

Accounts Receivable	Internal Controls
Billing	Intercompany Accounts
Bank Deposits	Inventory Control
Bank Statement Reconciliations	Journal Entries / Accruals
Budget Analysis – Cost Centers	Master Data: Vendors, Materials, Sources
Cash Applications	Month End Close
Cashier – Cash Controls	Payroll Processing
Fixed Assets	Staff Training

Accounts Payable

Account Reconciliations	Procurement Procedures
Credit Cards / Employee Expenses	Sales / Use Tax Returns
Full-Cycle Accounts Payable	Systems Conversion (SAP)
Invoice Discrepancy Resolution	Vendor Relations
Payment Monitoring / Verification	Wire Transfers

PROFESSIONAL BACKGROUND

CONFIDENTIAL CORPORATION, Anywhere, CA   **2001 – 2007**

Global supplier of confidential products and services
General Ledger Accounting Specialist, 2004 – 2007
Balance Sheet: Reconciled all accounts and subsidiary ledgers, including accounts payable, accounts receivable, and fixed assets.
Intercompany: Invoiced and reconciled for both domestic and international company locations.
Month End Close: Prepared reconciling and recurring journal entries. Compared cost center budgets to actual.
Fixed Assets: Tracked construction-in-progress and capitalized assets in accordance with GAAP.
Accounts Receivable: Assisted all functions, including cash applications and reconciling customer accounts.

Finance, Banking, and Insurance

SPECIAL PROJECT, SAP IMPLEMENTATION, 2005 – 2007
Team Lead – **Purchase to Pay:** Managed two other staff for successful implementation of Purchase to Pay process for SAP conversion.

Master Data: Set up and implemented Master Data accounts, including vendor, material, Product Information Record (PIR), and source listings.

Process Implementation and Documentation: Incorporated and revised existing purchasing and subcontracting processes into new system. Trained other team members.
Key User – General Accounting and Controlling: Resource for reviewing master data for general ledger setup. Assisted with GL account mapping for reporting and financial statement consolidation. Assisted users with cost center accounting. Assisted in transfer of accounts receivable and accounts payable to shared services department.

ACCOUNTS PAYABLE SPECIALIST, 2001 – 2004
Full-Cycle Payables: Handled all aspects of accounts payable, including general ledger coding.
Processed 100 checks per week, $2.5M per month.

Vendor Relations: Eliminated significant backlog for processing vendor and freight invoices that happened with job predecessor. Improved vendor relations by bringing payables up-to-date.
Process Improvement: Streamlined process for accounts payable invoices. Implemented effective Excel report to keep track of discrepant invoices.

ISYS MANUFACTURING, INC., Concord, CA   **1998 – 2001**
$50M manufacturer of electronic components for semiconductor industry

ACCOUNTING CLERK
Payroll: Processed full-cycle payroll for 130 salaried and hourly employees.

Accounts Payable: Performed lead role for full-cycle accounts payable with approximately 100 weekly checks.
Accounts Receivable: Handled full-cycle accounts receivable including billing, cash applications, labor applications, and general ledger entries.
Inventory Control: Tracked parts and finished goods inventory worth approximately $5M. Implemented improved procedures for shipping and receiving.

ORCHARD SUPPLY HARDWARE, Concord, CA   **1996 – 1998**

CASHIER INSTRUCTOR / BACKUP CUSTOMER SERVICE
Managed front-end store operations. Trained and scheduled all cashiers.

TECHNICAL EXPERIENCE

Microsoft: Word, Excel, PowerPoint
Applications: *SAP:* Vendor, Purchasing
        PRMS: Accounts Payable, Accounts Receivable, Vendors, Customer Masters, Journal Entries
        Payroll: ADP
        Other: MAS90, FAS Fixed Asset Software, T Rowe Price 401k system, Lotus Notes

Insurance Claims Adjuster

Career change résumé from police to insurance. Notice the target job is one in which many extant skills are transferable.

Andrew Moore, M.S.

H: 777-777-7777
Anywhere, NC

C: 999-999-9999
andrewmoore@anyserver.com

QUALIFICATIONS FOR INSURANCE CLAIMS ADJUSTER

Logical and analytical approach to identifying and resolving situations with high potential for conflict. Organized and creative, with solid approach to comprehensive information gathering.
Good listening skills, empathy, experience in negotiations, and ability to develop trust and open communication. Calm under pressure. Good balance between people and task orientation.
Committed to combining law enforcement background with education and training in leadership and organizational change.

CORE COMPETENCIES

- Conflict Resolution
- Courtroom Representation
- Incident Documentation
- Investigative Techniques

- Legal Compliance
- Needs Assessment
- Negotiating Techniques
- One-on-One Training

- Report Writing
- Risk Assessment
- Safety Principles
- Witness Questioning

EDUCATION

Pfeiffer University, Charlotte, NC
Masters of Science, Leadership and Organizational Change
Bachelors of Science, Criminal Justice

POLICE OFFICER BACKGROUND

ANY TOWN, North Carolina	2002 – 2003
ANOTHER TOWN, North Carolina	2001 – 2002
ANY CITY, North Carolina	1995 – 1999
ANOTHER CITY, North Carolina	1994 – 1995

ADDITIONAL BACKGROUND

ACADEMIC SABBATICAL	2003 – 2008
DS ATLANTIC CORP, Winston-Salem, NC	1999 – 2000
Instrument Operator	

PROFESSIONAL TRAINING

Selected in-service training, classes, seminars, and workshops:
Police Science ~ Investigation Techniques ~ Security ~ Evasive Driving ~ Reconnaissance
Surveillance Grade Crossing Accident Investigation ~ Photography ~ Family Violence
Child Abuse Rape Crisis Evidence ~ Public Relations ~ Public Speaking ~ Communication Skills

Stanly Community College, Albemarle, NC
Information systems security coursework

Non-Profit Fundraising Consultant

Senior re-entry résumé of a retired executive targeting the non-profit sector and showing he's done his homework.

NORMAN BEACON

555 Valley Glen Ridge • Valley Glen, California 91405
Home (818) 555-1234 • Mobile (818) 555-9876 • NormanBeacon@email.com

PUBLIC RELATIONS / COMMUNITY / FUNDRAISING CONSULTANT— NONPROFIT SECTOR

- Retired Corporate Executive, committed to providing expertise in communications to promote the public good.
- Combines distinguished career building and leading successful company growth with extensive background contributing efforts to charitable causes.
- Proven strengths in the fine art of communications and negotiations with the ability to establish confidence and trust, resolve conflicts, build consensus, and motivate parties with divergent opinions toward common goals.
- Excellent listening skills with focus on a "win/win" philosophy.
- Extensive network of contacts.

Verifiable Record of Raising Significant Amounts of Money for Charitable and Public Causes

PROFESSIONAL BACKGROUND

Personal Sabbatical—Travel, Community Involvement • 2006 to Present

WEST COAST SPECIALTY CONFECTIONS, Los Angeles, CA

Managing Partner / Chief Operating Officer • 1982 to 2006

Launched and directed activities of confectionary manufacturing company from start-up through 20 years of successful operations.

- Built business from initial capital investment of $10,000 to annual revenues in excess of $40 million.
- Established and nurtured key contacts with retail and wholesale operations on local, regional, and national level including major chain stores.
- Sourced vendors and contractors and directed manufacturing operations in U.S. and abroad.
- Negotiated with union and non-union personnel, consistently achieving a win/win outcome.
- Generated widespread goodwill for company though extensive, ongoing involvement with numerous community charitable organizations. Recognized by city for contributions.
- Named "Local Business of the Year" by *Valley Glen Business Journal.*

EDUCATION

B.A. in Humanities, UNIVERSITY OF CALIFORNIA, Los Angeles

COMMUNITY ACTIVITIES —Partial List

Fundraising Chair—Friends of Valley Glen Hospital
Platinum Donor, Chair of Steering Committee—Valley Glen Youth Association
Member, Past-Officer—Valley Glen Chamber of Commerce
Member, Board of Directors—Neighborhood Youth Industries, Inc.
President—Valley Arms Homeowners Association

ADDITIONAL INFORMATION

Foreign Languages—Fluent in Spanish
Computer Skills—PC and Mac Proficient on Microsoft Office Suite
Military—United States Army, Honorable Discharge
Activities & Hobbies—Los Angeles Marathon (annually since 1995), Golf, TennisEvent Planner

Event Planner

George wanted a job closer to home. Some of his past job titles did not fit with his career aspirations, and he wanted to focus on the specific skills needed for an Events Manager, so he used a functional style format.

George S. Easton
12 Lee Street, Middleburg, VA 20118
540-555-5470

PROFILE SUMMARY
Meeting Planning ▪ *Conferences* ▪ *International Events* ▪ *Fundraising* ▪ *Golf Tournaments*

Creative professional with expertise in all aspects of successful event/program planning, development, and management. Excel in managing multiple projects concurrently with strong detail, problem-solving, and follow-through capabilities. Demonstrated ability to manage, motivate, and build cohesive teams that achieve results. Sourced vendors, negotiated contracts, and managed budgets. Superb written communications, interpersonal and organizational skills. First-class client relation and teaming skills. Proficient in Access, Excel, PowerPoint, Outlook, MS Project, Publisher, MeetingTrak, and Corel WordPerfect.

PROFESSIONAL EXPERIENCE
Meeting Planning Management

Planned and coordinated government, association, and private conferences, meetings, events, and fundraisers. Coordinated all conference activities, workshops, meetings, tours, and special events. Trained, directed, and supervised teams to accomplish goals. **Saved $72,000 on most recent meeting.**

- As Team Leader, coordinated 10-26 annual workshops for Centers for Disease Control and Prevention.
- Coordinated 2004 National Conference on Smoking and Health. (2,000 participants)
- Organized 6,000-participant national annual conferences.
- Coordinated Global Scholarship Pre-Conference Training for 200 third-world participants.
- Developed and supervised education sessions at CSI's 2001 National Convention.
- Directed CSI's National Seminar Series.

Meeting Coordination

As Team Leader, coordinated production, distribution, and grading of exam materials. Supervised registration and tracking of continuing education units. Negotiated hotel and vendor contracts. Prepared and administered budgets. Arranged all on-site logistics, including transportation, accommodations, meals, guest speakers, and audiovisual support. **Consistently come under budget for each meeting planned.**

- Developed and maintained 5,000-person database.
- Developed, promoted, and implemented CSI's National Certification Program.
- Managed logistics for a Regional Pacific Training in Guam.

Fundraising

Team player in the development, promotion, and implementation of membership and retention programs for BUILD-PAC. Coordinated PAC fundraising events. Supervised high-donor club fulfillment benefits. Provided updated donor reports.

- Coordinated 2 PAC fundraising golf tournaments.

EVENTS MANAGEMENT EXPERIENCE
Conferences / Meetings / Program Coordinator   1997–Present

- Centers for Disease Control and Prevention/Office on Smoking & Health
- Tobacco Control Training & Technical Assistance Project
- Health & Human Services Department's Administration on Children, Youth and Families Grant Review Contract
- Food and Drug Administration
- Centers for Disease Control and Prevention/National Center for Health Statistics
- National Library of Medicine
- Housing & Urban Development Grant Review Contract
- CSI National Seminar Series
- CSI 1998 & 1999 National Conventions and Exhibits

PROFESSIONAL EMPLOYMENT
CORPORATE SCIENCES ■ Rockville, Maryland   2003–Present
Senior Conference Specialist

ROCKVILLE CONSULTING GROUP ■ Arlington, Virginia   2000–2003
Logistics Manager
Senior Conference Coordinator

CONSTRUCTION SPECIALISTS ASSOCIATION ■ Arlington, Virginia   1997–1999
Assistant Coordinator of Education Programs

NATIONAL ASSOCIATION OF PIPE WELDERS ■ Washington, D.C.   1997
Assistant Director, Fundraising

EDUCATION & CERTIFICATIONS
VIRGINIA POLYTECHNIC INSTITUTE & STATE UNIVERSITY ■ Blacksburg, VA
B.S. Exercise Physiology ■ 1996
Minor Psychology

Go Members Inc. MeetingTrak Certification ■ 2004

Certified Meeting Professional (CMP) – Pending Jan. 2005

PROFESSIONAL AFFILIATIONS
- Meeting Professionals International – Annandale Chapter (AMPI)
- Logistical Committee
- Educational Retreat Committee
- Member Services Committee
- Community Outreach Committee
- Connected International Meeting Professionals Association (CIMPA)
- DC Special Olympics – Volunteer
- Hands On DC – Volunteer
- SPCA of Northern Virginia – Volunteer

Publicist

This entry-level résumé positions the writer well for a position
in publicity and communications.

ANNIE SANCHEZ

5555 Lotus Drive • Encino, California 91436

(818) 555-1234 • AnnieSanchez@email.com

Recent Graduate Qualified for Positions in Publishing/Marketing
—Gained Valuable Experience as Publishing & Marketing Intern for Three Summers—

* Hard working and energetic with a proven ability to produce results in a fast-paced environment with critical deadlines. Outgoing and articulate communicator who works well with
  public and coworkers at all levels.
* Equally effective collaborating in a team setting as well as working independently.
* Learns quickly and enjoys challenges.

Strengths Include: Writing... Research & Analysis...
Problem Solving & Troubleshooting... Presentations

EDUCATION

Bachelor of Arts in Mass Communications; Minor in Journalism
UNIVERSITY OF CALIFORNIA, Los Angeles, CA; May 2008

PROFESSIONAL EXPERIENCE

DYNAMIC PUBLICATIONS/*SPORTS TODAY* MAGAZINE, Hollywood, CA • Summers 2006–2007
Assistant / Intern
Worked closely with Editor-in-Chief and Fashion Editor of teen-oriented magazine publication.
Prioritized and coordinated multiple assignments including transcriptions, research and follow-up.
Contributed story ideas that resulted in publication.
* Provided hands-on assistance to Fashion Editor at photo shoots. Contacted leading
  manufacturers to obtain sample merchandise; organized clothing for shoots; assisted with
  overall styling.
* Wrote articles for fashion feature of magazine. Arranged photo shoots for article including
  selecting locations and arranging staff housing. Attended editorial staff meetings, providing
  input on story.
* Contributed ideas for fitness feature. Wrote captions, explaining new trends in fitness
  training.

HOLLYWOOD MARKETING ASSOCIATES, Los Angeles, CA • Sept. 2005–May 2006
Assistant to Executive Vice President—Southern California Office
Gained valuable hands-on experience with national marketing and public relations organization.
* Provided broad range of assistance to Vice President in charge of Los Angeles office.
* Performed computer work, hosted clients, scheduled appointments, etc.
* Assembled press kits and EPK's.

MEDIA MANAGEMENT PROS, Los Angeles, CA • Summer 2004
Production Assistant
Assisted in coordinating makeup and wardrobe for television commercial productions.
* Coordinated wardrobe selections with set decorators.
* Arranged specific selections and appropriate sizes for individual models.
* Assisted location scout with identifying appropriate locations and negotiating fees.

ADDITIONAL INFORMATION

Computer Skills—Microsoft Office (Word, Excel, PowerPoint, Outlook), WordPerfect, Internet, E-mail
Foreign Languages—Bilingual English/Spanish

Human Resources

Joseph is someone with a psychology education transitioning into Human Resources.

JOSEPH D. MORTEN

167 HELMAN LANE • BRIDGEWATER, NEW JERSEY 08807
908.555.5555 (H) • 908.444.4444 (FAX) • JMORTEN439@AOL.COM

HUMAN RESOURCES / CORPORATE TRAINING
Supervision ~ Business Management ~ Employee Relations ~ Coaching

Energetic, reliable, and adaptable professional with a solid understanding of human resources, business operations, and various corporate environments. Proven abilities in creatively identifying methods for improving staff productivity and organizational behavior. Recognized for ability to incorporate innovative management techniques into a multicultural workforce.

Results-oriented professional with excellent communication and interpersonal skills. Accurately perform challenging tasks with precision and attention to detail. Excel at organizing and setting up new procedures, troubleshooting, and taking adverse situations and making them positive.

Competencies Include:
- Human Resources Management
- Operations Management
- Team building/Leadership
- Organizational & Project Management

- Training & Development
- Staffing Requirements
- Problem Resolution
- Employee Scheduling

Professional Experience

Waste Removal, *Plainfield, NJ (August 2000 – September 2005)*
CFA Administrator
Waste Removal is the nation's largest full-service waste removal/disposal company
- Maintained and monitored multiple databases for more than 120 pieces of equipment in the trucking company inventory.
- Generated accurate reports of budgets, repair costs, and personnel scheduling.
- Dramatically improved maintenance shop productivity through close budget monitoring.
- Served as a key link between management and mechanics, utilizing excellent interpersonal and communications skills. Acknowledged for improving the overall flow of information throughout the organization.
- Initiated, planned, and managed the implementation of high-turn inventory management systems and procedures. The new inventory system was credited with improving the operation of a very high-volume parts operation.
- Assumed a leadership role in the company by completely reorganizing the physical inventory process to assure greater accuracy and system integrity.
- Managed the successful integration of two new parts operations, turning a possible negative situation into a very positive one.

Easy Video Entertainment, *Colonia, NJ (March 1997 – August 2000)*
Store Manager
Retail video rental and sales chain with over 600 outlets and 5,000 employees worldwide
- Managed all daily store operations including a staff of 5 employees. Responsible for recruitment, hiring, firing, training, and scheduling of all staff members.
- Ability to train and motivate staff to maximize productivity, and control costs with hands-on management and close monitoring of store budgets.
- Attained a 25% increase in sales over a 12-month period, leading all 45 stores in the district. The store ranked 40th in overall sales volume of the 600 stores in the company.
- Maintained a consistent Top 20 ranking for sales of high-profit coupon books.
- Used excellent leadership, team building, and communication skills to develop subordinates and encourage cooperation and responsibility. Ensured compliance with corporate HR programs.
- Developed and implemented creative and aggressive promotional techniques that resulted in the store consistently exceeding its sales goals.

Education

BA ~ Psychology, FAIRLEIGH DICKINSON UNIVERSITY, Madison, NJ

Trainer

Casandra lost her job and needed to move into a higher-level position for increased compensation. She did not have a college degree, so highlighting her skills helped employers get a quick overview of her many talents . . . and it worked!

CASANDRA B. JEELES

555 Riverside Drive • Houston, Texas 77027
713-555-1234 • casbjeeles@bxy.net

PROFESSIONAL OBJECTIVE

Training/Performance Development

PROFESSIONAL PROFILE

- Proven leadership and supervisory experience with ability to lead multiple projects/teams simultaneously.
- Outstanding project planning and project management skills, meeting tight time constraints/deadlines.
- Solutions-driven manager, mentor, and coach who relates well with all types of people at all levels.
- Strong organizational and analytical abilities applied to achieve desired goals, objectives, and results.
- Unwavering commitment to excellence in building teams who are best of the best in serving others.
- Personal traits: professional; common sense; adaptability; focused; skilled trainer and team builder.

CORE COMPETENCIES

Passion for Customer Care Excellence:
- Instill a philosophy of immediate response to customer inquiries – no such thing as "do it tomorrow."
- Value each individual customer, exceeding expectations and paying diligent attention to small details.
- Act and serve with integrity and trust, essential ingredients for successful, long-lasting customer relations.
- Create an environment where customers are ecstatic with service, creating action-oriented advocates.

Motivating and Training:
- Analyze company culture and structure to pinpoint obstacles and create new pathways or adopt existing model to build an environment of solutions and forward movement.
- Recognize hidden solutions, already existing or external, through research, active listening, observation.
- Help personalize company vision and goals by implementing strategies to create ownership/advocates.
- Analyze and monitor sales figures and statistics to establish firm foundation for future growth.
- Identify the extraordinary among the team, systems, and practices and build upon strengths.

Team Building:
- *"My job is to make the team successful"* – accomplished by coaching, nurturing, and stretching to reach beyond an individual's comfort zone to maximize personal/professional excellence.
- Discover talents/gifts of individual team members and build upon those to maximize results.
- Create an environment to link team members' strengths as the beginning of all endeavors.
- Capitalize on company structure, budgets, and timelines to build a *"let's do it"* framework.

Managing and Supervising:
- Orchestrate a team, discover core values of individual members, and build consensus of goals.
- Analyze budgets and expenditures to align with company vision, mission, and direction.
- Automate and systematize rote and mundane functions to improve operating efficiencies.

Solutions Oriented – Analysis to Action:
- Thrive on converting obstacles into opportunities by recognizing root cause and developing solutions.
- Structure work environment where fear, failure, and blame are not responses and/or defenses.
- Incorporate active listening to unravel challenges and rebuild – be it systems, technology, or people.

EXPERIENCE / EDUCATION

- Inside Sales/Assistant to Director – Strigle, Inc., Houston, Texas, 2002–2006
- Senior Executive Club/Top Sales – Halley Distribution, Inc., Midland, Texas, 1994–2002
- Various administrative roles, Houston, Texas, 1989–1994
- Numerous leadership, management, and customer relations courses – company sponsored, 1986–2006

Operations/Human Resources Manager

Jason needed to transition from seasonal work with national fairs into a more traditional management career.

JASON CHAMBERS

1234 Main Street • Anaheim, California 55555
Home: (714) 555-5555 • Cellular: (714) 555-5551 • jchambers@chambers.com

Management Professional
Operations / Human Resources / Labor Relations / Staff Development

Dedicated organizational manager with track record of assuming positions of increased accountability. Background includes experience in industrial food service (world exposition food service management), restaurants, and catering. Proven leadership skills—able to recruit, retain, develop, and motivate employees to new levels of productivity. Communicate successfully and productively to any and all types of people. Excellent problem solver. Strong team orientation. Accomplished public speaker.

Core competencies include:

Verbal/Written Communications	Performance Evaluations	Prospective Employee Interviews
Relationship Building/Facilitation	Promotional Programs	Interpersonal Skills
Program Development	Policy Creation	Contract Negotiations

Particular Expertise in Boosting Profitability by Maximizing Sales and Reducing Costs

Employment History

XYZ EXPOSITION SERVICES-Costa Mesa, California   1989–2006
Leading provider of food service logistics and restaurant operations for world fairs and expositions.

Director of Personnel, Labor, and Human Resources / General Operations Manager
- 2005 French National Fair Exposition-Paris, France
- 2001 World Fair Exposition-Biel, Switzerland

Accountable for all phases of personnel management—hiring, staff development, evaluation, promotion, and separations. Created general employee contracts and work policy manuals. Controlled labor costs by optimizing staffing requirements according to customer visitations and by monitoring break times, clock-in/out accuracy, and on-the-clock productivity. Developed and monitored customer service systems. Created working relationships with government officials in European Union. Procured visas for core team members. Secured expo accreditation passes for all company employees.

Directed activities of all managers and assistant managers in supervision of multiple locations (8 in France, 10 in Switzerland) and up to 280 food service and facilities maintenance personnel. Also oversaw one beverage director to ensure full stocking and successful operating of all restaurants, bars, and food concessions. Reported directly to CEO.

Selected Contributions (French National Fair)
- Initiated full-scale recruitment of host-country hotel school interns. Secured a group of motivated general employees who were paid 20% less by law.
- Cut additional labor costs from 27% to 20%, significantly increasing net profit to investors. Company grossed $8.5 million in 6 months of operation.
- Streamlined staffing needs by re-engineering food service stations, allowing employees to multi-task.
- Discovered thousands of overpaid dollars by auditing every paycheck for inaccuracies.
- Increased sales in Mexican food concession. Designed innovative ticket system to reduce line wait. Simultaneously eliminated loss of impatient customer sales and boosted service capacity.
- Successfully interpreted and complied with all host country labor laws and regulations. Faced comprehensive labor policy audit by host country's top labor official. Passed with flying colors.

Selected Contributions (World Fair, Switzerland)
- Streamlined staffing needs by designing employee multi-task and partnership system.
- Discovered and broke multiple-employee theft ring at two separate concessions.

- Played key role in company meeting exposition revenue goals (grossed $11.25 million in 6 months with only 9 concessions) by facilitating open and productive communication with management-level and general employees.
- Became conversant with Swiss labor laws, culture, and practices. Resulted in productive, lasting international business relationships.

Operations Consultant
- 2007 Canadian National Fair Exposition-Vancouver, B.C., Canada *preparation in progress
- 1995 World Exposition-Osaka, Japan
- 1989 World Exposition-Lisbon, Portugal

Participated in formulation of management structure, labor policies, employee handbook, management and employee training handbook, and operating guidelines in preparation for expo.

GOURMET FOODS, INC.-Costa Mesa, California   1998–1999, 2002–2004, 2006

General Manager
Monitor customer service levels, employee performance, and labor costs. Track and evaluate daily sales. Responsible for prospective employee interviewing and hiring. Teach and facilitate communication skills. Supervise up to 50, including concession managers, counter help, cooks, and cashiers for 4 locations.

Selected Accomplishments
- Launched innovative ongoing promotions.

    ✓ Costa Mesa police and fire department discount program.
    ✓ Home-meal and catering menu program.
    ✓ "Daily Special" program.

- Improved customer service levels by retraining employees in the following areas: quick/personal attention to customers, cleaning without turning backs to customers, and interpersonal communication skills.

WORLD GYM-Anaheim, California   1989–1992

Sales Representative/Personal Trainer
Performed membership sales. Helped customers achieve fitness goals.

ZAURUS PIZZA-Costa Mesa, California   1986–1988

Assistant Operations Manager
Promoted from positions as counter help/delivery to oversee operations of 4 stores. Supervised roughly 70, including store managers, counter help, cooks, delivery personnel, cashiers, and dishwashers. Ensured store cleanliness, product availability and timely delivery, and customer satisfaction.

Computer Skills/Foreign Languages

Internet (Netscape Navigator, Internet Explorer)
E-Mail (Outlook, Outlook Express)
MS Word, Excel

Beginning Conversational French

Purchasing Director

Peter's résumé was shortened from a four-page résumé which listed 30+ bullets outlining responsibilities for each job, and no impact/achievements/value-add.

PETER M. RABBIT
333 Court Hill ▪ Underhill, NY 11111
(H) 111.111.1111 ▪ (C) 111.111.1111
ptrrbt@aol.com

PURCHASING DIRECTOR
SENIOR PROJECT MANAGER
SENIOR OPERATIONS MANAGER

Professional Summary

Driven operations leader offers extensive hands-on experience and a consistent track record in **exceeding goals** for large-scale domestic and international capital projects, **fostering growth** and **delivering strong and sustainable gains**. A self-starter with a proven ability to conceptualize and implement **innovative solutions**. **Technologically competent,** past achievements demonstrate a clear ability to utilize new, **cutting-edge technologies** as a means of updating processes/systems. **Highly effective leadership and motivating skills** support the development of cohesive teams (union and non-union) in the collaborative achievement of strategic goals. **Extensive experience** partnering with influential business leaders within successful organizations.

▪ CORE COMPETENCIES ▪

Business Planning	Financial Analysis	Quality Assurance
Business Process Re-engineering	Influencing Skills	ERP/MRP
Contracts Administration	Negotiation Skills	Supplier/Vendor Management
Cost Containment	Logistics Management	Systems Implementation
Efficiency Improvement	Project Management	Warehouse Management

Selected Achievements

- Initiated the development of a **first-ever computerized purchasing/inventory system** for the Newspaper Company resulting in substantial reductions on labor and materials costs; these improvements resulted in a request for support in the implementation of the system from the USA-based Newspaper. Subsequently consulted on the second successful implementation.
- **Reduced operating costs by $500,000 per year** by outsourcing an "in-house" printing department.
- Provided comprehensive capital procurement services for the **$300 million construction and start-up of two large daily newspaper printing press facilities.**
- **Significantly increased waste recycling revenues by $545,000 per year** through successful negotiations with individual recycling firms.
- Directed an **operating budget of over $180 million** during construction and operations of the **Famous World Exhibition.**
- Initiated the development and implementation of a **first-ever budget tracking and reporting system in support of a $90 million capital project**; this system accelerated the project's successful completion—**90 days ahead of schedule and $1 million under budget.**
- Shortly after assuming responsibility for Security operations, **reduced in-house theft, drug and alcohol abuse by 99%, while reducing costs $100,000 per year.**

Relevant Experience

Independent Consulting
2005 to Present
- **Sourced and introduced a comprehensive, cutting-edge finance management software solution,** which enabled a $5 million business to more effectively manage sales, inventory, and distribution.
- Established warehouse management procedures, facilitating highly effective **inventory planning and control** practices; **trained and coached warehouse crew.**
- Established the foundation for a **fully integrated logistics management function** consolidating inventory, warehousing, and distribution.

NEWSPAPER COMPANY, Manager, Procurement & Security
1991 to 2005
*Hired as Assistant Manager of Purchasing. Quickly demonstrated **aggressive turnaround management capability,** resulting in **significant increases in responsibility**—Fleet, Security, Facilities, and $40 million in newsprint inventories.*
- Established clear processes and procedures, and **centralized purchasing and inventory management** via first-ever electronic system in the southern newspaper system, **reducing costs by $500,000/year.**

- Introduced new technologies resulting in **increased efficiencies and cost-savings**; technologies included fax services and color scanning, which increased turnaround in ad presentation and makeup and **saved $125,000/year**.
- **Reduced annual operating costs by $500,000/year through offshore purchasing and vendor partnerships.**
- Successfully **sourced national and international vendors, negotiated and administered contracts** and executed **procurement strategies** on several large-scale capital projects: Development of a new $60 million facility; $97 million development project for implementation of new printing processes.
- **Directed international sourcing and managed logistics,** which included customs documentation and inspections.
- Served as **Project Manager in the design of a waste management system,** providing detailed specifications and managing project activities; **generated a significant increase in revenue.**
- **Overhauled the Security function**—outsourcing, modernizing equipment, establishing and training contract staff on new procedures and roles; significantly reduced costs, and nearly eliminated all incidences of theft.
- **Initiated and implemented the "pay in advance" system**—now used internationally among all newspapers—which contributed to a significant increase in revenue.
- **Revamped First Aid and Safety program,** and **implemented Assassination Protection Program.**
- Managed sale of assets from old facilities, building deconstruction, and **seamless relocation of 900 employees.**

WORLD EXHIBITION, Manager, Site Operations Procurement   **1987 to 1991**
World Exhibition's 6-month World Fair exhibition is orchestrated and attended by over 70 countries, each with its own on-site pavilion. Managed comprehensive procurement services for construction and start-up of operations. Held signatory responsibility for all purchases, and spearheaded profitable vendor partnerships.

- **Hired and established a procurement team and introduced new technology,** which facilitated shared communications and increased procurement and materials handling efficiencies; Successfully managed procurement activities throughout liquidation and site deconstruction.
- **Orchestrated first-ever buyback contracts** for heavy equipment and machinery utilized by the Exhibition, regaining a full 50% of the initial purchase price; negotiated and received free maintenance, providing additional cost savings; **negotiated service contracts** for site equipment and operations.
- **Demonstrated creative problem-solving skills,** which enhanced operations ability to provide ongoing entertainment, while significantly reducing operating costs.

PAPER COMPANY, Project Budget Controller/Buyer   **1984 to 1987**
Provided project support for a $90 million operations implementation.

- **Led the development of an innovative financial tracking and control system.**
- **Controlled spending and ensured consistent use of the system, enabling a perfectly balanced budget.**
- Identified an opportunity to apply for a tax break, **saving an additional $600,000** at project's end.

Previous Experience

BIGWIG COMPANY, Project Expeditor, 1982–1984
CHEMICAL COMPANY A, Project Buyer, 1981–1982
CHEMICAL COMPANY B, Project Buyer/Expeditor, 1979–1981
BIG DOG COMPANY, Materials Supervisor, 1978–1979

Technologies

Accpac, Crystal Report Builder, Dun & Bradstreet, EDI, Microsoft Office, Purchase Soft, RAL, Visio

Professional Development

North American Newspaper Purchasing Association
American Society for Industrial Security
School Institute: Business/Marketing Management Diploma

Peter M. Rabbit, page 2.

Logistics Manager

A powerful combination résumé that demonstrates a virtuoso grasp
of the supply chain function. Any employer with needs in this area
and at this level would want to talk to a person with these skills.

John William Wisher, MBA

**Expert leadership in cost-effective supply chain, vendor,
and project management within *Fortune* organizations.**

▤ 630.555.2653 ☎ 630.555.9117

2541 Bainbridge Blvd.
West Chicago, IL 60185
jwisher@ameritech.net

EXECUTIVE PROFILE

*A visionary, forward-thinking SUPPLY CHAIN AND LOGISTICS LEADER offering 20+ years of progressive
growth and outstanding success streamlining operations across a wide range of industries. Excellent
negotiation and relationship management skills with ability to inspire teams to outperform expectations. Proven record of delivering a synchronized supply chain approach through strategic models
closely mirroring business plan to dramatically optimize ROI and manage risk.*

Trust-Based Leadership *Vendor/Client Negotiations* *Cross-Functional Collaboration* *Supply Chain Mapping* *Financial Logistics Analysis*	**Supply Chain Strategy:** Successfully led over 500 supply chain management initiatives across a wide spectrum of businesses, negotiating agreements from $5K to $27M. Implemented technology solutions and streamlined processes to reduce redundancies and staffing hours, improving both efficiency and productivity. Industries include; automotive and industrial manufacturing, consumer goods, government and defense, healthcare, high-tech, and retail. **Industry Knowledge:** Extensive knowledge base developed from hands-on industry experience. Began career in dock operations with experience in Hub and Package Operations, multi-site retail operations management, to custom supply chain strategy development over 21-year career with UPS.
Contingency Planning *Risk Management* *Competitive Analysis* *Haz Mat Compliance*	**Supply Chain Process Costing:** Built several information packets on total cost of ownership (TCO) and facilitated several C-level negotiations to identify and confirm opportunities. Worked to increase awareness among stakeholders of efficiencies and cost-saving measures' ROI. Delivered $3.75M total cost savings to client base over three-year period. **Operations Re-organization:** Designed and implemented new sales force alignment and reporting structure; increased daily sales calls by 20%, reduced travel mileage 23%, and head count by nine; total annual cost savings of $920K.
Inventory Planning, Control, & Distribution *Recruiting/Training/ Development* *Project Management*	**Logistics:** Experienced across all modes of transportation; ocean, air freight, LTL, TL, mail services, and small package. Performs complex analysis to develop strategy based on cost and delivery requirements. **Project Management:** Implemented complete $1.2M redesign of 11 new UPS Customer Centers. Managed vendor and lease negotiations, developed budgets, training, and sales structure. All 11 centers up and operational on time and on budget.

Organizational Change Management	**Cost & Process Improvements:**
Distributive Computing	▸ Implemented complete warehouse redesign for a large optical distributor. Optimized warehouse operations through engineering a new warehouse design, integrating and automating technology, and synchronization of goods movement through ocean, air, ground, and mail services. Reduced transportation expense by 15%, increased production levels by 25%, reduced inventory by 15% and staffing by 20%.
Budget Management	
Labor Relations	▸ Built custom supply chain for a nationally recognized golf club manufacturer. Improved service levels by 30%, reduced damage by 45%, and integrated technology to support shipping process automation, reducing billing function staffing hours 50%.

PROFESSIONAL BACKGROUND

United Parcel Service (UPS), Addison, IL   **1986 – Present**
World's largest package delivery company and global leader in supply chain services, offering an extensive range of options for synchronizing the movement of goods, information, and funds. Serves more than 200 countries and territories worldwide and operates the largest franchise shipping chain, The UPS Store.

DIRECTOR / AREA MANAGER – SUPPLY CHAIN SALES, 2005–Present
Promoted to lead and develop a cross-functional sales force of 18 in consultative supply chain management services to Chicago-area businesses. Directs development of integrated supply chain management solutions across all modes of transportation, closely mirroring client business plans. Mentors team in Demand Responsive Model, a proven methodology to quickly align internal and external resources with changing market demands, situational requirements, and mission-critical conditions. Manages $100M P&L.

Accomplishments:
- Implements over 100 multimillion-dollar supply chain integrations per year with 14% annual growth on 8% plan.
- Develops future organizational leaders; four staff members promoted through effective mentoring and development.
- Choreographed a supply chain movement from the Pacific Rim for a global fast food chain to deliver 300k cartons to 15k locations all on the same day. Utilized modes of ocean, TL, air, and ground services, allowing for a national release synchronized to all locations on the same release date.
- Designed and implemented an automated reverse logistics program for a nationally recognized health food / supplement distributor. Automated returns process to reduce touches and costly staffing hours. Eliminated front end phone contact using technology and web automation.

MARKETING MANAGER, 2004–2005
Fast-tracked to streamline sales processes increasing performance. Performed analysis of sales territory, historical data, operations alignment, reporting structure, and sales trends to devise solutions. Managed and coached area managers in business plan development and execution of sales strategies. Delivered staff development in cost-reduction strategies and compliance requirements. Accountable for $500M P&L.

Accomplishments:
- Drove $500M+ in local market sales. Grew revenues 2004/2005 revenues 12% and 7% respectively.

RETAIL CHANNEL / OPERATIONS MANAGER, 2002–2004
Charged with turning around this underperforming business unit. Managed development and implementation of new retail strategy across northern Illinois. Re-branded UPS Customer Centers and The UPS Store. Performed vendor negotiations and collaborated with nine regions to support additional implementations.

Accomplishments:

- Developed key revenue-generating initiatives across multiple channels. Attained 65% growth in discretionary sales. Several strategies adopted across the national organization.
- Re-engineered inventory for over 1,000 drop-off locations, reduced lease expenses by 45% and inventory levels by 40% through weekly measurement, inventory level development by SKU, order process automation, and order consolidation.
- Implemented new retail sales associate structure in 1,100 locations; scored highest national service levels by mystery shoppers.
- Selected as Corporate team member on Mail Boxes Etc. acquisition integration.

PROJECT MANAGER, 2001–2002
Selected to support several underperforming business areas. Managed key segments of district business initiatives and compliance measures for 1,000 drop-off locations. Reported on status to corporate management. Supervised office staff of 16. Negotiated vendor and lease agreements.

Accomplishments:

- Rolled out and managed ongoing Haz Mat compliance program for all locations.
- Generated $6M in sales through cross-functional lead program and increased participation from 20% to 100%.
- Attained Union workforce sponsorship of support growth program through careful negotiations and persuasion.

Additional UPS Positions Include:

SENIOR ACCOUNT MANAGER, 1999–2001
Delivered $2.8M in growth on $1.1M plan, rated 3rd of 53 managers in revenue generation.

ACCOUNT MANAGER, 1997–1998
Top producer out of 53; $1.3M sales on $500K plan.

SERVICE PROVIDER, 1994–1996
Managed final service delivery to consumers; operated 378 hours under plan first year with zero accidents or injuries.

SUPERVISOR OF PACKAGE OPERATIONS, 1994
Managed 65 full-time service providers. Performed post-routine analysis, operating strategy development, compliance, payroll, service failure recovery, and new technology implementation. Met 100% DOT and Haz Mat compliance. Reduced post-delivery staffing time by 50% and missed pickups by 65%.

SUPERVISOR OF HUB OPERATIONS, 1988–1994
Managed up to 100 union employees and staff processing 75K pieces per day involving 40+ outbound bays. Performed complex staff scheduling and maintained low turnover rates. Designed new management reporting format reducing administrative time by 20% and improved load quality by 30%.

OPERATIONS DOCK WORKER AND TRAINING LEAD, 1986–1987

EDUCATION

MBA
National Louis University, Wheaton, IL, *4.0 GPA*

BA, Business, Supply Chain Management
Elmhurst College, Elmhurst, IL, *3.84 GPA, Magna cum laude*

Additional Specialized Courses:

- Supply Chain Mapping, 20 Hours
- Financial Logistics Analysis (FLOGAT), 10 Hours
- Hazardous Materials, 20 Hours
- Labor Relations, 30 Hours
- Managers Leadership School, 100 Hours
- Supervisors Leadership School, 100 Hours
- Managing from the Heart, 30 Hours

International Trade Manager

Nothing fancy, just the relevant information clearly laid out. The last four subheads at the end of the second page make this a powerful résumé from start to finish.

David M. Golden

943 Hartford Pike
Baltimore, MD 13257

(803) 555-1212 (Home)
dmgolden@yahoo.com

——— INTERNATIONAL TRADE COMPLIANCE PROFESSIONAL ———

TACTICAL MANUFACTURING OPERATIONS • INTERNATIONAL LOGISTICS • AUDITING • GLOBAL TRADE • TRANSPORTATION MANAGEMENT

Task-oriented, resourceful professional offering diversified management and leadership background highlighted by significant accomplishments governing global trade compliance. Innate ability to motivate and empower cross-functional groups to accomplish objectives and resolve complex import and export issues. Visionary and creative problem solver who controls cost and minimizes risks while simultaneously driving desired results for bottom-line profitability. Talent for analyzing business data and identifying opportunities to improve operational efficiencies and reduce ongoing expenses within domestic and international marketplaces.

——— CORE COMPETENCIES ———

- Strategic Business Planning
- Contract Negotiations
- Business Reengineering
- Regulatory, Compliance & Auditing
- Import and Export Operations
- Research and Data Management
- Transportation & Logistics
- Project Management
- Reporting & Administration

EDUCATION

Master of Business Administration—University of Southern Florida (3.7 GPA)
Bachelor of Science, Finance—The Pennsylvania State University

PROFESSIONAL EXPERIENCE

INTERNATIONAL TRADE INC., Baltimore, MD   2000 to Present
Senior Consultant, Policy & Compliance
Focal point leader and advisor for Trade Compliance Program within and across 120+ countries. Maintain knowledge of current import / export regulations, evaluate proposed regulatory changes, and write business impact and recommendation reports. Create manuals, guidelines, standard operating policies, internal control programs, and other tools needed for import / export compliance. Develop and conduct customs / export training programs for employees, customers, and third-party logistics providers.

Key Achievements:
- Discovered $1.5 billion in errors and other significant compliance deficiencies during international audit.

- Recognized as subject matter expert for development of numerous software applications. Automated and streamlined operations by at least 50% while simultaneously increasing global trade regulatory compliance.

- Conceived, developed, and implemented countless ideas for increasing Global Trade Compliance among numerous business units around the world, including immediate funding and IT resources. Successful in improving productivity and increasing due diligence for regulatory requirements.

AMERICAN FREIGHT CORPORATION, Lancaster, PA   1995 to 2000
Senior Transportation Analyst
Produced Request for Quotations for domestic and international transportation, freight forwarders, and other logistics services. Analyzed bid packages and participated in negotiations with carriers and logistics service contracts. Identified corrective actions for domestic and international shipments. Supervised and trained three staff members in export compliance, packaging, freight damage claims, and freight payment with full accountability for budget of over $4 million.

Key Achievements:

- Restructured and streamlined international transportation and logistics processes / procedures resulting in net savings of $8.3 million through initiatives with transportation and logistics impact assessments, import port-of-entry points, and port-of-export points.
- Slashed 5% on freight payments ($7 million) through efforts in auditing transportation / accounts payable.
- Played key role in leveraging global transportation, customs brokerage, and freight forwarding services.

PROFESSIONAL EXPERIENCE

ABC MANUFACTURING COMPANY, South Ridge, RI   1990 to 1995

Corporate Transportation Manager
Full P&L accountability for receiving, raw material inventory, and shipping departments. Managed prepared, and submitted applications to U.S. government agencies for approval of import and export licenses. Hired, trained, and supervised staff of 22 in raw material inventory, receiving, shipping, importing, exporting, regulatory compliance, and freight payment. Negotiated and managed contracts for domestic, international transportation, customs brokers, freight forwarders, and other logistics services.

Key Achievements:

- Saved $500,000 in immediate refunds and reduced all future duties by more than $2 million annually through initiating reclassification of company's imported products with United States Customs Office.
- Instrumental in streamlining operations, optimizing transportation and international activities along with implementing legal measures to comply with United States import and export regulations.
- Successfully classified products according to harmonized tariff schedule numbers, assigned Export Control Classification Numbers, and assured compliance to country-of-origin marking requirements, NAFTA regulations, and Valuation Rules for imported and exported merchandise.

CERTIFICATIONS

Certified United States Export Compliance Officer (CUSECO)—International Import-Export Institute
Certified in Transportation & Logistics (CTL)—American Society of Transportation & Logistics
Licensed United States Customs Broker—Department of Homeland Security / Customs & Border
    Protection

PROFESSIONAL AFFILIATIONS

Chairperson, American Society of Transportation & Logistics (AST&L)

Member, Institute of Internal Auditors (IIA)

Member, International Compliance Professionals Association (ICPA)

Operations Management and Human Resources

Petroleum Operations Supervisor

Military to civilian transition. The first third of the page shows he is
qualified and "gets" the target job.

MICHAEL W. MILLER

675 Bishy St. • Watertown, NY 13601 • millermichaelw@aol.com • 315.555.2345 Home
• 315.555.2347 Cell

FUEL DISTRIBUTION SYSTEMS SUPERVISOR, FOREMAN, OR SYSTEMS OPERATOR
Convoy Operations • *Staff Training & Leadership* • *Refueling Point Inventory Management & Control*

Top-performing, respected, and loyal petroleum operations supervisor possessing vast knowledge of petroleum operations. Expertise in supervision of pipeline and pump station operations, petroleum supply storage facilities, water supply and distribution systems, supply point and terminal operations, pipeline systems, water supply operations, and laboratory tests. Track record of excellence in leading, training, and developing staff; supervising maintenance activities; and property accountability. Recognized for outstanding performance and service and exceptional technical skill and discipline. Prepared to contribute in a dangerous environment. *Core competencies include:*

- Strategic Planning & Implementation
- Fuel Systems; Inspections
- Safety & Compliance
- Preventive Maintenance
- Employee Relations
- Recordkeeping & Administrative Functions
- Team Building & Leadership
- Organization & Time Management

PROFESSIONAL EXPERIENCE

U.S. ARMY, 1984–3/2008
Built impressive record of achievement and advancement through a series of progressively responsible positions leading petroleum operations functions and staff.

PETROLEUM OPERATIONS PLATOON SERGEANT, 2006–8/2008
Afghanistan

Supervised, trained, advised, inspected, and maintained responsibility for the health, morale, discipline, and welfare of 10 non-commissioned officers, and 41 enlisted soldiers, in petroleum operations at four separate locations in Afghanistan. Coordinated daily training requirements to meet unit refueling goals. *Group issued over 2.9 million gallons of aviation grade fuel with no safety issues and no damage to equipment or environment.*

Selected accomplishments:

- Converted four mismanaged areas into highly effective centers. Maintained an operational readiness rate above 97% on all ground vehicles. Managed responsibility for more than $8M of property.
- Assisted Platoon Leader in daily platoon functions, overseeing all training including convoy operations and providing battle-focused training and counseling.
- Directed construction of new living quarters for personnel.
- Served as the go-to person, continually sought out by leaders, subordinates, and peers throughout the organization for technical and tactical advise and expertise.
- Experienced zero accidents for entire period, due to stressing of the importance of safety.
- Developed a Soldier Study Board to encourage and assist staff in attending and passing boards.
- Awarded the Bronze Star Medal for meritorious service.

- From Aug. 2006 evaluation:
"Concerned, caring leader of the highest caliber … instilled confidence in his soldiers"
"Among the best … a unique NCO whose technical knowledge and experience are above his peers"
"Demonstrated unlimited potential … continue to assign to tough positions of increased responsibility"

PETROLEUM DISTRIBUTION TRAINER, 2001–2005
National Training Center, Ft. Irwin, California

Trained, coached, and observed platoon leaders, NCOs, and enlisted soldiers in the doctrinal employment of Forward Arming and Refueling Point (FARP) assets. Conducted after action reviews and debriefings for up to 10 units per year. Monitored and incorporated changes in operational policy and procedure. Scheduled and coordinated painting and maintenance overhaul of all team vehicles.

Selected accomplishments:

- Rapidly assessed operational and organizational strengths and weaknesses and provided complete programs for improvement.
- Coached and mentored new distribution platoon leaders. Provided quality after action reviews in one-on-one leadership format, as well as 3/5 platoon, small group format.
- Recognized for high degree of self-motivation and initiative, for providing exceptional leadership and training guidance, and for continual willingness to go the extra mile.
- Awarded the Meritorious Service Medal, Army Commendation Medal, and Army Achievement Medal. Received Certificate of Training Excellence, three Certificates of Achievement, Certificate of Appreciation, the Order of the Condor Award, and the Order of St. Michael medal for contributions to Army aviation.

PETROLEUM PLATOON SERGEANT, 2000–2001
Ft. Irwin, California

Shouldered responsibility for maintaining equipment valued in excess of $3M, including nine fuel tankers, nine tractors, two HEMTT's with trailer, a tanker aviation refueling system, two cargo trucks with tank, and pump unit. Accounted for supplies received, stored, and issued. Supervised, trained, and developed 16 soldiers and junior non-commissioned officers.

Selected accomplishments:

- Managed and directed a driver's training program which continuously qualified 100% of assigned personnel regardless of rank or MOS.
- Maintained accurate accounting of all bulk fuel issued.
- Ensured platoon received highest ratings during Aviation Fuel Inspections.
- Received an excellent performance rating as acting First Sergeant leading up to the Division Capstone Exercise.

** ** **

Additional experience as a Sergeant of a Support Platoon assigned to an attack helicopter cavalry squadron in the Republic of Korea, as Section Sergeant in a FORSCOM Petroleum Supply Company, as Supervisor in a refueling platoon, and as Section Sergeant and Fitness Trainer.

EDUCATION & CREDENTIALS

Graduate, Petroleum and Water Specialist ANCOC – Quartermaster School, Fort Lee, VA 1999
Graduate, Petroleum Supply Specialist Course BNCOC – Quartermaster School, Fort Lee, VA 1993
Graduate, Petroleum Supply Specialist Course – Quartermaster School, Fort Lee, VA 1987

Professional Development:

Specimen Collection Class – Fort Riley, KS 1996 **Hazardous Materials Training** (45 hrs.)
– Fort Riley, KS 1995
Environmental Officer Course (40 hrs.) – Health Consultants, Inc. 1993 **Bus Training School**
– Fort Story, VA 1989
Physical Inventory Management – Logistics Management College 1990 **Train The Trainer**
– Ft. Story, VA 1989
Primary Leadership Development – Armour School, Fort Knox, KY 1989 **Division Artillery**
Leadership Course – Schofield Barracks, HI 1986

Purchasing Manager

You get a great feel for the caliber of this candidate from the first third of the page. Get my attention that fast, and I'll read on.

Herman Keynes

5488 Sherman Drive
(818) 555-9880

Toluca Lake, CA 91455
Hkeynes818@email.com

PURCHASING

Buyer/Planner Skilled in Sourcing, Negotiations, and Inventory Management

➢ Expertise in purchasing, inventory planning/control, warehouse operations, and customer service.
➢ Skilled in sourcing and selecting suppliers, with a track record of consistently negotiating highest quality merchandise at favorable prices and terms.
➢ Accurate in monitoring inventory levels to minimize lead times, ensure accuracy, and contribute to efficient, cost-effective operations.
➢ Analytical, with excellent decision making strengths, team building and leadership qualities.
➢ Highly computer literate with experience on mainframes and PCs. Systems/applications include AS-400, CAPRMS, BPCS, COPS, UPS Online, Simbill, Microsoft Word, Excel, and Outlook; Internet, e-mail.

EXPERTISE

MRP ◆ JIT ◆ TQM ◆ ISO 9001 ◆ KanBan Inventory ◆ Vendor Sourcing, Selection, & Negotiations
Raw Material & Inventory Planning/Control ◆ Spreadsheets & Report Design/Preparation

PROFESSIONAL EXPERIENCE

MAJOR HEALTH PRODUCTS, Thousand Oaks, CA * 1998 to Present
$54 million international manufacturer and distributor of medical devices. Division of *Fortune* 100 company with 350 employees.

Buyer/Planner *(2000–Present)*
Oversaw material planning, inventory management, vendor sourcing/selection, and negotiation of pricing and delivery terms for components required for custom surgical kits, injection molded products, foam positioning products, and surgical kits. Worked closely with cross-functional teams including marketing, R&D, and product development. Processed material rejections and replacements; resolved quality and vendor problems; maintained intercompany transfers. Authorization for purchase orders up to $50,000.

- Served as key member of team in charge of transferring product line to Mexican manufacturing facility, implementing closure of Tennessee facility, transfer of inventory to Thousand Oaks facility, and transfer of new product line into facility — all within 10-month period.
- Reduced costs by $500,000 annually through new vendor sourcing and purchase negotiations.
- Identified and selected local vendors, reducing lead time by 50%.
- Implemented Kan Ban inventory management system.

Shipping Lead Man — Moebius Controls / Stilton Industries (1998–2000)
Supervised staff of 20 including warehousemen, fork-lift drivers, order pullers, and office staff. Responsibilities were diverse and encompassed overseeing order processing and shipment at 66,000 sq. ft. warehouse.
Maintained inventory transaction accuracy of 99%.
➢ Established procedures for online receipts of inventory to create live inventory transactions.
➢ Assisted management in closing and opening out-of-state distribution facilities.

EDUCATION / WORKSHOPS / SEMINARS

TQM (including problem solving, team skills, and conflict resolutions)
ISO 9001, GMP Overviews & Practices, Kaizen Blitz Training

Operations Manager

An executive's networking résumé. Not for job applications but a condensed version of deep skills for passing out to networking colleagues and contacts.

HOWARD MORRIS

249 Alpine St. #57 ◆ Morgan, CA 91677 ◆ (555) 555-9605 ◆ howard.morris@myemail.com

Operations Management

Information Technology · **Process Improvement** · **Financial Services**

"[The company President] wanted [to hire] someone who understood not only computers but also business and people – a management-level leader who could sell the changes to the staff, handle outside consultants, and make sure the company's choices positioned it for growth."
– Article titled "Hail to the Chiefs," *Inc. Technology Magazine*, Fall 1998

Profile of Qualifications

Highly accomplished visionary Executive with a solid background in operations, business development, information technology, staff training / development, change management, project management, and turnaround situations with large and small organizations in multiple industries. Results-oriented, decisive leader, with proven success in streamlining operations, reducing costs, and boosting profits. Thrive in a fast-paced, growth-oriented, highly competitive environment.

Core Competencies

- Visionary Leadership
- Operations Management
- Process Restructuring
- Project Management
- Technology Integration
- Business Development
- Market Identification
- Strategic Business Planning
- Turnarounds
- Strategic Alliances
- Staff Development
- Communication

Professional Experience

Project Manager / Process Improvement Manager
AT&T – Ferris, CA / KAVESH AND TAU – Morgan, CA (1999 to Present)

CIO / Vice President of Operations & Technology
ACT CONSULTANTS, INC. – Jordan, CA (1996 to 1999)

Vice President / Client Administrative Services
RESOURCE MANAGEMENT GROUP, INC. – Temple, CA (1995 to 1996)

Business Manager / Agent
NORTHWESTERN LIFE – Jarod, CA (1993 to 1995)

Project Manager / Systems Engineer
APPLE COMPUTER / MARKETING & SERVICES DIVISION – Long Beach, CA (1982 to 1993)

Education & Training

UNIVERSITY OF SOUTHERN CALIFORNIA – Los Angeles, CA
MBA in Finance & Marketing ◆ BS in Mechanical Engineering

Business ◆ Project Management ◆ Leadership ◆ Finance ◆ Management ◆ Sales
Customer Service ◆ Technical ◆ Product Information & Education

Professional Certifications: American Society of Pension Actuaries ERISA Consulting
Exams (Completed four exams; *first person in company history to pass all exams on first try*)
Registered Representative, Series 6 & 63, Life & Disability License
Certified Financial Planner Classes, UCLA (Completed two classes)

Community Leadership

Alumni Mentor, UNIVERSITY OF SOUTHERN CALIFORNIA – Los Angeles, CA (1995 to Present)

Executive Chef

Well structured, easy to read, and—because it is focused—
clearly represents a professional of some account.

JACKLYN LaFLAMME

Address   City, State Zip
Home Phone   Cell Phone   Email Address

EXECUTIVE CHEF

*Seeking to Leverage 15 Years of Management/Culinary Experience in Food Service Operations and
Passion for Food Preparation and Exemplary Guest Service in Executive Chef Position*

Quality-driven, guest-focused, and award-winning chef with a track record of building and maintaining optimal guest satisfaction and excellent productivity/profit performance. Place uncompromising focus on guest needs fulfillment while striving to meet and surpass corporate sales and production goals. Effective communicator, listener, and troubleshooter. Able to manage multimillion-dollar operations, prioritize multiple tasks in high-volume environments and relate to employees/guests with a wide range of backgrounds and personality types. Proficient in Execuchef, Cheftec, and MS Office suite applications; thorough knowledge of kitchen equipment.

Core competencies and knowledge base include:

- ✓ Front-of-House Management
- ✓ Banquet Operations
- ✓ Team Building/Leadership
- ✓ New Operations Launch
- ✓ Guest Satisfaction/Retention
- ✓ Food Preparation & Preservation
- ✓ Staff Training & Evaluation
- ✓ Menu Planning & Pricing
- ✓ Service Improvements
- ✓ Purchasing & Receiving
- ✓ Quality Assurance Standards
- ✓ Time/Resource Management

Professional Experience

COMPANY CONFIDENTIAL – Washington, D.C.   1998 – Present
Food operations included 2 restaurants, patio/café, 12,000 sq.ft. banquet and catering space, in-room dining for 314 rooms, and 100-person employee cafeteria.

EXECUTIVE CHEF

Senior Food Service Executive with full accountability and decision-making authority for all food/kitchen operational functions, directing staff of 3 managers, 3 sous chefs, and 7 dish staff. Hold additional roles as Director of Purchasing/Receiving for all food and non-alcoholic beverages and Executive Steward; signified as 1st Executive Chef in American division of company. Established and implemented all systems guiding kitchen operations, instituted sanitation policies and HAACP guidelines, and developed all menus for restaurants and banquet/catering functions.

- ✓ **New Systems Implementation –** Introduced software to manage inventory, labor/costing schedules, and recipe/plate costing, leading to 3.5% decrease in overall food cost, 4% reduction in kitchen labor cost, and overall increase in consistency.
- ✓ **Food Cost & Labor Reduction –** Generated over $84,000 in food cost savings since restaurant's opening (01/99) through price modifications, improvements in portion control, and negotiations with vendors to secure better purchasing deals, Reduced kitchen labor to annual rate of 9.84.
- ✓ **Operations Launch & Renovation –** Currently consulting with management on new hotel kitchen opening in 2004. Rewrote menus, designed recipes, trained cooking staff,

and set up other aspects of Courtyard by Marriott franchise. Directed 2 kitchen renovations to meet increased business.

✓ **Critic Reviews** – Led operations to receive outstanding reviews from leading local critics, including:

- *Washington Blade*, rated "Very Good"
- *Washington Times*, rated "Excellent"
- *Capitol Cuisine*, featured 2000, 2001, 2002
- *Sidewalk.Com*, rated "Best Pub in D.C."
- *City Paper*, rated "Very Good to Excellent"
- *AAA*, rated "3 Diamond Hotel"
- *Mobil*, rated "3 Star Property"
- *Where Magazine*, featured May, 2000

Professional Experience Continued

COMPANY CONFIDENTIAL – New Brunswick, NJ   1998/1993–1994
New Jersey's premier New Orleans-style restaurant with food sales exceeding $3 million annually.

EXECUTIVE CHEF (1998) **/ SOUS CHEF** (1993 – 1994)

Recruited for return after previously successful tenure as Sous Chef to lead all kitchen operations while assisting General Manager and Proprietor in developing strategies for profit and quality improvements. Supervised team of 170, created daily specials, and standardized written recipes and operational procedures.

✓ **Menu Planning & Design** – Developed new bar, late night, and café menus that provided additional revenue centers and led to $200,000 revenue increase; continued development on new menu of Creole and Acadian cuisine with modern influences.

✓ **Process Automation** – Introduced new inventory and recipe software that resulted in 3.2% decrease in overall food cost.

✓ **Formal Recognition** – Selected to Princeton University Garden State Great Chef Culinary Series; chosen as one of 5 "Great Chefs of New Brunswick" for City Market dining promotion/festival.

✓ **Restaurant Reviews** – Achieved excellent reviews from local critics and publications:

- *New Jersey Star Ledger*, "3 stars"
- *New Jersey Home News*, "4 stars"
- *NJ Home News Tribune*, "4 stars" "Best of Central New Jersey" 1998
- People Choice, "Best in the State"
- *New York Magazine*, "Best Beer Bar/Restaurant"

Education & Credentials

Professional Development Courses:

- ServSafe Train the Trainer Sanitation Course - National Restaurant Association - Washington, D.C. - 2002
- ServSafe Foodservice Sanitation Certification - National Restaurant Association - Washington, D.C. - 2001
- Diversity Awareness Skills Training Seminar - Jurys Washington Hotel - Washington, D.C. – 2001
- Big Tastes, Small Plates; Appetizers Class - The Culinary Institute Of America - August, 2003

Affiliations:
- National Restaurant Association (NRA) – 1997 – Present
- New Jersey Restaurant Association (NJRA) – Former member
- International Association of Culinary Professionals (IACP) – 2002 – Present
- Nation's Capital Chefs Association (NCCA) – 2002 – Present

Recognitions:
- Selected as an Honored Member in the American Registry of Outstanding Professionals 2002, 2003
- Won Second Place-People's Choice Award Chef's Gumbo Cook-Off 2003 - Sponsored by the Chesapeake Chefs Association - Sanctioned & certified by the American Culinary Federation
- Awarded 3rd Place *Entrée* Magazine's "Cooking with Beer" Dessert Contest - Sponsored by the New Jersey Restaurant Association - Judged by the Culinary Institute of America, 1994
- Selected as the Garden State Series guest Chef for Princeton University Culinary Great Chef Series, 1998

Presentations & Community Work:
- Hosting James Beard Foundation Fundraiser Dinner, 2003 – "Once In 100 Years" chef's dinner
- Featured on "The Best Of" on the TV Food Network – Washington, D.C.
- "Great Chef of New Brunswick" - New Brunswick Food & Music Festival
- Zoofari / Star Chefs, March of Dimes / Best Chef Fundraiser – Washington, D.C.
- Special Olympics Chef's Degustation Dinner – Washington, D.C.
- Mentor for the Marriott Charter Hospitality High School – Washington, D.C.
- Volunteer cook for Salvation Army at the Pentagon following September 11, 2001 terrorist attack

Operations Manager

Entry-level résumé targeting a specific job and successfully leveraging internship experience.

NATHAN W. BETHEL

4563 Woodstock Manor Road • East Otselic, NY 34216

(315) 555-2203 Cell • (315) 555-9897 Home • nwb4536@yahoo.com

BUSINESS MANAGEMENT PROFILE

• EXPERTISE IN WATER PARKS •

Operations/ Project Management • Staff Training & Management • Safety Initiatives

Dynamic, top-performing water park operations management professional with a broad range of business, organizational, and interpersonal skills. Natural leader, able to develop strong, easy working relationships with management, staff, and the general public to ensure positive, high-quality guest experiences. Expertise in company revenues through engendering customer loyalty. *Seeking part-time work while still a full-time student.*

Areas of Expertise

- Outstanding track record of strategic contributions in visioning, planning, strategizing, and accomplishment of a range of business-related initiatives, with significant success in developing emerging concepts into full-fledged, high-performance realities.

- Offer a valuable blend of leadership, creative, and analytical abilities that combine efficiency with imagination to produce bottom-line results. Proven success in planning, directing, and coordinating staff activities to maximize cost options and produce optimal outcomes.

- Calm under pressure; diplomatic and tactful with professionals and non-professionals at all levels. Recognized for ability to negotiate, manage, and deliver positive results and to readily transcend cultural and language differences.

- Technically proficient in use of Microsoft Office Word, Excel, PowerPoint, Outlook, on Windows and Macintosh platforms.

Relevant Professional Experience

WALT DISNEY WORLD – LIVERPOOL, NY   2006–2007

Professional Internship, Blizzard Beach

Recruited, following a productive four-month lifeguard internship, to contribute to the ongoing success of this popular Disney water park attraction.
Performed a variety of management-level functions and team-building training for staff, and developed key organizational systems to standardize strategic functions.

Key Contributions:

- Spearheaded, developed, created, and implemented the Blizzard Beach and Typhoon Lagoon Evacuation Operations Report, coordinating all strategic safety and evacuation information. Document included map of park, procedures, phone lists of all lifeguard stands, and inventory supply lists.

- Promoted the Disney anniversary theme of "A Year of a Million Dreams" by participating in the "Magical Moments" program to create special, unique, memorable guest experiences.

- Developed a signage system for the Lazy River to assist river patrons in finding their way through the park.

- Conducted monthly in-service staff trainings. Developed and delivered training materials on a variety of topics including CPR, team building, and water rescues.

- Selected to serve as a "Safety in Motion" (SIM) instructor, training staff in becoming aware of workplace safety issues and how to safely perform all required responsibilities.
- Achieved 100% completion of Blizzard Beach staff United Way Fundraising Drive.
- Assisted in planning and executing various events, including a get-to-know-you party for interns.

Lifeguard Internship

Served as one of 80 lifeguards at Disney's famous Blizzard Beach water park.

Received special training in the 10/20 Waterpark Rule of Lifeguarding (Ellis Lifeguard Training), and rotated throughout the water park with fellow staffers to provide assistance and protection to participants. Patrolled or monitored recreational areas on foot or from lifeguard stands. Rescued distressed people using rescue techniques and equipment. Contacted emergency medical personnel in case of serious injuries. Examined injured persons and administered first aid or cardiopulmonary resuscitation as required, utilizing training and medical supplies and equipment. Instructed guests in proper use of waterslides and other features and provided safety precaution information. Reported to the Lifeguard/Recreation Manager.

Key Contributions:

- Saved several lives in backboard and other types of rescues and resuscitations.
- Received many commendations for performance above and beyond the call of duty.

Manager, Miniature Golf

Completed internship in the Miniature Golf park to further develop management knowledge.

Oversaw a wide variety of staffing and administrative functions, supporting Disney initiatives and instructing others in company policies and procedures.

Education

Associate of Arts in Business Administration Candidate
PEACH COUNTY COMMUNITY COLLEGE, OTSELIC, NY
Anticipated Graduation, May 2008
Completed Organizational Leadership practicum at Walt Disney World, Orlando, Florida.
Serve as campus representative for the Walt Disney World Internship Program.

Ellis & Associates Lifeguard Training
WALT DISNEY WORLD, ORLANDO, FL

Focused, comprehensive, and well laid out, an overall easy, engaging read.

SAM MILLER

#2 Nowhere Court • New York, NY

(H) 973-555-1212 • (C) 973-555-1313 • résumés@arésumésolution.com

HUMAN RESOURCES MANAGER

~ Over 25 years of experience in Human Resources, Management, and Labor Relations ~

◆ ◆ ◆

Seasoned and accomplished Human Resources Management professional with strong background in leading, and managing HR initiatives. Proven senior-level experience in decision-making policy, direction business planning, government relations, and research. Talented in development and enforcement of policies and procedures. Skilled in analyzing staffing needs and creating effective solutions that result in maximized efficiency and reduced overhead. Exceptional interpersonal capabilities, able to cultivate relationships with clients, staff executives, and union leaders.

KEY PROFICIENCIES

Labor Relations	Arbitration Management	Union Negotiations
Policies and Procedures	Human Resource Functions	Budget Development
Staff Hiring	Management	Grievances

PROFESSIONAL EXPERIENCE

HUMAN RESOURCE SERVICES – New York, NY

STAFF MANAGER – LABOR RELATIONS   2001 – PRESENT

Direct all aspects of Labor Relations team through implementation of third step grievance, arbitration, NLRB, and labor relations training process. Research past bargaining minutes, history, and arbitration decisions to develop contract interpretations and clarify intent of collective bargaining agreements. Review grievance reports for identification of trends. Handle third step grievances, arbitrations, and bargaining preparation though research of background information for field labor managers and legal staff. Collaborate with union officials, Labor Relations Managers, and attorneys.

• Key member of team that served on National Bargaining Table with CWA and IBEW Unions in 2002.

XYZ CORPORATION– New York, NY

HR PARTNER – LABOR RELATIONS   1998 – 2001

Designed and implemented organizational budget. Oversaw monthly reports for operating budget results. Served as Labor Relations liaison for HR on performance development, benchmarking, merit review, and employee survey results. Facilitated the Employee Survey Results team, which analyzed the results of the survey, and prepared recommendations for action for the leadership team and LR organization based on the results. Directed performance management and merit review process for organization, while ensuring Labor Relations compliancy on budget and timeline. Managed communications to the union on numerous issues. Member of the LR leadership team.

Managed the development and maintenance of LR's 1999 operating budget, which was under ran by 19%, which allowed LR to contribute $1.5M to the overall HR budget reduction.

XYZ CORPORATION– New York, NY

BUNDLES PORTFOLIO ANALYST – AT&T ACCOUNTS RECEIVABLE MANAGEMENT   1997 – 1998

Analyzed accounts receivable portfolio results for long distance accounts, local bundled accounts, and wireless bundled accounts. Served as primary financial advisor for direct billing. Analyzed delinquent accounts. Calculated financial ratios for identification of trends, risk assessment, and performance evaluation. Prepared monthly presentations, through evaluation of AT&T's business performance against estimates. Examined uncollectible rates versus targeted objectives.

• Reconciled MultiQuest account adjustments in 2 Business Units, which yielded an annual $1.1 million improvement to uncollectible expense in one of the units.

XYZ CORPORATION– New York, NY

ASSISTANT MANAGER – HUMAN RESOURCES   1996 – 1997

Served as Human Resources Generalist for Law and Government Affairs organization. Oversaw staffing process from advertisement of open position though hiring and placement of candidate, which included telephone interview screenings. Advised clients on labor relations issues, benefits, leave of absence, performance management, employee misconduct, and terminations.

• Developed business/process assumptions and applied them to the existing Public Relations organization to create a plan for a new occupational design that maximized resources within the client group.

EDUCATION

Bachelor of Science – Business Administration   Nowhere University – New York, NY
Associate of Science – Business Administration   College of New Horizon – New York, NY
Certification – Secretarial   Katharine University – New York, NY
Contracts Administration Certification – Labor Relations   School of Industrial and Labor Relations, Cornell University – New York, NY

SOFTWARE KNOWLEDGE
MS Word • MS Excel • MS PowerPoint

Director of Recruiting

So *this* is what I might have been, had I kept my day job.
Clearly the writer really knows the recruitment business.

Anneke Smith　　　　2423 Fairfax Court　　　　Home: 248.555.2323
　　　　　　　　　　　West Bloomfield, MI 48322　　e-mail: annekes@aol.com

Director of Recruiting
Process Re-engineering / Project Implementation / Organizational Growth and Turnaround

Talented and forward-thinking senior recruitment leader with proven track record of success turning around company performance by distilling and managing processes, enhancing organizational structure, and developing skilled self-managed teams. Known as the "go-to" person for diverse organizational and process-related challenges. Confident and passionate individual with a mission to create "best in class" recruiting departments through comprehensive utilization of marketing tools and cutting edge sales practices.

✓ Project Implementation	✓ Strategic Planning	✓ On-boarding/Referral Programs
✓ Process Reengineering	✓ Sales and Marketing	✓ Role Competency Design
✓ Training and Development	✓ Recruitment Metrics	✓ Workforce Planning

Proven success collaborating with internal and external stakeholders to execute business-growth strategies that generate revenue and exceed client expectations. Demonstrate expert communication skills, analytical thinking, financial analysis, strategic planning, and business management capabilities.

PROFESSIONAL EXPERIENCE

A & E CORPORATION, *Bloomfield, MI*
A & E Corporation has been an innovative leader in Recruitment Process Outsourcing (RPO) for over a decade. A & E offers innovative recruiting, consulting, and staffing solutions.

Recruitment Process Outsourcing Manager　　　　　　　　　　　　6/2006 to present
- Design the recruitment and sourcing strategies to support the strategic, operational, and business plan for the company. Influence senior business executives on strategy, resources, hiring forecasts, and capacity planning.
- Establishand oversee maintenance of effective candidate sourcing channels and both internal and external résumé tracking systems to speed the process of identifying qualified candidates and tracking effectiveness and efficiency metrics.
- Assistwith proposal generation, implementation, training, and daily oversight of key account service delivery teams, overall delivery of key account results, and the management and nurturing of client relationships to deliver the highest caliber client results.
- Provide timely feedback to management and clients regarding workload and accomplishments, ensuring accuracy of data and timely, thorough completion of assignments.

SMITH & WILLIAMS CONSTRUCTION, INC., *San Francisco, CA*
Established as a general contractor in 1961, and consistently ranked among the largest local Contractors by the San Francisco Business Journal, *the Top 400 Contractors and the Top 100 Design/Builders in the nation by* Engineering News Record.
Vice President, Recruiting　　　　　　　　　　　　　　　　　　1/2005 to 6/2006
Designed, implemented, and oversaw 230-person corporate recruiting function. Reported directly to the CEO and provided strategic direction and tactical follow-up on all levels of hiring. Established executive construction talent pipeline through direct networking, cold-calling, online niche boards, and an employee referral program.
- Managedthe internship program and volunteered to represent student construction organizations establishing a future flow of qualified construction management majors.
- Improved the "candidate experience" by instituting full life cycle recruiting to the company.
- Spearheaded company-wide skills matrix to aid in succession planning and resource management.
- Partneredwith IT to create and launch career site to meet OFCCP and EEOC compliance requirements.
- Orchestrateda comprehensive multi-prong employee retention process overhaul.
- Establisheda 30-60-90 new employee review process, introduced buddy system and re-engineered new hire on boarding procedures, reducing communication breakdowns and ensuring employees' complete preparedness for first day of employment.

START UP AIR, *Dulles, VA*
A low-cost airline based in Fairfax County, Virginia (near Washington, D.C.) that operated from 1989 until 2002.
Recruiting Manager 12/2003 to 12/2004
Hired to develop and implement a large-scale recruiting function for a pre-launch start-up airline to support 2000 hires. Assisted with the creation and management of a $1M advertising budget. Presented detailed and comprehensive reports and analysis on staffing metrics including attrition, program results, time-to-fill, and recruiter performance. Assisted with creation and follow-through of function's new Sarbanes-Oxley narrative.
- Exceeded 2004-headcount targets by 20%, employing 2000 external and 500 internal employees.
- Conducted months of research, built a business case, and gained C-level buy in for the implementation of an applicant microsite, which significantly increased the ease and effectiveness of the baggage handler screening process. Developed tool questions based on role competencies, and rolled out "plug-and-play" microsite to *www.startupair.com.*
- Dismantled and rebuilt all hiring processes and procedures to accommodate AAP, EEOC, and OFCCP guidelines with an eye towards the U.S. government's newest definition of an applicant and conducted quarterly internal audits to ensure compliance.
- Created a robust Employee Referral Program (ERP) that propelled referrals to 13% of total hires resulting in lower cost-per-hire for hourly airport employees.
- Implemented legally defensible behavioral interviewing with recurrent training for hiring managers, resulting in a significant reduction in EEOC claims.
- Designed and implemented a measurement tool to assist with monitoring the "candidate experience," ensuring a positive experience and takeaway after interviewing with Independence Air and increasing candidate satisfaction levels 20%.
- Designed and implemented a Service Level Agreement (SLA) greatly impacting the time-to-offer metric by eliminating communication disconnects. Time-to-offer on corporate hires went from 65 days to 30 days.
- Influenced two major internal departments to utilize in-house recruiting function rather than headhunting services, resulting in a savings of approximately $300K in 2004.

TNET COMMUNICATIONS, *Dulles, VA*
TNET Communications provides leading voice, data, converged, and managed services for businesses, enterprises and carriers who need a proven, responsive and cost-effective alternative to traditional service providers.
Staffing Manager (promoted to full-time in July 2001) 8/2000 to 12/2003
Promoted to take nationwide 37-market telecommunications corporate, technical and sales recruiting efforts for 1200-member organization to the next level. Reported to multiple VPs/Directors and charged with maintaining order through chaos of company's bankruptcy filing.
- Orchestrated and launched organizational measurements and metrics against specific and desired corporate outcomes.
- Engaged external agencies and internal recruiters in a massive hiring effort for top performers in sales arena meeting the business objective of 300 hires in a time frame of 3 months, dramatically impacting sales for the last quarter.
- Introduced SLA to firmly establish the recruitment strategy, reducing time-to-offer by 5 days. Significantly reduced time-to-offer to 27.01 and time-to-start to 40.01 after the initiative implementation completion.
- Successfully established solid customer service best practices and hired 700 sales employees.
- Reduced offer turnaround to a 5-day administrative cycle from a 2–3 week cycle.
- Implemented technical pre-screen process to eliminate unqualified candidates to meet OFCCP and EEOC guidelines.

PRIOR ENGAGEMENTS

CONCERT/FOLIO FN/BRITISH STANDARDS INSTITUTE/MANPOWER

Recruiter 3/1996 to 8/2000
Utilized both traditional and non-traditional search resources and techniques to identify and target top talent professionals including cold-calling, advertising, networking, and professional associations.
- Sourced, reviewed, and screened résumés for a variety of technical and corporate positions.
- Conducted preliminary IT candidate interviews and arranged for subsequent interviews with hiring managers and clients.
- Expanded growth of business by initiating direct placement contracts and placements service.

Emerging Technologies Executive

Louis Edwards
1234 Ocean Road • Wilmington, NC 97979 • (999) 999-9999 • louis@email.com

Emerging Technologies Globalization Executive
Deal Maker / Market & Product Strategist / Business Developer / Negotiator

Results-driven and innovative Telecommunications Industry Executive with a 20+ year successful track record driving revenue growth and winning market share primarily in turnaround, start-up, and high growth situations. Consistently deliver strong and sustainable revenue gains through combined expertise in Strategic Business Planning, Product Management, Market Strategy, Contract Negotiations, and Customer Relationship Management. Recognized for exceptional ability to assess business unit capabilities, identify and implement appropriate business and product re-engineering measures thus assuring bottom line growth. Rare ability to establish the organization's vision, develop "C" level relationships and negotiate the deals that guarantee success.

Key Accomplishments

- "C" level relationship builder with a track record personally negotiating contracts with companies such as Xerox, Lockheed Martin, Bank of America, Morgan Stanley, EDS, Visa, Oracle, Microsoft, Nortel, Boeing, Nordstrom, and The Gap.
- Consistent track record developing contracts and terms that utilized company capabilities and met customer needs, including the first prepaid international contract. This allowed the company to accelerate into the international market achieving $1+ billion in revenue. This approach became the industry standard.
- Turned around an underperforming business unit lacking leadership by redesigning and motivating the sales and services teams, successfully recovering 60% of the lost accounts and adding new business to increase revenues to $5+ million annually in the first 12 months.
- Conceived and coordinated the global account management process; identified customer needs and product capabilities, spearheaded product and service level agreement changes to win the first global contract. Not only did this grow market share from 7% to 100% and revenue from $330,000 to $6 million per month, it set new industry standards in global business practices.
- Revitalized a product offering by identifying and implementing an International Reseller Channel, re-engineering the existing product through the addition of a conversion process adding packaging enhancements and aligning a service/support structure extending the product life by 2 years and capturing a potential revenue of $10 million annually.
- Within 45 days, conceived and implemented a National Accounts Program, establishing pricing model, sales organization structure, and customer service delivery format, successfully increasing revenue from $12 million to $27 million per month. This program became the standard for the entire company.
- Led the company's new technologies market development (VPN, Web Hosting, co-locating Internet) securing sales in excess of $15 million within 6 months.

Employment Summary

Software Company, Inc.   2004 – Present
Vice President, Business Development and Alliances, Philadelphia, PA
Recruited to drive the product development process and expand market reach through the implementation of an international reseller channel and strategic business alliances.

- Negotiated contracts with Fuji Xerox, Xerox, Accenture, and Lockheed Martin, capturing $10 million in potential revenue.
- Managed the renegotiation of two existing alliances that will net the company at least $2 million over the next 12 months.
- Established a new technology relationship with Open Text extending the company's reach in the Life Sciences market.

International Telecom, Inc.   1997 – 2004

Regional Vice President National Accounts, Nashville, TN

Recruited to develop a major account program and subsequently developed a national account program. Responsibilities included full P&L, $20 million operational budget, and more than 250 personnel.

- During a 15-company acquisition period, including the ITI acquisition (the largest in Telecom history), consistently exceeded all business objectives.
- Managed the best corporate A/R and bad debt levels, achieved outstanding customer retention level of 94% and managed corporation's lowest employee turnover rate of 10%.
- Developed and implemented a National Account Program expanding revenues within the first year from $180 million to $260 million and achieved Top Regional Vice President award for outstanding revenue increase.
- Averaged a 21% annual internal revenue growth and was selected to the President's Club from 1998 through 2003 by continually identifying new business opportunities and establishing the right teams, resources, and support to grow the organization and meet the customer's expectations.

ABC Telecom, Inc.   1995 – 1997

Executive Director – Global Accounts, California

Promoted to manage the Western U.S. team of 139 sales and support staff, 5 direct reports and to oversee 35 national accounts.

- Managed and negotiated $750 million in contracts with "C" level players including BOA, Visa, Microsoft, The Gap, Sun, Apple, Oracle, AMD and Nordstrom. Grew market share from less than 15% to 48% in two years.
- Averaged 122% of revenue target every year.

ABC Telecom, Inc.   1992 – 1995

Branch Manager, California

Recruited to grow and manage the Bank of America account, successfully leading a team of 39 cross-functional members.

- Grew annual sales and revenue from $3.6 million to $80 million within two years, attaining 100% market share.
- Spearheaded largest commercial sale in ABC history, valued at $400 million, successfully converting the entire Bank of America network to ABC in less than 6 months while maintaining 100% customer satisfaction.

BS&S   1986 – 1992

Field District Manager, San Francisco, CA

- Consistently exceeded quota, averaging 112% and made President's Club every year while in sales/sales management positions.
- As staff member for the President of BS&S Information Systems, was responsible for revenue and issues for all national accounts west of the Mississippi, approximately 200 accounts, achieving 109% of the revenue quota.

BS&S   1983 – 1986

National Account Management, BS&S Headquarters, New York, NY

- Negotiated and implemented the largest state government equipment contract, valued at $20 million.
- Named to Management Development Program (top 2% of all management personnel), recognized for superior executive and leadership potential.

Education

Bachelor of Arts, New York University

Career Development: Intensive 18-week BS&S account management and product training seminar

Management

JANE B. URATA

3131 CARMEL ROAD • SAN DIEGO, CALIFORNIA 92109
HOME: (858) 555-0234 • CELLULAR: (858) 555-0235 • E-MAIL: JU_ARBORIST@PLANTNET.COM

New Business Development • Strategic Partnerships • Product Marketing
Accomplished Senior Executive with a strong affinity for technology and a keen business sense for the application of emerging products to add value and expand markets. Proven talent for identifying core business needs and translating into technical deliverables. Launched and managed cutting-edge Internet programs and services to win new customers, generate revenue gains, and increase brand value.

Unique combination of technical and business/sales experience. Articulate and persuasive in explaining the benefits of e-commerce technologies and how they add value, differentiate offerings, and increase customer retention. Highly self-motivated, enthusiastic, and profit-oriented.

Expertise in Internet services, emerging payment products, secure electronic commerce, smart card technology, and Java.

AREAS OF QUALIFICATION

Business

- Sales & Marketing • Business Development • Strategic Initiatives
- Business Planning • Project Management • Strategic Partnerships
- Business & Technical Requirements • Revenue Generation
- Contract Negotiations • Relationship Management

Technical

- Electronic Commerce • Encryption Technology • Key Management
- Public Key Infrastructure • Firewalls • Smart Cards • Stored Value
- Digital Certificates • Internet & Network Security • Complex Financial Systems
- Authorization, Clearing, Settlement • Dual and Single Message

PROFESSIONAL EXPERIENCE

ABC Credit Card Corp., San Diego, CA   *2002 to Present*
E-COMMERCE AND SMART CARD CONSULTANT

- Developed strategic e-commerce marketing plans for large and small merchants involving Web purchases and retail transactions using a multifunctional, microcontroller smart card for both secure Internet online commerce and point-of-sale offline commerce.
- Combined multiple software products for Internet and non-Internet applications: home banking, stored value, digital certificates, key management, rewards & loyalty program, PCS/GSM cell phone, and contactless microcontroller with RF communications without direct POS contact.
- Consulted on business and technical requirements to define new e-commerce products and essential deliverables for ABC Credit Card, valued at $2.5 M, supporting and enhancing Internet transactions.
- Analyzed systems relating to the point of sale environment in the physical world and at the merchant server via the Internet for real-time authorization, clearing, and settlement.
- Managed projects including the requirements management system for electronic commerce products affecting core systems: authorization, clearing, and settlement. Provided expertise about business and technical issues regarding SET and the Credit Card Payment Gateway Service.

218

Communications Technology Corporation, Miami, FL   *1997 to 2002*
MANAGER OF WESTERN REGION CHANNEL PARTNER PROGRAM

- Developed and maintained business relationships with large *Fortune* 500 customers and partners that use or resell client-server software for applications and contracts involving e-commerce and smart card technology for a variety of Internet/intranet products: home banking, EDI, stored value, digital certificates, key management, perimeter defense with proxy firewalls, secure remote access.
- Negotiated an exclusive contract with one of the largest government and commercial contractors in the industry, projected to generate $2–4 million over a 24–36 month period. Contract includes secure remote access, telecommuting, secure health care applications.

Avanta Corp., Miami, FL   *1993 to 1997*
SENIOR SOFTWARE ENGINEER / SOFTWARE INSTRUCTOR

- Designed new programs and trained software engineers in object-oriented analysis and design using UML. Solutions were implemented in C++ in a UNIX environment.
- Managed a software engineering group of 53 individuals. Developed in-house program that saved over $150,000 in training costs for state-of-the-art communications system software development.
- Received Peer Award for outstanding performance; earned a performance evaluation rating of 4.2/5.0.
- Developed and maintained C and C++ communication software in a UNIX environment.
- Created curriculum and course materials that reduced overall training costs by more than $150,000. Coordinated and presented software training programs.

EDUCATION AND CREDENTIALS

- B.S., Electrical Engineering, University of Miami: Emphasis, software engineering; Minor: Psychology. President of the Sigma Sigma Fraternity
- Top Secret Security Clearance with Polygraph

Management

Senior Technology Executive

BRENDA FRANKS

95 Lane Road   Los Angeles, CA 900071   (888) 888-9888   Bfran@yahoo.com

SENIOR TECHNOLOGY EXECUTIVE
Project Management ◆ Multimedia Communications & Production ◆ MIS Management

Exceptionally creative management executive uniquely qualified for a digital media technical production position by a distinctive blend of hands-on technical, project management, and advertising/communications experience. Offers a background that spans broadcast, radio, and print media; fully fluent and proficient in interactive and Internet technologies and tools.

Proven leader with a strength for identifying talent, building and motivating creative teams that work cooperatively to achieve goals. Highly articulate with excellent interpersonal skills and a sincere passion for blending communications with technology. Capabilities include:

- ◆ Project Planning & Management
- ◆ Account Management & Client Relations
- ◆ Multimedia Communications & Production
- ◆ Information Systems & Networking
- ◆ Conceptual & Creative Design
- ◆ Work Plans, Budgets, & Resource Planning
- ◆ Department Management
- ◆ Interactive / Internet Technologies
- ◆ Technology Needs Assessment & Solutions
- ◆ Team Building & Leadership

PROFESSIONAL EXPERIENCE

LaRoche Investments, Inc., Los Angeles, CA   *1989 – Present*
VICE PRESIDENT OF MIS (2000 – Present)
ASSISTANT VICE PRESIDENT OF IT/CORPORATE COMMUNICATIONS   (1995 – 2000)
CORPORATE COMMUNICATIONS OFFICER   (1991 – 1995)
ASSOCIATE   (1989 – 1991)

Advanced rapidly through a series of increasingly responsible positions with this U.S. based, European investment group. Initially hired to manage market research projects, advanced to plan and execute corporate communications projects, and in 1995, assumed responsibility for spearheading the introduction of emerging technologies to automate the entire company.

Current scope of responsibility is expansive and focuses on strategic planning, implementation, and administration of all information systems and technology. Lead technical staff members, manage budgets, select and oversee vendors, define business requirements, and produce deliverables through formal project plans. Manage systems configuration and maintenance, troubleshoot problems, plan and direct upgrades, and test operations to ensure optimum systems functionality and availability.

Technical Contributions
- • Pioneered the company's computerization from the ground floor; led the installation and integration of a state-of-the-art and highly secure network involving 50+ workstations running on 6 LANs interconnected by V-LAN switching technology.
- • Defined requirements; planned and accelerated the implementation of advanced technology solutions, deployed on a calculated time frame, to meet the short- and long-term needs of the organization.
- • Orchestrated the introduction of sophisticated applications and multimedia technology to streamline workflow processes, expand presentation capabilities, and keep pace with the competition.
- • Administered the life cycle of multiple projects from initial systems/network planning and technology acquisition through installation, training, and operation. Saved hundreds of thousands in consulting fees by managing IS and telecommunication issues in-house.

Business Contributions
- Created and produced high-impact multimedia presentations to communicate the value and benefits of individual investment projects to top-level company executives. Tailored presentations to appeal to highly sophisticated, multicultural audiences.
- Assembled and directed exceptionally well-qualified project teams from diverse creative disciplines; collaborated with and guided photographers, videographers, copywriters, script writers, graphic designers, and artists to produce innovative presentations and special events.
- Performed market research and analyses to determine risks and feasibility of multiple investment projects valued at up to $150 million. Developed and recommended tactical plans to transform vision into achievement.

Broadcast, Print, and Radio Advertising & Production   *1974 – 1988*
DIRECTOR OF ADVERTISING, Schwarzer Advertising Associates, New York, NY (1986 – 1988)
ADVERTISING ACCOUNT EXECUTIVE, Schoppe, New York, NY (1987) / Rainbow Advertising, Brooklyn, NY (1984 – 1986) / Marcus Advertising, Phoenix, AZ (1983 – 1984) / WCHN, WTYR, AND WSCZ, Boston, MA (1982 – 1983) / WFDX-TV, WFDX-FM, WKLU, WERS, WQRT, Lehigh Valley, PA (1974 – 1981)
WRITER/PRODUCER, RADIO PROGRAMMING, WPTR, Detroit, MI (1974)

   Early career involved a series of progressive creative and account management positions spanning all advertising mediums: multimedia, television, radio, and print. Worked directly with clients to assess complex and often obscure needs; conceptualized and developed advertising campaigns to communicate the desired message in an influential manner.

Achievement Highlights
- Designed, wrote, produced, and launched advertising campaigns that consistently positioned clients with a competitive distinction. Developed a reputation for ability to accurately intuit and interpret clients' desires and produce deliverables that achieved results.
- Hand-selected and led creative teams consisting of graphic designers, artists, musicians, talent, cartoonists, animators, videographers, photographers, and other freelancers and third-party creative services to develop and produce multimillion-dollar advertising campaigns.
- Won accolades for the creation, production, and launch of a 4-color fractional-page advertisement that generated the greatest response in the history of the publication. Honored with a featured personal profile recognizing achievements.
- Developed and applied a unique style and advertising philosophy that accounted for the nuances of human psychology and utilized innovative, brainy, and sometimes startling techniques to capture attention and influence the target market.

EDUCATION & TRAINING

A.A.S. Broadcast Production, Russ Junior College, Boston, MA, 1974
Continuing education in Marketing Research and Broadcast Production, 1984 – 1986
The School of Visual Arts, New York, NY

TECHNICAL QUALIFICATIONS

Innate technical abilities and interest in emerging technologies and digital communications. Trained and fully versed in all aspects of network design, implementation, installation, and maintenance. Advanced skill in the installation, configuration, customization, and troubleshooting of software suites and applications, hardware, and peripherals within the Windows environment (3.x, 95, 98, NT 3.5, NT 3.51, NT 4). Proficient with most Web development, multimedia, word processing, spreadsheet, graphic/presentation, and database tools and applications.

Management

Manager

The creative layout is appealing and breaks up the dense data in the first half page. It's all there: Target Job, Performance Profit, Core Competencies, and even an endorsement.

KEN DAVENPORT

864 Bentley Road ◆ Campbell, CA 95008 ◆ 408-555-0606 ◆ kendaven@sbcglobal.net

Electronic Manufacturing Management Performance Profile
Delivering value to the "bottom line" by recognizing and maximizing opportunities.

Customer-driven manager with more than 15 years of electronic manufacturing services experience involving operations, finance, project management, materials management, and supply chain management, including 6 years managing cross-functional teams and customer relationships. Skilled at evaluating complex issues, identifying key elements, creating an effective action plan and guiding its execution. MBA in Finance and General Management. APICS-certified: CPIM and CSCP.	**Core Strengths & Expertise:** • **Revenue & Profit Increases** • **Cost Reduction & Cost Avoidance** • **Process & Efficiency Improvement** • **Customer Relationship Management** • **Contract Development & Negotiation** • **Team Building & Leadership** • **Materials & Supply Chain Management** • **P&L Management** • **Metrics Management & Analysis**

Consistently promoted to positions with increasing responsibility. Recognized by management as a key contributor, with comments such as the following: *"Ken is a strategic thinker. He is respected as a role model of integrity—he sets a good example for others to follow. He knows how to get things done through channels. Ken's good judgment has helped him identify several opportunities for the company; he not only recognizes opportunities but takes decisive action to make the most of them."*

PROFESSIONAL EXPERIENCE

High-Tech Circuits, Inc., San Mateo, CA   1998–Present; 1989–1997

Business Analyst, Business Unit Financial Analyst *(2006–Present)*
Perform extensive analysis and reporting for a business unit group of 300+ employees. Key actions and accomplishments include the following:

- Revitalized the Time Clock project, which was behind schedule. Established close interaction with offsite project manager and completed assembly, installation, and testing ahead of schedule. Recognized for contribution to efficiency improvement and more effective plant operation.
- Compiled and updated quarterly customer QBR reports using Excel pivot tables and Access database information. In addition, generated and reported quarterly bonuses for employees.

Business Unit Manager *(2003–2006)*
Managed a challenging $25 million/year account and approximately $18 million of materials to maintain profitability. Major areas included forecasting, contract negotiations, supplier performance, financial management, and HR issues. Developed and coordinated activities of cross-functional teams. Key actions and accomplishments included the following:

- Spearheaded revision and execution of full manufacturing contract within 4 months versus expected 6-12 months.
- Grew revenue 330% in fiscal year 2006.

Business Unit Coordinator *(2001–2003)*
Managed accounts valued at $12 million per year. Interacted with customers to ensure high satisfaction. Contributed to cost-reduction and efficiency improvements that included developing Excel macros to use purchasing and inventory data more efficiently and an Access database to track ECN changes and impact.

Master Planning Supervisor *(1998–2001; 1996–1997)*

Established rules, procedures, tools, and techniques to move plant from prototype to volume production. Managed master scheduling for multiple programs, as well as work cell material management and metrics. Key actions and accomplishments included the following:

- Achieved smooth transfer of $30+ million program to another facility through detailed material transactions and planning.
- Reduced excess inventory by $400,000 and increased inventory turns 20%.
- Originally earned promotion from Master Planner position within less than a year.

Previous positions: Master Planner; Accounting Manager

Peterson Laminate Systems, Phoenix, AZ   1997–1998

Production/Scheduling/Inventory Manager

Served as a member of Plant Leadership Team and as High Performance Work Team coach for Shipping department. Additional actions and accomplishments included the following:

- Participated in Kaizen event that promoted continuous improvement and elimination of waste by initiating changes that included reducing product travel from 5,000 to 2,000 feet.
- Contributed to $500,000 inventory reduction and 98% on-time shipping record.

EDUCATION & CERTIFICATION

Master of Business Administration-Finance & General Management
Boston University, Boston, MA

Bachelor of Science-Accounting
Northeastern University, Boston, MA

Certified in Production & Inventory Management (CPIM): earned in less than one year
Certified Supply Chain Professional (CSCP): earned in less than 6 months
APICS, Alexandria, VA

PROFESSIONAL AFFILIATION

Member, American Production & Inventory Control Society

COMPUTER COMPETENCIES

MS Office: Word, Excel (including pivot tables and macros), PowerPoint, Access; Visio; SAP ERP

Management

Marketing Director

Good one-page networking résumé for an executive that captures the big points; wouldn't be used to make a serious pitch but for getting the word out, useful.

Terri Williams

Los Angeles, CA 90066 ▫ (310) 390-7943 ▫ isom@verizon.net

Strategic Marketing Director

Identifies and establishes footholds in new markets

Innovative business development leader offers 12 years of international expertise identifying market opportunities, defining market strategies, developing reseller channels, and establishing profitable distribution networks. Collaborative by nature; works within teams to build strong relationships and strategic business partnerships. Experienced across a range of industries; create competitive advantage by taking the lessons learned from one industry and applying to others.

Areas of Expertise

Business Development ~ Relationship Building / Strategic Partnerships ~ Marketing ~ Channel Management
Strategic Market Planning ~ Reseller Channels ~ Distribution Networks ~ Market Penetration ~ Market Growth
Program Development & Management ~ Marketing Communications ~ Brand Awareness ~ Market Research

PROFESSIONAL SUMMARY

Ontario Market Development Group, San Francisco, CA (1996–Present)
International Business Development Manager

> Helped more than 300 Quebec-based companies penetrate the US market

Assist various Ontario-based industries (technology, food, environmental, and others) in penetrating and developing distribution networks within the US market. Define and identify market opportunities, analyze and create market entry strategies, establish and manage market development plans, develop key contacts, recruit agents and distributors, make formal introductions, train companies in promoting their businesses, craft and manage promotional programs and events, perform market research, and generate valuable business intelligence. Initiate and implement licensing, OEM, and other partner relationships. Teach companies how to identify, negotiate, and establish reseller networks.

- Identified, qualified, and selected appropriate markets and distribution channels for 800+ companies; developed strategic business and marketing plans for 150 clients.
- Planned, coordinated, and managed promotional events that have generated tens of millions of dollars in new revenues for Ontario-based businesses; 1999 Hollywood animation promotion generated $34M (Canadian) in contracts.
- Developed network of high-level, strategic contacts in numerous industries; taught companies to profit through channel distribution.

California Computer, Los Angeles, CA (1992–1995)
Sales Support Administrator

Coordinated reseller channel strategy implementing channel marketing programs for printers, plotters, and other peripheral products. Supported 15 outside sales representatives and 1 international subsidiary, helped resellers understand and leverage marketing programs, managed accounts, resolved conflicts between sales channels and internal departments, and provided world-class customer service.

- Improved marketing program tracking and reporting time 30% through automation.

EDUCATION

Master of Business Administration—International Management & Marketing
University of California—Los Angeles

Bachelor of Arts—Economics
University of Florida, Gainesville

Marketing Director

Strong combination-style résumé. Target job followed by relevant credentials and section detailing mission-critical core competencies.

TINA JOHNSON, MBA

22761 River Bank Drive Reston, Virginia 20165
703-555-7667 (h) • 703-555-6840 (m) • tinajohnson14@comcast.net

Online and Brand Marketing Strategist/Director

Over 20 years experience in every facet of marketing in positions such as marketing director, consultant, and/or owner with a solid successful background in traditional and entrepreneurial venues. Use a real-world approach to problem solving and a deep well of experience to meet the challenges of this fast-paced function.

◆ Demonstrateproject planning and management skills in supremely high-stress scenarios where failure is not an option and the wrong decision could deliver substantial client loss.

◆ Utilize a consultative approach to assess client needs and provide "turnkey" solutions and programs that meet the client's strategic goals.

◆ Possessstrategic business sense, an uncompromising work ethic, and a natural sincerity to help create consistent, "magic" marketing solutions and win loyal support from clients, partners, managers, and business owners.

◆ Possessdeep expertise in branding, managing and positioning product lines, and implementing innovative marketing messages that drive revenue and bring unique product "stories" to the community.

MBA - Marketing - Rutgers University, New Jersey • **BS in Business Administration** - College of New Jersey, New Jersey

Results-Oriented Catalyst:

◆ Builta packaged employee communication strategic roll-out plan for Montgomery General Hospital, partnered with senior internal HR leaders and directed launch time frame for new employee subscription benefit (PepPods, an online emergency preparedness and personal home record system).

◆ Metwith potential investors on behalf of Zigzag.net, marketed online learning management system to military and law enforcement professionals, and identified a $1 million investor who was ultimately secured.

◆ Developedfrom inception to implementation an interactive kiosk concept whereby banking clients received instant product and service information during busy bank periods, receiving praise from customers nationwide during testing and rollout.

Marketing and Events Planner:

◆ Created and launched the AT&T "No More Excuses" multimedia cell phone campaign, the most successful January campaign to date in company history.

◆ Assistedin locating creative team to design Mascot Percy's character costume. Lined up stimulating children's entertainment musicians and artisans, and food and health screening vendors, and launched direct mail campaign to the Mercy Health Plan members, resulting in an impressive 900-person turnout.

◆ Organizedand launched a hugely successful White Glove Car Wash charity grand opening event, and donated a portion of the proceeds to the Make-a-Wish Foundation.

Multi media Marketing Strategist:

◆ Createdthe Magistar public corporate identity, including the marketing language on the corporate website, trade show participation strategy, and public relations presentations.

◆ Establishedstrong rapport with TMC Labs editor who agreed to conduct an extensive product evaluation and testing, resulting in a rave product review for Magistar in the January 2001 issue of *Internet Telephony Review* entitled "VoIP 'Click-to-Talk Shootout'"

Gifted Leader:

Developed a turnkey fundraising program for immediate online client use complete with a fundraising microsite, fundraising, sales and pricing procedures, and training and sales support materials such as scripts and FAQs. Improved the volume and quality of traffic to ActiveMedia client websites from search engines via "natural" search results, raising their resulting online rank, and improving their click-through numbers.

THE RIVER BANK GROUP • Marketing Consultant – Reston, VA • 2001–present
MAGISTAR • Director, Brand Marketing (VOIP) - Reston, VA • 1999–2001
NATIONS BANK/BARNETT BANK, INC. – Advertising Project Manager - Jacksonville, FL • 1997–1998
URBAN DESIGN, INC. – Director of Marketing - Philadelphia, PA • 1994–1995

Online Faculty at UNIVERSITY OF PHOENIX • 2002–2003

Facilitated asynchronous online undergraduate courses in Marketing, Integrated Marketing Communications, Management, and Organizational Behavior. Developed marketing rich content and designed final group project, whereby students created a viable business and marketing plan and delivered presentation to final class.

Senior Finance Manager

Here the target job title, giving instant focus to the reader, is immediately followed by bolded credentials highlighting relevant skills.

BOB JOHNSON

5401 68th Street ◆ Lubbock, TX 79424
Home: 203-000-0000 ◆ Cell: 913-000-0000 ◆ Email: bobjohnson@hotmail.com

SENIOR FINANCE MANAGEMENT EXECUTIVE / CFO

17+ Years of Progressive Experience, Including Position as CFO for Global Division of Wal-Mart
MBA in Finance; Graduate of Wal-Mart Financial Management Program; Green Belt Certified
Executive Board Member for Several Asian Financial Services Companies

Senior-level finance executive/CFO with track record of directing and re-engineering large-scale corporate finance functions. Strategic analyst, forecaster, and planner with proven risk assessment and sound decision-making background.

Core Financial & Executive Knowledge/Skill Areas Include:

Corporate Finance Management	Acquisitions & Divestitures	Financial Forecasting & Modeling
Corporate Reorganization Affairs	Financial Analysis & Reporting	International Financial Affairs
Cost Reduction & Avoidance	Risk Assessment Management	Banking & Investor Relationships
Senior Executive Collaboration	Team Building & Leadership	Multi-Location Operations Leadership

PROFESSIONAL EXPERIENCE	***WAL-MART, 1989 – Present*** *Progressed through increasingly responsible positions and challenging assignments over 17-year period, demonstrating ability to generate quantifiable results on national and international scale.* **Global Financial Planning & Analysis Leader** – Wal-Mart Insurance (2004–Present) Currently lead financial reporting and forecasting functions for $10 billion Revenue Insurance division with $40 billion in assets. Supervise local and international (India) team. Work hand-in-hand with CFO and CEO on mission-critical objectives and serve as primary point of contact to Corporate Finance organization. Create reports for BOD Audit Committee and CEO reviews. Assist top-level senior management in key strategic communication and presentation activities. **Challenges: Bring heightened visibility to key business information within complex, restructured organization. Improve financial reporting methods (previously lacking insightful analysis) to provide better view for senior management and Board into financial health of large operations.**
FINANCIAL FORECASTING & REPORTING	Built Center of Excellence team that took charge of financial reporting for $100 million in expenses, leading to significant improvements in cost control and immediate benefits to business operations. Led successful forecasting improvements through design and development of new modeling tools; instituted new SG&A reporting infrastructure for ~$800 million cost base.
MERGERS & ACQUISITIONS	Played key role in supporting largest re-insurance transaction in history (Wal-Mart Insurance sale to Swiss RE), performing due diligence functions to facilitate process.
EXECUTIVE MANAGEMENT SUPPORT	Provided value-driven recommendations and support to Chief Financial Officer and Chief Executive Officer, including preparation of strategic communication and presentation materials for delivery at Board of Directors and other key meetings.

	Chief Executive Officer – Wal-Mart Hong Kong (2002–2004) Hand-selected for return to top leadership position following previously successful management tenure with Wal-Mart Capital Hong Kong, overseeing team of 150–160. Held full P&L responsibility for Consumer Financial Services Operations ($600 million in assets, $200 million in revenues) consisting of Mortgage, Personal Loans, and Automobile Financing divisions. Functioned as Capital's Lead Representative to Hong Kong Monetary Authority and Finance House Association of Hong Kong. **Challenges: Engineer turnaround for underperforming business affected by heavily saturated financial services market in Hong Kong and SARS epidemic, with continual downsizing initiatives.**
NEW BUSINESS DEVELOPMENT	Transformed Hong Kong's mortgage strategy by strengthening operations and launching new product introductions, generating 30% growth in asset base as a result.
COST REDUCTION & AVOIDANCE	Achieved $1.5 million cost savings through several productivity improvement solutions, including outsourcing and rationalization initiatives, leading to fulfillment of turnaround goals.
	Chief Executive Officer – Wal-Mart Finance Indonesia/Malaysia (2000–2002) Promoted to hold full P&L accountability for Finance Indonesia, directing multi-branch platform with 800+ team members. Directed Credit Card, Personal Loans, and Automobile Financing divisions. Served as Board member for several Asian leading financial services businesses. Challenges: Reverse 5-year history of declining profits as operations emerged from Asian economic crisis of late 1990s. Restructure debt necessitated by difficulties of commercial financing customers. Drive improvements for low employee morale.
OPERATIONS TURNAROUND	Met turnaround objectives by leading Indonesian business to first profitable year in 5 years by growing credit card/personal loan revenues and customer base over 150%.
BUSINESS DEVELOPMENT	Launched Visa co-brand credit card with largest bank in Indonesia that became #1 Visa-issued card in Indonesia during 2001.
QUALITY ASSURANCE	Utilized Six Sigma processes to improve operations through collection autodialers, application scanning, and system migration to Vision+
EDUCATION & CREDENTIALS	Masters of Business Administration in Finance UNIVERSITY – New York, NY (1997) Bachelor of Science in Information Technology
Professional Development	Financial Management Program (FMP) Information Management Leadership Program (IMLP) Six Sigma Green Belt Training & Certification Financial Analysis for Business Development

Management

227

Receptionist

With this résumé, Keisha had no trouble finding another
job after her last employer moved out of state.

Keisha A. Jackson

1305 Lakeshore Drive ◆ Apartment 10-B ◆ Chicago, IL 00000 ◆ (555) 555-5555 ◆ kaj200@netmail.com

PROFILE

Responsible and dedicated office professional with 15 years of experience in heavy-volume, fast-paced environments. Cooperative team player who enjoys working with people and utilizing direct telephone contact. Detail-oriented, thorough, and accurate in taking and relaying information. Well-organized to handle a variety of assignments and follow through from start to finish. Strong work ethic, with eagerness to learn and willingness to contribute toward meeting a company's goals.

- ◆ Visitor reception and routing
- ◆ Multi-line phone system operations
- ◆ Data entry and retrieval (Word and Excel)
- ◆ Customer relations
- ◆ Sales department support

- ◆ Account maintenance/reconciliation
- ◆ Order processing and billing
- ◆ Research and resolution of problems
- ◆ Regular and express mail distribution
- ◆ Office supplies and forms inventory

WORK HISTORY

CONCORD GROUP, INC., CHICAGO, IL   1998–2007
Personal and commercial insurance company
Receptionist
- ◆ Represented the prestigious image of this company in a high-profile position requiring public contact with important clients in the sports and entertainment field as well as various other industries.
- ◆ Entrusted with opening the office daily and handling confidential material.
- ◆ Operated 24-line Premiere 6000 phone system, routing calls/faxes appropriately, and relaying messages accurately. Saved managers' time by screening unwanted calls.
- ◆ Reorganized shipping room to run more efficiently and operated automated labeling/tracking system (Powership), processing 5 to 50 outgoing packages daily.
- ◆ Ensured prompt delivery of express packages.
- ◆ Took initiative to update insurance certificates on computer.
- ◆ Participated in hiring a new assistant and trained her in company procedures.

PAPERCRAFT USA, CHICAGO   1994–1997
Nation's largest distributor of specialty paper
Telephone Account Coordinator (Customer Service Representative)
- ◆ As one of 80 employees in a busy call center averaging 200 incoming calls per hour, handled the ordering process, billing, and issuing credits or rebills to ensure accurate account records.
- ◆ Consistently achieved excellent scores in the mid-90s on monitored activities.
- ◆ Provided support to sales representatives all over the country.
- ◆ For four months in 1996, assisted the product director, creative director, and vice president of sales, providing them with daily sales activity reports and analyses, pricing updates, and sales strategy presentations for company's two divisions.
- ◆ Processed invoices and deliveries for international shipments.

HJR VENDING COMPANY, CHICAGO, IL   1992–1994
Distributor of confectionery items sold in vending machines
Customer Service Representative
- ◆ Worked in a team of six, processing telephone orders from individuals and retailers, including four house accounts. Resolved billing discrepancies.
- ◆ Offered information on promotions and discounts, which encouraged larger orders.

THE PLAYHOUSE, CHICAGO, IL   1987–1997
Director of Day Care Center
- ◆ While raising a family, owned and operated a full-service day care center for preschool children.
- ◆ Administered all aspects of the business (billing, accounts payable, accounts receivable, and maintaining client files).

Office Support Professional

Janet is a long-time (15 years) worker within the veterinarian field who successfully moved into an administrative assistant's job in a medical office. She sent out one résumé and got the job.

JANET COOPER

813-555-9988 • JCOOPER@EMAIL.COM
2833 Newsome Road, Valrico, FL 33594

OFFICE SUPPORT PROFESSIONAL
Receptionist ... Clerk ... Administrative Assistant

EXPERTISE

Records Management

Customer Liaison

Front Office Operations

Workflow Planning / Scheduling

Troubleshooting / Problem Solving

Inventory Control

COMPUTER SKILLS

- Microsoft Word
- Cornerstone Proprietary Contact Management Software

TRAINING

Eastern States Conference in Orlando – Annual training for receptionists and managers

---

Top-performing office assistant with a reputation for professionalism, integrity, creativity, resourcefulness, and competence. Superior communication and listening skills. Strong client focus, with attention to detail and excellent follow-through.

SELECTED CONTRIBUTIONS

- Redesigned administrative processes to streamline functions, eliminate redundancy, and expedite workflow. Initiated the conversion from manual processes to a fully computerized office. Implemented the automated Gevity HR Payroll Program.
- Improved customer service by developing a new client survey, soliciting feedback to quickly resolve client complaints and ensure top-quality service and satisfaction.
- Launched an employee-of-the-month incentive program to build unity and promote outstanding customer service.

PROFESSIONAL EXPERIENCE

Practice Manager – 1993 to 2006
Receptionist – 1992 to 1993
COMPLETE ANIMAL HOSPITAL, Tampa, Florida
(Veterinary clinic comprised of 6 doctors, 10 technicians, and 7 receptionists with annual revenues of $1.4 million)
Oversaw scheduling, managed inventory, and trained receptionists. Accountable for financial reports including daily deposits, monthly billings, and collections.

Receptionist – 1990 to 1992
WILLIAM SMITH, DVM, Fayetteville, North Carolina
(One-doctor veterinary clinic, 2 technicians, 2 receptionists)
Professional and cheerful first point of contact. Broad-based experience in answering multiple telephone lines, scheduling appointments, and filling prescriptions.

RELATED EXPERIENCE

Administrative Assistant
CENTEL BUSINESS SYSTEMS, Fayetteville, North Carolina

Clerking Assistant
OSTEOPATHIC SCHOOL OF MEDICINE
Ohio University, Athens, Ohio

Office Assistant (Initial Résumé)

After interviewing Barbara, it became clear that she did more than her résumé reflected. Aside from her initial résumé being poorly formatted, it lacked focus, an interesting summary, and a content-rich presentation of her experience.

BARBARA WINSTON
190-12 Arthur Avenue, Brentwood, NY 11717
• • • 631-555-5555 • • •

OBJECTIVE

TO OBTAIN AN OFFICE ASSISTANT POSITION, ENABLING ME TO UTILIZE MY SKILLS AND DEVELOP CAREER PROGRESSION.

SKILLS

WORD PERFECT 5.0 AND 6.0
LOTUS 123
MICROSOFT WINDOWS 98
KEYBOARDING
DICTAPHONE, OFFICE PROCEDURES
KNOWLEDGE OF BUSINESS AND ORAL COMMUNICATIONS
MEDICAL FORMATS
WORK HISTORY

12/01 to Present

SIX AREAS UNIVERSITY, BRENTWOOD, NY
LIBRARY CLERK

ORGANIZING CIRCULATION DESK. ATTENTION TO DETAIL, EDITING, DATA ENTRY, XEROXING, FAXING, FILING, ASSISTING STUDENTS WITH RESEARCH, ADMINISTERING TESTS.

3/99 to 6/00

BRENTWOOD SCHOOL DISTRICT, BRENTWOOD, NY
TEACHER'S AIDE / CLERICAL

ASSISTED TEACHERS WITH SPECIAL EDUCATION STUDENTS, COMPUTER LAB, LUNCH ROOM MONITOR, PERFORMED DUTIES IN PUBLICATIONS DEPARTMENT, CLERICAL DUTIES SUCH AS COLLATING, HAND-INSERTING, AND PROOFREADING.

EDUCATION

10/97

SECRETARIAL SCHOOL OF AMERICA
MORRISTOWN, NY
Certificate In Information Processing
CUMULATIVE GPA – 3.6

1/85

JOHN WILSON TRAINING SCHOOL
BRENTWOOD, NY
Certificate In Medical Assisting

EXCELLENT REFERENCES AVAILABLE UPON REQUEST

Office Assistant (Revised Résumé)

The result of this before-and-after résumé is dramatic in many ways. It has gone from a confusing document to a personal marketing tool that clearly expresses Barbara's objective. Most importantly, the experience section has become very detailed and interesting to read.

BARBARA WINSTON
190-12 Arthur Avenue, Brentwood, NY 11717 ◆ 631-555-5555 ◆ BWinston@aol.com

Seeking a position in the capacity of **OFFICE SUPPORT ASSISTANT** within a general business or medical office environment, bringing the following experience, skills, and attributes:

◆ ◆ ◆

Extensive experience working in general public, educational, and medical office settings.
Interface well with others at all levels including patrons, patients, professionals, children, and students.
Caring and hardworking with excellent interpersonal communication, customer service, and office support skills.
Windows 98/DOS, MS Word, Dictaphone, CRT data entry, basic Internet skills, and medical terminology.

Work Experience

Circulation Desk Associate, Six Areas University, Brentwood, NY   **12/00 – Present**
Provided diversified information services and research assistance to the general public and student populations

- ◆ Assisted patrons in obtaining a broad selection of books, periodicals, audio-visuals, and other materials.
- ◆ Catalogued library materials, prepared bibliographies, indexes, guides, and search aids.
- ◆ Performed multifaceted general office support, and administered academic placement tests.

Teacher's Aide / Office Assistant, Brentwood School District, Brentwood, NY   **3/96 – 6/00**
Assigned to the Publications Department, Computer Lab, Special Education Resource Room, and Lunch Hall

- ◆ Assisted grade-level teachers with diversified clerical support in areas of document proofreading, duplication, collating and distribution, classroom management, student monitoring, and miscellaneous assignments.
- ◆ Easily established rapport with students, and interfaced well with parents and school-wide faculty members.

Nursing Assistant, Our Lady of Consolation, West Islip, NY   **6/90 – 1/96**
Physical Therapy Aide, Mother Cabrini Nursing Home, Dobbs Ferry, NY   **3/85 – 6/90**

Held the following combined responsibilities at Our Lady of Consolation and Mother Cabrini Nursing Home:

- ◆ Obtained vital signs and followed up with timely and accurate medical records-keeping procedures.
- ◆ Interfaced extensively with patients, staff personnel, orthopedic surgeons, and neurologists.
- ◆ Observed and reported changes in patients' conditions and other matters of concern.
- ◆ Performed ambulatory therapeutic treatments such as range of motion, gait training, and whirlpool baths.
- ◆ Transported patients to and from the hospital for emergency care and scheduled tests.
- ◆ Ensured the proper use of equipment and medical devices such as wheelchairs, braces, and splinters.
- ◆ Assisted patients with personal hygiene, grooming, meals, and other needs requiring immediate attention.
- ◆ Maintained sanitary, neatness, and safety conditions of rooms in compliance with mandatory regulations.

Education

Certificate, Information Processing, 1997
SECRETARIAL SCHOOL OF AMERICA, Morristown, NY

Certificate, Medical Assisting, 1985
JOHN WILSON TRAINING SCHOOL, Brentwood, NY

BRENDA FORMAN
45 Duquesne Street
Parlin, New Jersey 08859

Residence: 732-555-4681

CUSTOMER SERVICE PROFESSIONAL

SENIOR CUSTOMER SPECIALIST • BILLING • CREDIT

Shipping and Dispatching • Inventory Control

Top-performing customer service specialist with more than 20 years experience in diverse environments. Outstanding reputation for keeping and maintaining excellent customer service standards. Experienced in working with high volume calls and answering intricate inquiries.

Train and observe other customer service staff. Take pride in order processing accuracy and efficiency; receive excellent customer feedback. Punctual in meeting deadlines. Interact with the President of my present company on a daily basis. Known to go the "extra mile" for customers and colleagues. Dedicated, efficient, task-oriented employee.

Perform the functions of Order Processing Specialist, Diversified Account Specialist, and Crediting/Billing Specialist. Skilled planner with the ability to analyze client needs and achieve objectives. *Professional strengths include:*

- Customer Service
- Shipping Receiving
- Manufacturing Processes
- Troubleshooting Accounts
- Leadership/Supervision
- Sales Force Support
- Accounts Receivable
- Inventory Control Functions

- Pricing/Quoting Customers
- Processing Orders
- Expediting Deliveries
- Tracking
- Special Attention Order Entry
- Customer Service Observations
- Billing
- Written Reports

BUSINESS EXPERIENCE

EDWARD SMITH, Cranbury, NJ   2000 – Present
Senior Customer Service Representative and Trainer
Team Leader

- Currently serve as a Team Leader for this fine art and supplies manufacturer. Responsible for training and observation of other customer service employees. Lead customer service meetings and prepare written reports of findings.
- Replace supervisor in her absence.
- Ensure that discounts are applied correctly, and credits are entered in a timely fashion.
- Work with orders from start to completion. Interact daily with Daler-Rowney sales force and district manager.
- Handle customer requests. Take orders via fax, place on our system, send to purchasing; then send to warehouse, edit order, bill, print, and send to customers.
- Process all orders from Wal-Mart, our largest customer, through an EDI system.
- Work with Internet order processing systems including Microsoft Orbit program, Navision Financial Program, Trading Partners, Retail Link, Microsoft Word, and Excel.

BRENDA FORMAN PAGE TWO

- Attend trade shows and handle special orders in the field. Work with export customers.
- Print back order reports on a weekly basis. Work with potential new clients and their sales representatives regarding administrative work.
- Process numerous order per day including 500–1,000 keyed lines. Write reports in Microsoft Excel and Word.
- Responsible for the issuance of all return authorization numbers and UPS call tags. Research credits and input information into our system.

ROLL INDUSTRIES, Cranbury, NJ   **1991–2000**

Shipping/Receiving Coordinator
Customer Service Representative

- Responsible for a wide range of shipping/receiving and customer service functions for this *Fortune* 500 carpet manufacturer. Handled an extremely high call volume. Processed orders, answered customer inquires, tracked inbound/outbound shipments, expedited deliveries, and set up delivery schedules. Prepared UPS shipments and participated in cycle counting and quarterly inventories.
- Attended trade shows and expedited special attention orders.
- Coordinated with and supported sales representatives in the field. Performed cash receipt reconciliations and resolved customer complaints, disputes, or discrepancies.
- Received Employee of the Month Award out of 300 people.

CONTINENTAL LIFE INSURANCE, Plainfield, NJ   **1989–1991**

Customer Service Representative

- Responsible for pricing/quoting customers, answering phone inquiries, processing orders, and expediting deliveries along with troubleshooting accounts.

CHILDCRAFT, Plainfield, NJ   **1988–1989**

Customer Service Representative

- Duties similar to above. Position required ability to work in a high-pressure/fast-paced environment.

ACTION TUNGSTROM, East Brunswick, NJ   **1985–1988**

Shipping/Receiving Coordinator/Accounts Receivable Clerk

~ LETTERS OF RECOMMENDATION AND REFERENCES UPON REQUEST ~

Retail Manager

Scott needed a résumé that would highlight his strong retail
and store management experience.

SCOTT KELLY

761 Stoneham Avenue
Woburn, MA 01801

(781) 555-6093
ScottKelly3@hotmail.com

RETAIL ~ SALES & MANAGEMENT

Successful retail manager with over 14 years of experience in Sales, Purchasing/Buying, Customer Service, Inventory Management, Merchandising, Staff Recruitment, and Supervision. Proven ability to increase sales revenue and improve profitability through effective sales consultation, merchandising, purchasing, and inventory management. Demonstrate a high level of motivation and enthusiasm in all aspects of work.

- **Record of improving sales, successfully introducing new products, and growing customer base.** Expanded business for large volume – wine specialty – liquor establishment.
- **Excellent leadership skills**—can communicate effectively with employees and motivate them to perform at their best. Can set direction for the team. Hands-on approach to training.
- **Established record of dependability and company loyalty.**
- **Experience in both general merchandising and specialty retail sales.** Extensive knowledge of the wine industry including suppliers, distributors, and consumers; extensive product knowledge.

PROFESSIONAL EXPERIENCE

Manager (General Operations), *O'Leary's Discount Market,* Woburn, MA   **1996–present**

Direct the daily operation of a high-volume liquor/wine specialty store, servicing over 1,000 customers per week. Manage staff of 15 in the areas of sales and customer service, cash management, budgeting, sales forecasting, employee relations, merchandising, promotions, and security.

- Steadily increased revenues through strong focus on customer service, excellent merchandising, and teamwork.
- Attracted new clientele to store through the development of a full-service wine department. Expanded product line, increased sales and special-order purchasing by implementing specialized sales methods, such as promotional wine-tasting events.
- Established strong reputation in the area as leader for extensive wine inventories at competitive pricing, including regularly stocked hard-to-find selections.
- Trained staff in selling through increased product knowledge and food and wine pairing.
- Participated regularly in trade tastings, shows, and vintner dinners, including Westport Rivers Vineyard, Nashoba Valley Vineyard, Prudential Center and World Trade Center events.

Manager (Stock and Display), *Ames Department Stores,* Boston, MA   **1994–1995**

Managed a staff of 12 in a large, national general merchandise store. Marketed and sold products; developed merchandise and promotional displays; maintained stock levels.

- Increased profits through effective displays and merchandising.
- Improved operations through effectively supervising daily staff assignments.

Stock/Inventory Manager, *Beantown Gift,* Boston, MA   **1992–1994**

Managed purchasing and supervised sales staff for a high-traffic specialty gifts store.

- Expanded customer base by offering a wide range of attractive product displays and creating a welcoming atmosphere that increased the comfort level of patrons.
- Supervised staff of three, ensuring quality of store display and product inventory levels.

Additional experience includes entry-level inventory/shipping-receiving position at Boston University (1990-1982).

Merchandise Buyer

The use of a title and keywords list allows the reader to see exactly what Mary's objective is and the scope of her skills in relation to the position of interest. Notice the keywords are very specific rather than general attributes.

Mary J. Sanders

111 East End Avenue • Elmhurst, New York 55555 • (555) 888-0000 • shop2drop@retailworld.net

Assistant Buyer

Skilled in areas of:

- Wholesale / Retail Buying
- Product Merchandising
- Inventory Replenishment
- Product Distribution and Tracking
- Sales Analysis & Reporting
- Regional Marketing Campaigns
- Information Systems
- Vendor Relations
- Order Management

Professional Experience

Merchandise Buying / Coordination

- Report directly to London-American's Director of Sales, providing support in areas of commodities buying and merchandising activities that reach annual sales volumes of $3 million for the division.
- Collaborate with multiple buyers to facilitate the marketing efforts of new products, and development of promotional calendars, product launches, and employee incentive programs.
- Maintain open lines of communication between manufacturers, sales teams, vendors, and warehousing personnel to expedite product orders, distribution, and problem resolutions.
- Reported directly to the Senior Buyer of Steinway Bedding in charge of day-to-day retail merchandise buying and merchandising activities impacting bedding sales across 37 Northeast locations.
- Successfully trained 45+ Steinway employees on a complex LAN database management system.

Sales Tracking, Analysis, & Reporting

- Perform LAC's weekly sales analysis activities on regional/local transactions, achieving a recovery of $1,800,000 from 2001 to 2007 resulting from identification and resolution of accounting discrepancies.
- Develop sales books reflecting product lines, monthly promotions, discontinued items, order forms, and transparencies utilized by sales teams and personnel throughout 26 store locations.
- Formulate price breakdowns and track sales levels to determine product volume adjustments, replenishments, and allocations with a demonstrated proficiency in internal networking systems.
- Researched, compiled, and recorded Steinway's historical data to develop innovative sales strategies through close examination of inventory and product availability, pricing, and store promotions.

Work History

Assistant Buyer / Sales Analyst   7/00 – Present
LONDON-AMERICAN COMMODITIES, LTD. (LAC), Valley Stream, New York

Assistant Buyer / Merchandise Coordinator   4/96 – 7/00
STEINWAY BEDDING, Woodbury, New York

Education

Associates in Science, Business Management, 1996
STATE UNIVERSITY of NEW YORK at COBLESKILL

Sommelier

Angelica's résumé was tricked out to look like a menu.

Angelica Merceau
242 W. 103rd Street, Olathe, Kansas 66206
Phone: 913-555-2323 Email: wineangel@yahoo.com

Sommelier Extraordinaire

Piedmonts by the Bay, San Francisco, CA
Master Sommelier, September 2001 – Present

➤ Expertise in all aspects of wine, including regions of the world and their products, grape varietals, fortified wines, methods of distillation, international wine law, cigar production, and proper storage and handling.
➤ Manage wine inventory averaging over 12,000 bottles, worth $2,550,000.
➤ Supervise and personally train staff of 25 sommeliers and wine stewards in pairing wines with cuisine, presentation of wine, brandies, liqueurs, and cigars, and selection, preparation, and placement of glassware.
➤ Coordinate all wine-tasting events, and varietal seminars.
➤ Handle all client inquiries and complaints.

Bordeaux Steak House, New York, NY
Sommelier, May 1999 – January 2001
Lead Wine Steward, December 1997 – May 1999

➤ Supervise and train staff of wine stewards in all aspects of wine presentation, pairing with cuisine, and glassware selection and placement.
➤ Choose appropriate cuisine and wine pairings, assist clients in selection of wines, brandies, liqueurs, cigars, properly present and decant wines, and select and place stemware.

Education, Certifications and Professional Development:

➤ Columbia University, New York, NY
B.A. Food History, May 1997
➤ Court of Master Sommeliers, Napa, CA
Master Sommelier, 2001
➤ International Sommelier Guild, Grand Island, NY
*Sommelier Diploma Program, 1999
*Wine Fundamentals Certificate, Level II, 1999
*Wine Fundamentals Certificate, Level I, 1998
➤ Sommelier Society of America, New York, NY

Varietal Courses:
*Cabernet Sauvignon, 1999
*Sauvignon Blanc, 1999
*Chardonnay, 1999
*Merlot, 1999
*Sangiovese, 1999
*Syrah, 1998
*Pinot Noir, 1998
*Riesling, 1998

Professional Memberships

➤ *Association de la Sommellerie Internationale (ASI)*
Member, 2001 – Present
➤ *The Sommelier Society of America*
Member, 1999 – Present

Restaurant Server

Valerie uses an "Outstanding Achievements & Recommendations" section to bring attention to her strengths, and she has done a nice job in identifying the type of restaurants in which she has gained experience.

Valerie W. Butler

333 S.E. Riveredge Drive • Vancouver, Washington 33333
222-222-2222 cell • home 555-555-5555

❧Server❧

Professional Profile

Energetic and highly motivated **Food Server** with extensive experience in the food service industry. Expertise lies in working with the fine dining restaurant, providing top-quality service, and maintaining a professional demeanor. Solid knowledge of the restaurant business with strengths in excellent customer service, food and wine recommendations.

Get along well with management, coworkers, and customers. Well-developed communication skills, known as a caring and intuitive "people person," with an upbeat and positive attitude. Highly flexible, honest, and punctual, with the ability to stay calm and focused in stressful situations. Committed to a job well done and a long-term career.

Outstanding Achievements & Recommendations

- Served notable VIP clientele including clients associated with Murdock Charitable Trust.
- History of repeat and new customers requesting my service as their waitress.
- Known for creating an atmosphere of enjoyment and pleasure for the customer.

"...Valerie was warm, friendly, kind and very efficient.
We didn't feel rushed – she handled our requests and
we appreciated her genuine 'May I please you' attitude...."

Related Work History

Waitress • Banquets • Heathman Lodge • Vancouver, Washington • *2005–present*
Northwest seasonal cuisine.

Banquets • Dolce Skamania Lodge • Stevenson, Washington • *2004–2005*
Casual to fine dining restaurant.

Waitress • Hidden House • Vancouver, Washington • *1996–2004*
Exclusive fine dining restaurant.

Waitress • Multnomah Falls Lodge Restaurant • Corbett, Oregon • *1995–1996*
Historic Columbia Gorge Falls restaurant serving authentic Northwestern cuisine.

Waitress • The Ahwahnee at Yosemite National Park • California • *1 year*
World renowned award-winning fine dining restaurant – sister lodge to Timberline Lodge.

Customer Service Representative

Well laid out. Everything important is up front and center.

JUANITA FLORES

1523 Wisteria Avenue • Sherman Oaks, California 91423

Residence (818) 555-5555 • Mobile (818) 555-1234 • jflores555@email.com

Customer Service Representative / Administrative Support Specialist

—Bilingual English / Spanish—

Highly reliable professional who consistently demonstrates integrity and sound judgment.

Verifiable record of low absenteeism and punctuality; performs tasks with enthusiasm and efficiency.

Well organized with good time management habits; completes assignments in a timely and accurate manner.

Works well independently as well as collaboratively in a team environment.

Reputation for exceptional customer relations; easily establishes trust and rapport with public, demonstrating good listening skills and compassion.

Strong problem solving abilities; can be counted on to follow through to resolution.

Computer Skills: Windows, Microsoft Office (Word, Excel, PowerPoint)

PROFESSIONAL EXPERIENCE

Administrative Assistant, Trust Division • 2005 to Present

CITIBANK, Los Angeles, CA

Provide outstanding customer service handling and directing incoming telephone calls, assisting clients with inquiries and requests, and processing trust account transactions.

Directly support two vice presidents and team of trust specialists with administrative and clerical tasks.

Administrative Assistant • 2001 to 2005

LA OPINION NEWSPAPER, Los Angeles, CA

Provided sales and administrative support to advertising account executives. Assisted customers with inquiries and marketing information in Spanish and English.

Performed translation services.

Handled English and Spanish language correspondence.

Apartment Building Manager • 2001 to 2004 (*concurrent with above*)

SHERMAN PARTNERS PROPERTIES, Sherman Oaks, CA

Collect rents, ensure grounds and units are well maintained, prepare vacancies for rental, screen applicants, and write up rental agreements.

EDUCATION

LOS ANGELES VALLEY COLLEGE, Valley Glen, CA

Major: Business Administration—currently attending

UNIVERSIDAD MICHOACANA DE SAN NICOLAS DE HIDALGO, Mexico

Completed two years of studies in International Business

Steamfitter

Fred had experience in highly specialized jobs. His expertise
and training were attractively emphasized with graphic lines.

Fred G. Jamisen

9999 Abernethy Road • Oregon City, Oregon 99999
555-555-5555

Steamfitter

Professional Profile

Highly skilled, conscientious, and precise **Steamfitter** with over 6 years experience and 10,000+ hours of training in all aspects of Steamfitting. Familiar with all required codes, appropriate use of equipment, steamfitting techniques, safety standards, and proper procedures to prevent injuries. Proficient in reviewing plans, blueprints, and specifications for steamfitting projects with proven ability to provide expert recommendations. Well-developed troubleshooting skills with accurate and precise repairs. Experienced EMT willing to volunteer EMT services on the job. Excellent communication skills, personable, trustworthy, adaptable, and committed to a long-term career.

Expertise and Training Includes:

- Air Conditioning and Refrigeration Systems and Equipment
- Boilers
- Commercial and Industrial
- Conduit Flex, Duct, and Controls
- Electrical and Electronic Contracting
- HVAC, Air Conditioning, and Refrigeration
- Instrumentation
- Outdoor Installations
- Overhead and Underground
- Process Systems and Equipment
- Steam and Heating Systems and Equipment
- Troubleshooting and Maintenance
- Welding Processes including Orbital Welder Arc 207
- Wire Pulling, Wiring Devices, Removal, and Finish

Licenses

Pressure Vessel and Boiler License Class V • *State of Oregon*
United Association of Steamfitters • *Local 290*

Employment History

Steamfitter • United Association of Steamfitters • Portland, Oregon • *6 years*
Assignment to various companies and projects as needed.

Paper Machine Operator • Crown Zellerbach Corp. • West Linn, Oregon • *11 years*
previously owned by James River and Simpson Paper Company
EMT *(Emergency Medical Technician)* • Served as volunteer EMT for the paper mill.

Sales Representative • Pepsi Bottling Company • Portland, Oregon • *8 years*
Beverage sales.

Military

U.S. Army • **Specialist E-4 – Nuclear Missile Technician** • *Honorable Discharge* • *1979*

Education

Associates of Applied Arts • **Humanities**
Carroll College • Helena, Montana *and* Clackamas Community College • Oregon City, Oregon

TOM PARSONS

52 Dune Drive
Matawan, NJ 07747

732.555.3896
E-mail: DTJNPAR@AOL.COM

AUTOMOTIVE SERVICE MANAGER

Twenty-three years successful customer service management experience within the automotive industry; proven track record meeting challenges and creatively solving a variety of problems. Extensive knowledge of automotive warranty policies and procedures. Decisive hands-on manager with an interactive management style able to lead several service teams and administrative staff. Ability to motivate employees' performance levels and develop rapport with diverse audiences; excellent employee relations. Developed excellent product and service knowledge throughout career. Computer-literate with experience of Microsoft Office. Broad-based responsibilities and knowledge include:

- Customer Service
- Problem Solving
- Leadership, Supervision, & Training
- Service Repair Analysis
- Safety & Quality Control
- Warranty Expertise

- Product Knowledge
- Conflict Resolution
- Team Building
- Service Accounting (Expenses/Revenues)
- Technical Knowledge/Efficiency
- Operational Policies & Procedures

PROFESSIONAL EXPERIENCE

KEASBY NISSAN & SUBARU, Keasby, NJ ~ 1992 to Present
Service Manager

- Direct reports include 35 staff (Service Advisors, Service Teams, Cashiers, Receptionists, Lot Attendants, & Detailers)
- Manage Nissan and Subaru Service Departments while supervising service advisors and administrating client issues; ensure customer satisfaction.
- Solve product issues for both departments while working with company representatives and senior management.
- Improve department productivity and solve warranty issues when necessary.
- Monitor departmental budget, taking correct actions when required.
- Oversee the development and implementation of new Subaru franchise, and obtain required certification for service department.
- Achieve 2.2 hours per service order ratio for each customer.
- Eliminate expense and waste while reducing employee time-schedule loss.
- Perform repair order analysis, and monitor team efficiency improving shop utilization and work in process ratios.
- Analyze monthly owner first reports for Nissan, and communicate findings with staff.

ESSEX COUNTY NISSAN, Stanhope, NJ ~ 1987 to 1992
Service Manager

- Direct reports included 13 staff (Service Advisors, Service Teams, Cashiers, Lot Attendants, & Detailers)
- Oversaw entire Service Department ensuring complete customer satisfaction.
- Communicated with Nissan Service Representatives regarding product issues and warranty concerns.
- Improved departmental productivity, implementing several new programs.
- Conducted repair order and service department analysis.
- Substantially increased service revenues and volume by 60% during first fiscal year.
- Maintained warranty expenses within manufacturers' guidelines.
- Transferred to another location to manage larger department.

HAYNES NISSAN, Bloomfield, NJ ~ 1982 to 1987
Service Consultant

- Handled and wrote over 20+ customer service orders per day.
- Sold service and maintenance plans to clients.
- Coordinated service orders with technical staff ensuring quality control through entire service process.
- Prepared final accounting of orders.
- Implemented first statewide service team model for dealerships.
- Transitioned to new organization after company purchase.

Heavy Equipment Driver

Treavor was interested in driving heavy equipment in the Middle East.

TREAVOR BLACK
9999 CR7555 + Rolling Hills, Texas 79000
(999) 999-9999 + (806) 777-7777 (C)

+ DRIVER / HEAVY EQUIPMENT +

PROFILE

- Skilled driver with Class A Commercial Driver's License (CDL), Expires 1/29/08
- Over two million miles driving commercial vehicles loaded with general or refrigerated freight.
- Superior driving / safety / inspection record and on-time delivery.
- Excellent health and physical condition.
- Mechanically inclined and maintenance-minded.
- Customer-service oriented; personable with instructional communication skills.

VEHICLE EXPERTISE

• Several tractor / trailer rigs including refrigerated vans	32 years
• National 2003 Flatbed Trailer	3 years
• 2006 2T Ford F550 with Jerr-Dan Bed, Hydraulic Winch, Diesel	1 years
• 2004 35T Pete Wrecker with Nomar Bed, Hydraulic Winch, Diesel	3 years
• Racetrack road graders and water trucks	13 years

TRUCKING EXPERIENCE

Truck Driver, ROLLING HILLS WRECKER, Rolling Hills, Texas   2003 – present
Clean up heavy equipment wreck sites and transport vehicle remains to Rolling Hills Wrecker storage facility. In addition to using wrecker with hydraulic winch, utilize refrigerated vans, cow trailers, flatbed trailers, and Jaws of Life, as situation requires. Interface with customers and insurance providers. Maintain daily log and State / Federal paperwork. Worked dispatch and accepted management responsibilities as needed.

- Receive consistent raises due to outstanding performance.
- Underwent police background check to secure driver's position.

Truck Driver, GORGE TRANSPORT, Rolling Hills, Texas   2000 – 2001
Leased refrigerated truck to haul produce and meat products throughout California, Washington, Oregon, and Texas. Worked 12–14 hour days; maintained daily logs and trip sheets; and hired own loaders (lumpers) at docks.

Owner / Driver, BLACK TRUCKING, Rolling Hills, Texas   1993 – 2000
Leased out transport truck during summers to clients that included Blackcrest Transportation, WWW Trucking, and Gorge Transport. Drove during winters.

OTHER EMPLOYMENT

Promoter, SUN CITY SPEEDWAY, Sun City, Texas (summers)	2002 – 2003
Manager / Promoter, PLAINS SPEEDWAY, Rolling Hills, Texas (summers)	1990 – 2002
Auctioneer, Panhandle Texas Area	1996 – 2002

EDUCATION

High Plains College, Rolling Hills, Texas, Real Estate License	1998
Buddy Lee Auctioneer School, Freeze, Montana, Auctioneer	1996

Material Handler

Glenda used her "Outstanding Accomplishments and Achievements" section to bring strong focus to her capabilities.

Glenda Pension

356 N.E. Musical #303 • Portland, Oregon 88888
Email: pen333333@attbi.com • 555-555-5555

Material Handler

Professional Profile

Energetic, highly motivated, and organized Material Handler with extensive experience in purchasing, inventory control, and shipping / receiving. Strong liaison and negotiator for improving product delivery and lowering expenses. Well developed tracking and research abilities. Outstanding communication skills. Personable, independent, and committed to producing top-quality work. Positive and upbeat attitude; get along well with coworkers and management. Thoroughly enjoy a challenge and committed to a long-term career.

Experience Includes

• Accuracy	• Import	• Order Pulling	• Quality Assurance
• Customer Service	• Inventory Control	• Ordering	• Receiving
• Dedication	• Liaison	• Organization	• Shipping
• Export	• Negotiator	• Purchasing	• Tracking

Outstanding Accomplishments and Achievements

- Advocated to get certification through Quality Control to achieve FAA approval on specific products.
- Secured credit, due to my personal reputation, for a company in Chapter 11 bankruptcy.
- Negotiated effective contracts to obtain product shipment with little or no shipping charges.
- Recaptured thousands of dollars in warranty monies for company.
- Developed and implemented inventory tracking system.
- Reorganized and set up efficient stock room.

Professional Experience

Enlargement Printer • Qualex, Inc. • Portland, Oregon • *2003–2007*
Temporary Associate • Manpower • Portland, Oregon • *2002–2003*
Inbound Auditor / Quality Control • Columbia Sportswear • Portland, Oregon • *2001–2002*
Warehouse Tech / Quality Control • Dr. Martins Airwair • Portland, Oregon • *1999–2001*
Records Clerk • America West Airlines • Phoenix, Arizona • *1998*
Purchasing Agent • MarkAir Express, Inc. • Anchorage, Alaska • *1996–1998*
Japan Airlines Liaison for Inventory Management by Alaska Airlines
    Alaska Airlines • Anchorage, Alaska • *1994–1996*
Purchasing Manager / Warranty Administrator / Inventory Control
    Stateswest Airlines – USAIR Express • Phoenix, Arizona • *1991–1994*

Education and Training

Beechcraft Warranty Training • Indianapolis, Indiana • *2001*
Various classes offered by OSHA and Japan Airlines
Hazardous Materials Training • San Francisco, California • *1995*
Business *emphasis* • University of Alaska – Anchorage • Anchorage, Alaska • *1995*

Apartment Management (Joint Résumé)

Pamela and Katherine needed a combined résumé for use in applying as Team Managers. This format was highly effective.

Pamela Heshe ❧ Katherine Heshe

1234 S.E. 23rd Avenue · Rhododendron, Oregon · 555-555-5555

Apartment Managers

PROFESSIONAL PROFILE

- Highly motivated, dynamic, and energetic with over 30 combined years experience successfully working with diverse personalities.
- Experienced management and maintenance of various houses and plexes.
- Possess strong organizational skills and effective paper processing techniques.
- Expert bookkeeping abilities.
- Skills include: Minor repairs, simple plumbing, light electrical, painting, pool maintenance, landscaping, strong maintenance and clean-up experience.
- Effective in pre-qualifying new lease applicants and collecting rents in a timely fashion.
- Personable, loyal, honest, committed, creative, able to maintain property impeccably, and get along well with tenants and management.
- Able to be bonded, if necessary.
- Computer literate.

Pamela Heshe

EMPLOYMENT HISTORY

Medical Assistant • Portland, Oregon • *1993–2007*
- OHSU Sellwood/Moreland Clinic • *2002–2007*
- Medical Temporaries • *1993, 1994, 1998, 2000, 2002*
- Mount Tabor Medical Group • *1999–2000*
- Dr. Samuel Miller • *1994–1998*

EDUCATION

Medical *Emphasis* • *1988*
- Clackamas Community College
  Oregon City, Oregon

Graduate
- Portland Community College
  Portland, Oregon

Graduate
- Oregon X-Ray Institute
  Portland, Oregon

Katherine Heshe

EMPLOYMENT HISTORY

Accounting Manager / Administrative Assistant
- National Metal Distributors, Inc. • *2003–2004*
  Vancouver, Washington

Bookkeeper • *2001–2003*
- Aerospace & Corrosion International
  Vancouver, Washington

Letter Carrier • *1979–2000*
- United States Postal Service
  Portland, Oregon

MILITARY

United States Air Force • *1974–1978*
- Disbursement Accountant

EDUCATION

Elliott Bookkeeping School • *2001*
Accounting • *1979*
- Portland Community College
  Portland, Oregon

Fitness Trainer

Anna has a great start in her career as a fitness trainer with super client results that are detailed in the résumé for an action-packed, results-oriented document.

Anna Mead
5235 N. Halsey Drive, Richmond, Texas 77853 • 256-555-7772 • fitness77@sbcglobal.net

Physical Fitness Specialist

BACHELOR of SCIENCE KINESIOLOGY
December 2004
Texas A&M University   *College Station, Texas*

PROGRAMS DEVELOPED

- Volleyball League
for health club members

- Women's Self Defense

- "Silver Hearts"
group exercise class for mature members over sixty years of age

- "HealthPlex Holiday Challenge"

- "Suit Up for Summer"

- Personalized exercise programs for clients

- "Tiny Mites"
gymnastics for preschool

- "Gymnastic All-Stars Cheerleading Program"

GROUP EXERCISE CLASSES

- Yoga for Fitness

- Muscle Pump

- Rock Bottoms

- Aquafit

Proficient in the use of PC and Macintosh computers.

Motivated and driven

FITNESS SPECIALIST

brings eighteen months of ENERGETIC professional training experience to health and wellness programs yielding enthusiasm, commitment, and results.

SELECTED ACHIEVEMENTS

- Develop strong and strategic weightlifting program for male clients.

- Implement customized fitness programs for group and individual clients.

- Manage personal training programs, results, and profiles for 13 clients.

PROFESSIONAL CERTIFICATIONS

- IDEA Personal Trainer • YogaFit Certified Instructor
- CPR & First Aid • NSCA & ASCM Professional Member

PROFESSIONAL PHYSICAL FITNESS EXPERIENCE

EXERCISE PHYSIOLOGIST
- **Develop, produce and implement** internal and external marketing plans.
- **Instruct and create** programs for Cardiac Rehabilitation Phase III members.
- **Organize** Fitness Team and Health Assessment Testing schedules
- **Exceed expectations** and **deliver excellent customer service.**

PERSONAL TRAINER
- **Develop** personalized exercise programs for each client.
- **Monitor** the transition and progressions of each client into new, more effective exercises.
- **Prepare** exercise prescriptions.

FITNESS INSTRUCTOR
- **Instruct** various Group Fitness and Yoga classes.
- **Conduct research** on the latest trends and newest exercises.

GYMNASTICS COACH
Head Level Five Compulsory Coach

CLIENT PROFILES

Profile: Female, age 33 – Stay-at-home mom
Goal: Lose weight and get in shape after birth of baby.
Results: Within 4 months, weight: 147 to 128 lbs; body fat: 30.8% to 18.9%

Profile: Senior male, age 57 – Retired
Goal: Exercise to maintain and get the benefits for his heart.
Results: Developed regulated fitness program to reach target heart rate.

Profile: Female, age 40 – Professional
Goal: Lose weight (100 lbs.) and get in shape.
Results: Lost 12 lbs. and 14 inches in a six-week period.

PROFESSIONAL EXPERIENCE

ABM HEALTHPLEX – Richmond, Texas   **January 2005 – Present**
UNITED GYMNASTICS – Richmond, Texas   **2001 – 2004**
SPELLING GYMNASTICS – Richmond, Texas   **1999 – 2001**

Everyday Jobs

245

Aesthetician

Anita is an aesthetician moving up in her chosen profession.

ANITA KELLER

9001 E. Aspen Drive, Fountain Hills, AZ 85233
480/555-0000 • akeller@123.net

PROFILE

An experienced state-licensed **Aesthetician** seeking a rewarding career opportunity in a service-driven, team-centered spa / resort setting.
Consistently exceed client expectations; recognized for a gentle, soothing touch with a pleasant attitude, while demonstrating capability in areas of:

- skin care / facials • body treatments / wraps • waxing • lymphatic drainage • chemical peels • masks
- aromatherapy • multivitamin treatments • makeup • acupressure and Oriental massage treatments

Familiar with a wide product range including:

- Dermalogica • Murad • Obagi • Trucco • Jan Marini • Epicuren • Bio Elements
- Biomedics • Skinceuticals • MD Forte • Neo Clean • Magica

Licensure:

- State of Arizona Aesthetician License
- State of California Aesthetician License

AESTHETICIAN EXPERIENCE

HUDSON WILLIAMS DAY SPA, 3/03 – 7/06   Palm Springs, California
NITA FOSHEE, 4/03 – 7/06   Costa Mesa, California
Aesthetician
Working by appointment, provided comprehensive aesthetology services, from oxygen facials and anti-aging skin treatments, to waxing, body wraps, and aromatherapy for these upscale spas.

- Noted for customer service excellence to build a loyal customer base.

OTHER

PARSONS AGENCY, 7/06 – Present   Fountain Hills, Arizona
Personal Assistant
Provide production support for advertising agency, monitoring media placement, preparing and analyzing invoices and coordinating / scheduling talent for ads.

- Additionally serve as **makeup artist / stylist** on location / photo shoots to maximize visual impact.

EDUCATION

International Dermal Institute   Los Angeles, California
Continuing Education in Aesthetology 2005
Classroom and hands-on training in:

- European Skin Care Techniques • Vitamin Therapy for Skin Health • Aromatherapy • Body Therapy
- Wellness Therapies for Body, Mind, and Spirit • Results-oriented Tips for Maximum Prescriptive Retailing

Walters International School of Beauty   Costa Mesa, California
Aesthetology Certificate Program (600 hours) 2003
Course work encompassed:

- Microdermabrasion • Salt Glow Body Scrub
- Advanced Skin Care • Makeup Techniques
- Color Theory • Contouring and Corrections
- European Skin Care Techniques • Vitamin Therapy for Skin Health
- Aromatherapy • Body Therapy
- Wellness Therapies for Body, Mind, and Spirit
- Results-oriented Tips for Maximum Prescriptive Retailing

The New Executive Résumé

Traditional thinking has it that résumés only get a cursory first-time reading (about 45 seconds, and 90 percent of that time spent on the first page), rarely get thoroughly examined, and so consequently all résumés must be as brief as possible. The standard chant for professionals who think constantly about these matters says this: "One page for every ten years experience and never more than two pages." This still holds true for the majority of professionals, but not for all.

In certain quarters I may be regarded as a résumé heretic, because I believe that for some professionals in some situations such as senior technologists, scientists, and certain medical professionals—as well as many Director level, most VPs, and just about all C-suite executives—this rule no longer holds true; in fact, adhering to it can be a detriment to a successful job search.

The practical issues creating the need for this change are really quite simple: The increasingly complex requirements for more senior jobs creates the need for adequate reflection of these multifaceted competencies in a written document.

Such competency must be shown through ever-deepening experience supported by steadily increasing responsibility and illustrated by achievement. Management expertise and its achievements separate from professional and market sector skills also need clear illustration; additionally there are the necessities of professional visibility through publishing, speaking, and other leadership roles that are relevant in many senior level jobs. For example, I recently advised a big Pharma COO with a half-page history of board appointments, all of which had utmost relevance given his target job. Science is one of the "publish or perish" professions, and you'll see a résumé example in the next few pages that contains almost a full page addressing publications, presentations, and professional affiliations; in such instances, mass adds weight.

Let's take a moment to recall the roles your résumé plays in a successful job search: It gives you an achievable focus (without which you cannot be successful); It opens doors; it acts as a road map for interviewers; and it is your spokesperson long after the last interview is over. In short, the thinking that goes into the focus and execution of your résumé has a significant impact on every facet of your successful job search. Not surprisingly for professionals in the higher ranks of some professions, an adequate story sometimes cannot be told in two pages, and cramming it in with 9- and 10-point fonts is certainly not the answer—the people in a position to hire such candidates are simply not going to struggle with the fine print.

At the same time the Internet has changed the face of recruitment advertising in at least two dramatic ways:

1. Space is no longer an issue, so recruitment advertising has changed from a few terse lines to hundreds and sometimes thousands of words.
2. The descriptors used in the recruitment advertising and job descriptions increase the need for a data-dense résumé—one that is going to be retrieved from the résumé databases because it uses the right keywords in adequate frequency to catch the attention of the database spiders.

Putting these considerations together: The complexity of some professional and most executive work, along with the need to communicate effectively by using the traditional device of the résumé in the new electronic media, has birthed knowledge-era executive résumés of considerable length and density.

My thinking has changed to such a degree on this issue that in my private coaching practice, where I work with senior professionals on the national and international stage, I am suggesting, encouraging, supporting, and approving data-dense résumés in the three-to-eight-page range, because these résumés are clearly necessary to hit home runs for players in the major leagues.

Executive résumés will still get a cursory first-time review, whether they come directly to human eyes or are dragged up by keywords from a database. This means that, just as much as ever, a résumé needs to be clearly focused on a specific job with that first page screaming understanding, capability, and achievement in the target area of expertise.

When the first résumé page communicates clearly and contains a compelling message, the subsequent pages will get read with serious attention. The established standards of clarity and brevity (wherever possible) still hold; it's just the complexity of work at the higher levels that has increased and requires explanation. So résumé length for today's executive becomes a clear-cut issue of form following function.

The examples you'll see in the next few pages are courtesy of my colleagues at the Phoenix Career Group *(www.phoenixcareergroup.com)*, where we work with executives like this every day. If you are in need of powerful executive documents, Phoenix or MartinYate.com is the place to go.

Senior-Level Corporate Executive

DONALD T. THOMAS

2009 Churchill Drive
Aliso Viejo, CA 92656
donaldthomas@gmail.com

Home: 949-555-9396   Mobile: 949-555-2709

SENIOR-LEVEL EXECUTIVE
FINANCE, CORPORATE STRATEGY, & DEVELOPMENT
Expert in Leading & Partnering Corporate Finance with Enterprise Strategies, Initiatives, Transactions, & Goals

PROFILE & VALUE

Strategic Finance Expert—Dynamic CFO with extensive experience and exceptional success in conceiving, planning, developing, and executing strategic and tactical finance initiatives that drive top-line performance and bottom-line results. Technically proficient in all aspects of the finance and accounting functions, and expert in partnering corporate finance with enterprise strategies, initiatives, and objectives.

Corporate Strategy & Development Specialist—Characterized as a rare visionary, strategist, and tactician. Consistent originator of bold, innovative business strategies that have extraordinary results on growth, revenue, operational performance, profitability, and shareholder value. Heavy transactions background including startup financing, industry rollup, merger of equals, acquisition, and sale.

Consummate Management Executive—Top-performer and valuable contributor to corporate executive teams. Extremely versatile with high-caliber cross-functional management qualifications, experience-backed judgment, and excellent timing. Outstanding role model. Talented team builder, mentor, and leader.

Diverse Industry & Situational Experience—public and private; small and *Fortune* 500; startup, rapid growth, turnaround, post-IPO, post-acquisition integration, bankruptcy—consulting services, real estate, hospitality, resort/vacation property, travel companies doing business in highly regulated industries in U.S., European, and global arenas.

Extraordinary Personal Characteristics—Articulate, intelligent, ambitious, self-driven, and creative. Outstanding corporate ambassador to customers, industry groups, regulatory bodies, private investors, Wall Street analysts, board members, and other internal and external stakeholders. Speak conversational French and German.

QUALIFICATIONS & EXPERTISE

Vision, Strategy, Execution, & Leadership

Strategic Corporate Finance

P/L & Performance Improvement

Financial Forecasting, Analysis, & Reporting

Cost Analysis, Reduction, & Control

Treasury, Tax, Internal Audit

GAAP, SEC, & Statutory Reporting

Corporate Development & Strategic Alternatives

Due Diligence, Deal Structuring, & Negotiation

Financial & Legal Transactions

Growth Management & Business Development

Organizational Design & Transformation

Turnaround & Restructure

Crisis & Change Management

Internet Strategies & IT Projects

Team Building & Leadership

Investor, Analyst, & Board Relations

Executive Advisory & Decision Support

PROFESSIONAL EXPERIENCE

DTT Management Consulting, San Diego, CA   2000 to Present
Successful Management Consulting Firm—Significant Repeat Business and Value-Added Partner to Leading Consulting Firms (e.g., Alix Partners, PKF Consulting)—Retained by Start-up, Small-Cap, and Fortune *500 in US, UK, and ASIA*

PRINCIPAL

Operate an independent firm specializing in the delivery of a full-range of consulting services—strategic business planning; strategic finance; corporate strategy, development and financing; organizational design; operational and financial turnaround; marketing; and market research and strategy. Identify and acquire new business, and manage all aspects of the project lifecycle—from scope of work through provision of deliverables, follow-up, and relationship management—for large-scale, long-term projects. Engaged by corporate clients representing a broad-range of industry sectors—travel and tourism; hospitality; real estate development; marketing services; and technology and Internet.

Management Successes
- Leveraged professional reputation contacts worldwide to build and grow a successful management consulting firm.
- Acquired significant repeat business and positioned the firm as a value-added partner to high-profile management consulting firms in the U.S. and U.K. (e.g., ABC Partners, DEF Consulting).

Key Engagements
- **Turnaround & Change Management**—Retained (by principal consultancy group) to evaluate a key strategic business unit of a $500 million resort/vacation sales company in Chapter 11. Performed in-depth analyses of operations, identified deficiencies and risks, and presented recommendations for restructure and turnaround of call center operations, program management, inventory control, and member services functions. Engagement contract was extended to serve as Chief Business Architect during execution and post-C11 transition/recovery phases.
- **Operational Start-up & Financing**—Retained by U.K.-based client of a $10 million marketing services business to advise and participate in creating a business plan, raising capital, and executing a startup in the global event management and incentives sector.
- **Corporate Strategy & Finance**—Retained by independent U.S. resort developer to determine the viability and ROI of expanding into international markets. Analyzed business, financial, marketing, competitive intelligence, and geopolitical issues impacting the world tourism and hospitality sectors. Pinpointed key target markets, and authored business strategy and financial plan for launch of a luxury boutique hospitality brand.
- **Corporate Strategy**—Engaged in joint consultancy project with ABC Consulting in developing a full-scale corporate strategy plan for $500 million public hospitality company. Researched and analyzed internal and external organizations, market opportunities, competitive differentiators, business models, and challenges.

CDE Group, Ltd., London, England   1999 to 2000
Venture Capital–Backed Dot-Com Start-up Operating in a Niche Sector—Fine Arts and Antiques Online Sales/Auction

MANAGING DIRECTOR

Held full P&L accountability—recruited by and reported to the investor group and Chairman of the Board—for an early-stage Internet company. Developed and executed strategy, managed finance and operations, directed sales and marketing, steered technology development, and managed relationships with internal and external stakeholders. Led a core team of three executives—Director of Sales, Director of Operations, Manager of Finance & Administration—and provided indirect oversight to team of 18 in sales, operations, IT, finance, and administrative roles.

Strategy & Leadership Successes
- Revised corporate strategy to leverage core competencies—a well-established network of dealerships and virtually unlimited source of product—and position the firm as inventory and distribution solution to another company.
- Conceived and executed viable exit strategy—vs. minimum requirement of additional 2+ years' investment to achieve break-even—by identifying a buyer and negotiating sale of the company to a U.S.-based business. Provided investors with ROI on their original investment/commitment of 660%+.

STUV Corporation, Inc., Orlando, FL   1997 to 1999
$500 Million Company—One of Largest Resort and Vacation Development/Sales Companies in U.S.—in Rapid Growth Through International Expansion, Strategic M&A, Industry Rollup, and IPO

VICE PRESIDENT—BUSINESS DEVELOPMENT

Key member of the executive committee—retained in company's buyout of U.K.-based LSI Group—in charge of the strategic and tactical business development activities during period of dynamic growth and change. Crossed-over functional lines to address product development, marketing, branding, sales, corporate communications, legal, and regulatory matters. Administered $10 million business development budget. Reported directly to the CEO/COO, led a team of five Director-level executives, and interfaced with Board of Directors, Wall Street analysts, and strategic alliance partners.

Strategy & Leadership Successes
- Led the company's single most significant post-IPO strategic initiative—conceptualization, development, and execution of transformation of the company's infrastructure, business model, product offering, and marketing strategy—without negative impact on sales, operational performance, or customer service during execution.
- Shifted the business model and organizational structure—from a disconnected collection of resort properties—to a membership-based vacation sales company with an exclusive, points-based vacation product, and strong value proposition with single marketing message.

Business Development Results
- Credited with personal contributions to explosive growth—from $330 million in 1997 to $500 million in 1999—by spearheading the development and rollout of an innovative vacation ownership product and complementary offerings.
- Expanded market reach and brand recognition by initiating and leveraging relationships with high-profile strategic business partners—American Airlines, Time Warner, HSN, MemberWorks, and others in the travel, hospitality and marketing services industries.

XYZ, Ltd., Lancaster, England   1994 to 1997
$65 Million, Privately Held Enterprise—One of Largest Vertically Integrated Vacation Ownership Companies in Europe—Specializing in Development and Management of Resorts, and Marketing and Sales of Timeshares and Travel Services

DIRECTOR—BUSINESS DEVELOPMENT (1995 to 1997)
CHIEF FINANCIAL OFFICER (1994 to 1995)

Held two key executive positions on the management team—both reporting to CEO (one of two principal shareholders)—following a major debt restructure, physical relocation, and preparation for sale. As CFO, managed all aspects of the corporate finance and administration functions (including treasury, tax, statutory reporting, and internal audit) for headquarters and 10+ overseas branches. Directed the preparation and analysis of financial statements, budgets, forecasts, desktop "dashboards," and other essential management reports. Hired, trained, mentored, and managed a team of 28 including three senior financial and accounting professionals.

As Director of Business Development, identified, created, and capitalized upon both innovative and traditional business opportunities. Conceived, developed, and managed strategic and tactical messaging, branding, marketing, sales, and relationship-building initiatives. Directed product development, positioning, and go-to-market strategies, and launched a series of breakthrough concepts and techniques—trial membership, incentive-driven referral program, customer/prospect profiling, direct-to-consumer sales, interactive multimedia presentations.

Strategy & Business Development Successes
- Key contributor to providing deep due diligence to ABC in its purchase of LMN Group—activities and relationships that led to recruitment to executive position with the acquiring company.
- Credited with personal contributions (strategy, finance, operations, business development)—to growth—from $40 million to $65 million—profitability—from 5% pre-tax margin in 1994 to 11% in 1997—and shareholder value—from $15 million to $55 million at sale of the company in mid-1997.

Finance & Operations Results
- Built and managed a best-in-class finance and accounting function. Managed the complete turnaround of the corporate finance organization to include new systems, technologies, processes, and personnel.
- Provided the executive team and stakeholders with comprehensive, meaningful decision support by restructuring virtually all financial reporting systems.

WXY Group, London, England   1987 to 1994
One of London's Largest Public Accounting and Business Consulting Practices—Professional Services for Entrepreneurial Public and Private Companies in Real Estate, VC Funding, Hospitality, and Leisure Travel Sectors

Rapidly Advancing Levels of Seniority to:
MANAGER—CORPORATE FINANCE & INVESTIGATIONS DEPARTMENT (1992 to 1994)

Managed client engagements involving deep due diligence for numerous acquisition and funding transactions. Provided a full range of advisory services and functions including creating/opining on corporate development strategies, authoring business plans, preparing projection models, and performing operational and financial assessments. Developed expertise in fraud and litigation support, debt workout, and internal audit. Interfaced with firm's Partners, investment bankers, private investors, senior-level corporate executives, board members, industry specialists, and regulatory officials.

Key Engagements
- **Debt Restructure**—Contributed to restructure of £100+ million debt with complex asset security position.
- **Fraud Investigation & Litigation**—Provided support on several high-profile engagements including collapse of a private financial services firm (represented WXY as the client) and a Formula One motor racing team.
- **Corporate Recovery**—Contributed to financial and operational turnaround of several hospitality and leisure firms.

EDUCATION & CREDENTIALS

British Chartered Accountant—ACA—(CPA equivalent), Institute of Chartered Accountants in England and Wales
G Mus (Hons)—Four year degree in Music (with honors), Royal Northern College of Music, Manchester, England
Training in Corporate Finance and Treasury, Association of Corporate Treasurers

PROFESSIONAL AFFILIATIONS

Institute of Chartered Accountants in England and Wales (ICAEW); American Resort Development Association (regular speaker and panelist at conventions) (ARDA); American Marketing Association (AMA); San Diego Chamber of Commerce; Association of Chartered Accountants in the U.S. (ACAUS); American Real Estate Society (ARES); and Financial Management Association (FMA)

Executive Résumés

DONALD T. THOMAS

donaldthomas@gmail.com

HIGHLIGHTS OF A CAREER IN EXCELLENCE
Addendum to Résumé

EXCELLENCE IN CORPORATE STRATEGY & TURNAROUND

Managing Director—early-stage Internet start-up

Challenge   Revise corporate strategy and turnaround operational and financial performance of a venture capital-backed, early-stage start-up—fine arts and antiques dot-com.

Actions   Evaluated the original business plan against actual conditions and projected outcomes based on multiple scenarios. Created and executed a decisive strategy for "repackaging" the company's value proposition as an inventory and distribution solution to larger companies. Halted overspending, implemented strict financial controls, restructured operations, and re-engineered business processes.

Results   Provided investors with viable business strategies and alternatives, and at their direction, executed an exit strategy through the successful sale of the company for $10 million in stock. Provided investors with 660% ROI on their original investment/commitment.

Strengths   I am a turnaround specialist—I can rapidly assess a complex business situation, formulate a solution that meets overall commercial objectives (even if the solutions are a radical departure from initial direction), and inspire and gain buy-in for dynamic change.

EXCELLENCE IN STRATEGY & BUSINESS DEVELOPMENT

VP—Business Development, large resort development and sales company

Challenge   Lead high-profile, mission-critical strategic business initiative—characterized by COO as "betting the ranch"—to restructure and transform a $500 million resort and vacation development and sales company.

Actions   Developed and executed strategies, and planned and managed on virtually all cross-functional aspects of the business. Steered development of an appealing customer value proposition in an innovative product offering—"Club Main Attraction" a points-based vacation club—communicated through a clear, strong brand and marketing message. Partnered with legal counsel in structuring products that met state/federal regulatory guidelines. Built and led a team of top-performing strategic marketing professionals to execute rollout to 1,000+ person sales force.

Results   Exceeded expectations of founders/executive management and Wall Street analysts—rewarded in 1999 for exceptional corporate contributions by receipt of a specially created Award for Vision—in conceiving and driving innovation in corporate strategy, infrastructure, and product marketing.

Strengths   I am a true visionary and talented business leader who is always originating new concepts, innovating bold strategies, creating opportunities, and applying highly developed finance, marketing, business management, and people skills to take on huge challenges and overcome daunting challenges.

EXCELLENCE IN COST REDUCTION & PERFORMANCE IMPROVEMENT

CFO—large European, vertically integrated vacation ownership company

Challenge   Resolve serious financial and operational performance issues—increasingly high costs and productivity bottlenecks in the travel and reservations division.

Actions   Streamlined divisional operating processes, realigned key personnel, and updated and improved the payment processing and banking functions by establishing a relationship with a high-tech banking institution.

Results   Improved customer service while slashing invoicing and collection costs—from 10% to <5% and $5 million; and as volume grew to $25+ million, reduced the ratio even further—and created seamless connectivity in processes, communications and culture between the division and the rest of the organization.

Strengths   I am an expert in leveraging best practices, technologies, and relationships to enable and maintain inter-organizational cohesiveness and operational performance excellence.

EXCELLENCE IN DECISION SUPPORT

CFO—leading European resort developer

Challenge   Provide comprehensive, meaningful, and accurate decision support to the principals of a privately held, multisite resort development and sales enterprise.

Actions   Led complete restructure of the corporate finance and accounting organization, and all related systems, controls, processes, and technologies. Introduced sophisticated forecasting, analysis, and reporting tools, restructured the financial reports, refined the budgeting/variance analysis process, and implemented open-architecture accounting IT solutions/applications. Rebuilt, retrained, and mentored the 28-person finance and accounting team, and advised senior-level management in optimal utilization of new financial information.

Results   Created and led a top-notch finance and accounting organization that produced timely, precise, meaningful financial and operational data—executive decision support and departmental financial accountability credited with the company's realization of 65% improvement in profitability (despite zero revenue growth) within one year of implementing new corporate finance regime, and delivery of significant ROI in successful sale of the company two years later.

Strengths   I am valuable to any corporate executive team through my ability to provide mission-critical decision support, and I am proficient in building and leading best-in-class finance and accounting organizations.

EXCELLENCE IN STRATEGIC & TACTICAL BUSINESS DEVELOPMENT

Director of Business Development—European vacation ownership company

Challenge   Continue to grow revenue and market share despite dramatic changes in the European vacation ownership sector—new legislation impacting multiple areas of the business model (ban on down-payment at point of sale, expanded disclosure requirements, statutory cancellation period).

Actions   Went to senior sales executives with a new sales model—multimedia technology, new sales showroom environment, upgraded sales presentation and collaterals—and gained approval from shareholders for investing in the strategic and tactical innovations.

Results   Distinguished the company as an industry leader—first vacation ownership company (in both U.S. and U.K.) to utilize new technology-enabled sales/communication tools—a significant feature in sale of company. Maintained corporate revenue performance while reducing cancellation rates by 5%+.

Strengths   I am continuously devising ways to drive growth, operational performance, and profitability—despite any internal or external challenge. With acute understanding of the marketplace, I am able to create and execute business development strategies and tactics that put my company in front of the competition.

EXCELLENCE IN TURNAROUND & CHANGE

Consultant—international resort and vacation timeshare company

Challenge   Restore financial and operational health to a key strategic business unit—an SBU critical to the survival of the company—for an enterprise in post-Chapter 11 transition.

Actions   Contributed industry and business unit expertise (personally created, developed and exceeded performance objectives during period of 1997 through 1999) to a joint venture consulting engagement with ABC Partners (turnaround specialists). Evaluated existing operations and mapped-out a new strategy, organizational structure, business model (personal property vs. deeded real estate) and culture.

Results   Delivered the plan for putting in place a robust organizational structure with best-practices for risk management, inventory utilization, call center operations, program management, financial reporting, and member communications/satisfaction. Retained on extended contract to serve as Chief Architect (reporting to Interim CEO) to contribute cross-functional leadership to ongoing project phases. Received second extension (reported to permanent executive committee) to manage post-C11 integration of the U.S. and European programs. Combined annual cost savings of turnaround initiatives exceeded $5 million annually.

Strengths   In addition to industry expertise—resort and vacation timeshare—I bring the full complement of business and finance management qualifications. I am quick to identify and create solutions to complex business issues, and am proficient in managing large-scale, long-term, mission-critical projects.

Executive Résumés

SAMUEL HARRINGTON, Ph.D.

VA Dept. of Health & Human Services
Public Health Laboratories
6 Hazen Drive, Fairfax, VA 22033
Office: 800-555-5555
harringtons@dhhs.state.va.us

1012 South Street
Fairfax, VA 22033
Home: 571-555-5555
Cell: 571-555-5555
harringtonsam@aol.com

SENIOR EXECUTIVE—SCIENTIST
Chief Science Officer—Executive Director—Program Manager—Senior Scientist/Researcher
Biotechnology Enterprises—Molecular Research & Diagnostics Organizations

CAREER PROFILE & DISTINCTIONS

- Dynamic, entrepreneurial business professional with high-caliber general management qualifications ... strong orientations in finance and technology ... proven leadership talents. Led the startup of three biotechnology R&D organizations and turned around an existing test / surveillance laboratory.

- Accomplished senior-level scientist and recognized innovator in modern technical and managerial strategies, principles, methodologies, and processes for the biotech industry. Designed and developed numerous scientifically / commercially significant diagnostic reagents and assays.

- Professional experience spanning diverse clinical and technical settings; private biotech firms ... large R&D operations ... public health organizations ... hospitals ... academic facilities ... federally funded Homeland Security projects.

- Accustomed to, and effective in high-profile scientist executive roles ... managing large organizations ... overcoming complex business/technical challenges ... gaining respect from competitors and peers ... communicating complex concepts to technical and non-technical audiences ... maintaining impartiality in politically charged environments ... fostering consensus and generating cooperation from multicultural, multidisciplinary teams.

- Confident, assertive, diplomatic, and outgoing with exceptional communication, public speaking, and interpersonal relations skills. Multicultural, bilingual professional—speak fluent Arabic and English.

MANAGEMENT QUALIFICATIONS

Entrepreneurial Vision, Strategy, & Leadership
Financial Planning & Management
Program & Project Management
Staff Training, Development, & Supervision
Team Building, Mentoring, & Leadership

P&L and Operations Management
Budget Planning, Analysis, & Control
Process Design / Improvement—Business & Technical
Technology Investments & Solutions
Marketing, Communications, & Public Relations

AREAS OF EXPERTISE

Molecular Diagnostics R&D
Disease Investigation & Management—Infectious & Genetic
Laboratory Management Quality Improvement & Assurance
Advanced Laboratory Procedures & Technologies
Homeland Security Strategies, Policies & Programs

Molecular-Based Surveillance
DNA Fingerprinting & Gene Banking
Regulatory Affairs & Compliance—CLIA, CAP
GLP, CQA, CQI
Crisis / Emergency Preparedness & Response

PROFESSIONAL EXPERIENCE

State of Virginia, Fairfax, VA   1999 to Present

STATE MOLECULAR BIOLOGIST
Department of Health & Human Services, Public Health Laboratories (PHL)

Hold full P&L accountability for Virginia's only public health reference laboratory—infectious disease testing and surveillance services, bioterrorism detection, prevention, and response—serving the state's 1.2 million citizens. Manage all aspects of business operations (e.g., strategic planning, budgeting, financial reporting, staffing, workflow, administrative affairs, internal/external customer service, quality, regulatory reporting / affairs). Provide technical and managerial oversight to six primary areas of laboratory operations: test development, disease surveillance, disease outbreak investigations (including emerging infections, air-water-food-borne infections), and testing for biothreat organisms / bioterrorism. Manage $600K capital budget and $250K annual budget for operations. Lead a three-person management team and provide indirect supervision to seven technical and non-technical support employees.

DIRECTOR OF MOLECULAR DIAGNOSTICS—State of Virginia—*Continued:*

Management & Leadership Successes:

- Put the State of Virginia "on the map" in the U.S. biotech industry. Distinguished the facility as one of the best labs in the nation, and one of the first public health organizations to receive federal funding for bioterrorism testing and preparedness.

- Evolved a very basic laboratory operation into a dynamic scientific organization staffed with talented, highly trained professionals utilizing state-of-the-art technologies and contemporary methodologies to perform sophisticated testing and surveillance of emerging infections.

- Led an ambitious campaign to secure $600K+ investment in technology (state and federal sources). Achieved financial accountability and discipline throughout the organization in order to maximize ROI.

- Equipped the organization and prepared the staff to handle both routine and emerging infections (including potential bioterrorism organisms) despite the challenges of operating under serious financial and staff constraints.

- Converted the test development strategy from a successive to concurrent approach. Re-engineered laboratory processes and workflows enabling completion of 80,000+ tests in FY 2001/2002.

- Designed and led intensive training and career development programs—trained / qualified four professionals in advanced molecular testing—and provided team coaching and one-on-one mentoring.

- Served as an effective representative / spokesperson for the organization to internal and external parties—scientific community, state / federal agencies (CDC, FDA, USDA, other public health laboratories), regulatory officials, media, and the public—and continue to advocate on behalf of the MDX / PHL and its activities, budgets, personnel, and projects.

Clinical Projects & Achievements:

- Distinguished as the state's top-ranking science officer providing consulting, advisory, and leadership services on matters related to molecular diagnostics.

- Led the entire development cycle—design, validation, application, training, troubleshooting—of molecular diagnostics-based assays for rapid investigation, diagnosis, and surveillance of emerging / re-emerging infectious diseases including E. coli, salmonella, West Nile virus and Noro virus.

- Participated in validation of new rapid tests developed by CDC for BT organisms including anthrax, smallpox, and the emerging virus responsible for SARS.

Columbia University Medical Center (CUMC)—Mailman School of Public Health, New York, NY   1992 to 1998

PROGRAM COORDINATOR—DEVELOPMENT
Division of Molecular Diagnostics

Key member of a seven-person management team for a key division within this large, diverse health-care conglomerate—2nd largest medical center in New York and largest in northeastern area—comprised of several regional hospitals and specialty institutions (including Columbia Cancer Institute and Starzl Transplant Institute). Managed the business, clinical, and technology aspects of test development. Led a team of 13 full-time technologists.

Management Achievements:

- Established the MDX developmental laboratories from the ground up—lab was a model followed by other laboratories throughout the U.S.—and provided the vision and operational framework for accommodating emerging technologies and future expansion

- Contributed to planning, development, and control of annual budgets of nearly $1 million for operations—including $200K for capital equipment.

- Developed/presented formal training programs—one-month courses in lecture and wet lab formats—to physicians on topics related to emerging/advanced molecular diagnostics methodologies, technologies, and applications.

Clinical Projects & Achievements:

- Developed DNA fingerprinting method to distinguish between closely related isolates of *Legionella pneumophila*—causative pathogen for Legionnaire's Disease. Existence of this technique thwarted potential litigation (six-figure damage claim) by a former patient against the hospital.

- Developed test for identifying four most common gene mutations of Gaucher Disease among Ashkenazi Jewish populations. Delivered $110K+ per year in revenue from laboratory test fees.

The Methodist Dallas Transplant Institute (MDTI), Dallas, TX   1995 to 1998

SCIENTIST/CONSULTANT

Contributed expertise in molecular diagnostics to a multidisciplinary team of professionals—immunology, molecular biology, genetics, cell biology, other disciplines—working clinical R&D activities for the oldest/largest comprehensive international organ transplant programs in the world (a division of the University of Texas Medical Center). Developed customized specialty reagents utilized in research at the Institute.

Clinical Projects & Key Accomplishments:

- Developed 2-hour assay—vs. existing test requiring 24+ hours—for detecting presence of low-level HCV in donated livers to be used in transplantation.

- Established custom oligonucleotide design and synthesis service. Generated $150K+ in annual revenue (commercial value exceeded $300K).

Applied Genetics Laboratories, Inc. (AGL), Melbourne, FL   1991 to 1992

PROJECT LEAD/STAFF SCIENTIST

Managed a five-year, $2.5 million project funded by the National Institute of Environmental Health Sciences (NIEHS) for R&D of early cancer detection/treatment methods. Provided technical and managerial oversight to all aspects of the project lifecycle. Tracked and controlled project budgets. Supervised four laboratory technologists.

Clinical Projects & Key Accomplishments:

- Designed and executed protocols for searching for TSGs in mice genome and detecting mutations enabling early diagnosis of cancer in humans.

- Participated in presenting annual project report to National Institute of Environmental Health Sciences in North Carolina.

Kuwait Institute for Scientific Research, Shwaikh, Kuwait   1985 to 1987

RESEARCH SPECIALIST
Department of Biotechnology

Established and managed Kuwait's first molecular genetics laboratory. Developed research strategies and managed projects. Provided consulting/advisory services on business and scientific issues. Built and led a team of 10 scientists, and hired/managed administrative support staff.

Research Projects & Key Accomplishments:

- Distinguished as the only molecular biologist in Kuwait, and independently started and managed mission statement, business/clinical strategy, business/laboratory operations, policy/procedure formation, budget, staff, equipment for this, the first molecular genetics laboratory in the country.

- Co-Principal Investigator on three-year, $480K+ project involving establishment of basic tools and methodologies for subsequent production of high-value compounds—single cell proteins—for use as animal feed supplements.

TEACHING EXPERIENCE

University of Virginia, Hampton, VA   2000 to Present

ADJUNCT ASSOCIATE PROFESSOR
Department of Microbiology

Served in a consulting role as a biotechnology subject-matter expert. Led presentations to faculty and graduate students on topics related to molecular diagnostics, public health, and bioterrorism. Provided advice on technical issues and made recommendations for academic/scientific programming.

Florida State University, Tallahassee, FL   1987 to 1991

RESEARCH ASSOCIATE

Supervised graduate students and taught undergraduate coursework in chemistry. Worked with senior scientists on projects.

TEACHING EXPERIENCE—*Continued:*

Kuwait University Faculty of Medicine, Jabriya, Kuwait   1985 to 1987

LECTURER

Provided classroom and laboratory instruction in biochemistry and molecular biology to undergraduate students. Led/participated in scientific research with focus on rheumatic fever.

EDUCATION

Ph.D.—Medical Biochemistry, West Virginia University, Morgantown, WV, 1983
MS—Biochemistry, Duquesne University, Pittsburgh, PA, 1979
B.Sc.—Biochemistry, Kuwait University, Khaldiya, Kuwait, 1977

PUBLICATIONS—*a partial list*

Samuel Harrington. Molecular Diagnostics of Infectious Diseases: State of the Technology. *Biotechnology Annual Review,* Elsevier Publishing Company (2000).

Samuel Harrington, Robert Lanning, David Cooper. Rapid detection of hepatitis C virus in plasma & liver biopsies by capillary electrophoresis. *Nucleic Acid Electrophoresis Springer Lab Manual,* Dietmar Tietz (ed), Springer-Verlag, Heidelberg (1998).

Samuel Harrington, William Pasculle, Robert Lanning, David McDevitt, David Cooper. Typing of *Legionella pneumophila* isolates by degenerate (D-RAPD fingerprinting. *Molecular and Cellular Probes,* 9 405-414 (1995).

John A. Barranger, Erin Rice, **Samuel Harrington,** Carol Sansieri, Theodore Mifflin, and David Cooper. Enzymatic and Molecular Diagnosis of Gaucher Disease. *Clinics in Laboratory Medicine,* 15 (4) 899-913 (1995).

Samuel Harrington, Robert W. Lanning and David L. Cooper. DNA Fingerprinting of Crude Bacterial Lysates using Degenerate RAPD Primers (D-RAPD). *PCR Methods and Applications.* 4 265-268 (1995).

Samuel Harrington, Carol A. Sansieri, David W. Kopp, David L. Cooper and John A. Barranger. A new diagnostic test for Gaucher Disease suitable for mass screening. *PCR Methods and Applications,* 4 (1) 1-5 (1994).

David L. Cooper, **Samuel Harrington.** Molecular Diagnosis: a primer and specific application to Gaucher disease. *Gaucher Clinical Perspectives,* 1 (3) 1-6 (1993).

PRESENTATIONS—*a partial list*

Samuel Harrington and Krista Marschner. "A new, two-hour test for *Bordetella pertussis* using the SmartCycler," 103rd General Meeting of the American Society for Microbiology (ASM), Washington, DC, May 2003.

Samuel Harrington. "Methods & Applications of DNA Fingerprinting Techniques," Five 1- and/or 2-week-long workshops presented at the University of Puerto Rico, 1997 through 2003.

Samuel Harrington and Denise Bolton. "Development of a duplex real time RT-PCR test for surveillance of West Nile and Eastern Equine Encephalitis viruses using the SmartCycler," 102nd General Meeting of the American Society for Microbiology (ASM), Salt Lake City, UT, May 2002.

D.K. Voloshin, A.W. Pasculle, S.P. Krystofiak, **S. Harrington** and E.J. Wing. "Nosocomial Legionnaire's disease: an explosive outbreak following interruption of hyperchlorination," Interscience Conference on Antimicrobial Agents and Chemotherapy, San Francisco, CA, October 1995.

S. Harrington. "Genetic identification technologies: PCR and DNA fingerprinting," Second UN-sponsored Conference on the Perspectives of Biotechnology in Arab Countries, Amman, Jordan, March 1993.

S. Harrington, G. L. Rosner, D. L. Cooper and J. A. Barranger. "A new PCR-based diagnostic test for Gaucher Disease (GD)," Amer. J. Hum. Genet. 53 (supplement) 1755, 1993.

Bahr, G., **Harrington, S.,** Yousof, A., Jarrar, I., Rotta, J., Majeed, H. and Behbehani, K. "Depressed lymphoprolypherative responses in vitro to different streptococcal epitopes in patients with chronic rheumatoid heart disease," Conference on Infectious Diseases in Developing Countries, Kuwait City, Kuwait, March 1987.

PROFESSIONAL AFFILIATIONS

Member, American Society for Microbiology—ASM   Member, Association for Molecular Pathology—AMP
Consultant, INTOTA Corporation   Member, Council of Healthcare Advisors, Gerson Lehrman Group

Executive Résumés

Senior Executive–Scientist (addendum)

SAMUEL HARRINGTON, Ph.D.

VA Dept. of Health & Human Services
Public Health Laboratories
6 Hazen Drive, Fairfax, VA 22033
Office: 800-555-5555
harringtons@dhhs.state.va.us

1012 South Street
Fairfax, VA 22033
Home: 571-555-5555
Cell: 571-555-5555
harringtonsam@aol.com

Leadership Addendum—Science & Management

Dr. Samuel Harrington brings exceptional value through the combination of his core management qualifications, leadership talents and scientific knowledge, proficiency, and experience. He continues to develop his cross-functional general management skills and remains on the cutting-edge of scientific advancements and contemporary topics in biotechnology.

BUSINESS MANAGEMENT & ORGANIZATIONAL LEADERSHIP
—Strategies, Initiatives, Contributions, & Successes—

Much more than a scientist, Dr. Harrington is a management professional who is experienced and successful in directing organizations, programs, projects, and teams. He brings strategic perspective, business acumen, sound judgment, and financial discipline to private and public organizations involved in the life sciences/biotechnology fields.

"His work ethic is exemplary and his professional demeanor a model for others to emulate."
David L. Cooper, Director, Division of Molecular Diagnostics, University of Virginia Medical Center

"The quality of Samuel's work is exceptional ... and he excels in this area [communications]."
Chief, VA Public Health Laboratories

Organizational Development & Leadership

Dr. Harrington has provided both technical and managerial leadership to scientific organizations, and over the course of this 20+-year career, he has:

- Established the Virginia Public Health Laboratory as an important participant/contributor in the national biotech industry.
- Led the complete organizational startup of the MDX developmental laboratory for the Division of Molecular Diagnostics at the University of Virginia Medical Center.
- Contributed the vision, technical expertise, and business management capabilities to create and direct Kuwait's first molecular genetics laboratory.

Business & Finance Management

Dr. Harrington's ability to achieve operational and financial performance objectives within the departments he leads has made significant contributions to the ROI, profitability, and value of the larger organizations. As demonstrated by his track record, Dr. Harrington takes personal responsibility for all general business, daily operations, and budgeting/cost control initiatives. For example, he has:

- Authored and executed the business plan for the MDX molecular development laboratory for the University of Virginia Medical Center (UVMC), and integrated it into the main organizational structure.
- Participated in planning, administering, and controlling the $1 million operating budget for the Division of Molecular Diagnostics at UVMC.
- Achieved all budgetary performance objectives and gained financial discipline within the Virginia PHL.

Laboratory Operations Management

With more than 20 years' of academic, research, and management work in science, Dr. Harrington is well-qualified in establishing, staffing, managing, and improving the performance of laboratory operations/organizations. For example:

- Manage all aspects of operations—including disease surveillance, disease outbreak investigations, test development, and testing for biothreat (BT) organisms—in a "best in class" public health laboratory.
- Established Virginia's first Microbial Gene (DNA) Bank.
- Modernized and improved performance in key operational areas—productivity, efficiency, personnel qualifications, quality, compliance—for the State of Virginia's PHL.

BIOTECHNOLOGY / BIOMEDICAL RESEARCH, DEVELOPMENT, & DIAGNOSTICS
—Projects, Activities, Contributions, & Achievements—

"[Samuel Harrington's] strengths [include]... scientific knowledge and technical expertise, quality of work, initiative, sense of humor, and ability to get along with people."

"[Dr. Harrington] set up an RT-PCR procedure for West Nile Virus which brought much praise to the PHL for its ability to quickly deal with a developing public health problem."

"[Dr. Harrington] has shown a great deal of initiative in learning about Virginia's infectious disease needs and developing molecular procedures for their detection and identification."
Chief, VA Public Health Laboratories

Dr. Harrington's career is focused on Infectious Disease, Molecular Diagnostics, and Genetic Disorders.

<u>**Molecular Diagnostics of Infectious Diseases**</u>

Dr. Harrington's work in molecular diagnostics of infectious diseases has involved extensive research, surveillance, testing, assay development, and publication. He is proficient in the utilization of sophisticated laboratory methodologies, techniques, and technologies including, but not limited to: DNA fingerprinting (PFGE, Ribo Printing, PCR-based fingerprinting – RAPD/AFLP); DNA/RNA sequencing; PCR (including Real Time, RT-PCR, multiplex); oligonucleotide primer/probe design and synthesis; Southern hybridization; molecular cloning; and recombinant DNA technologies.

- Developed a two-hour RT-PCR test for the detection of *B. pertussis* directly from crude clinical specimens, thereby eliminating the need for traditional labor-intensive, time-consuming specimen processing (DNA extraction) step. Laboratories across the U.S. (e.g. SC, OK, FL, others) and Europe (Germany and Spain) have requested permission to use this test in their laboratories, and a Canadian diagnostics company has expressed interest in participating with validation studies. Presented this work at the 103rd General Meeting of the American Society for Microbiology in Washington, D.C., May 2003.

- Developed and presented (at the 102nd General Meeting of the American Society for Microbiology in Salt Lake City, UT, May 2002) a duplex RT-PCR test for surveillance of West Nile and Eastern Equine Encephalitis viruses using SmartCycler.

- Developed and managed the design, validation, application, test, and troubleshooting of molecular diagnostics-based assays for rapid identification and surveillance of emerging infectious diseases for the State of New Virginia PHL.

- Distinguished the NH PHL as one of the first labs in the U.S. to participate in proficiency testing (RT-PCR) for SARS utilizing a RT-PCR test developed by the CDC—validated test is being performed routinely at VA PHL.

- Developed a RT-PCR test for the rapid detection of the food-borne pathogen Noro (Norwalk) virus from human stools using melt-curve analysis of the amplified product—several PHLs have requested permission to use this test in their facilities.

- RNA isolated from mosquito pools inhibits West Nile virus real-time RT-PCR. Presented findings at the 3rd International Conference on Emerging Infectious Diseases in Atlanta, Georgia in March 2002.

- Investigation of simultaneous outbreaks of *S. pneumoniae* and *H. influenzae* in major medical center. Presented abstract at the 6th Annual PulseNet Update Meeting in Ann Arbor, Michigan in April 2002.

- Molecular Diagnostics of Infectious Diseases: State of the Technology. Invited article summarizing emerging technologies and applications in the rapid diagnosis of disease. Published in *Biotechnology Annual Review*, Elsevier Publishing Company, 2000.

- Rapid detection of hepatitis C virus in plasma and liver biopsies by capillary electrophoresis. In: *Nucleic Acid Electrophoresis Springer Lab Manual*, 1998.

- Developed and co-presented an abstract entitled "Nosocomial Legionnaire's disease: An explosive outbreak following interruption of hyperchlorination," presented at the Interscience Conference on Antimicrobial Agents and Chemotherapy in San Francisco in October 1995.

- Co-developed "Depressed Lymphoprolypherative Responses *in vitro* to Different Streptococcal Epitopes in Patients with Chronic Rheumatoid Heart Disease," presented at the Conference on Infectious Diseases in Developing Countries held in Kuwait in March 1987.

Molecular Diagnostics of Genetic Diseases

Either independently or as a member of a team of multidisciplinary professionals, Dr. Harrington has conducted a wide range of scientific research/experimentation, developed mutation screening assays, written/published numerous articles, and delivered presentations covering a vast spectrum of areas related to genetic diseases.

- Developed mutation screening and detection assays for a number of genetic diseases such as breast cancer (BRCA-1 mutation screening), Fanconi's anemia, Canavan's disease, Factor V Leiden, Fragile X syndrome, and Huntington's disease.
- Molecular Diagnosis: a primer and specific application to Gaucher disease. *Gaucher Clinical Perspectives* 1 (3) 1-6, 1993
- Phenotype, Genotype, and the treatment of Gaucher Disease. *Clinical Genetics*. 49 111-118, 1996.
- Enzymatic and Molecular Diagnosis of Gaucher Disease. *Clinics in Laboratory Medicine*. 15 (4) 899-913, 1995.
- A review of the molecular biology of glucocerebrosidase and the treatment of Gaucher disease," *Cytokines and Molecular Therapy*, 1995.1 149-163, 1995.
- A new diagnostic test for Gaucher Disease suitable for mass screening. *PCR Methods and Applications* 4 (1) 1-5, 1994.

BioSecurity

Dr. Harrington champions interest and involvement in the conduct of scientific research and development, especially diagnostic test development and validation, of organisms and pathogens potentially used in biological terrorism/warfare. His work makes him of significant value to organizations and programs involved in related medical practice and public health programs, actions, projects, and policies—to ultimately bridge the gap between public health specialists/organizations, the public, government agencies/intelligence community, and primary care providers.

In April 2003, the U.S. House of Representatives overwhelmingly approved President Bush's "Project Bioshield," solidifying national interest and commitment to preparedness against potential bioterrorism attack.

- Distinguished the Virginia Public Health Laboratory (VA PHL) as one of the first in the U.S. to be awarded funding for bioterrorism testing and preparedness.
- Established the MDX laboratory as the first PHL in the U.S. to use SmartCycler for the development and routine testing of emerging infections including BT organisms—enabling the laboratory to participate in validation studies with CDC and Lawrence Livermore National Laboratory in developing assays for BT organisms.
- Implemented and supervised internal proficiency testing—within CDC protocols—and personnel cross-training programs at the VA PHL.
- Initiated VA PHL's participation in PulseNet (National Molecular Sub-Typing Network for Food-Borne Disease Surveillance), a network of laboratories (including CDC, FDA, USDA, state and local PHLs) adhering to standardized microbial surveillance procedures using Pulsed Field Gel Electrophoresis (PFGE) in performing gene sub-typing—a membership of particular importance to being equipped to respond to potential bio-terrorism threats/incidents.
- Adopted CDC-based anthrax testing procedures, facilitating VA PHL's selection as a testing beta site by the Lawrence Livermore National Laboratory.
- Led Virginia's participation in President Bush/CDC's strategy for immunizing public health workers and first responders against smallpox—including ensuring the capacity for testing for the vaccine strain of Smallpox and other related viruses.

DNA Fingerprinting & Gene Banking

- Established Virginia's first microbial DNA bank with 1,000+ DNA and RNA samples from various pathogens—food-borne pathogens, West Nile virus, hepatitis C virus, Noro virus isolates—each containing nucleic acids in one or more formats: highly purified genomic DNA or RNA, immobilized (aerosol-resistant) purified DNA, agarose DNA plugs (ready for PFGE analysis), and viable organism (whenever possible).
- Developed and presented several one- to two-week long workshops on methods and applications of DNA fingerprinting techniques at the University of Puerto Rico during the years of 1997 through 2003.

<u>DNA Fingerprinting & Gene Banking</u>—*Continued:*

- Developed a DNA fingerprinting method to distinguish between closely related isolates of *Legionella pneumophila*, the causative pathogen for Legionnaire's Disease—providing the only way to track the transmission of this pathogen from patients to hospital rooms/hospital rooms to patients. A six-figure liability suit against the University of Virginia Medical Center (University Hospital) was thwarted as a result of the availability of this technique.

- Coauthored an abstract on tDNA-PCR amplification of species-specific polymorphic bands in *plasmodium faciparum, plasmodium berghei* and *plasmodium yoelii* at the University of Puerto Rico in San Juan, 2001.

- Authored "Typing of *Legionella pneumophila* isolates by degenerate (D)-RAPD fingerprinting," published in *Molecular and Cellular Probes*, 1995.

- Coauthored and presented "Microsatellite Analysis (MSA) Using the Polymerase Chain Reaction (PCR) of Paraffin Embedded Material for Distinction of Tissues From Different Individuals," at the United States and Canadian Academy of Pathology (USCAP) Specialty Conference in Toronto, Canada in March 1995.

- Authored "DNA Fingerprinting of Crude Bacterial Lysates using Degenerate RAPD Primers (D-RAPD)," published in *PCR Methods and Applications*, 1995.

- Authored and presented "Genetic identification technologies: PCR and DNA fingerprinting" at 2nd UN-sponsored Conference on the Perspectives of Biotechnology in Arab Countries, held in Amman, Jordan in March 1993.

<u>Other Biomedical Research</u>

- Authored, "Prediction of biologic aggressiveness in colorectal cancer by p53/K-ras-2 topographic genotyping," published in *Molecular Diagnosis*, 1996.

- Authored, "Distribution and evolution of CTG repeats at the myotonin protein kinase gene in human populations," published in *Genome Research*, 1996.

- Authored "Loss of heterozygosity in spontaneous and chemically induced tumors of the B6C3F1 mouse," published in *Carcinogenesis*, 1994.

- Authored "Identification of allelic loss in liver tumors from the B6C3HF1 mouse," published in *Cell Biology Supplement*, 1992.

- Authored, "Antibody levels and in vitro lymphoproliferative responses to streptococcus pyogenes erythrogenic toxin A mitogen of patients with rheumatic fever," published in *Clinical Microbiology*, 1991.

- Authored, "Isolation and characterization of developmentally regulated sea urchin U2 snRNA genes," published in *Developmental Biology*, 1991.

- Authored, "The U1 snRNA gene repeat from the sea urchin (*Strongylocentrotus purpuratus*): The 70 kilobase tandem repeat ends directly 3' to the U1 gene," published in *Nuclear Acids Research*, 1991.

- Authored "A developmental switch in the sea urchin U1 RNA," published in *Developmental Biology*, 1989, and presented at the American Society for Biochemistry and Molecular Biology meeting held in San Francisco in January 1989.

- Authored, "Isolation and characterization of tandem repeated U6 genes from the sea urchin *Strongylocentrotus purpuratus*," published in *Biochemistry Biophysics*, 1994, and presented at the Developmental Biology of the Sea Urchin meeting in Woods Hole, MA (August 1988) and at the Annual Meeting of Florida Biochemists in Miami in February 1988.

- Authored, "Modified nucleosides and the chromatographic and aminoacylation behavior of tRNA^{ile} from *Escherichia coli C6*," published in *Biochemistry Biophysics Acta*, 1988.

Special Reports

Once in a very long while a new idea comes along in the world of job-hunting. The Special Report is one of those ideas. It presents you as an expert in your field without overtly saying you are job-hunting, and as such gets the reader to create an initial impression of you that is very different from that of a typical job seeker. A special report is not for everyone, but if you really know your business and you like to write, this can be a very helpful tool to add to your job-hunting arsenal.

A Special Report has the appearance of a newspaper, newsletter, or trade magazine article that focuses on a commonly recognized challenge in your profession; but rather than mass publication it is created by you to send directly to end users. You create it by using your professional knowledge and packaging it in a written document. Just about anyone in your field who receives one will read a well-written and properly edited special report, and at the end they'll get to read the résumé of the person who created it. While a résumé gets very little initial time investment, your report can have the reader building a respectful relationship with you even before they know you are available and looking. Special reports have titles like:

Computer Conversion: Plan it, Move on it, and Roll it out!

Three simple things you can do that double the effectiveness of your school resource center

Research reveals little-used sales technique that dramatically improves product sales in financial investment market

Ten simple actions any FCM, BD, Bank, Prop Trading, and/or Treasury Director can take to head off trouble at the pass

Seven Secrets of the Successful Waitperson

Special reports all aim to help the reader solve problems, make money, save money, or save time. Think of them as departmental reports, position papers, or articles (whichever works best for you), where the goal is to give the reader some useful information they can actually use. This is why a special report is not for everyone. You have to know your stuff and enjoy the writing process, but as I always say, anyone can write so long as they don't have a so-called life! If this is you (at least the part about having an affinity for writing) read on; you will not only learn a new job-hunting technique you'll be contributing to your professional credibility and visibility in ways that reach well beyond this job hunt.

In the space available here, I can't show you how to write short, job-hunting-oriented, nonfiction articles—a.k.a. Special Reports. Instead, I'll explain the basic structure and packaging and then refer you to a couple of additional resources.

What Goes into a Special Report?

- A benefit-oriented title
- An introduction
- The body copy usually in the form of "tips" or "mistakes to avoid"
- Author info (usually, your résumé)
- A binding

The key to this Trojan horse approach is to include your résumé with contact information in the author information section. If your résumé isn't right for the job, you can use a biography that highlights information you feel is more relevant to the reader; in this instance you'll be able to cut and paste one of your broadcast letters without the salutation.

The proper length is up to you, and opinions differ. Some will tell you that special reports can be as long as you like, and I have seen some that run to 6,000 words (about ten pages). Personally, I think you should keep your report to between 600 and 1,000 words—in other words, about the length of a regular newspaper column (or the length of this section on what goes into special reports, which runs about 1,000 words). I say this for two reasons:

- Writing takes time away from the main thrust of your job-hunting activities, and you cannot allow this great secondary approach to affect your focus.
- You don't want to share everything you know about a particular subject on paper; you want to be able to continue the conversation in person with yet more information to share.

There is another benefit to this approach. Job offers usually go to the person who turns a one-sided examination of skills into a two-way conversation between professional colleagues. The nature of the special report goes a long way toward defining you as someone quite different from almost every other candidate.

If you look at the examples below and think that this might be a useful approach for your needs, but you feel you need more help, go to *www.salarynegotiations.com*, the Web site of longtime career consultant Jack Chapman, who developed the whole Special Report idea.

If you do try this as an additional approach for your job hunt, you will be able to re-use the fruits of your efforts. You can submit your article for publication to professional newsletters and magazines, and you can turn it into a presentation. In fact, your notes for the special report simultaneously form the outline of a business presentation. So even outside of the context of your job hunt, this approach of putting your professional expertise into a different delivery medium can have a significant impact on your professional visibility and credibility.

Now look at these samples.

SPECIAL REPORT EXAMPLE #1: WAITRESS

BACKGROUND:

With NO experience directly as a waitress, Christine, a college freshman, got hired. She had only been a hostess at "23"—Michael Jordan's Restaurant near the University of North Carolina. She had observed waiters and waitresses, and she had definite ideas about what differentiated the satisfactory from the excellent. She wanted to "jump over" the menial waitress positions and get hired by an upscale, four-star restaurant (read: big tips!). This way, she positioned herself as an exceptional waitress who had the boss's viewpoint of the job.

TITLE: Christine's Four Keys to an Excellent Waitperson

EXCERPT FROM INTRODUCTION:

Excellent waiter, waitress? It's not all that complicated to be just a satisfactory waitperson. Practically anyone can write down an order and bring food to the table. Surprisingly, it's not all that hard to be an outstanding waitperson, either—but not everyone does it. I've put down my thoughts here on the 4 keys to excellence on the job as I see it. It will help you get an idea of my philosophy.

EXCERPT FROM RULES SECTION:

Key #3 *There's always a way to get people what they want.*

When you know that customers want more than just food, that they want a pleasant time as well, possibilities arise. As hostess at 23, waitstaff would often complain to me about customers ordering things not on the menu, or prepared a certain way. When, out of curiosity, I checked it out with the cooks, they almost always said, "No problem." So it was the waitperson creating a problem for a customer—that problem didn't exist! I find that if you put your mind to it, there's always a way to keep the customer satisfied.

OUTLINE OF THE REST OF THE REPORT:
Key #1: Remember that your job is not "things to do," but people to take care of.
Key #2: The friendlier you are, the friendlier the customers will be.
Key #3: There's always a way to get people what they want.
Key #4: It's a job for you, but it's a business for your boss.
Summary

RESULTS: Christine leapfrogged into a fine-dining (and fine tip-ping) job.

SPECIAL REPORT EXAMPLE #2: SALESMAN

BACKGROUND:
Mike's success at sales came from meticulous attention to detail (read: boring!), but he turns that dull skill into a reason to be hired! His report shows how astoundingly elementary your report "rules" can be and still make an indelible impression. (His first rule is, "Answer the Phone.") He focused on software sales to financial investors, but this type of report could be applied to almost any type of sales. Mike also got the Hiring Decision Makers' attention in the cover letter by mentioning that theirs was one of the firms he called in his "secret shopper" research.

TITLE: Research Reveals Little-Used Sales Technique That Can Dramatically Improve Sales [to the Financial Investment Market.]

EXCERPT FROM INTRODUCTION:
Recently I undertook a research project to determine how companies might improve their sales. I called several companies and said, "I would like to buy your software."

It was astonishing to me that from over twenty companies, I only reached someone knowledgeable about the product 14 percent of the time. Equally surprising was that only 28 percent of the organizations had someone return my call. Almost 40 percent didn't bother to send me any information. And even when they did, only 4 percent followed up with a phone call.

This confirmed my hunch. Just by applying a sales principle I've used for 18 years, namely follow-up consistency, any one of these firms could experience a dramatic increase in sales. Here is how consistent follow-up can be easily applied in five areas to increase sales. I'm embarrassed at how basic these actions are, but remember—only 14 percent of my calls reached a salesperson!

EXCERPT FROM RULES SECTION:
Follow-up Consistency Rule #1: ANSWER THE PHONE.

Having a dedicated line that is answered by a knowledgeable, helpful, friendly, live human being is essential in sales. No voice mail allowed! Not every line needs to be answered this way (although that's nice if you can afford it), but each and every call from potential customers must receive this follow-up consistency.

On one of my calls an operator informed me she could not take my name and address for information—that would have to be handled by a salesperson. She then informed me that she could not transfer me to a salesperson because they were all gone for the rest of the day. It was 11 A.M.!

QUESTION: Have you called your own sales line recently? What happened next?

OUTLINE OF THE REST OF THE REPORT:

Rule #2: Return messages.

Rule #3: Send the materials.

Rule #4: Don't just call the prospect, get through.

Rule #5: Never discard the names of prospects.

Summary

RESULTS: Mike got interviews with EVERY ONE of the 20 firms he had called as a "secret shopper." He got job offers from two of them.

SPECIAL REPORT EXAMPLE #3: FINANCIAL INVESTMENT SERVICES CFO

BACKGROUND:

Scott was seeking a high six-figure CFO job in the investment field. Billion-dollar scandals at Enron, MCI WorldCom, and Tyco had just occurred so his report caught people's attention. His simple techniques to prevent these catastrophes were powerfully linked up with the war stories attached to each rule.

TITLE: How to Uncover Financial and Operational Trouble Before Your P&L Blows Up . . . Ten Simple Actions Any FCM, BD, Bank, Prop Trading, and/or Treasury Manager or Director Can Take to Head Off Trouble at the Pass

EXCERPT FROM INTRODUCTION:

When a company is in or about to be in trouble, there are *always* flashing yellow warning lights. The good news is that *problems rarely travel alone*. Usually they create a pattern of circumstances that aren't individually recognized as problems, but when the puzzle pieces are assembled—wham! It's an open invitation to red ink. It may be up to you to recognize enough of those pieces in time to stop the entire puzzle from being completed.

For the past 20 years, as a troubleshooter CFO or COO at financial services firms, I've learned to read the signs. And what are some of those signs?

EXCERPT FROM RULES SECTION:

Rule #2: *Pay attention to your checks after they're cashed and cleared.*

How are they endorsed?

Your employees? The ones who can't trade because you won't let them? Why is one or more of their checks endorsed over to a third party or brokerage firm—is this a hidden trading account in their own name?

Your customer? Why are multiple checks for identical amounts drawn on a single customer's account and endorsed over to multiple third parties? Unregistered pool? What if one of those third parties is your employee in a position to allocate trades or initiate commission rate or brokerage rate changes in your computer system?

Your vendor? Why are checks always endorsed to the name of a company you don't recognize? Is it an innocent d/b/a or are you dealing with a middleman who is marking up goods or services you could get for less by going direct?

OUTLINE OF THE REST OF THE REPORT [FOUR SAMPLES OF THE TEN RULES):

Rule #1: Periodically, sort your name and address file. Look for dual-identity payments.

Rule #3: Review a month of original trade tickets, blotters, out-trade sheets. Slowly. It's worth it.

Rule #6: Use simple line graphs to compare periods. It's easy to be caught up in the day-to-day.

Rule #9: Regularly review IB/RR/AP/Broker/Trader Payouts. Without exception, the most consistent source of hidden losses is linked in some way to Payouts.

RESULTS: Scott's report opened doors to networking interviews with "heavy hitters" in his field, which led to his new job.

SPECIAL REPORT EXAMPLE #4: SHIPPING TERMINAL MANAGER

BACKGROUND:

Keith worked for Yellow Freight. Besides getting all the trucks loaded, unloaded, and on the road on time, he also loved to catch cheaters—people collecting disability who weren't really disabled. His title is very intriguing and benefit-oriented.

TITLE: A Simple Way to Put a Couple Hundred Thousand Dollars Right to the Bottom Line: Watch People Who Aren't There, Make Sure Nothing Happens

EXCERPT FROM INTRODUCTION:

This report's title says that if you watch people who aren't there and make sure nothing happens, you can save money. I have found that a few simple techniques to watch people who are out because of injuries, and a few principles of safety to make sure that nothing (bad) happens, will put $200,000 or more to the bottom line each year.

EXCERPT FROM RULES SECTION:

Rule #1: Call at Odd Times

When I have a man out, I'll put in calls every once in a while ostensibly to get some information. "Where is that bill of lading?" "Truck #3 seems to be acting up, how did it run for you?" At 2:30 in the afternoon, or home at night. I'll remind them their doctor's appointment is tomorrow. They soon learn they will be caught if they aren't home.

This cuts costs because besides clipping the wings of the ones who are playing hooky, saving time off, or receiving disability payments, it also alerts the 80 percent with real injuries that if they ever want to fake it, that they'll have a hard time.

OUTLINE OF THE REST OF THE REPORT [FOUR SAMPLES OF THE RULES]:

Rule #2: [Watch people...] Make them come in to the facility.

Rule #3: [Watch people...] Call the Bluff of "Regular Offenders."

Rule #4: [Nothing happens...] Have safety meetings led by peers, not supervisors.

Rule #7: [Nothing happens...] Reward safety in teams to create peer pressure for safety.

RESULTS: The report was the focus of several telephone networking conversations, which led to interviews and a great job.

Making Your Résumé Scannable

In today's electronic world, you need both a "keyword-conscious" paper résumé that is scannable, and an electronic résumé that can be sent via e-mail and is database-compatible. When you mail your résumé to a company, it is a paper document. In order for a company to quickly and effectively transform your résumé to an electronic format they scan, or digitize, it.

Here's what happens behind the scenes: A company receives your paper résumé and they place it in a scanner that takes a picture of it. When you fax your résumé to a company, the fax machine will act just like a scanner and create a file with a picture of your résumé. A software program called OCR (optical character recognition) is then applied to that picture of your résumé. The OCR software tries to identify parts of that picture that represent letters, numbers, and symbols. Knowing that recruiters and employers use this technology means that you must create your print résumé to operate within the technical capabilities of the software. The software capability improves almost monthly, but that doesn't mean that every company always has the latest version of the best program, so we will err on the side of conservatism. Here are some general rules to follow to assure that your print résumé is indeed scannable:

- Always avoid paper with a dark or even medium color, a colored border, heavy watermark, or graining—plain white paper is best.
- Be circumspect about adding borders around a document or around a section of text in the résumé. The OCR software could identify the outline as a single character and omit the entire content of that section.
- Do not use columns—when scanned, the order of words will be out of sequence and that could hurt the effectiveness of your keyword sections.
- Do not use fonts smaller than 10 point; 12 point is ideal. If the employer experiences difficulty in scanning your résumé, you will not receive a polite phone call asking you to resubmit it.

When Should You Use a Scannable Résumé?

Anytime you are mailing or faxing your résumé to a company, assume that it will be scanned. Always use the "fine mode" setting when faxing your résumé; this will result in better resolution and allows the OCR to optimize the digital conversion. Many companies do not print faxed résumés, but instead convert them directly to digital. Also, most PCs now come with standard software that allows the user to fax and receive documents without ever having to print them.

CAREER CONSULTANTS AND RÉSUMÉ WRITING SERVICES

APPENDIX · APPENDIX · APPENDIX · APPENDIX · APPENDIX · APPENDIX

A

As part of your job search, you might feel the need to look into getting extra help from a professional résumé writer and/or a career counselor. A professional in the field might be able to help you develop a more polished layout or present a particularly complex background more effectively.

As in any other profession, there are practitioners at both ends of the performance scale. I am a strong believer in using the services of résumé writers and career consultants who belong to their field's professional associations. They tend to be more committed, have more field experience, and have an all-around higher standard of performance, partly because their membership demonstrates their commitment to the field and partly from the ongoing

educational programs that these associations offer to their members.

The three major associations in the résumé-writing field are: the Professional Association of Résumé Writers (PARW, *parw.com*), the National Résumé Writers Association (NRWA, *nrwa.com*), and Career Masters Institute (CMI, *www .cminstitute.com*). All three associations have hundreds of members and provide ongoing opportunities for members to gain mentoring experience and additional training. They all offer résumé-writing certification and operate e-mail list servers for members with access to e-mail.

Two important smaller organizations are CertifiedRésuméWriters .com and CertifiedCareerCoaches .com. These two Web sites are designed to connect job seekers with certified career professionals who meet specific résumé writing and career coaching needs. All of the résumé writers on these two sites are active members of one or more of the above associations and have taken the time to achieve accreditation in different aspects of the résumé writing and career coaching process.

Finally there is the Phoenix Career Group *(www.phoenixcareergroup.com)*, a small group of highly qualified and exceptionally credentialed career management consultants and résumé writers spread all over North America.

Martin Yate, Executive Career Strategist
E-mail: *martin@knockemdead.com*
Martin Yate, CPC
Typically works with C-level and C-level-bound professionals facing challenges in the areas of Job Search, Interviewing, and Career Strategy.

Phoenix Career Group
www.phoenixcareergroup.com
Debbie Ellis, CPRW, CRW
Serving career-minded professionals to senior executives, the Phoenix Career Group is a one-of-a-kind consortium of 15 industry-leading professionals specializing in personal branding, résumé writing, career management coaching, research, and distribution.

This is a by-invitation-only marketing consortium of independents who all know each other through membership in other groups. Although I do not offer these one-on-one services myself, I am a member of Phoenix solely for the camaraderie and value I receive from rubbing shoulders with a select group of mature and committed professionals.

The following is a list of career consultants and professional résumé writers. All of these have contributed to the *Knock 'em Dead* books and are members of one or more of the above groups.

100PercentRésumés
www.100percentrésumés.com
Daniel J. Dorotik, Jr. NCRW
Global career development service specializing in the preparation of résumés, cover letters, and other associated career documents. In addition to traditional formats, prepares online-compatible documents for Internet-driven job searches.

A First Impression Résumé Service
www.résuméwriter.com
Debra O'Reilly CPRW, CEIP, JCTC, FRWC
Debra provides job-search and career-management tools for professionals, from entry level to executive. Areas of specialty include career transition and the unique challenges of military-to-civilian conversion.

A Résumé For Today
www.arésuméfortoday.com
Jean Cummings M.A.T., CPRW, CEIP, CPBS
Distills complex hightech careers into potent, memorable, and valuable personal brands. Provides résumé writing and job search services to executives and managers seeking to advance their careers in high tech.

A Résumé Solution
www.arésumésolution.com
Becky Erdelen
1716 Clark Lane
Barnhart MO 63012
(636) 464-4544
e-mail: *Becky@arésumésolution.com*

A Word's Worth Résumé and Writing Service
www.keytosuccessrésumés.com
Nina K. Ebert CPRW/CC
Serving clients since 1989, A Word's Worth is a full-service résumé and cover letter development/career coaching company with a proven track record in opening doors to interviews.

A+ Career & Résumé, LLC
www.careerandrésumé.com
Karen M. Silins CMRS, CCMC, CRW, CECC, CEIP, CTAC, CCA
Expertise includes career document development, career exploration and transition, assessments, job search methods, networking, interviewing, motivation, dressing for success, and career management strategies.

Abilities Enhanced
www.abilitiesenhanced.com
Meg Montford MCCC, CMF, CCM
Helps enable radical career change, as from IT trainer to pharmaceutical sales rep and technical writer to personal trainer. Career coaching and résumés by a careers professional since 1986.

Advanced Résumé Services
www.résuméservices.com
Michele Haffner CPRW, JCTC
Résumés, cover letters, target mailings, interview coaching, and search strategy/action plan development. Specialty is mid- to senior-level professionals earning $75K+. Complimentary critique. Over 10 years of experience. Guaranteed satisfaction.

Advantage Résumé & Career Services
www.CuttingEdgeRésumés.com
Vivian VanLier CPRW, JCTC, CCMC, CEIP, CPRC
Full-service résumé writing and career coaching serving clients throughout the U.S. and internationally at all levels. Special expertise in Entertainment, Management, Senior Executives, and Creative and Financial Careers.

Arnold-Smith Associates
www.RésuméSOS.com
Arnold G. Boldt CPRW, JCTC
Offers comprehensive job search consulting services, including writing résumés and cover letters; interview simulations; career assessments and coaching; and both electronic and direct-mail job search campaigns.

A&E Consulting

www.aspire-empower.com
Laura Labovitch
45722 Wellesley Terrace #330
Sterling VA 20166
(703) 942-9390
Fax; (703) 406-0587
e-mail: *aspireempower@gmail.com*

A Successful Career

www.ablueribbonrésumé.com
Georgia Adamson
1096 N. Central Ave
San Jose CA 95128
(408) 244-6401
e-mail: *success@blueribbonrésumé.com*

Brandego LLC

www.brandego.com
Kirsten Dixson CPBS, JCTC
Creates Web Portfolios for executives, careerists, authors, consultants, and speakers. Includes experts in branding, career management, multimedia, copywriting, blogging, and SEO to express your unique value.

Career Directions, LLC

www.careeredgecoach.com
Louise Garver JCTC, CPRW, MCDP, CEIP, CMP
Career Directions, LLC, is a full-service practice specializing in résumé development, job-search strategies, and career-coaching services for sales and marketing executives and managers worldwide.

Career Ink

www.careerink.com
Roberta Gamza JCTC, JST, CEIP
Offering career marketing and communication strategy services that advance careers. Services include precisely crafted résumés and customized interview training sessions that persuade and motivate potential employers to action.

Career Marketing Techniques

www.polishedrésumés.com
Diane Burns CPRW, CCMC, CPCC, CFJST, IJCTC, CEIP, CCM
A career coach and résumé strategist who specializes in executive-level military conversion résumés and federal government applications. She is a careers industry international speaker and national author.

Career Solutions, LLC

www.WritingRésumés.com
Maria E. Hebda CCMC, CPRW
A certified career professional, she helps people effectively market themselves to employers and position them as qualified candidates. Provides writing and coaching services in résumé and cover letter development.

Career Trend

www.careertrend.net
Jacqui Barrett MRW, CPRW, CEIP
Collaborates with professionals and executives aspiring to ignite their careers or manage transition. The owner is among an elite group holding the Master Résumé Writer designation via Career Masters Institute

Cheek & Cristantello Career Connections, LLC

www.cheekandcristantello.com

Freddie Cheek M.S. Ed., CCM, CPRW, CRW, CWDP

Resource for résumé writing and interview coaching with 25 years' experience satisfying customers and getting results. Creates accomplishment-based résumés that help you achieve your career goals.

Confidentcareer.com

www.confidentcareer.com

Divya Gupta

(630) 364-1848

e-mail: *divya@confidentcareer.com*

Create Your Career

www.careerist.com

Joyce Fortier CCM, CCMC

Company collaborates with clients as a catalyst for optimum career success. Services include résumé and cover letter services, and coaching services, including job search techniques, interview preparation, networking, and salary negotiation.

Creating Prints

www.creatingprints.com

Rosa Vargas

3799 Millenia

Orlando FL 32839

(407) 802-4962

e-mail: *Rvargas@creatingprints.com*

Dynamic Résumé Solutions

www.dynamicrésumésolutions.com

Darlene Dassy

14 Crestview Drive

Sinking Spring PA 19608

(610) 678-0147

e-mail: *Darlene@dynamicrésumésolutions.com*

ekm Inspirations

www.ekminspirations.com

Norine T. Dagliano FJST, Certified DISC Administrator

More than 18 years of comprehensive and individualized career transition services, working with professionals at all levels of experience. Specializes in federal job search assistance, assisting dislocated workers, and career changers.

Executive Essentials

www.career-management-coach.com

Cindy Kraft CCMC, CCM, CPRW, JCTC

Prepares professionals and executives to outperform the competition. Top-notch marketing documents, a focused branding strategy, and job search coaching result in a multifaceted, effective, and executable search plan.

Executive Power Coach

www.ExecutivePowerCoach.com

Deborah Wile Dib CPBS, CCM, CCMC, NCRW, CPRW, CEIP, JCTC

Careers-industry leader helps very senior executives stand out, get to the top, and stay at the top. Executive brand development, power résumés, and executive power coaching services since 1989.

Guarneri Associates

www.Résumé-Magic.com

Susan Guarneri NCC, NCCC, LPC, MCC, CPRW, CCMC, CEIP, JCTC, CWPP

Comprehensive career services—from career counseling and assessments to résumés and cover letters—by full-service career professional with top-notch credentials, 20 years of experience, and satisfied customers.

Greenbrand

www.1greenbrand.com

Kevin Morris

168 SW Oakwood Court

Lake City FL 32024

(386) 623-5124

e-mail: *kmorris@lani.net*

JobWhiz

www.JobWhiz.com

Debra Feldman B.S., M.P.H.

Personally arranges confidential networking appointments delivering decision makers inside target employers. Engineers campaign strategy, innovates positioning, and defines focus. Banishes barriers accelerating job search progress. Relentless follow-up guarantees results.

The Loriel Group—CoachingROI: RésuméROI

www.RésuméROI.com

Lorie Lebert CPRW, IJCTC, CCMC

A full-service career management provider, offering personalized, confidential support and guidance; moving client careers forward with focused customer service.

The McLean Group

Don Orlando MBA, CPRW, JCTC, CCM, CCMC

Puts executives in control of the career they've always deserved. Personal, on-demand support that helps busy managers get paid what they are worth.

e-mail: *yourcareercoach@aol.com*

Mil-Roy Consultants

www.milroyconsultants.com

Nicole Miller CCM, CRW, IJCTC, CECC

Creates the extra edge needed for success through the innovative design of dynamic résumés and marketing tools that achieve results.

Partnering For Success, LLC

www.résumés4results.com

Cory Edwards CRW, CECC, CCMC

Résumé writer and career coach currently achieving 98 percent success rate getting clients interviews. Specializing in all résumés, including federal, SES, postal, and private sector from entry-level to executive.

Résumé Impressions

www.résuméimpressions.com

Melissa Kassler

540 West Union Street, Suite 4

Athens OH 45701

(740) 592-3993

Fax: (740) 592-1352

e-mail: *résumé@frognet*

Résumés Etc

www.cnyrésumés.com

Terrie Osborn

PO Box 454

Central Square NY 13036

(315) 676-3315

e-mail: *tosborn@twcny.rr.com*

Résumés for Less

www.RésumésForLess.com

Gwen Harrison

5847 North 9th Ave, Suite A113

Pensacola FL 32504-9312

(800) 706-2942

Fax: (800) 706-2942

e-mail: *résumé@frognet*

RésuméRighter

www.RésuméRighter.com

Denise Larkin CPRW, CEIP

A mount-a-campaign, market-yourself, total-job-search support system. They promise to: Present your qualifications for best advantage, write an attention-grabbing cover letter, and coach you to ace your interview.

Résumé Suite

www.résumésuite.com

Bonnie Kurka CPRW, JCTC, FJST

Career coach, résumé writer, speaker, and trainer with more than 11 years' experience in the careers industry. Specializes in mid- to upper-level management, IT, military, and federal career fields.

The Résumé Writer

www.therésuméwriter.com

Patricia Traina-Duckers CPRW, CRW, CEIP, CFRWC, CWPP

Fully certified career service practice offering complete career search services, including personalized civilian/federal résumé development, business correspondence, Web portfolios, bios, CVs, job search strategies, interview coaching, salary research, and more.

Tools for Transition

www.toolsfortransition.com

Irene Marshall

38750 Paseo Padre Parkway, #C1

Fremont CA 94536

(510) 790-9005

Fax: (510) 315-3132

e-mail: *irene@toolsfortransition.com*

Write Away Résumé and Career Coaching

www.writeawayrésumé.com

Edie Rische NCRW, JCTC, ACCC

Creates targeted résumés and job search correspondence for clients in every vocation, and specializes in helping others discover their "Authentic Vocation," shift careers, and resolve issues using "QuantumShift" coaching.

APPENDIX · APPENDIX · APPENDIX · APPENDIX · APPENDIX · APPENDIX · APPENDIX ·

B

INTERNET RESOURCES

These are really Knock 'em Dead Internet resources, with links to Web sites in twenty-two job search and career-management categories.

You'll find the big job banks, profession specific sites for eighteen major industries, associations, entry level, executive, minority sites and more. You'll discover tools that help you find companies, executives, and lost colleagues, plus sites that help you choose new career directions or find a super-qualified professional résumé writer, job, or career coach.

To save time, you can come to the knockemdead.com website, where you can click on each of these resources and be connected directly—no more typing in endless URLs!

Association Sites

www.ipl.org
The Internet Public Library. Lots of great research services of potential use to your job search. This link takes you directly to an online directory of professional associations.

www.weddles.com
Peter Weddle's employment services site also offers a comprehensive online professional association directory.

Career and Job Coaches

www.knockemdead.com
Martin Yate CPC Executive Career Strategist
E-mail: *martin@knockemdead.com*

Martin typically works with C-level and C-level bound professionals facing challenges in the areas of Job Search, Interviewing, and Career Strategy.

www.phoenixcareergroup.com

A private, by invitation only, association of seasoned and credentialed coaches, of which I am a member. I know all the Phoenix consultants professionally, and I'm proud to know most of them personally; they're the finest you'll find.

www.certifiedcareercoaches.com

A Web site that features only certified career coaches.

www.certifiedrésuméwriters.com

A Web site that features only certified résumé writers.

Career Assessments

www.analyzemycareer.com

A well-organized and comprehensive career choice online testing site.

www.assessment.com

A career choice test which matches your motivations against career directions. I've been using it for a number of years.

www.crgleader.com

Links to career planning and choice tools. The first free career choice test listed wasn't very helpful, but the site has other good resources.

www.careerplanner.com

Affordable RIASEC oriented career choice testing by an established online presence.

www.careertest.us

Allows you to take online career tests and get reports in minutes.

www.college911.com

Helps you find colleges based on your interests. No career choice tests; rather a site you might want to visit after you have a general sense of direction.

www.livecareer.com

Home page says it's free, and the free report is okay as far as it goes, which is not very far. To get a full report you will pay $25 and there are also premium options, but you don't know this until you have spent 30 minutes taking the test! Despite this sleight of hand, a good career choice test with comprehensive reports.

www.princetonreview.com

A $40 online test; this is a good solid test and the site is easy to navigate.

www.rockportinstitute.com

Excellent career choice tests for all ages. Although priced on a sliding scale dependent on income, they start at $1,500 for someone earning 40K a year or less.

www.self-directed-search.com

This is the famous SDS test developed by John Holland. An extremely well-regarded test, and at just $9.95 it's a great deal.

Career Choice and Management Sites

www.acinet.org

A site that offers career choice and advancement advice via testing for job seekers at all levels. Has good info on enhancing your professional credentials.

www.phoenixcareergroup.com

A premier site featuring deeply experienced and credentialed career counselors available for consultation on an hourly basis.

www.quintcareers.com
Career and job-search advice.

www.rileyguide.com
Excellent site for job search and career management advice. It's been around for years and is run by people who really care.

Career Transition
Military Transition

www.destinygroup.com
A great site for anyone transitioning out of the military. The number 1 post-military careers site.

www.corporategray.com

www.taonline.com
Military transition assistance.

Other Transition

www.careertransition.org
For dancers once their joints go.

College and Entry Level Job Sites

www.a1education.com
Directories and links for colleges and graduate schools, test prep, financial aid, and job search advice.

www.aboutjobs.com
Links and leads for student jobs, internships, recent grads, expats, and adventure seekers.

www.aftercollege.com
Internships and co-ops, part-time and entry level, Ph.D.s and post-docs, teaching jobs, plus alumni links.

www.backdoorjobs.com
Short-term and part-time adventure and dream jobs.

www.blackcollegian.com
Premier site for black college students and recent graduates; help and sensible advice in areas of concern for the young professional.

www.campuscareercenter.com
Job search, career guidance, and advice on networking for transition into the professional world.

www.careerfair.com
Career fair directory.

www.collegecentral.com
A networking site for graduates of small- and medium-size community colleges.

www.collegegrad.com
A comprehensive and well-thought-out site full of good information for the entry-level job seeker; probably the best in the entry-level field.

www.collegejobboard.com
A top job site for entry-level jobs; includes jobs in all fields.

www.collegejournal.com
Run by the *Wall Street Journal*, it's a savvy site for entry-level professionals, with lots of resources.

www.collegerecruiter.com
One of the highest traffic sites for students and recent grads with up to three years' experience. Well-established and comprehensive job site.

www.ednet.com
Reports on college aid, college selection, career guidance, and college strategy.

www.entryleveljobs.net
It's been around since 1999, and it does have jobs posted, though much is out of date.

www.graduatingengineer.com
A site for graduating engineers and computer careers.

www.internshipprograms.com
A good site if you are looking for an internship.

www.jobpostings.net
The online presence of one of the biggest college recruitment magazine publishers in North America; includes jobs across U.S. and Canada.

www.jobtrak.com
Now owned by Monster, it's their presence in the entry level job market.

www.jobweb.com
Owned and sponsored by the Association of Colleges and Employers. It's a great way to tap into the employers who consistently have entry level hiring needs.

www.snagajob.com
For part time and hourly jobs.

College Placement and Alumni Networks

www.mcli.dist.maricopa.edu
Resource for community college URLs.

www.utexas.edu
Resource for locating college alumni groups.

Diversity Sites

janweb.icdi.wvu.edu
Job Accommodation Network: a portal site for people with disabilities.

www.bilingual-jobs.com
Like the name says: a site for bilingual jobs, in America and around the globe.

www.blackcollegian.com
Premier site for black college students and recent graduates; help and sensible advice in areas of concern for the young professional.

www.business-disability.com
Run by the National Business and Disability Council, job search through listings of member organizations, post résumés, career events, and internships.

www.bwni.com
Businesswomen's network.

www.christianjobs.com
Full-featured employment Web site focusing on employment within the Christian community.

www.diversitylink.com
Job site serving women, minorities, and other diversity talent.

www.eop.com
The online presence of the oldest diversity recruitment publisher in America. For women, members of minority groups, and people with disabilities.

www.experienceworks.org
Training and employment services for mature workers, 55 and older.

www.gaywork.com

A job site featuring a résumé bank and job postings for gay men and women.

www.hirediversity.com

Links multicultural and bilingual professionals with both national and international industry sectors. Clients primarily consist of *Fortune* 1000 companies and government agencies.

www.imdiversity.com

Communities for African Americans, Asian Americans, Hispanic Americans, Native Americans and women. No jobs or overt career advice, but lots of links for members of minority communities on issues that affect our lives.

www.latpro.com

The number-one employment source for Spanish- and Portuguese-speaking professionals in North and South America. The site can be viewed in English, Spanish, or Portuguese. Features both résumé and job banks.

Executive Job Sites

www.netshare.com

Been around since before the Internet with tenured management; really understands and cares about the executive in transition. Job banks, resources, etc.

www.6figurejobs.com

Solid and well-respected site; includes job banks, resources, etc. A warning: Some of their career advice seems very nonspecific and geared to selling services.

www.careerjournal.com

Run by the *Wall Street Journal* with all the bells and whistles, this is an excellent executive transition site.

www.chiefmonster.com

Monster's site aimed at the executive area, though it's difficult to differentiate from the rest of the brand. Comprehensive job postings.

www.execunet.com

One of the top executive sites (along with Netshare, 6 Figure, and the *WSJ* site). Job banks and resources. Founder Dave Opton has been around a long time and runs a blog with interesting insights.

www.futurestep.com

Korn Ferry is the search firm behind the site. You can put your résumé in their database, which is not a bad idea.

www.spencerstuart.com

Executive site for eminent search firm Spencer Stuart. You can put your résumé in their database.

www.theladders.com

Like pretty much all the executive sites, you pay for access. Good job board and aggressive marketing means this site has become a player in the space very quickly.

Finding Companies

flipdog.monster.com

www.corporateinformation.com

In addition to having an alphabetical listing of over 20,000 companies, you can also research a country's industry or research a U.S. state. Also, if you register with the site, it will allow you to load the company profile. Within the address section, you will find a link to the company's home page.

www.eliyon.com

www.goleads.com

www.google.com

www.infospace.com

www.searchbug.com

www.superpages.com

www.wetfeet.com

General Job Sites

flipdog.monster.com

hotjobs.yahoo.com

www.4jobs.com

www.americasjobbank.com

www.bestjobsusa.com

www.career.com

www.careerboard.com

www.careerbuilder.com

www.careerhunters.com

www.careermag.com

www.careers.org
Good one-stop site for job search resources.

www.careershop.com

www.careersite.com

www.directemployers.com

www.employment911.com

www.employmentguide.com

www.employmentspot.com

www.job-hunt.org
Excellent site with sensible in-depth advice on
job search and career management issues.

www.job.com

www.jobbankusa.com

www.jobfind.com

www.jobwarehouse.com

www.jobweb.com

www.localcareers.com

www.mbajungle.com
Site for current entry level-ish and future
MBAs.

www.monster.com

www.nationjob.com

www.net-temps.com

www.quintcareers.com

Diversity Job-Seeker Career, Employment, Job Resources

www.snagajob.com

www.sologig.com

www.summerjobs.com

www.topusajobs.com

www.truecareers.com

www.vault.com

www.wetfeet.com

www.worklife.com

Job Posting Spiders

www.indeed.com

www.jobbankusa.com

www.jobs.just-posted.com

www.jobsearchengine.com

www.jobsniper.com

www.worktree.com

International Sites

www.ukjobsnet.co.uk
UK Jobs Network: the easiest way to find vacancies throughout the United Kingdom.

www.4icj.com

www.careerone.com.au

www.eurojobs.com

www.gojobsite.co.uk

www.jobpilot.com

www.jobsbazaar.com

www.jobserve.com

www.jobstreet.com
Asia-Pacific's number 1 job site.

www.monster.ca
Monster Canada

www.monster.co.uk
Monster UK: England's number 1 job site.

www.overseasjobs.com

www.reed.co.uk

www.seek.com.au
Australia's number 1 job site.

www.stepstone.com

www.topjobs.co.uk

www.totaljobs.com

www.workopolis.com
Canada's number 1 job site.

Job Fairs

www.careerfairs.com
CareerFairs.com is the fastest one-stop Internet site for locating upcoming job fairs and employers. In some cases you can even find the specific positions you desire and the specific positions you are trying to fill.

www.cfg-inc.com
Career Fairs for all levels: Professional and General, Health Care, Technical, Salary, Hourly, and Entry to Senior Level.

www.preferredjobs.com

www.psijobfair.com

www.skidmore.edu

Networking Sites

network.monster.com

socialsoftware.weblogsinc.com
This blog maintains a comprehensive listing of hundreds of networking sites. If you want to check out all your networking options, this is the place to start.

www.40plus.org
Chapter contact information.

www.alumni.net

www.distinctiveweb.com

www.eliyon.com
Helps you find people and companies.

www.execunet.com
An extensive network of professionals with whom you can interact for advice, support, and even career enhancement through local networking meetings. To locate meetings near you (U.S. and the world), check under 'Networking' on their Web site.

www.fiveoclockclub.com
National career counseling network.

www.fiveoclockclub.com
Network with members and alumni
database.

www.rileyguide.com

www.ryze.com
Helps people make connections and expand
their networks. You can network to grow
your business, build your career, and find
a job. You can also join networks related to
your industry for free.

www.tribe.net

www.womans-net.com

www.linkedin.com

Newspaper Sites

newsdirectory.com
Links to newspapers (global).

Profession
Specific Sites
Advertising, Public Relations,
and Graphic Arts

www.adage.com

www.adweek.com
Adweek Online

www.amic.com
Advertising Media Internet Center

www.creativehotlist.com

Communication Arts

www.prweek.net
pr week

Aerospace and Aviation

www.aerojobs.com

www.avcrew.com

www.avjobs.com

www.spacejobs.com

Agriculture and Horticulture

www.agricareers.com

www.fishingjobs.com

www.hortjobs.com

Broadcast, Communications,
and Journalism

www.b-roll.net

www.cpb.org
Corporation for Public Broadcasting

www.crew-net.com

www.journalismjobs.com

www.telecomcareers.net

www.womcom.org
AWC Online

Business, Finance, and
Accounting

www.accounting.com

www.bankjobs.com

www.brokerhunter.com

www.businessfinancemag.com

www.careerbank.com

www.careerjournal.com

www.cfo.com

www.efinancialjobs.com

www.fei.org

www.financialjobs.com

www.jobsinthemoney.com

Education

www.aacc.nche.edu
American Association of Community Colleges

www.academic360.com

www.academiccareers.com

www.chronicle.com

www.higheredjobs.com

www.petersons.com

www.phds.org

www.teacherjobs.com

www.ujobbank.com

www.wihe.com
Women in Higher Education

Engineering

www.asme.org

www.chemindustry.com

www.engineeringcentral.com

www.engineeringjobs.com

www.engineerjobs.com

www.enr.com
Engineering News Record Magazine

www.graduatingengineer.com

www.ieee.org

www.mepatwork.com

www.nsbe.org
National Society of Black Engineers

www.nspe.org
National Society of Professional Engineers

www.swe.org
Society of Women Engineers

Entertainment, TV, and Radio

www.castingnet.com

www.eej.com
Entertainment Employment Journal

www.entertainmentcareers.net

www.showbizjobs.com

www.themeparkjobs.com

www.tvandradiojobs.com

www.tvjobs.com

Healthcare

www.accessnurses.com
Travel nursing jobs

www.allnurses.com

www.dentsearch.com

www.healthcaresource.com

www.healthjobusa.com

www.hirehealth.com

www.jobscience.com

www.mdjobsite.com

www.medcareers.com

www.nurses123.com
Nurses can use this site to find nursing jobs across the United States.

www.nursetown.com

www.nursing-jobs.us
Nursing jobs in the United States.

www.nursingcenter.com

www.nursingspectrum.com

www.physemp.com

Human Resources

www.hrjobnet.com

www.hrworld.com

www.jobs4hr.com

www.shrm.org

www.tcm.com

IT and MIS

www.computerjobs.com

www.computerjobsbank.com

www.dice.com

www.gjc.org

www.mactalent.com

www.tech-engine.com

www.techemployment.com

www.techies.com

Legal

www.emplawyernet.com

www.ihirelegal.com

www.law.com

www.legalstaff.com

www.theblueline.com

Nonprofit

www.execsearches.com

www.idealist.org

www.naswdc.org

www.nonprofitcareer.com

www.opportunityknocks.org

Real Estate

www.realtor.org

Retail, Hospitality, and Customer Service

www.allretailjobs.com

www.chef2chef.net

www.chefjobsnetwork.com

www.coolworks.com

www.hcareers.com

www.leisurejobs.com

www.resortjobs.com

www.restaurantrecruit.com

www.supermarketnews.com

Sales and Marketing

www.careermarketplace.com

www.jobs4sales.com

www.marketingjobs.com

www.marketingmanager.com

www.marketingpower.com

www.salesheads.com

www.salesjobs.com

Science, Chemistry, Physics, and Biology

www.biocareer.com

www.biospace.com

www.bioview.com

www.bmn.com

www.eco.org

www.hirebio.com

www.medzilla.com

www.microbiologistjobs.com

www.pharmacyweek.com

Recruiter Sites

www.kellyservices.com

www.kornferry.com

www.manpower.com

www.napsweb.org
A job seeker can search the online directory by state, specialty, or by individual. Be sure to check out the headhunters who are designated C.P.C.s—the few but the best.

www.randstad.com

www.recruitersonline.com

www.rileyguide.com

www.snelling.com

www.spherion.com

www.staffingtoday.net
Search the database by state, skills, and type of services you need (temporary/permanent/ profession) and it will tell you about staffing services companies in your area.

www.therecruiternetwork.com

Reference Checking

www.allisontaylor.com

Researching Companies

bls.gov

iws.ohiolink.edu
A place for getting started with company research.

iws.ohiolink.edu
Helpful in understanding industry research.

newsdirectory.com

www.competia.com

www.fuld.com

www.industrylink.com

www.learnwebskills.com
A business research tutorial that presents a step-by-step process for finding free company and industry information on the Web. This online course will enable you to learn about an industry, and locate company home pages.

www.quintcareers.com
The quintessential directory of company career centers.

www.quintcareers.com
Guide to researching companies, industries, and countries.

www.thomasregister.com

www.vault.com
Company research.

www.vault.com
Industry list.

www.virtualpet.com
Teaches you how to learn about an industry or a specific company.

Résumé Creation

Knockemdead.com
E-mail: *martin@knockemdead.com*

www.phoenixcareergroup.com

certifiedrésuméwriters.com

parw.com

Résumé Distribution

www.résumémachine.com

Salary Research

www.jobstar.org

www.salary.com

www.salaryexpert.com

Telecommuting

www.homeworkers.org

www.jobs-telecommuting.com

www.tdigest.com

www.tjobs.com

Web Résumés/Portfolios

www.brandego.com

www.qfolio.com

APPENDIX · APPENDIX · APPENDIX · APPENDIX · APPENDIX · APPENDIX

C

RÉSUMÉ KEYWORDS

The keyword verbs on pages 69–70 describe your working actions, while the keyword nouns and phrases that follow showcase those actions in desirable work settings. Inclusion of these words will definitely have a favorable impact on the reception of your electronic job search correspondence. Read the profession-specific nouns for your field, and ask yourself: Have I done work in this area? If the answer is yes, ask yourself: Is it detailed in my résumé?

If you possess experience in an area not captured on your résumé, describe that experience. The goal isn't to create a résumé that includes lots of keywords at the expense of an accurate description of your background; you are simply making sure that your résumé is the most powerful it can be. Once online, the important thing is to have the screening software work for you, pulling your résumé back from cyberspace into the hands of employment managers—where it actually matters. Remember, you can always add keywords to the keyword/skill set area of your résumé, and it takes only a little effort with no need to reformat.

Administration

administration
administrative
  infrastructure
administrative processes
administrative support
back office
budget administration
client communications
confidential correspondence
contract administration
corporate record keeping
corporate secretary
customer liaison
document management
efficiency improvement
executive liaison
executive officer support
facilities management
front office operations
government affairs
liaison affairs
mail and messenger services
meeting planning
office management
office services
policy and procedure
product support
productivity improvement
project management
records management
regulatory reporting
resource management
technical support
time management
workflow planning/
  prioritization

Association and Nonprofit Management

advocacy
affiliate members
board relations
budget allocation
budget oversight
community outreach
corporate development
corporate giving
corporate sponsorship
education foundation
educational programming
endowment funds
foundation management
fundraising
grassroots campaign
industry association
industry relations
leadership training
marketing communications
media relations
member communications
member development
member-driven organization
member retention
member services
mission planning
not-for-profit
organization(al) leadership
organization(al) mission
organization(al) vision
policy development
political affairs
press relations
public policy development
public/private partnerships
public relations
regulatory affairs

research foundation
speakers bureau
special events management
volunteer recruitment
volunteer training

Banking

asset-based lending
asset management
audit examination
branch operations
cash management
commercial banking
commercial credit
consumer banking
consumer credit
correspondent banking
credit administration
credit analysis
debt financing
deposit base
depository services
equity financing
fee income
foreign exchange (FX)
global banking
investment management
investor relations
lease administration
letters of credit
liability exposure
loan administration
loan processing
loan quality
loan recovery
loan underwriting
lockbox processing
merchant banking
nonperforming assets

portfolio management

receivership

regulatory affairs

relationship management

retail banking

retail lending

return-on-assets

return-on-equity

return-on-investment

risk management

secondary markets

secured lending

securities management

transaction banking

trust services

unsecured lending

wholesale banking

workout

Customer Service

account relationship
 management

customer communications

customer development

customer focus groups

customer loyalty

customer management

customer needs assessment

customer retention

customer satisfaction

customer service

customer surveys

field service operation

inbound service operation

key account management

order fulfillment

order processing

outbound service operation

process simplification

records management

relationship management

sales administration

service benchmarks

service delivery

service measures

service quality

telemarketing operations

telesales operations

Engineering

benchmark

capital project

chemical engineering

commissioning

computer-aided design (CAD)

computer-aided engineering
 (CAE)

computer-aided
 manufacturing (CAM)

cross-functional team

customer management

development engineering

efficiency

electrical engineering

electronics engineering

engineering change order
 (ECO)

engineering documentation

environmental engineering

ergonomic techniques

experimental design

experimental methods

facilities engineering

fault analysis

field performance

final customer acceptance

hardware engineering

industrial engineering

industrial hygiene

maintenance engineering

manufacturing engineering

manufacturing integration

methods design

mechanical engineering

nuclear engineering

occupational safety

operating and maintenance
 (O&M)

optics engineering

plant engineering

process development

process engineering

process standardization

product design

product development cycle

product functionality

product innovation

product life-cycle
 management

product manufacturability

product reliability

productivity improvement

project costing

project management

project planning

prototype

quality assurance

quality engineering

regulatory compliance

research and development
 (R&D)

resource management

root cause

scale-up

software engineering

specifications

statistical analysis

systems engineering
systems integration
technical briefings
technical liaison affairs
technology development
test engineering
turnkey
work methods analysis

Finance, Accounting, and Auditing

accounts payable
accounts receivable
asset disposition
asset management
asset purchase
audit controls
audit management
cash management
commercial paper
corporate development
corporate tax
cost accounting
cost avoidance
cost/benefit analysis
cost reduction
credit and collections
debt financing
divestiture
due diligence
employee stock ownership
    plan (ESOP)
equity financing
feasibility analysis
financial analysis
financial audits
financial controls
financial models
financial planning

financial reporting
foreign exchange (FX)
initial public offering (IPO)
internal controls
international finance
investment management
investor accounting
investor relations
job costing
letters of credit
leveraged buyout (LBO)
liability management
make/buy analysis
margin improvement
merger
operating budgets
operational audits
partnership accounting
profit gains
profit/loss (P&L) analysis
project accounting
project financing
regulatory compliance
    auditing
return on assets (ROA)
return on investment (ROI)
revenue gain
risk management
shareholder relations
stock purchase
strategic planning
treasury
trust accounting
work papers

General Management, Senior Management, and Consulting

accelerated growth

acting executive
advanced technology
benchmarking
business development
business re-engineering
capital projects
competitive market position
consensus building
continuous process
    improvement
corporate administration
corporate communications
corporate culture change
corporate development
corporate image
corporate legal affairs
corporate mission
corporate vision
cost avoidance
cost reduction
crisis communications
cross-cultural
    communications
customer-driven
    management
customer retention
efficiency improvement
emerging business venture
entrepreneurial leadership
European economic
    community (EEC)
executive management
executive presentations
financial management
financial restructuring
global market expansion
high-growth organization
interim executive
leadership development

long-range planning

management development

margin improvement

market development

market-driven management

marketing management

matrix management

multifunction experience

multi-industry experience

multisite operations
    management

new business development

operating infrastructure

operating leadership

organization(al) culture

organization(al) development

participative management

performance improvement

policy development

process ownership

process re-engineering

productivity improvement

profit & loss (P&L)
    management

profit growth

project management

quality improvement

relationship management

re-engineering

reorganization

return-on-assets (ROA)

return-on-equity (ROE)

return-on-investment (ROI)

revenue growth

sales management

service design/delivery

signatory authority

start-up venture

strategic development

strategic partnership

tactical planning/leadership

team building

team leadership

total quality management
    (TQM)

transition management

turnaround management

world class organization

Healthcare

acute care facility

ambulatory care

assisted living

capital giving campaign

case management

certificate of need (CON)

chronic care facility

clinical services

community hospital

community outreach

continuity of care

cost center

electronic claims processing

employee assistance
    program (EAP)

emergency medical systems
    (EMS)

fee billing

full time equivalent (FTE)

grant administration

healthcare administrator

healthcare delivery systems

health maintenance
    organization (HMO)

home healthcare

hospital foundation

industrial medicine

inpatient care

long-term care

managed care

management service
    organization (MSO)

multihospital network

occupational health

outpatient care

patient accounting

patient relations

peer review

physician credentialing

physician relations

practice management

preferred provider
    organization (PPO)

preventive medicine

primary care

provider relations

public health administration

quality of care

regulatory standards
    (JCAHO)

rehabilitation services

reimbursement program

risk management

service delivery

skilled nursing facility

third-party administrator

utilization review

wellness programs

Hospitality

amenities

back-of-the-house operations

banquet operations

budget administration

catering operations

club management

conference management

contract F&B operations

corporate dining room

customer retention

customer service

food and beverage operations (F&B)

food cost controls

front-of-the-house operations

guest retention

guest satisfaction

hospitality management

inventory planning/control

labor cost controls

meeting planning

member development/ retention

menu planning

menu pricing

multiunit operations

occupancy

portion control

property development

purchasing

resort management

service management

signature property

vendor sourcing

VIP relations

Human Resources

Americans with Disabilities Act (ADA)

benefits administration

career pathing

change management

chief talent officer (CTO)

claims administration

college recruitment

compensation

competency-based performance

corporate culture change

cross-cultural communications

diversity management

equal employment opportunity (EEO)

employee communications

employee empowerment

employee involvement teams

employee relations

employee retention

employee surveys

expatriate employment

grievance proceedings

human resources (HR)

human resources generalist affairs

human resources partnerships

incentive planning

international employment

job task analysis

labor arbitration

labor contract negotiations

labor relations

leadership assessment

leadership development

management training and development

manpower planning

merit promotion

multimedia training

multinational workforce

organization (al) design

organization (al) development (OD)

organization (al) needs assessment

participative management

performance appraisal

performance incentives

performance re-engineering

position classification

professional recruitment

regulatory affairs

retention

safety training

self-directed work teams

staffing

succession planning

training & development

train-the-trainer

union negotiations

union relations

wage & salary administration

workforce re-engineering

Human Services

adult services

advocacy

behavior management

behavior modification

casework

client advocacy

client placement

community-based intervention

community outreach

counseling

crisis intervention

diagnostic evaluation

discharge planning

dually diagnosed

group counseling

human services

independent life skills
   training

inpatient

integrated service delivery

mainstreaming

outpatient

program development

protective services

psychoanalysis

psychological counseling

psychotropic medication

school counseling

social services

social welfare

substance abuse

testing

treatment planning

vocational placement

vocational rehabilitation

vocational testing

youth training program

**International Business
Development**

acquisition

barter transactions

channel development

competitive intelligence

corporate development

cross-border transactions

cross-cultural
   communications

diplomatic protocol

emerging markets

expatriate

export

feasibility analysis

foreign government affairs

foreign investment

global expansion

global marketing

global market position

global sales

import

intellectual property

international business
   development

international business
   protocol

international financing

international liaison

international licensee

international marketing

international subsidiary

international trade

joint venture

licensing agreements

local national

market entry

marketing

merger

multichannel distribution
   network

offshore operations

public/private partnership

technology licensing

start-up venture

strategic alliance

strategic planning

technology transfer

**Law and Corporate
Legal Affairs**

acquisition

adjudicate

administrative law

antitrust

briefs

case law

client management

contracts law

copyright law

corporate by-laws

corporate law

corporate record keeping

criminal law

cross-border transactions

depositions

discovery

due diligence

employment law

environmental law

ethics

family law

fraud

general partnership

intellectual property

interrogatory

joint venture

judicial affairs

juris doctor (JD)

labor law

landmark decision

legal advocacy

legal research

legislative review/analysis

licensing

limited liability corporation
   (LLC)

limited partnership

litigation

mediation

memoranda

mergers

motions

negotiations

patent law

personal injury

probate law

risk management

shareholder relations

signatory authority

strategic alliance

tax law

technology transfer

trademark

trade secrets

transactions law

trial law

unfair competition

workers' compensation
litigation

**Law Enforcement
and Security**

asset protection

corporate fraud

corporate security

crisis communications

crisis response

electronic surveillance

emergency planning &
response

emergency preparedness

industrial espionage

industrial security

interrogation

investigations management

law enforcement

media relations

personal protection

public relations

safety training

security operations

tactical field operations

white collar crime

Manufacturing

asset management

automated manufacturing

capacity planning

capital budget

capital project

cell manufacturing

computer integrated
manufacturing (CIM)

concurrent engineering

continuous improvement

cost avoidance

cost reductions

cross-functional teams

cycle time reduction

distribution management

efficiency improvement

environmental health and
safety (EHS)

equipment management

ergonomically efficient

facilities consolidation

inventory control

inventory planning

just-in-time (JIT)

kaizen

labor efficiency

labor relations

lean manufacturing

logistics management

manufacturing engineering

manufacturing integration

manufacturing technology

master schedule

materials planning

materials replenishment
system (MRP)

multisite operations

occupational health & safety
(OH&S)

on-time delivery

operating budget

operations management

operations re-engineering

operations start-up

optimization

order fulfillment

order processing

outsourcing

participative management

performance improvement

physical inventory

pilot manufacturing

plant operations

process automation

process redesign/
re-engineering

procurement

product development and
engineering

product rationalization

production forecasting

production lead time

production management

production output

production plans/schedules

productivity improvement

profit & loss (P&L)
management

project budget

purchasing management

quality assurance/quality
control

quality circles

safety management

safety training

shipping and receiving
   operation
spares and repairs
   management
statistical process control
   (SPC)
technology integration
time and motion studies
total quality management
   (TWM)
traffic management
turnaround management
union negotiations
value-added processes
vendor management
warehousing operations
workflow optimization
workforce management
work in progress (WIP)
world class manufacturing
   (WCM)
yield improvement

Public Relations and Corporate Communications

advertising communications
agency relations-directed
brand management
brand strategy
broadcast media
campaign management
community affairs
competitive market lead
community outreach
conference planning
cooperative advertising
corporate communications
corporate identity

corporate sponsorship
corporate vision
creative services
crisis communications
customer communications
direct mail campaign
electronic advertising
electronic media
employee communications
event management
fundraising
government relations
grassroots campaign
investor communications
issues management
legislative affairs
logistics
management
   communications
marketing communications
market research
media buys
media placement
media relations
media scheduling
merchandising
multimedia advertising
political action committee
   (PAC)
premiums
press releases
print media
promotions
public affairs
publications
publicity
public relations
public speaking
sales incentives

shareholder communications
special events
strategic communications
   plan
strategic planning
strategic positioning
tactical campaign
trade shows
VIP relations

Purchasing and Logistics

acquisition management
barter trade
bid review
buy vs. lease analysis
capital equipment acquisition
commodities purchasing
competitive bidding
contract administration
contract change order
contract negotiations
contract terms and
   conditions
cradle-to-grave procurement
distribution management
economic ordering quantity
   methodology
fixed price contracts
indefinite price/indefinite
   quantity
international sourcing
inventory planning/control
just-in-time (JIT) purchasing
logistics management
materials replenishment
   ordering (MRO)
   purchasing
multisite operations
negotiation

offshore purchasing

outsourced

price negotiations

procurement

proposal review

purchasing

regulatory compliance

request for proposal (RFP)

request for quotation (RFQ)

sourcing

specifications compliance

subcontractor negotiations

supplier management

supplier quality

vendor partnerships

vendor quality certification

warehousing

Real Estate, Construction, and Property Management

acquisition

Americans with Disabilities
  Act (ADA)

asset management

asset valuation

asset workout/recovery

building code compliance

building trades

capital improvement

claims administration

commercial development

community development

competitive bidding

construction management

construction trades

contract administration

contract award

critical path method (CPM)
  scheduling

design and engineering

divestiture

engineering change orders
  (ECOS)

environmental compliance

estimating

facilities management

fair market value pricing

grounds maintenance

historic property renovation

industrial development

infrastructure development

leasing management

master community
  association

master scheduling

mixed-use property

occupancy

planned-use development
  (PUD)

portfolio

preventive maintenance

project concept-driven

project development

project management

project scheduling

property management

property valuation

real estate appraisal

real estate brokerage

real estate development

real estate investment trust
  (REIT)

real estate law

real estate partnership

regulatory compliance

renovation

return on assets (ROA)

return on equity (ROE)

return on investment (ROI)

site development

site remediation

specifications

syndications

tenant relations

tenant retention

turnkey construction

Sales/Marketing/ Business Development

account development

account management

account retention

brand management

business development

campaign management

competitive analysis

competitive contract award

competitive market
  intelligence

consultative sales

customer loyalty

customer needs assessment

customer retention

customer satisfaction

customer service

direct mail marketing

direct response marketing

direct sales

distributor management

emerging markets

field sales management

fulfillment

global markets

high-impact presentations

incentive planning

indirect sales

international sales

international trade

key account management

line extension

margin improvement

marketing strategy

market launch

market positioning

market research

market share ratings

market surveys

mass merchants

multichannel distribution

multichannel sales

multimedia advertising

national account
   management

negotiations

new market development

new product introduction

product development

product launch

product life-cycle
   management

product positioning

profit & loss (P&L)
   management

promotions

public relations

public speaking

revenue growth

revenue stream

sales closing

sales cycle management

sales forecasting

sales training

solutions selling

strategic market planning

tactical market plans

team building/leadership

trend analysis

Teaching and Education Administration

academic advisement

accreditation

admissions management

alumni relations

conference management

curriculum development

e design

education administration

enrollment

extension program

field instruction

grant administration

instructional media

instructional programming

intercollegiate athletics

lifelong learning

management development

peer counseling

program development

public/private partnerships

recruitment

residential life

scholastic standards

student-faculty relations

student retention

student services

textbook review

training and development

Transportation

agency operations

cargo handling

common carrier

container transportation

customer delivery operations

dedicated logistics operations

dispatch operations

distribution management

driver leasing

equipment control

facilities management

fleet management

freight consolidation

freight forwarding

import operations

inbound transportation

line management

load analysis

logistics management

maritime operations

outbound transportation

over-the-road transportation

port operations

regulatory compliance

route management

route planning/analysis

safety management

terminal operations

traffic planning

transportation management

transportation planning

warehouse management

workflow optimization

INDEX

The bestselling job-search series that will help you land the job you want!

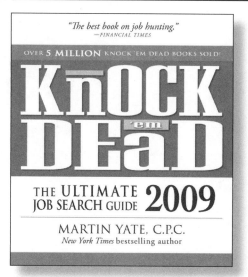
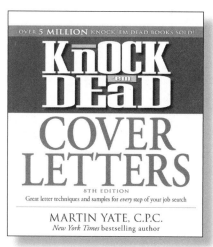